RACIAL RECONSTRUCTION

AMERICA AND THE LONG 19TH CENTURY

General Editors: David Kazanjian, Elizabeth McHenry, and Priscilla Wald

Black Frankenstein: The Making of an American Metaphor
Elizabeth Young

Neither Fugitive nor Free: Atlantic Slavery, Freedom Suits, and the Legal Culture of Travel
Edlie L. Wong

Shadowing the White Man's Burden: U.S. Imperialism and the Problem of the Color Line
Gretchen Murphy

Bodies of Reform: The Rhetoric of Character in Gilded-Age America
James B. Salazar

Empire's Proxy: American Literature and U.S. Imperialism in the Philippines
Meg Wesling

Sites Unseen: Architecture, Race, and American Literature
William A. Gleason

Racial Innocence: Performing American Childhood from Slavery to Civil Rights
Robin Bernstein

American Arabesque: Arabs and Islam in the Nineteenth Century Imaginary
Jacob Rama Berman

Racial Indigestion: Eating Bodies in the Nineteenth Century
Kyla Wazana Tompkins

Idle Threats: Men and the Limits of Productivity in Nineteenth-Century America
Andrew Lyndon Knighton

Tomorrow's Parties: Sex and the Untimely in Nineteenth-Century America
Peter M. Coviello

Bonds of Citizenship: Law and the Labors of Emancipation
Hoang Gia Phan

The Traumatic Colonel: The Founding Fathers, Slavery, and the Phantasmatic Aaron Burr
Michael J. Drexler and Ed White

Unsettled States: Nineteenth-Century American Literary Studies
Edited by Dana Luciano and Ivy G. Wilson

Sitting in Darkness: Mark Twain, Asia, and Comparative Racialization
Hsuan L. Hsu

Picture Freedom: Remaking Black Visuality in the Early Nineteenth Century
Jasmine Nichole Cobb

Stella
Émeric Bergeaud
Translated by Lesley Curtis and Christen Mucher

Ethnology and Empire: Languages, Literature, and the Making of the North American Borderlands
Robert Lawrence Gunn

The Black Radical Tragic: Performance, Aesthetics, and the Unfinished Haitian Revolution
Jeremy Matthew Glick

Racial Reconstruction: Black Inclusion, Chinese Exclusion, and the Fictions of Citizenship
Edlie L. Wong

Racial Reconstruction

Black Inclusion, Chinese Exclusion, and the Fictions of Citizenship

Edlie L. Wong

NEW YORK UNIVERSITY PRESS
New York and London

NEW YORK UNIVERSITY PRESS
New York and London
www.nyupress.org

© 2015 by New York University
All rights reserved

References to Internet websites (URLs) were accurate at the time of writing.
Neither the author nor New York University Press is responsible for URLs
that may have expired or changed since the manuscript was prepared.

ISBN: 978-1-4798-6800-1 (hardback)
ISBN: 978-1-4798-1796-2 (paperback)

For Library of Congress Cataloging-in-Publication data, please contact
the Library of Congress.

New York University Press books are printed on acid-free paper,
and their binding materials are chosen for strength and durability.
We strive to use environmentally responsible suppliers and materials
to the greatest extent possible in publishing our books.

Manufactured in the United States of America

10 9 8 7 6 5 4 3 2 1

Also available as an ebook

CONTENTS

List of Illustrations	vii
Acknowledgments	ix
Introduction: Black Inclusion / Chinese Exclusion: Toward a Cultural History of Comparative Racialization	1
1. "Cosa de Cuba!": American Literary Travels, Empire, and the Contract Coolie	17
2. From Emancipation to Exclusion: Racial Analogy in Afro-Asian Periodical Print Culture	69
3. American Futures Past: The Counterfactual Histories of Chinese Invasion	124
4. Boycotting Exclusion: The Transpacific Politics of Chinese Sentimentalism	175
Conclusion: Against Historicism: James D. Corrothers and Speculations on Our Racial Futures	224
Notes	239
Index	279
About the Author	293

ILLUSTRATIONS

I.1.	Flyleaf illustration, *Truth versus Fiction; Justice versus Prejudice*	2
1.1.	"Celestial Cubans"	33
1.2.	Cedula de Libres de Color for José Puchal	35
1.3.	Contrata for He Fu (Eduardo)	44
1.4.	Chinese translation of Contrata for He Fu (Eduardo)	45
1.5.	Newspaper clipping pasted into letter from Richard H. Chinn to Eliza McHatton Ripley	55
2.1.	Nast, "The Civilization of Blaine"	74
2.2.	Title page, *Life and Adventures of James Williams*	81
2.3.	Nast, "The Nigger Must Go" and "The Chinese Must Go"	123
3.1.	Keller, "San Francisco A.D. 1900"	134
3.2.	Keller, "A Fresh Eruption of the Pacific Coast Vesuvius"	165
4.1.	Walter, "There's Millions in It"	179
4.2.	Case file 10025/36 (Ju Toy)	180

ACKNOWLEDGMENTS

I have incurred innumerable debts to the many friends, colleagues, and librarians who helped me bring this book to life over the long course of research and writing. First, I would like to acknowledge the institutions that supported my work. A generous yearlong fellowship from the National Endowment for the Humanities provided me with the resources to conduct archival research at the Bancroft Library at the University of California–Berkeley and the Hargrett Rare Book and Manuscript Library at the University of Georgia. I wrote a majority of the book with the assistance of a Research and Scholarship Award from the Graduate School, University of Maryland. As the book neared completion, I received additional assistance from the College of Arts and Humanities, University of Maryland, Subvention Fund as well as the Department of English, University of Maryland. I am grateful to my department chair, William Cohen, for his continued support.

I would not have been able to complete this book without the encouragement, intelligence, and guidance of the many friends and colleagues who helped direct my thinking and research over the years. Brent Edwards, Saidiya Hartman, David Eng, Stacy Klein, and Christine Chism offered helpful professional guidance as this book first took shape. The Rutgers Center for Historical Analysis seminar on "Vernacular Epistemologies" (2009–2010), organized by Julie Livingston and Indrani Chatterjee, gave me the opportunity to share early work with a perceptive cohort of interdisciplinary scholars whose insights and suggestions helped reshape and expand the contours of the book. At different stages of the project, Ryan Kernan and Shuang Shen provided me with invaluable translation assistance, and Sonali Perera was unstinting in her encouragement throughout the process. I must also thank Herman Bennett, Matthew Sandler, Michael Schoeppner, Hester Blum, and Sunny Yang and Nancy Bentley of the American Studies reading group at the University of Pennsylvania for inviting me to their campuses to present my work. The feedback I received from the audiences that attended my talks at the CUNY Graduate Center (as a participant in the conference "Middle Passages: History and Poetics"), the Center for the Study of Race and Ethnicity at Columbia University, the California Institute of Technology, Penn State University, and the University of Pennsylvania challenged me to further refine my ideas. I offer special thanks to Eric Hayot, who graciously shared his work with me during my visit to Penn State. The wonderful participants at the University of Maryland's "Race, Law, and American Literary Studies: An Interdisciplinary Conference" (2012), especially Brook Thomas, Nan Goodman, Hoang Phan, Alfred Brophy, and Jeannine DeLombard, receive my deepest gratitude for their intellectual engagement, suggestions, and encouragement. My colleagues at the University of Maryland, including Ralph Bauer, Robert Levine, Mary Helen Washington, Christina Walter, Jonathan Auerbach, Brian Richardson, Peter Mallios, Sangeeta Ray, and Orrin Wang, have fostered my work in myriad significant ways. They welcomed me to Maryland with warmth, generosity, and good humor and provided me with the intellectual support to complete this book.

I would like to thank Eric Zinner at New York University Press, who reprised his role from my first book and, with Alicia Nadkarni, guided this second book through the lengthy publication process. I was fortunate to work with a wonderfully responsive copyeditor, Andrew Katz. Marisa Louie, an archivist with the National Archives at San Francisco, also offered indispensible assistance and provided me with the case files for *United States v. Ju Toy*. Shawn Saremi, the Department of English IT coordinator, also gave me invaluable technical assistance when I needed it most. My thanks too to Priscilla Wald and Gordon Hutner for providing me with forums to test out and share early portions of this book, which appeared in somewhat different forms, in *American Literature* and *American Literary History*.

There are certain individuals whom I am deeply fortunate to have in my life. Since graduate school, Hsuan Hsu has remained the closest of my intellectual interlocutors. He is a generous friend and inspiring scholar. Hsuan read through my manuscript piecemeal, and the book benefited enormously from his thoughtful insights. Matt Cohen also offered incredibly incisive suggestions at key moments in the manuscript's composition. I would not have completed this project without the kindness, understanding, and camaraderie of Cathy Paiste, Jae Suh, Mike Ferguson, Linda Chandler, Stafford Gregoire, Robert Soza, and my wonderful Philadelphia friends Jena Osman, Amze Emmons, Josephine Park, James Ker, Adalaine Holton, and James Salazar. Noel Warren patiently suffered through the latter stages of the project, offering both emotional and intellectual support as the manuscript was finalized. And, lastly, this book is dedicated to my father, King Tong Wong, and my family, So Man, Edson, Edlen, Nolan, and Audrey Wong. I am also grateful for my extended family, King Kui, Linda, Edwin, Eddie, and King Luen Wong, as well as my godmother, Violet Hoffer. This book was written for them all.

Introduction

*Black Inclusion / Chinese Exclusion:
Toward a Cultural History of
Comparative Racialization*

Published in 1902, the pro-Chinese pamphlet *Truth versus Fiction; Justice versus Prejudice: Meat for All, Not for a Few* marks the last of the great public debates over Chinese exclusion before its indefinite extension in the U.S. and its newly acquired Pacific territories. A stinging rebuttal to the American Federation of Labor's influential anti-Chinese tract, *Some Reasons for Chinese Exclusion. Meat versus Rice: American Manhood against Asiatic Coolieism. Which Shall Survive?* (1902), *Truth versus Fiction* sought to counteract the alarmist discourse of Yellow Peril, which depicted Chinese labor migrants as deindividualized Asiatic masses threatening to overwhelm American industry and civilization.[1] A flyleaf from *Truth versus Fiction* features a striking unsigned political cartoon depicting Uncle Sam mediating a stand-off between Chinese immigrants eagerly awaiting to disembark from a steamship and a crowd of men figured as "squareheads," an ethnic slur designating immigrants from Germany, Scandinavia, and the Netherlands, angrily protesting their arrival (see figure 1.1). The Reconstruction Amendments and the extension of nominal citizenship to black freedmen did not break the constitutive link between whiteness and citizenship, as the racial exclusion of Chinese (and later all so-called Asiatic races) from immigration and naturalization helped establish the whiteness (or Americanization) of new European immigrants. The formal processes that produce U.S. citizens entailed the production of American racial identities or racial formations.[2] By critically figuring the protesting men as ethnicized "squareheads," the pamphlet reveals how becoming "American" involves assignment to a particular racial identity and internalizing an exclusionary understanding of race and nation.[3]

1

Figure 1.1. Flyleaf illustration, *Truth versus Fiction; Justice versus Prejudice: Meat for All, Not for a Few* (Washington, DC, c. 1902) (Courtesy of the Bancroft Library, University of California–Berkeley)

Specifically, *Truth versus Fiction* references the work of the largely unsung Jewish immigration reformer Max J. Kohler to distill one of the most lasting racial formations from the era. In defending Chinese immigration and naturalization rights, it critically observed, "Nor can any one explain why the black man should enjoy all the 'rights of men,' and the man whose skin is yellow be treated by the law as an outcast because of such difference of shade."[4] The pamphlet uses the dialectical configuration of black inclusion / Chinese exclusion to critique a failed American racial democracy at the dawn of the twentieth century. In limning the contours of this seeming racial paradox, *Truth versus Fiction*, however, elides the racial policy of Jim Crow and its systematic undermining of black political rights in advocating inclusion for nonwhite, nonblack Chinese immigrants. In holding up Chinese inclusion as an unrealized Republican ideal, the pamphlet evades the question of how black inclusion into the category of formal citizenship had neither mitigated racial inequality nor racially subordinated American identities, particularly in the wake of the U.S. Supreme Court ruling in *Plessy v. Ferguson* (1896).[5] By upholding the constitutionality of de jure racial segregation, *Plessy* affirmed whiteness as the condition of full citizenship. Black citizens may inhabit the political space of the nation, but they cannot participate fully within it. Inclusion into abstract or formal citizenship did not entail substantive rights, as black Americans faced continued exclusion on the basis of their differentiated inclusion into citizenship.[6] As a rhetorical figure, the dialectical configuration of black inclusion/Chinese exclusion is significant for what it both hides *and* reveals about U.S. racial formations in the era of emancipation. Dialectic designates "a relationship that simultaneously embodies antagonism and interdependence, that develops over historical time, and that links the small-scale and large-scale (or 'micro' and 'macro') dimensions of social life," writes Howard Winant.[7] In thus challenging federal efforts to fix and stabilize U.S. racial identity, the pamphlet marshals one of the most lasting racial formations from the era, marking the limits of Reconstruction race radicalism and inaugurating a fundamental shift in U.S. immigration policies that lasted until the Immigration and Nationality Act of 1965.

By the end of the nineteenth century, this dialectical configuration of black inclusion/Chinese exclusion had become an oft-referenced rhetorical figure in popular and legal discourses, structuring persuasive arguments both for *and* against Chinese political rights and black racial inequality. For example, Justice John Marshall Harlan's oft-celebrated dissent in *Plessy v. Ferguson* marshaled this dialectic to exemplify the legal inconsistencies of black-white racial segregation. Harlan utilized the metaphor of "color-blindness" and its logic of impartiality—borrowed from the brief of the lead attorney for the plaintiff, Albion Tourgée—to inveigh against the discriminatory intent of "equal but separate" accommodations.[8] In thus disputing the constitutionality of black-white segregation, Harlan imagined a different scene of cross-racial contact to emphasize the contradictions of the Louisiana statute. In his now oft-quoted words, "There is a race so different from our own that we do not permit those belonging to it to become citizens of the United States. Persons belonging to it are, with few exceptions, absolutely excluded from our country. I allude to the Chinese race. But, by the statute in question, a Chinaman can ride in the same passenger coach with white citizens of the United States, while citizens of the black race" are banned from the same privilege.[9] Harlan's counterfactual thought experiment limns the contours of a racial formation that first took shape in the overlapping contexts of the so-called Negro Problem and the Chinese Question. By emphasizing Chinese difference as a "race" reclassified by the 1870 Naturalization Act and reinforced by the Chinese Exclusion Acts as "aliens ineligible to citizenship," Harlan sought to combat the "sentiment of alienism," in writer George Washington Cable's words, directed against black citizens in the wake of Reconstruction.[10] Harlan enfolded black racial difference within the embrace of national identity; yet this romance of black-white national reunification reinforced the exclusion of another proscribed race as he redrew the color line to demarcate U.S. citizens from Chinese aliens who were politically inassimilable to the nation but not (it would appear) to the unstable legal category of "whiteness" at the time. In rejecting racial "caste" legislation, Harlan marshaled the dialectic of black inclusion / Chinese exclusion against black-white segregation, investing this racial formation with new vigor in Jim Crow America.

Racial Reconstruction: Black Inclusion, Chinese Exclusion, and the Fictions of Citizenship explores the cultural genealogies of this dialectical configuration linking together immigration and citizenship struggles in the long shadow of slavery, abolition, and Reconstruction. The end of black chattel slavery did not end racism but "drove it into new terrain, reconfigured it, and inaugurated a new phase in its history," as Arif Dirlik argues.[11] Resurgent antiblack violence in the Reconstruction South attested to the belated temporality of racial equality in social—if not strictly legal—fact. Black citizenship and male suffrage constituted a dramatic shift from past U.S. racial policy, yet new forms of racialization emerged in its wake. Reconstruction facilitated these monumental shifts with the 1870 Naturalization Act, which amended the 1790 Naturalization Act limiting naturalization to "free white persons." It added the category of "African nativity and . . . descent" to reflect black enfranchisement while maintaining the primacy of whiteness for racial eligibility to naturalization. This postemancipation realignment of racial exclusion also reenergized a discourse of Christian civilization, which deemed Chinese and Native Americans as unredeemable heathens and consequently morally unfit for political participation in the future of America's Manifest Destiny. At the end of the century, the Chinese Exclusion Acts and subsequent U.S. Supreme Court rulings on Chinese immigration cases completed the redefinition of the Asiatic as the categorically excluded. Meanwhile, the national debate over the "Chinese Question" further intensified the contradictions of black inclusion in the era leading to *Plessy v. Ferguson* and beyond. The dialectical configuration of black inclusion / Chinese exclusion shaped Reconstruction and its conflicted political and cultural legacies, providing the framework through which black citizens and Chinese immigrants became differentially racialized subjects within the nation.

The complex histories of slavery and Reconstruction influenced the course of Chinese immigration to the U.S., especially at the level of representation. Narration and other representational practices mediate the experiences of nation and nationality. The archive of Chinese exclusion and the debates over Chinese fitness for citizenship became part of the broader story about who did and did not belong to the newly reunified nation. In the wake of the Civil War, emancipation ushered a new paradox into American life and thought: it nullified one kind of property relation—the buying and selling of chattel slaves—to consecrate, according to the historian Amy Dru Stanley, the "market as a model of social relations among free persons" who voluntarily sold their labor as property.[12] The end of the transatlantic slave trade and slavery facilitated wide-scale labor crises in the Western Hemisphere, as the lucrative agricultural economies of the U.S. South and the British and Spanish Caribbean drove demands for easily replaceable workers who were both cheap and plentiful. Labor-strapped planters looked toward China and its teeming population as a source of labor replenishment. The British West Indies first began importing Chinese and South Asian indentured labor in what became popularly known as "coolieism." By 1847, as the now-contraband slave trade waned, Cuba also began experimenting with Chinese contract labor as a supplemental labor force in addition to legal chattel slavery on the island. Cuban plantation owners—some of whom were Confederate expatriates such as Eliza McHatton Ripley—sought out Chinese contract labor as emancipation threatened. Chapter 1 discusses how their efforts to represent and control Chinese contract labor resembled the more familiar tactics of managing the representation of slavery as a patriarchal institution while constantly guarding against slave revolt. National debates over the American use of Chinese labor based on the Cuban example intensified as sectional tensions over the future of slavery threatened to erupt into Civil War. Chinese coolieism thus emerged in an Atlantic world that had yet to see the end of black chattel slavery or the racialized legal and political structures that seemed to ensure its indefinite continuation.

In the decades between the end of the Civil War and the heyday of the Progressive era, debates about and representations of Chinese immigrants to the U.S. often identified Chinese labor as a form of servile labor, analogizing it to the black chattel slavery it was supposed to replace. *Racial Reconstruction* unfolds from the analogy embedded in the term "coolie-slave" that came into frequent use in the national debates over the "Chinese Question." From popular fiction to congressional debates, coolieism came to mark all forms of Chinese labor migration even though Chinese contract labor (common throughout Cuba and Peru) was outlawed in the U.S. (with the 1885 Foran Act, or Alien Contract Labor Law). Anti-Chinese agitators called on the "coolie-slave" to mobilize the patriotic memory and moral indignation of abolitionism for the purpose of protecting and empowering white labor, especially as the Republican Party reformed itself during Reconstruction and as conflicts between labor and capital heightened. They defended Chinese Exclusion as an antislavery, proimmigrant measure in a U.S. committed to freedom, free labor, and free trade. By placing Chinese immigration within the framework of Atlantic slavery and emancipation, this book illuminates how the radical reconstruction of post–Civil War citizenship, geopolitics, and national belonging led to the ratification of America's first race- (and gender-) specific immigration law. The passage and administration of the Page Act (1875) and the subsequent Chinese Exclusion Acts, which barred the entry of Chinese laborers and prohibited their naturalization, marked the beginning of America's modern immigration system and its transformation into what the historian Erika Lee calls a "gatekeeping nation."[13]

Racial Reconstruction focuses on Chinese racialization and its intersections with African American and (to a lesser degree) Native American subject formations. It intervenes in several overlapping fields of interdisciplinary scholarship: Afro-Asian comparative racialization, race and immigration law, and race and labor history. To that end, *Racial Reconstruction* makes use of materials from multiple archives that are usually not in conversation with each other, including political cartoons, print journalism, legal cases and contracts, official investigations, travelogues, sensational fiction, and sentimental literature. It draws from them a comparative analytic for understanding American race, racialization, and identity formations in the long nineteenth century. Chapter 1 brings the pioneering work of Evelyn Hu-DeHart, Moon-Ho Jung, Walton Look Lai, Lisa Lowe, and Lisa Yun on the figure of the Asiatic "coolie" into critical conversation with U.S. labor histories and the sociological analyses of Michael Omi and Howard Winant. By exploring the Afro-Asian analogy embedded in the term "coolie-slave," chapter 1 lays the historical groundwork for subsequent chapters examining how nativist labor activists, legislators, jurists, and African American and Chinese American writers drew on Afro-Asian comparisons to shore up and/or contest the links between U.S. citizenship and whiteness. Specifically, *Racial Reconstruction* follows the "comparative turn" in American race and ethnicities studies and increasingly in gender and sexuality studies.[14]

Race making *and* gender control were constitutive of Chinese immigration regulation. Recent work such as Nayan Shah's *Stranger Intimacy: Contesting Race, Sexuality, and the Law in the North American West* (2011) has challenged the heteronormative fiction of the nuclear family as a "conceptual crutch that renders any other form of kinship and household structure pathological, aberrant, and incompatible with cultural support and political privilege."[15] Presented as an antiprostitution law, the Page Act controlled Chinese women's immigration and reproduction under the aegis of Christian morality and paved the way for subsequent class-based racialized restriction measures. It policed Chinese family formation and strengthened perceptions of Chinese men as unnatural bachelors and sexual deviants. This regulation of gender and sexuality provided a central framework for the production of race and racial meaning in the U.S. "Racialized immigration," as Lowe argues, "along with American empire, [is] part of a longer history of the development of modern American capitalism and racialized democracy."[16] In thus situating the phenomenon of Asian immigration as "racial formation, as economic sign, and as an epistemological object," Lowe's early theorization of an Asian American critique called for an "inquiry into the *comparative* history of racialization."[17]

Race is a relational concept, and immigration law—as it was first forged in relation to the "Chinese Question"—fundamentally shaped the boundaries of race in the U.S. This book emphasizes what the legal scholar Devon Carbado calls the "multiracial social dynamics of inclusion and exclusion" to reveal the significance of immigration law and foreign policy as understudied contexts for understanding African American racial formation on the one hand and slavery and Reconstruction as equally underappreciated contexts for understanding Asian American racial formation on the other.[18] *Racial Reconstruction* attends to these overlapping and divergent histories of U.S. racial formations in its efforts to reconfigure the black-white binary of the U.S. "color line." The dominance of the black-white binary often overshadows the complex interrelations between and among other racial formations, perpetuating a racialized hierarchy within our national history. Recent interdisciplinary scholarship such as Leslie Bow's *Partly Colored: Asian Americans and Racial Anomaly in the Segregated South* (2010) and Natalia Molina's *How Race Is Made in America: Immigration, Citizenship, and the Historical Power of Racial Scripts* (2014) has begun exploring the linked experiences of interstitial ethnic groups, including Mexican Americans, Asian American, and Native Americans located beyond and between the structural logics of black-white segregation and for whom the color line was continually redrawn.[19] In this vein, *Racial Reconstruction* seeks to understand the necessarily contingent contours of African American and Asian American race relations, law, and cultural production. It tracks the elaboration of black inclusion/Chinese exclusion across a variety of discursive registers as Reconstruction America underwent geographical expansion and bureaucratic consolidation.

Comparative racialization studies have begun to change how we think about race and its multiple and contradictory meanings across different periods of U.S. history. There have been a number of recent contributions to this important trend in thinking about comparative constructions of race and cross-racial solidarities and antagonisms. In literary studies, the publication of the 2008 *PMLA* special issue "Comparative Racialization" helped forge this critical shift by positioning it against existing frameworks of multiculturalism and interracialism on the one hand and ethnic nationalisms on the other. In particular, earlier work on Afro-Asian comparative racialization, such as Vijay Prashad's *Everybody Was Kung Fu Fighting: Afro-Asian Connections and the Myth of Cultural Purity* (2001), Bill Mullen's *Afro-Orientalism* (2004), and Andrew Jones and Nikhil Singh's special issue of *positions: east asia cultures critique, The Afro-Asian Century* (2003), has focused largely on twentieth-century writers and thinkers, emphasizing revolutionary—indeed, at times utopian—forms of anticolonial transpacific polyculturalism and political collaborations.[20] More recent literary scholarship such as Crystal Anderson's *Beyond the Chinese Connection: Contemporary Afro-Asian Cultural Production* (2013), Helen Jun's *Race for Citizenship: Black Orientalism and Asian Uplift from Pre-Emancipation to Neoliberal America* (2011), and Julia Lee's *Interracial Encounters: Reciprocal Representations in African and Asian American Literatures, 1896–1937* (2011) has begun to offer more critical perspectives on Afro-Asian solidarities and cross-racial identifications.[21] For example, Jun's provocative study explores how the pursuit of citizenship rights in competition led to the development of two distinct racial discourses, "black Orientalism" and "Asian uplift," which African Americans and Asian Americans leveraged against each other to prove their fitness for citizenship.[22] And while this book also casts a critical eye on the romance of Afro-Asian alliance, it also builds on the analytics for articulating racial difference—indeed, differential thinking—honed in U.S. race and ethnicity studies to explore cross-racial and transpacific connections and sympathies that resisted reinscribing racially homogenizing stereotypes and misperceptions.

Racial Reconstruction adds to and critically intervenes in this cultural scholarship on Afro-Asian comparative racialization. Specifically, the book emphasizes aspects of immigration law and legal culture and inflects its study through comparable developments in critical legal studies under the aegis of critical race theory, an interdisciplinary analytical framework that, among other things, seeks to understand the sociolegal constructions of race and racial power. This book investigates the varied mechanisms by which citizens and immigrants were assigned and invested with race and racial identities. It also explores how national debates over the "Chinese Question" and the sensationalist cultural materials that it produced influenced a series of U.S. Supreme Court cases, including *Chae Chan Ping v. U.S.* or the Chinese Exclusion Case (1889) and *Fong Yue Ting v. U.S.* (1893), that established congressional plenary power over immigration regulation, as studied in chapter 3. The plenary power doctrine continues to shape federal constitutional authority over immigration today. In this aspect, the book builds on the historian Najia Aarim-Heriot's *Chinese Immigrants, African Americans, and Racial Anxiety in the United States, 1848–82* (2004) while emphasizing the role of cultural productions in the dissemination of racial ideas about the "Chinese Question" and "Negro Problem" and in resistance to them.[23] Furthermore, by exploring the protest fiction published in China objecting to the extension of Chinese exclusion (in chapter 4), this book extends the national and historical frameworks of current scholarship to consider the global repercussions of U.S. domestic policies on Chinese immigration. In this fashion, *Racial Reconstruction* attends to the complex dynamics of U.S. racial formations at the precise moment at which national debates over black citizenship and Chinese immigration became ideologically articulated with U.S. expansion into the Asia Pacific. The historically contextualized readings that follow reveal broader methodological issues that speak to current theorizations of "comparative racialization" and comparative knowledge productions about race within regional, national, and transnational cultural contexts.

Immigration policies shape American understandings of national membership through specific forms of racial exclusion, as the historian Mae M. Ngai argues in *Impossible Subjects: Illegal Aliens and the Making of Modern America* (2003).[24] Chinese exclusion—the exception that proved the rule—helped the United States redefine itself as a free nation in the wake of racial slavery. Long-standing Chinese struggles against discriminatory state laws on the Pacific Coast, followed by two decades of battles against increasingly stringent federal exclusion laws, generated a vast archive of Chinese immigration case law, policies, and writings charting the rise of immigration administration and the transformation of the U.S. into a modern bureaucratic state. Such racialized exclusions tempered the liberal ideology of U.S. citizenship founded on

Lockean-based notions of universal natural rights, birthright citizenship, and membership through voluntary political allegiance. The San Francisco circuit court first ruled against Chinese naturalization in the case *In re Ah Yup* (1878), and this racialized ban was later incorporated into the 1880 U.S.-China Treaty (or the Angell Treaty) and the federal Chinese exclusion laws that soon followed.[25] Later, in *United States v. Wong Kim Ark* (1898), the U.S. Supreme Court upheld the citizenship of Chinese born on U.S. soil, yet it continued to prohibit Chinese and later Japanese and South Asians from naturalization, deeming all Asiatic immigrants to be unnaturalizable noncitizens.[26] By the end of the nineteenth century, U.S. racial exclusions located people of Chinese descent in the liminal position of existing both within and without the political community of the nation, subject to U.S. jurisdiction yet without the protection of its laws and Constitution. Thus, the U.S. simultaneously embraced a broad, universal definition of national membership based on native birth and voluntary allegiance *and* an exclusionary policy of Asiatic racial differentiation.[27]

In arguing for the centrality of race and racial formations in the making of modern America, this book insists that U.S. racial formations should be studied in different registers and through comparative and transnational approaches. Two years after *Plessy v. Ferguson*, the U.S. began its overseas empire with the annexation of Hawaii, followed by Puerto Rico, Guam, and the Philippines in the Spanish-American War (1898), as it brought into alignment white supremacy and imperial rule. Territorial aggrandizement in the Asia Pacific threw into deeper relief the contradictions embedded within and organizing the law and politics of Chinese exclusion in the U.S. In efforts to stabilize the racial-legal borders between the U.S. mainland and its overseas territories, the federal government extended Chinese exclusion to Hawaii (in the 1898 Hawaiian-U.S. Treaty of Annexation) and the Philippines (in 1899 at the onset of the Philippines-American War and as law in 1902). The extension of Chinese exclusion to the Asia Pacific territories further exacerbated the racial cleavages within U.S. citizenship, provoking additional debate over what constituted membership in the expanding republic. In a series of opinions known as the Insular Cases (1901–1922), the U.S. Supreme Court again reaffirmed the uneven, racialized application of the Constitution—indeed, the legal framework established in *Plessy*—as it judged subjects of these unincorporated foreign territories to be U.S. citizens in matters of discipline and taxation yet ineligible to full protection under the Fourteenth Amendment.[28] The modern era of U.S. race relations inaugurated by *Plessy*'s doctrine of "equal but separate" was not isolated from the global forces of imperialism and colonialism. *Racial Reconstruction* shifts the prevailing axis of race and freedom from North-South to East-West and argues that Afro-Asian racial formations were transregional and transnational processes that mutually constituted each other in complex relation to an emergent post–Civil War ideology of contract freedom. Thus, the book's comparative structure is both formal in its exploration of law and literature and geopolitical in its efforts to bring Pacific Rim studies to bear on Black Atlantic studies. Resisting the tendency to plot American history as the movement from slavery to freedom, this book recuperates those overlooked intellectual and cultural forces that propelled historical continuity and change across the divide of the Civil War and Reconstruction.

By emphasizing the relational character of U.S. racial formations, *Racial Reconstruction* explores how black and Chinese writers first began challenging the idea of America and Americanization as radical Reconstruction dismantled and reformulated the foundational narratives of white racialized citizenship and national identity. Specifically, chapters 2 and 4 chart various ways in which African American, Chinese American, and Chinese writers and commentators (often across the English-Chinese language divide) invented new comparative analytics for understanding racial formations within regional, national, and transpacific contexts. Racialization works relationally through association and differentiation, and these writers took on and adapted various ideologically inflected literary forms—travelogue, print journalism, oratory, sensational fiction, and sentimental literature, in which raced and gendered classifications were defined *and* defied. They sought to account for incommensurability and difference in the processes of comparison, as new forms of relationality between and among long-standing categories, such as slave and free, white and nonwhite, citizen and alien, and the domestic and foreign were forged in the wake of emancipation, increased immigration, and imperial expansion.[29] American literary culture thus gave powerful expression to the dynamics of contact, exchange, negotiation, and conflict that attended the social relations between Chinese immigrants and black and white Americans across regional and national borders.[30]

Chapter 1 mines an underexamined archive of Anglo-American travelogues of Cuba to explore the literary and cultural construction of the Chinese "coolie" as a transatlantic racial formation enmeshed both in the geopolitics of U.S. empire and in national debates over labor versus capital. Controversies over U.S. participation in the lucrative "coolie trade," involving the transport of thousands of Chinese laborers to Cuba and Peru, intensified as sectional tensions over the future of slavery threatened to erupt into Civil War. During this time, a steady stream of personal narratives recounting travels to Cuba made their way into U.S. print with the great boom following Narciso López's widely publicized filibustering expedition to the island and culminating in the 1890s with a flood of books by those who went to Cuba to cover the Spanish-American War. American travelers to Cuba, from the abolitionist Richard Henry Dana and Maturin Murray Ballou (editor of the *Boston Daily Globe* and *Ballou's Pictorial Drawing-Room Companion*) to the Confederate slaveholder Eliza McHatton Ripley sought to answer the question of whether Chinese contract labor constituted a form of slavery or a transition to free labor. The unresolved categorical ambivalence in defining Chinese contract labor lay at the heart of the coolie's figurative significance in the U.S. cultural imaginary. Drawing on Ripley's collected personal papers held at the University of Georgia's Hargrett Rare Books and Manuscript Archives, the chapter reads these travel accounts with and against the Chinese testimonies recorded in the 1876 *Cuba Commission Report* (by a Chinese government-appointed, multinational official investigative commission) and the Chinese American activist and journalist Wong Chin Foo's narrative of a "fugitive coolie" to investigate how these narratives absorbed, refracted, and influenced changing American ideas about slavery, racial citizenship, and free labor, specifically as they took shape in the ideology of contract and the concepts of self-ownership and free will associated with it. These texts helped disseminate the specter of the Chinese "coolie-slave," which shaped U.S. debates over slavery and later became a potent symbol of the enduring legacy of slavery in Reconstruction America.

Chapter 2 connects U.S. expansionist desires in the Caribbean to the racial geopolitics of the Pacific Coast after news of the California gold strike catalyzed Chinese labor immigration to the U.S. By broadening Reconstruction to encompass the West and its "Chinese Question," chapter 2 draws on a diverse range of texts by African American and Chinese American writers, including James Williams, William H. Newby, Frederick Douglass, Yan Phou Lee, and Wong Chin Foo. In juxtaposing lesser-known figures from early African American and Asian American print histories, this chapter investigates the analogization of blacks and Chinese in popular discourse and how these writers negotiated and contested these homogenizing racial representations in oratory and print journalism. As the "Chinese Question" became nationalized in the 1870s, racialization became expressed through an exclusionary discourse of Christian civilization (in opposition to Orientalized heathenism), which came to define the boundaries of acceptable and unacceptable racial difference in the U.S. Shaped by experiences in multiracial California, black writers such as Williams and Newby wrote against Chinese exclusion, representing it as an outgrowth of the racial proscriptions that they had faced during slavery. They acknowledged the complex political histories (and futures) that they shared with indigenous and other racialized groups in the U.S., while Chinese American writers such as Wong and Lee struggled to disarticulate the powerfully racializing discourse of heathenism that helped sustain the dialectic of black inclusion / Chinese (and Native American) exclusion in the wake of Reconstruction.

By the final decades of the nineteenth century, the notion of an Asiatic threat was well established in U.S. culture, in part through the popularization and propagation of Yellow Peril fears in visual and print media. A product of the Pacific Coast anti-Chinese movement, invasion fictions depicting Asiatic aggressors conquering the West first began appearing in print in the 1880s. Chapter 3 teases out the racial fictions and counterfactual imaginings of this popular yet understudied subgenre of Chinese invasion fiction. From legal discourse, including *Chae Chan Ping v. U.S.*, to the once-popular but largely forgotten novels of Pierton W. Dooner, Robert Woltor, Arthur Dudley Vinton, and Marsden Manson and the short stories of more recognized writers, including

Jack London, James D. Corrothers, and Vachel Lindsay, the invasion trope came to dominate U.S.-China relations and public discussions of and federal policies on the "Chinese Question." In combating negative portrayals of white lawlessness and anti-immigrant violence, these texts projected the anxiety of white displacement from labor markets to displacement from the country. Of all the cultural materials studied in this book, the Chinese invasion subgenre's Janus-faced depictions of Chinese labor migrants as abject coolie-slaves *and* villainous fifth-column agents of foreign aggression embodied most vividly the contradictions of American modernity. In linking industrial modernization to national dissolution, the invasion narrative offered a nonteleological vision of American Manifest Destiny as it imagined China as the horizon of industrialized capitalism.

U.S. relations with China underwent another dramatic shift as Progressive-era industrialists began focusing on China as an outlet for surplus overproduction and its teeming populace as future consumers of American manufactures. However, restrictive federal legislation against Chinese immigrants began to conflict with these fantasies of commercial expansion into the Asia Pacific. Chapter 4 engages a range of Chinese literary productions, including Lin Shu's Chinese translation of Harriet Beecher Stowe's antislavery masterpiece, *Uncle Tom's Cabin; or, Life among the Lowly* (1901), the Chinese boycott novel *The Bitter Society* (1905) in partial English translation (by June Mei and Jean Pang Yip in the *Amerasia Journal*), and the self-identified Chinese American Edith Maude Eaton's English-language writings on the North American Chinese. It situates these readings in two overlapping domestic and foreign contexts: the 1905 Chinese boycott of U.S. goods protesting the extension of Chinese exclusion laws to Hawaii and the Philippines and the infamous immigration case of *United States v. Ju Toy* (1905), which denied a U.S. citizen of Chinese descent access to courts to challenge admission and reentry decisions made by immigration inspectors. *Ju Toy* effectively ended decades of Chinese legal protest against exclusion laws. By reading Chinese immigration case law and U.S. foreign policy with and against the reform-based fictions of writers of Chinese descent in the U.S. and abroad (in English and in translation from Chinese), chapter 4 illuminates how the growth of U.S. immigration administration and the rise of the modern bureaucratic state reshaped the meaning of race, citizenship, and nation after colonial expansion into the Asia Pacific.

Racial Reconstruction ends with a conclusion that delineates, in brief, the promise of historical counterfactualism, ending by way of a critical recasting of the Chinese invasion subgenre studied at length in chapter 3. Serialized in the NAACP's *Crisis* magazine, the African American writer James D. Corrothers's two-part tale "A Man They Didn't Know" (1913–14) turned Yellow Peril on its head, revealing its buried racial histories and ideological forms. Corrothers's speculative fiction pushed the counterfactual imaginary of Chinese invasion to its limit, plying the disruptive potential of an Asiatic threat to America in his efforts to challenge the meaning of whiteness and existing racial hierarchies in a world reshaped by *Plessy v. Ferguson* and the global diffusion of white supremacist ideologies. In experimenting with historical mutability, Corrothers's tale reconfigures the relationship between the past and possible futures of race and racialization in the U.S. and suggests some new directions for immigration and comparative racialization studies in the current conjuncture.

1

"Cosa de Cuba!"

American Literary Travels, Empire, and the Contract Coolie

In 1871, the Charleston banker George W. Williams authored *Sketches of Travel in the Old and New World* (1871) after a lavish two-month tour of Cuba, the "Queen of the Antilles." His narrative typified the countless American travelogues of Cuba that found their way into print over the course of the nineteenth century. Beginning in 1847, Cuba's experiment with Chinese contract labor—popularly referred to as coolieism—became a particular fascination for these American travelers. Their narratives sought to answer the question—most concisely formulated by Evelyn Hu-DeHart—of whether Chinese contract labor constituted a form of slavery or a transition to free labor. "I am surprised to see so many Chinamen scattered throughout the Island," writes Williams. "They are brought here by the cargo, in English and Yankee ships, and sold into ten or more years of slavery!" He continues, "You see them loaded with the cruel Spanish chain, for rebelling, when they ascertain how shamefully they have been imposed upon. Oh, for a Harriet Beecher Stowe, to write a Chee-Chow-Wang romance upon the cruelty to this deluded people! It is a horrid thing, according to modern philanthropy, to steal wild Africans, but a blessing to kidnap the educated Chinaman, and sell him into slavery."[1] Merging Orientalism with New World discourse, Williams's droll, sentimentalized appeal sought to educate Americans about the true nature of so-called free Chinese contract labor, as the U.S. began to define the meaning of postemancipation freedoms, often in relation to colonial Cuba, where experiments with Chinese labor appeared closely connected with—and possibly coconstitutive of—black chattel slavery.[2]

This chapter mines an archive of American travelogues to explore the literary and cultural construction of the Chinese "coolie-slave" as a circum-Atlantic racial formation. The analogy embedded in this term influenced the course of U.S. empire in the Caribbean as well as national debates over the "Labor Question" and Chinese immigration. In the nineteenth century, a steady stream of personal narratives recounting travels to Cuba made their way into U.S. print, including Richard Henry Dana's well-received *To Cuba and Back* (1859), Maturin Murray Ballou's *History of Cuba; or, Notes of a Traveller in the Tropics* (1854) and *Due South; or, Cuba Past and Present* (1885), John Abbott's *South and North; or, Impression Received during a Trip to Cuba and the South* (1860), Julia Ward Howe's *A Trip to Cuba* (1860), R. W. Gibbs's *Cuba for Invalids* (1860), Cornelia H. Jenks's *The Land of the Sun; or, What Kate and Willie Saw There* (1861), J. Milton Mackie's *From Cape Cod to Dixie and the Tropics* (1864), Samuel Hazard's *Cuba with Pen and Pencil* (1871), Julia Louisa Matilda Woodruff's *My Winter in Cuba* (1871), James O'Kelly's *The Mambi-Land; or, Adventures of a Herald Correspondent in Cuba* (1874), J. W. Steele's *Cuban Sketches* (1881), and Eliza McHatton Ripley's *From Flag to Flag* (1889), culminating in the 1890s with a flood of books by those who went to Cuba to cover the Spanish-American War (1898).[3]

As a genre, travel literature performed powerful acts of national symbolization as it staged the consolidation of national culture through the representative figure of a traveler in foreign lands. The literary theme of travel not only gave expression to American territorial ambitions in Cuba. It also became a "discursive means for managing a national culture's concern with internal social differences and change," as the U.S. grappled with slavery and abolition.[4] Moreover, feminist scholars have long noted that women travelers occupying tenuous relations to authority—narrative and otherwise—staged difference and sameness in ways that both challenged and diverged from male-authored travelogues.[5] This was especially true in the case of Ripley, a Confederate slaveholder who fled to Cuba after the Civil War. This diverse corpus of Cuban travelogues, ranging from humorous sketches to political journalism and ethnography, helped shore up American attitudes and ideas about the changing relations of race, gender, and labor, while their sustained popularity throughout the century attested to long-standing U.S. expansionist interests in the Caribbean.

This chapter focuses on two narratives, Dana's *To Cuba and Back* and Ripley's *From Flag to Flag*, which represent the antinomies of American political and aesthetic responses to Cuba's Chinese experiment. It pays particular attention to Ripley's management of sexuality, marriage, and Cuban plantation home life, both in practice and in narrative, as key elements of postemancipation discussions of personal freedom. Reformers initially welcome indentured Chinese as a transitional labor force, facilitating the passage from slavery into a wage-labor economy. However, American travelers' eyewitness accounts of wide-scale abuse and contract violations began turning international public opinion against the use of Chinese labor in Cuba. In response, the Chinese government sent a mixed commission of British, French, and Chinese officials to Cuba to investigate the conditions of contract labor. Published in English translation, the resultant 1876 *Cuba Commission Report* furthered the indelible association between black chattel slavery and Chinese labor that later influenced U.S. immigration legislation and public debates over Chinese exclusion.[6] The blending of enslaved black with indentured Chinese labor was, in the oft-repeated refrain of the humorist travel writer and Civil War veteran Samuel Hazard, "Cosa de Cuba!" (Thing of Cuba).[7] By reading these travel accounts with and against the Chinese testimonies recorded in the *Cuba Commission Report* and by the Chinese American newspaperman Wong Chin Foo, this chapter investigates how the "coolie" shaped American ideas about slavery, racial citizenship, and free labor, specifically as they took shape in postemancipation liberal philosophies of contract freedom.

Controversies over American participation in the lucrative "coolie trade," involving the transport of thousands of Chinese contract laborers to Cuba and Peru intensified in the U.S. as sectional tensions over the future of slavery threatened to erupt into Civil War. The specter of a new slave trade in Asiatic coolies helped shape antebellum American debates over domestic slavery in largely understudied ways.[8] It raised the problem of racial definition in U.S. federal policies against the contraband foreign slave trade, and it later became a potent symbol of the enduring afterlife of slavery in Reconstruction-era debates over immigration restriction and control. Analogies between enslaved blacks and Chinese laborers structured U.S. critiques of Cuban coolieism before the Civil War, and their significance intensified after the abolition of slavery, as labor demands grew more acute in the agricultural, postbellum South. This chapter excavates the circum-Atlantic contours of the "Afro-Asian analogy," as the "contract coolie" gave way to the specter of the "coolie-slave." These relations of influence between the U.S. and Cuba reveal underexamined hemispheric circuits of comparative knowledge production about race and racial formations. For Dana, the "Coolie problem" emerged as an unexpected permutation of the "strange system" of unfree labor "by which one man is enthroned in the labor of another race, brought from across the sea," whereas Ripley, fleeing the fall of the Confederacy, turned to Cuba to shore up shifting ideologies of race and slavery.[9] In these long-standing debates over the form and significance of Chinese labor in Cuba, competing proslavery and abolitionist discourses, racial imaginaries, colonial epistemologies, and laws collectively constructed the figure of the Chinese "coolie." The coolie came to represent an alternate racialized labor form that embodied the contradictions and disjunctive temporalities of U.S. emancipation. Was the coolie a throwback to slavery's past or a harbinger of freedom's future?

The Chinese Experiment

Cuba suffered periodic labor shortages after a series of bilateral Anglo-Spanish treaties led to the abolition of the transatlantic slave trade in the Spanish Caribbean. In Cuba, a robust contraband slave trade emerged that continued as late as 1867.[10] The U.S. Civil War helped hasten the end of this contraband trade, as the withdrawal of U.S. ships and capital combined with a British blockade of West African ports stemmed the supply of new slaves to Cuba's expanding sugar industry.[11] According to Sidney Mintz, modern sugar plantations became an "industrial enterprise" combining labor-intensive agricultural work with factory work in the sugar mills, and continuous capital accumulation demanded a steady supply of cheap and plentiful labor.[12] In the face of a growing labor crisis, commentators such as John Thrasher, the U.S.-born filibusterer and editor of the short-lived government-suppressed Cuban newspaper *El Faro*, noted that the "Spanish Government in Cuba has declared that its duty is to increase the supply of labor in that island at all hazards.... Great exertions are being made ... to bring in European, Indian, and Asiatic laborers.... Its declared policy is to reduce the price of labor."[13] Cuban planters began looking toward China's teeming population as a viable source of labor replenishment, "delaying the inevitable crisis that would have set in with the end of the slave trade and making it possible for the plantation economy to continue to prosper," according to Hu-DeHart.[14] At midcentury, one self-described "Yankee" traveler to Cuba speculated that "it would not be strange to see them [Chinese], at some future time, occupying the place of the negroes in all agricultural districts."[15]

The coolie trade emerged in an Atlantic world that had yet to see the end of black chattel slavery or the political structures that seemed to ensure its indefinite continuation. In 1806, as Britain debated the abolition of the transatlantic slave trade, Chinese contract labor was first introduced into the West Indies in the short-lived "Trinidad experiment," which imagined Chinese labor as a buffer against black slave rebellion and a means to expand West Indian sugar production.[16] By 1838, Britain had turned to India, importing a million South Asians to Mauritius in British East Africa and the plantation economies of British Guiana, Trinidad, Jamaica, Suriname, and Fiji just as Chinese laborers first began arriving to Cuba.[17] Moreover, British colonial incursions into the long-fabled China market, culminating in the Anglo-Chinese Wars or the Opium Wars (1839–1842, 1856–1860), further catalyzed this Chinese outward migration.[18] In Cuba, Chinese labor served as both substitute for and supplement to black chattel slavery. It facilitated the restructuring of long-standing colonial labor systems, helping to stabilize *and* undermine existing colonial orders.[19] In Lowe's insightful formulation, the Chinese appeared as a "collective *figure*, a fantasy of 'free' yet racialized and indentured labor" central to the development, following Michel Foucault, of "a modern racial governmentality."[20] Thus, the "coolie" helped sustain a narrative of historical transition from slavery to free labor in Cuba even as it troubled the "social and cultural dualisms" at the heart of a long-standing colonial slave society, which tethered legal status and identity to a racial hierarchy that parsed legal and social rights according to whether the individual was considered "de color."[21]

American ships helped transport up to 225,000 Chinese laborers to Cuba and Peru between 1847 and 1874.[22] Largely originating in the infamous Portuguese transit port of Macao, Chinese coolies awaited shipment in guarded barracoons, and their transport vessels followed a lengthy six-month route crossing the Indian and Atlantic Oceans to

Cuba in what was known as *la trata amarilla* (the yellow trade) in Spanish.[23] American vessels quickly surpassed the British, Spanish, French, and Portuguese in the transport of primarily male Chinese laborers. British vessels dominated the shipping of South Asian labor, which involved the transport of men along with widows, married couples, and families, unlike its Chinese counterpart.[24] Joseph Conrad's novella *Typhoon* (1900–1901) fictionalized this nefarious commerce as it imagined the calamitous journey of the steamship *Nan-Shan* transporting two hundred Chinese "coolies," "all seven-years'-men."[25] As a furious hurricane engulfs the *Nan-Shan*, British Captain MacWhirr's incredulous reply to his first mate's growing concern over the safety of the Chinese locked in the darkness of the damaged and flooded "'tween deck" reveals the logic of commodification that underwrote the global commerce in coolies. "Never heard of a lot of coolies spoken of as passengers before," exclaims MacWhirr. "Passengers, indeed! What's come to you?"[26] By century's end, coolieism had come to name a racialized servile labor regime akin to the African slavery that it was imagined to supplant.

In the 1850s, U.S. newspapers had begun to remark with increasing distress on the prevalence of "Northern freighting ships" "from the ports of New York and Boston" engaged in the transport of "Chinamen Coolies" to Cuba.[27] For these outraged commentators, the transport of Chinese by American vessels constituted a circumvention of the 1808 Slave Trade Act, which prohibited the "transport from any of the coasts or kingdoms of Africa, or from any other foreign kingdom, place or country, or from any sea, any negro or mulatto or person of color . . . in any ship, vessel, boat, or other water-craft, for the purposes of holding, selling, or otherwise disposing of such person as a slave, or to be held to service or labor."[28] Additional legislation in 1820 enforced this ban, declaring participation in the foreign slave trade to be an act of piracy punishable by death. As the slavery controversy spilled into sectional violence, the Chinese coolie raised the problem of racial definition in U.S. federal policies against the contraband foreign slave trade.[29] "We do an immense business in Coolie transportation," observed William Lloyd Garrison's *Liberator*, "and sometimes do it horribly."[30] Ballou's Boston-based story paper *Flag of Our Union* took an even stronger stance as it portrayed Chinese indentured or contract labor as a "system of labor-stealing ... countenanced and encouraged by England, France, and Spain; and even American vessels are engaged in the butcher-business of transporting these victims of falsehood, fraud, and force, to their place of doom."[31]

Critics called for a radical reinterpretation of the existing federal law against the foreign slave trade to include the Chinese coolie as highly publicized mutinies and suicides aboard U.S. vessels strengthened associations between coolie transport and the banned foreign slave trade in the minds of American readers.[32] In 1855, three hundred Chinese laborers en route to Peru perished of suffocation during a violently suppressed revolt aboard the Boston-based *Waverly*.[33] The following year, antislavery northerners introduced the Coolie Trade Prohibition Act in Congress, but southern opposition repeatedly delayed its passage until after Confederate secession.[34] In 1862, Abraham Lincoln finally signed the "Act to prohibit the 'Coolie Trade' by American citizens in American Vessels" just months before the Emancipation Proclamation, which fundamentally changed the character of the Civil War by linking it to the issue of slavery.[35] The Coolie Trade Prohibition Act might be viewed as America's last slave-trade regulation and its first federal immigration restriction, as Moon-Ho Jung observes.[36] After the abolition of legal slavery, the regulation of Chinese labor migration inaugurated a new era of U.S. federal control over immigration.[37] Forged in the sectional struggle over slavery, the Coolie Trade Prohibition Act explicitly differentiated human importation from immigration as it established certification of voluntary emigration as the fundamental condition of entry to the U.S.

American Travels to Cuba

The travel narrative was one of the most commercial and well-liked forms of nineteenth-century writing, and American visitors to Cuba were among the most prolific contributors to the genre.[38] These travelogues offered some of the most detailed, firsthand accounts of Chinese coolies in Cuba, and they played a significant role in shaping American public opinion of Chinese labor immigration to the West in general. The great boom in U.S. travel accounts of Cuba dates from 1850–1865, following General Narciso López's widely publicized failed filibustering expedition to the island. These travel books found a guaranteed market in the U.S., as Cuban exiles turned New York and New Orleans into centers for both Hispanophone publishing and independence movements against Spanish colonial rule throughout Latin America and the Caribbean, as Rodrigo Lazo and Kirsten Silva Gruesz have documented.[39] These Cuban anticolonialists often forged unlikely alliances with American imperialists in advocating U.S. annexation. Cuba had been the object of U.S. purchase offers for three decades, and it was not unusual for commentators such as the editor of the *New Orleans Picayune* to portray U.S. annexation of Cuba as Cuban independence from Spain.[40] In the 1840s, Cuba became even more tightly drawn into the sphere of U.S. economic influence when the rise of French and German beet-sugar cultivation closed European markets to Cuban sugar. The U.S. became Cuba's sole overseas market.[41] Moreover, Cuba's proximity to the U.S. led expansionists to claim its location as essential to American Manifest Destiny, for "its possession would give us command of the Archipelago and all the neighboring seas, so that on island and continent, land and water, our power would be supreme."[42]

As the threat of secession and Civil War loomed, debates over the future of slavery and the possibility of emancipation in the U.S. became structured as much by sectional politics as by the prospect of Cuba becoming a slaveholding state in the Union.[43] Arguments for annexation often cut across deeply divisive regional and political lines, as secessionists and unionists, abolitionists and slaveholders laid various political and moral claims on Cuba.[44] The island nation, writes the historian Matthew Pratt Guterl, "entered the Southern imagination . . . as a future state in the republic, destined to be absorbed by the supposedly predestined advance of Southern slavery into the global South."[45] After the onset of the Civil War, Confederates such as Ripley looked to Cuba to shore up their old plantation way of life in the face of new race and labor ideologies.[46] Even proannexation travelogues by antislavery northerners such as Ballou began to naturalize the geographical contiguity between the U.S. and Cuba to argue for the island's inevitable absorption into the Union. "Naturally belonging to this country by every rule that can be applied," writes Ballou, "Cuba will ere long be politically ours."[47] Another travelogue confidently declared that Cuba "is inevitably bound to become one of the States of our Confederacy."[48]

In this fashion, the island functioned as a "powerful site for imagining alternative models of race, nation, and empire, even as Cuba was integral to the creation of an explicitly racialized U.S. imperialism," as Caroline Levander argues.[49]

American travelogues of Cuba influenced the shape of these imperial fantasies as extended visits to sugar estates worked by African slaves and Chinese coolies became an established convention of the genre. The sighting of a Matanzas sugar plantation with its characteristic *ingenio*—the sugarhouse steam works—confirms the romantic fantasy of a "tropical, rich, sugar-growing, slave-tilled Cuba" that Dana had long envisioned in his mind's eye: "The plantation life that I am seeing and about to see, tells the story of Cuba, the Cuba that has been and that is" (95, 96). Travelogues constructed slaves and coolies as aesthetic objects, naturalizing them to the exotic landscape in relation to each other.[50] For example, British travelogues of the postemancipation West Indies reinvented the picturesque as a disciplinary "aesthetic mode" "of apprehending, rendering, and controlling" South Asian coolies as the colonies' newest source of labor, according to Amar Wahab.[51] American accounts often juxtaposed the coolie's alien strangeness against the black Creole slaves' New World assimilation. In an 1871 travelogue, Julia Woodruff (under the pseudonym W. M. L. Jay) recalls accosting a Yankee engineer at Ingenio Santa Sofía while on a tour of Matanzas: "I asked some questions relative to the comparative efficiency of slave and coolie labor." The Yankee's impressions were not in the least complimentary. "The coolies do know a leetle the most," he informs Woodruff, "but they are apt to be cross-grained, ugly chaps (to be sure, it's no wonder, considerin' how they're treated); and then they don't mind up and killing themselves, when they git mad, any more'n I do paring my nails. I'd rather have ten niggers to manage, than one Chinaman, by a long chalk."[52] As the abolition of slavery brought about a labor crisis in the agricultural South, Cuba's experiment with Chinese contract labor became even more significant to American readers. By the 1880s, well after the demise of the Old South, no American visit to Cuba was complete without such a tour of a sugar estate worked by coolies and slaves. Ballou's 1885 travelogue advised readers that the "visitor should not fail to make an excursion to some representative plantation, where it is impossible not to be much interested and practically informed" (49).

After the U.S. abolished legal slavery, Cuba's ongoing exploitation of Chinese coolies offered American annexation advocates additional moral justification for empire in the Caribbean.[53] The Quaker serial *Friends' Intelligencer* observed that "visitors to Cuba, during this past winter, have had enlarged opportunities of noting the condition of the Cooly apprentices, of whom thousands swarm everywhere on that lovely island."[54] Such widely disseminated accounts of the slave-like conditions of Chinese coolies in Cuba helped bolster moral arguments for U.S. annexation, while affirming the newly reunified U.S. as a beacon of freedom and humanitarianism in the hemisphere.[55] For example, Williams's tongue-in-cheek call for a "Harriet Beecher Stowe, to write a Chee-Chow-Wang romance" marshaled the idea of coolie liberation as just cause for U.S. imperial intervention in the Spanish Caribbean. American travelers, unlike their British counterparts, were not ideologically invested in restoring the colonial symbolic order of the Caribbean colonies they visited.[56] They were far more likely to depict Cuba and its strange system of Chinese coolieism as chaotic and disordered, demanding U.S. intervention. In this fashion, Ballou's *History of Cuba* depicted the Spanish colony languishing in "political darkness" and yearning for the "independence and freedom" of its Republican neighbor. "To go hence to Cuba," he writes, "is not merely passing over a few degrees of latitude in a few days' sail,—it is a step from the nineteenth century back into the dark ages" (216). Cuba's failed experiment with Chinese labor only lent additional support to the growing consensus that the slaveholding island had become a retrogressive anachronism in an increasingly free and liberalizing Atlantic world.

Fictions of Contract Freedom: Richard Henry Dana's *To Cuba and Back*

From the 1850s to 1870s, American perspectives regarding the Cuban experiment with Chinese contract labor became increasingly negative, as contract ideology came to dominate postemancipation U.S. political discourse. Initially, writers such as Dana had hailed the Cuban experiment as an odd permutation of the Atlantic "slave racial capitalism" requiring further study, but such curiosity turned into outright rejection as writers became increasingly convinced of the experiment's failure.⁵⁷ In reviewing recent travel accounts, the *Friends' Intelligencer* concluded that "this scheme of slavery, every feature of which is worse in all particulars than negro servitude, sickens the traveler in Cuba at every turn."⁵⁸ Chinese contract laborers were, in its words, "oriental slaves . . . nominally, for seven years; but, substantially, for life, since no provision is made for restoring them to their homes."⁵⁹ This system of contract labor amounted "to little less than slavery in a new form," in the words of the Quaker serial *Friends' Review*, as Chinese laborers became strongly linked to the black chattel slaves whom they were supposed to supplant.⁶⁰ This deep figurative association between Chinese labor and slavery in the American popular imaginary held devastating consequences for the national debates over Chinese exclusion studied in chapter 2.

Of the earlier travelogues, Dana's popular 1859 account of his three-weeks journey throughout Cuba was perhaps the most influential, given its extended investigation of Chinese contract labor as a new development in the regimes of racialized unfree labor and capitalist expansion in the Caribbean. The Massachusetts-born Dana was a prominent abolitionist lawyer who had helped establish the antislavery Free Soil Party in 1848 and later unsuccessfully defended (with the African American lawyer Robert Morris) the Virginia slave Anthony Burns in one of the most controversial cases to come under the infamous 1850 Fugitive Slave Act. Dana's visit coincided with the Thirty Millions Bill—an expansionist proposal to purchase Cuba from Spain, pending before Congress. The *Little's Living Age* review of Dana's travelogue noted the timeliness of the publication, given the way in which subjects pertaining to Cuba had "become complicated through that restless desire in the United States for extension of territory."⁶¹ Reviews and extractions of Dana's travelogue in antislavery newspapers such as the *Liberator* and the *Friend* focused on its contributions to ongoing debates over the future of American slavery if Cuba was to be annexed.⁶² "As a Northerner, and averse to slavery," concludes one review, "Mr. Dana is decidedly hostile to any plan for including Cuba within the Union."⁶³

The Cuba that Dana discovers is a "motley multitude of whites, blacks, and Chinese" (157). These "intermeshed transculturations" of New World plantation societies were a source of both attraction and repulsion for American travelers who viewed them as essential elements of Cuban difference from the U.S.⁶⁴ In Havana, the strange sight of "men of an Indian complexion, with coarse black hair" arrests Dana's attention (53). For many American travelers such as Dana, the sighting of Chinese laborers in Cuba was marked by ambivalence and disorientation, which served to heighten the exotic appeal of Chinese difference. Dana mistakes the Chinese as "native Indians, or of mixed blood," but later realizes that they are "Coolies, . . . the victims of the trade, of which we hear so much about": "I am told there are 200,000 of them in Cuba, or, that so many have been imported, and all within seven years" (53). Dana's effort at racial classification and the misattribution of the Chinese as indigenous Indians connects to long-standing colonial efforts to manage the creolized mixing of laboring populations.⁶⁵

Chinese laborers occupy a central place in Dana's experience of Cuba. On morning walks to the Havana sea baths, he espies files "of Coolies, in Chinese costume, marching, under overseers, to their work or their jail" (71). Coolies "dressed in the common shirt, trowsers and hat" serve as the "brakemen on the train" from Matanzas to the interior of the country (90).⁶⁶ American accounts emphasized the pervasiveness of Chinese coolies throughout Cuba, unlike comparable British travelogues of the West Indies, which depicted South Asian coolies as largely contained to plantation estates.⁶⁷ In an effort to "give the reader an idea [of Cuba], if he doesn't go there himself," Hazard's *Cuba with Pen and Pencil* depicts Chinese coolies as fully integrated into all aspects of the colonial economy. For example, he describes in detail the "cooley making cigarettes" in a La Honradez tobacco factory, Chinese peddlers roaming Havana streets, "a highly intellectual and intelligent *Chinois* boy" who served as his male "chamber-*maid*" in Matanzas, and gangs of "negroes and Chinese" working the Cobre Mountains copper mines, before he offers the obligatory discussion of Chinese labor in sugar production—a requisite of the American travelogue of Cuba.⁶⁸

Dana's early fascination with Chinese contract labor was not unusual, for "nearly every visitor to Cuba," according to Guterl, "studied the Chinese, the most confusing addition, they thought, to the political economy of slavery."⁶⁹ For Dana, Chinese contract labor offers a unique opportunity to investigate the permutations of an Atlantic slave system in decline. The language of romanticism fuses with economic pragmatism as Dana sets out to understand "this strange development of the domination of capital over labor," traveling to sugar plantations in Matanzas and a "mart of Coolie in the Cerro" (53–54) to witness it firsthand. Dana's visit to the "Coolie jail, or market, where the imported Coolies are kept for sale" offers him "a strange and striking exhibition of power" (196). By emphasizing the coercive nature of Chinese contract labor, Dana contradicts spirited defenses of coolieism, which claimed, in the words of one official, that "the Chinese are universally regarded in the island as free laborers under a civil contract, . . . and on the completion of the stipulated term of service, they are at liberty either to remain in Cuba, or to return to their own country."[70] Tellingly, Dana's extended discussion of Chinese contract labor comes in a chapter titled "Slavery," which defines coolieism as a form of unfree labor tantamount to black chattel slavery:

> The Cuban authorities assume them to be free men, making voluntary contracts, and do no more. That they are kept in strict confinement until sold, and then kept to labor by force, there is no doubt. I suppose there is as little doubt that the form of a contract is gone through with, which binds them to all labor for eight years, at four dollars per month and their board and two suits of clothes annually. It is not yet eight years since their introduction; and it remains to be decided what this contract amounts to. That they can be forced into a servitude for life, if it is for the interest of their purchasers to force them to it, and the government does not interfere energetically, there can be as little doubt. . . . Their presence in Cuba adds another distressing element to the difficulties of the labor question, which hangs, like a black cloud, over all the islands of the West Indies. (242–244)

For Dana, coolieism masked "servitude for life" in the trappings of contract, long valorized as the guarantor of free society in the Western legal and philosophical tradition. The form and significance of Chinese contract labor in Cuba troubled Americans such as Dana who sought to understand the shifting relations between race and labor under modern capitalism and to imagine the possible consequences of abolition for U.S. society at large.[71]

Cuba's experiment with Chinese labor revealed how forms of free labor secured by "voluntary contract," in Dana's words, emerged as largely continuous with (rather than opposed to) enslaved labor in the plantation systems of the Atlantic world. Of all the travelogues, Dana's *From Cuba and Back* most forcefully emphasizes the strangeness of Chinese indentured or contract labor as an ambiguous intermediary form of so-called free labor. Unlike black chattel slaves, Chinese laborers were not legally defined as commodities; however, their labor was imagined as property subject to the processes of commodification in exchange for a wage. This wage legally entitled a *patrón* or employer to the time and industry (however forcibly extracted) of his Chinese laborer, and this entitlement to labor was represented as distinct from the entitlement to persons under slavery.[72] This exchange, noted one impassioned critic, "reduc[es] human labor to the list of marketable commodities—making it an object of purchase and sale, and holding it, subject to the various vicissitudes which attend stocks, provisions, dry goods and other articles of commerce."[73]

In Cuba, the bilingual labor contract embodied this logic of commodification. Colonial regulations accorded the *patrón* the right to sell and resell contracts at will. "The striking peculiarity of these contracts is," explains William Ashmore of the American Baptist Missionary Union, "that they are . . . like notes of hand, and become negotiable, because the service is pledged, not to the agent alone, but to *the holder of the contract*." He continues, "To all practical purposes the paper constitutes a substitute for a deed of sale in all countries where slavery exists."[74] Labor contracts were often transferred from one *patrón* to another, although planters such as Ripley's brother commonly spoke of purchasing Chinese *laborers* (rather than their labor *contracts*).[75] In 1874, Chinn paid $700 in gold for six Chinese laborers from another planter who "bought 6 Chinese to make a trial and not being pleased wished to sell them again."[76] Thus, Chinese contract labor was largely commensurable with black chattel slavery yet legally defined as a "free" alternative to enslaved labor. The logic of commodification, as Stephanie Smallwood explains, "secures particular ways of seeing, evaluating, classifying, and representing things that emphasize fixed, uniform, stable characteristics, so as to render their commensurability self-evident and thereby facilitate their easy circulation and exchange as commodities in the market economy."[77] American travelers such as Dana were troubled as much by how the Cuban experiment revealed the logic of commodification at the heart of free contract labor as by how this commodification functioned as a discursive system.[78]

Such experiments with Chinese coolies in the Atlantic world—specifically, in the Spanish Caribbean—helped reshape understandings of contract and free labor before and especially after U.S. abolition, revealing another facet of the heterodox negotiations over nineteenth-century contract studied in Amy Dru Stanley's influential work *From Bondage to Contract: Wage Labor, Marriage, and the Market in the Age of Slave Emancipation* (1998), which explores how contract became the "dominant metaphor for social relations and the very symbol of freedom" in the age of emancipation.[79] Abolitionists, as Stanley argues, "drew on contract to describe the changes in their world and to distinguish between the commodity relations of freedom and bondage."[80] For these abolitionists, contract functioned as more than a worldview. It designated a social relation resting on "principles of self-ownership, consent, and exchange," in which "the negation of chattel status lay in . . . selling one's labor as a free market commodity, and in marrying and maintaining a home."[81] Accounts of Chinese contract labor in Cuba unsettled contract ideology at the moment of its emerging prominence in American political discourse, drawing attention to the forms of coercion, dependency, and constraint intimately bound up with the promise of contract.

The commodification of Chinese contract labor in Cuba conflicted with Enlightenment traditions of liberal thought foundational to Western law and society. William Blackstone's *Commentaries on the Laws of England* had long defined contract in terms of consent and reciprocity based on exchange, although exchange itself need not be of perfect equivalents, as the equities of contract, like the market, were self-regulating.[82] In antebellum America, the deepening sectional struggles over slavery, as Stanley writes, further "infused the principles of self ownership, consent, and exchange with new ideological urgency."[83] The figure of the "contract coolie" thus problematized the antislavery identification of contract with personal freedom and social justice with the fulfillment of contract.[84] John Locke's *Second Treatise of Civil Government* (1690) had long asserted that "freedom from absolute, arbitrary power, is so necessary to, and closely joined with a man's preservation, that he . . . cannot, by compact, or his own consent, enslave himself."[85]

In a nation reshaped by Civil War and abolition, American writers began more forcefully analogizing Chinese contract labor in Cuba to black chattel slavery, anomalizing it as a relic of slavery's past. For example, a *New York Times* editorial encouraged U.S. readers along with the Chinese government to oppose "a system of contract labor which has been so shamefully abused." "If America and England stand together in their opposition to this new slave trade," the editorial urged, "it, like its predecessor, will soon be extinguished."[86] In U.S. popular and political discourses, the renominalization of the Chinese contract laborer as the "coolie-slave" sought to expunge the specter of coercion—indeed, the fundamental unfreedom of contract relations—from the growing orthodoxy of contract freedom in Reconstruction America.

Writing from the vantage of Reconstruction, later travelogues by American writers and journalists confirmed Dana's early fears. Chinese coolies were no longer the harbingers of free labor but the "wretched" byproducts of Cuba's old slave system (Ballou 38–39). A Bostonian who wintered in Cuba, Ballou depicts coolie importation as a continuation of black chattel slavery, a source of cheap labor to "supply the places of the constantly diminishing slaves" (61). In charting the history of the "coolie system," Ballou's 1885 *Due South* analogizes Chinese importation to the now-defunct African slave trade, excoriating it as a similar "fraud and an outrage upon humanity" (62). Sent to cover the Ten Years' War, the *New York Herald* correspondent O'Kelly, likewise, lumps together "negroes and Chinese" as collective figures for a now-obsolete system of slave labor: they are "wretched beings, ignorant and degraded to the last degree, without a spark of that manly independence which is so marked a feature of the working classes in free countries."[87] Such postbellum narratives often positioned coolies and slaves as equivalent forms of unfree labor, but they also made a point of asserting a lack of intimacy between the two racialized groups. Like Ballou in *Due South*, O'Kelly strains to parse the differences between Chinese contract labor in Cuba and free labor in the U.S., concluding the "experiment of Chinese labor" to be a failed one.[88]

The vexed figure of the Chinese contract laborer thus stood as an archetype of the wage slave, a centerpiece of the anticapital discourses of American labor reformers in the industrialized North for whom the purchase of labor (as an unalienable essence of man, according to some

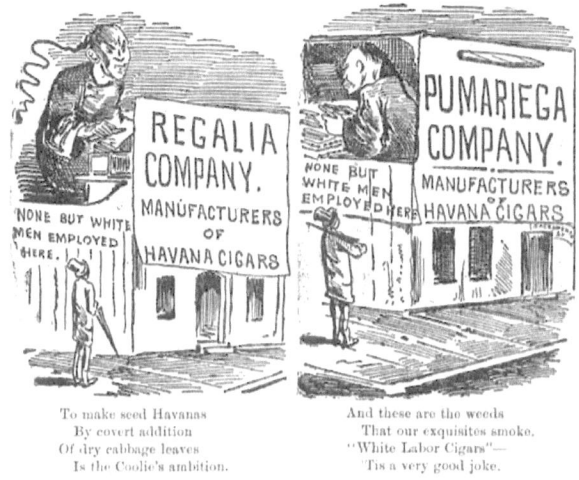

Figure 1.1. "Celestial Cubans," *Wasp* 2 (August 1877–July 1878): 267 (Courtesy of the Bancroft Library, University of California–Berkeley)

workingmen) was tantamount to the purchase of the laborer himself.[89] Debates over the nature and form of Chinese contract labor rehearsed aspects of the claim, increasingly popularized by the "Labor Question," that wage work constituted a form of bondage, as labor activists began to attack contract as a paradigm of free social relations.[90] The complex links between waged work and chattel bondage were first forged in the vigorous debates over the Chinese contract labor system in Cuba (and American participation in it). However, American labor activists, facing Chinese "cheap" labor brought in to break industrial strikes, aggressively disarticulated their struggle against the commoditization of labor and loss of self-entitlement entailed in the wage contract from earlier protests over coolieism in the Spanish Caribbean.[91] In a telling political cartoon, "Celestial Cubans" (1877–1878), the anti-Chinese *San Francisco Wasp* (over which Ambrose Bierce assumed editorship in 1881) offered satirical commentary on the nature of Chinese contract labor in Cuba by highlighting the incongruity of coolieism as a putative form of free "white" labor in signage that reads, "None but white men employed here" (see figure 1.1).[92] Postbellum labor movements marshaled a discourse of contract servitude first honed in the long-standing debates over the nature and form of Chinese contract labor in Cuba.[93] These efforts to challenge the authority of contract as an organizing principle of free society drew on the symbolism of wage slavery purified of reference to Cuba's failed experiment with Chinese contract labor.

As noted by critics and advocates alike, the feature that distinguished Chinese from black enslaved labor lay in the legal instrument of the written labor contract. "The circumstance that 'contracts' are made with the Coolies has been persistently put forward as establishing a wide gulf between the Coolies and slaves," observed one critic.[94] Styled as a "voluntary emigrant," the Chinese laborer was recognized "in the class of persons legally capable of contracting for themselves," unlike black slaves, who were categorized "with minors, insane persons, etc., who have no recognized legal right to act for themselves" under Cuban law.[95] As Lisa Yun argues, the Chinese testimonies collected by the Cuba Commission in 1874 reveal a pervasive struggle over these "document papers."[96] The *patrón* often held the contracts and *cedulas* (identification papers) of their Chinese laborers, who, unable to prove their identities or the fulfillment of contracts, were often coerced into laboring without compensation well beyond the terms of their original agreements.[97] For example, Ripley held onto the Cedula de Libres de Color number 249, dated October 1868, for her twenty-year-old Chinese cook, José Puchal, which she brought back to the U.S., where it found its way into her collected family papers (see figure 1.2).[98]

Commodification operated as a discursive system, and Cuba created a vast system of legal documentation to help facilitate the labor coercion implied by, but not explicitly expressed in, the contract. In 1872, the *New York Herald* correspondent O'Kelly observed that "colored people and coolies were constantly compelled to exhibit their permit to travel; and, in several cases, men were arrested on account of some irregularity in their papers."[99] Often in collusion with government officials, planters falsely claimed Chinese laborers as runaways and forced them to recontract if they did not have official "freedom papers" stipulating the completion of contracts. In some cases, corrupt officials simply forced laborers to relinquish their legal papers, deeming them as false.[100] Given the significance of these documents, testimonial accounts recorded in the *Cuba Commission Report* often represented the contract as the figurative and literal embodiment of the asymmetrical relations of racialized colonial power in Cuba.[101]

Figure 1.2. Cedula de Libres de Color for José Puchal, number 249, October 1868 (Carton 10, Thomas Hubbard McHatton Family Papers; courtesy of the Hargrett Rare Books and Manuscript Library, University of Georgia Libraries)

Thus, to many observers, the voluntary contract structuring Chinese labor in Cuba was a grotesque perversion of the self-ownership and free will of contract relations.[102] Indeed, the 1874 Chinese Commission to Cuba declared the contract's "various clauses evincing a certain consideration for the interests of the Chinese" to be "empty words" (81). Both preceding and paralleling U.S. struggles over the "Labor Question," these early investigations into Chinese contract labor in Cuba reveal the complex ways by which contract, as Stanley has argued, "served as a legitimating symbol for social relations in which inequality was either cloaked by exchange or said to arise from consent."[103] "The coolie system, which was latterly substituted for that of the importation of Africans," notes Ballou, "was commenced in 1847, but it was only slavery under another form, being in point of humanity even more objectionable" (271–273). To northern critics such as Ballou, coolieism was more reprehensible than black chattel slavery was: it was coerced servitude legitimated through the legal artifice of contract. Indeed, proslavery southern ideologues such as J. D. B. DeBow of *DeBow's Review* and antislavery advocates such as Dana had long concurred on this point: coolieism involved the desecration of free will associated with contract.[104] By 1872, the year of O'Kelly's visit to Cuba, "there was no pretense on the part of any one to regard them [coolies] in any other light than as slaves."[105] To these various commentators, Chinese coolieism was slavery under the guise of contract freedom. It revealed the specter of the coercion and alienation that lay at the heart of all contract relations in the age of emancipation.[106]

Confederates in Cuba: Eliza McHatton Ripley's *From Flag to Flag*

Eliza McHatton Ripley's 1889 autobiographical narrative of life and travels, *From Flag to Flag: A Woman's Adventures and Experiences in the South during the War, in Mexico, and in Cuba*, vividly illuminates the transnational links that bound the U.S. South to the Atlantic world of coolies and slaves. Eliza and James Alexander McHatton were members of an elite "transnational planter class" whose social and economic well-being was bound as much to the futurity of slavery in U.S. as to its continuance in the hemisphere.[107] A former Confederate, Ripley's narrative of ten years' residence in Cuba as the co-owner with her brother of a large sugar estate offers a powerful counternarrative to earlier accounts of Chinese contract labor circulated by northern antislavery writers such as Dana and Ballou. Unlike these other travelers, Ripley participated in the society that others merely observed. A spirited defense of Chinese contract labor, *From Flag to Flag* presents one of the most detailed accounts of coolieism from the perspective of an American *patrón* or employer in Cuba. This section reads Ripley's narrative of her life and travels against the grain and in the context of her collected personal papers held at the University of Georgia's Hargrett Rare Books and Manuscript Archives to illuminate the circum-Atlantic struggles over race and gender, slavery and freedom elided from her published account. In practice and in the narrative, Ripley reveals the centrality of gender, sexuality, and labor to the domestic management of racialized populations. Her emphasis on marriage, home life, and the Cuban plantation household also contributes to Reconstruction-era debates over individualism and contract freedom.

From Flag to Flag charts Ripley's movements from Civil War–era Louisiana, Texas, and Mexico to Cuba, where she along with other Confederate exiles sought to reestablish the slaveholding society lost in the Civil War. Significantly, Ripley makes no mention of the U.S. North, specifically New York, where she lived until her death in 1912 after leaving Cuba in 1873. This unspoken region serves as the site of her narrative production and literary reception and, like other occluded aspects of her life in Cuba, helped shaped the story of sectional and racial reconciliation and national progress that Ripley sought to disseminate in print. Like other writers, Ripley capitalized on the broad postwar memorial impulse in literary publication. She published *From Flag to Flag* during a resurgence of interest in the Civil War. One review numbered the volume among the many "literary souvenirs of the Confederacy . . . perpetually cropping up, now in one form, now in another."[108] Shortly before her death, Ripley completed a second nostalgic account of the Old South published posthumously as *Social Life in Old New Orleans* (1912).[109] Having lost the war, Confederates such as Ripley sought to win the battle over cultural memory in their literary efforts to dominate interpretations of the Civil War, from its costs and causes to its legacies and meanings for the reunited nation, according to Coleman Hutchison.[110]

Ripley manages the contradictions of authority staged in women's travelogues by constructing a narrative that successfully performs the southern delicacy required of white femininity in the face of the harsh realities of managing a racialized slave plantation in Cuba. *From Flag to Flag* aligns itself with the plantation romance with its portrayals of mischievous "darkies" and the affectionate bonds between mistress and slave. This genre grew in popularity with regional rapprochement and the emerging architecture of Jim Crow in the postwar American South.[111] Ripley begins by describing the idyllic past of her Louisiana plantation home, where she arrived as a young bride one decade before the Civil War.[112] Back then, reminisces Ripley, "the fields were dotted with groups of busy and contented slaves, and their cabins resounded with the merry voices of playing children" (1). Reviewers lauded the unique female perspective of the book and its glimpses into the "interior life of the Confederacy, the domestic sufferings and hardships . . . which overtook thousands of Southern families."[113] The narrative lays bare the "inside of the Confederacy . . . in a way to make the heart quiver," applauded the *Critic*.[114] Ripley's sympathetic portrait of Confederate domesticity sought to offset potential criticism of her efforts to extend a slaveholding way of life in Cuba that had passed from U.S. soil.

The McHattons fled their Arlington plantation after Union forces seized control of the state capital at Baton Rouge. A moderate Democrat, Ripley's husband co-owned a Mississippi plantation with the Illinois senator Stephen A. Douglas, and partial blindness relieved him from active service in the Civil War.[115] The McHattons faced the "only alternative, voluntary exile," after Union Commander Nathaniel Banks took steps to abolish slavery in Union-occupied areas of Louisiana.[116] Against Union orders, the McHattons surreptitiously transferred their slaves into the safekeeping of Ripley's brother in Texas and Mexico. No doubt they saw this as a means to stem the dangerous "querulous discontent" among their now "contraband" human property (Ripley 30). In December 1862, the McHattons joined the "hundreds of refugees fleeing . . . from their . . . homes," traveling westward to northeastern Mexico along the Gulf Coast (31, 33, 41). This border area became a strategic center for Confederate commerce and mercantilism, particularly for the Union blockade-running cotton trade in which the McHattons were involved (76).

Ripley held a deep investment in slaveholding paternalism, and her narrative betrays few traces of the struggles she faced maintaining the fiction of affective reciprocal ties between slave and mistress as legal slavery in the U.S. came to an end. Posted from Mexico and Cuba, Ripley's personal correspondences help flesh out her complicated negotiations with the slaves she smuggled out of the U.S. They belie her literary efforts to construct a romantic narrative of slavery's past. During her "wandering life" in Mexico, Ripley offers humorous reflections on the racialized curiosity that she and her enslaved maid Delia offered to local Mexicans, for whom Ripley was "the first *white* woman and [her] attendant the first *black* one the generation had seen" (74, 52). Steeped in romantic racialism, these humorous sketches sought to offset the significance of later instances of slave intransigence and willful self-assertion. While in Mexico, Delia took advantage of Mexican law, which abolished slavery and decreed slave importation illegal in 1829, to emancipate herself from the McHattons. According to Ripley's narrative, Delia "disappeared the morning we left Piedras Negras to return to Texas" (70). After Delia's escape, the McHattons took steps to prevent any additional losses to their human property. Ripley wrote her sister with news concerning her two other domestic slaves, Martha and Zell. "They both behave exceedingly well," she observes, "but we whispered the thing once, and concluded he was less secure than she and maybe we had better send him to H[avana] to stay there until we go over—then we have a *nigger sure*."[117] In a preemptive gesture, the McHattons send Zell away from Mexico, preferring to secure their chattel property on Cuban soil.

Largely elided from the published narrative, these letters reveal the tense undercurrents structuring the relationship between mistress and slaves, as Ripley strove to maintain authority over slaves who were no longer her legal property. Once apprised of the McHattons' intention to migrate to slaveholding Cuba, another household slave, named Humphrey, following Delia, refused to leave Mexico. He went even further, calling on Mexican officials to prevent Ripley from transporting Martha, who was only fourteen at the time. "Humphrey," according to Ripley, "complained that Martha was about to be taken to Cuba without her consent. By the aid of an interpreter, the *alcalde* questioned the young girl closely" (76–77). Martha and Zell were entitled to their freedom in Mexico and the U.S. after abolition; however, Ripley took advantage of their youth to conceal the implication of traveling to Cuba, where slavery remained legal until 1886. The adolescent Martha, panicked by the prospect of separation from her mistress and life alone in Mexico, according to the narrative, "burst into tears and implored to be permitted to 'go with Miss 'Liza,'" thus convincing the official "that she was under no compulsion" (77).

Within weeks of the fall of the Confederacy, the McHattons joined the great exodus of Confederate officers and their families who fled to Cuba, fearing the extent of Union reprisals for their actions.[118] According to Ripley, the American-owned Hôtel Cubano in Havana was "thronged with Confederates as homeless as ourselves" (80). Soon thereafter, the McHattons decided to take advantage of the island's mature slave economy to resume their Louisiana plantation life. They purchased a heavily mortgaged one-thousand-acre plantation named Desengaño (roughly, "disenchantment"), located near Matanzas, which was once made infamous for the brutal repression of a rumored slave revolt known as Conspiración de La Escalera (1843–1844).[119] At this point in the narrative, Ripley formally introduces the two household slaves whom she had smuggled from the U.S., among the other "little belongings" that she had managed to transport from Louisiana. "As the lives of these two devoted and faithful servants were interwoven so closely with our own," announces Ripley, "it might be well to give them a more personal introduction." She continues, "Martha was a mulatto whose profile, albeit no beauty, strangely resembled that of the famous St. Cecilia; while Zell was a full-blooded creole negro, black as ebony, tall, broad-shouldered, with a big mouth, full of dazzling ivories—one of the best-natured, jolliest souls that ever lived" (94). Once in Cuba, Martha and Zell take a prominent role in the narrative. Their depiction as dialect-speaking stock character types drawn from the racialist conventions of the plantation romance popularized by the likes of Joel Chandler Harris and Thomas Nelson Page belie their key roles in facilitating Ripley's transition into the mistress of Desengaño. Quickly fluent in Spanish, Martha and Zell mediate between the English-speaking Ripley, the Chinese contract laborers, and Creole Cuban slaves who spoke a "mixture of bad Spanish and African jargon" (97).

Cuba had long served as a refuge for slaveholders such as Ripley fleeing the social and political upheavals of revolution and emancipation. In the wake of the Haitian Revolution, French émigrés fleeing Saint-Domingue settled in nearby Cuba, where they helped establish the island's first *cafetals* or coffee estates. Hazard writes in his tour of Cuba, "My future host, like most of the inhabitants of this section of the country, was a descendant of the old original French settlers, refugees from the terrible massacres of St. Domingo, who, coming to the island of Cuba, settled themselves, as much as possible, in their old occupations of sugar-making and coffee-growing."[120] The Haitian Revolution transformed Cuba from a society with slaves into a slave society.[121] Roughly sixty years later, slaveholding Cuba again provided refuge for Confederates such as the McHattons fleeing the end of slavery on U.S. soil. In Cuba, they tried to reconstitute their Old South plantation with a racialized labor force that included their smuggled American slaves, black Creole Cuban slaves, and Chinese coolies. And just as French émigrés from Haiti brought coffee cultivation to Cuba, the McHattons brought planting technologies from Louisiana to their Los Palos plantation.

They imported "Louisiana subsoil plows," which at that time, according to Ripley, were "unheard-of innovations, and so at variance with any cultivation ever before seen" (100). Tellingly, Ripley's narrative links their successful modernization of sugarcane cultivation with the introduction of Chinese coolies onto a plantation long overworked by slave labor. After securing Desengaño, McHatton went to "Havana . . . to secure the only kind [of labor] available—Chinese coolies" (105). In the McHattons' native Louisiana, labor-strapped planters also had begun experimenting with Chinese workers in their search for an ideal "cheap" plantation labor force as Civil War and federal occupation radically reshaped sugar cultivation in the state.[122] According to Jung, debates over the viability of Chinese labor as a replacement agricultural workforce dominated debates over the economic future of the New South.[123]

Two decades before the publication of *From Flag to Flag*, Ripley had weighed in on this debate, touting the benefits of Chinese labor as an alternative to black labor. Introducing Ripley as "a native of this city—certainly a long time resident—and known to many of our best people as one of the most elegant, intelligent and accomplished of her sex," a supplement to the *New Orleans Times* quoted at length from articles that she had penned while in Cuba for *Hearth and Home* under the pseudonym "Siempre Fiel."[124] In them, Ripley interjected herself into the national discussion over the "Chinese Question," claiming expert knowledge given her management of Chinese contract labor as mistress of Desengaño. "So much is being said nowadays about Chinese labor," she writes, "that we propose to 'say our say,' and we have the advantage of most talkers on the subject—that of experience."[125] She offers fulsome praise of Chinese contract laborers as "valuable servants" in her domestic household and in all aspects of sugarcane cultivation:

> As planting was our business years ago in Louisiana, planting became our business also in Cuba. Half our working force is negroes, the other half Chinese—Chinese under contract to serve for eight years. They make good farm-laborers even in this hot climate. After the first year, they bear as much fatigue and exposure as the native. They are industrious and frugal; their monthly wages of four dollars in gold supplies them with tobacco, of which they are very fond. Soap—for they are cleanly also—an occasional handkerchief, or an extra shirt, all their necessary supplies,

food, clothing, bedding, medical attendance, etc., are furnished them by contract, besides four dollars in gold, payable monthly.[126]

For Ripley, Chinese contract labor is both an efficient alternative to and modern improvement on the now-outmoded system of black chattel slavery. "Long before a Chinese understands enough of a foreign tongue to make his simplest wants known," Ripley concludes, "he understands and fulfills the duties faithfully that a negro grows gray trying to perform."[127] In this comparative assessment, Ripley produces the fiction of racial discreteness between Chinese and black in order to assess the differences among these racial types. Reiterated in *From Flag to Flag*, Ripley's advocacy of the more skilled Chinese over black labor also anticipates the rise of a modern racialized division of labor.[128] In a show of sectional partisanship, Ripley, addressing herself to ongoing "Yankee" efforts to encumber such "voluntary emigrants from China to the United States," retorts, "we would advise our Yankee friends not to hinder the 'coming servant'; he will do more work, for less wages, and live more comfortably on it, and be more contented, than one out a thousand of the present laboring class in their midst."[129] Ripley not only juxtaposes Chinese against black labor in the South but positions Chinese against white worker in the North, limning aspects of the debates over racialized labor competition that would infuse organized labor, Populist, and Progressivist calls for Chinese exclusion.

In *From Flag to Flag*, Ripley's Desengaño functions as a microcosm of the struggles over race, labor, and immigration that engulfed the U.S. in the 1870s and 1880s, struggles that spanned her residence in Cuba and New York up to the publication of her autobiographical narrative. McHatton returned to Desengaño with "thirty-five newly imported coolies" and accompanied by "Zell, whom he summoned to Havana to interpret from English into Spanish; and Ramon, a Chinese, whose term of service on the plantation was drawing to a close, to interpret from Spanish into Chinese" (109). Starved and traumatized during the harrowing passage from China to Cuba, the coolies arrived ill and unfit to work and soon became refractory given the harsh conditions of their plantation labor. Ripley addresses her account to an American readership facing its own "Chinese Question":

The new crowd presented a grotesque appearance. Beardless, and with long pig-tails, loose blouses, and baggy breeches, they looked like women. Stolid, quiet, and undemonstrative as Indians, they tumbled out of the wagon that had been sent to the depot for them. Having been months on the voyage, packed in a coolie-ship, and fed on light rations of tea and rice, they were in no physical condition to work, or to endure the showers that were already beginning to be of daily occurrence; so some light occupation in the vicinity of the house was assigned to them, and when a poor fellow rubbed his stomach, rolled up his eyes, and patted his head, he was forthwith marched to the infirmary and dosed. From long privation on ship, with the stimulation of climatic change, they were so voracious that, if permitted to eat all the food craved, they would have gorged themselves to death. (109)

In her initial encounter, Ripley feminizes Chinese racial difference as specifically nonblack. In the fashion of Dana's travelogue, Ripley likens the Chinese to the "undemonstrative . . . Indians" yet distinguishes them from the black chattel slaves already bound to the plantation. She also explicates at length on the nature of the labor contract as another point of differentiation from the "negroes, direct descendants of imported Africans," who labored alongside the Chinese (115). Ripley even held onto contract number 159, which was made in her name for the twenty-five-year-old Chinese contract laborer He Fu (in Pinyin translation) from Guangdong and renamed "Eduardo" in Cuba.[130] In Macao, near the Lunar New Year in January 1868, He Fu signed the eight-year contract, which was later signed over to Ripley and her brother in Cuba on June 13, 1868. A handwritten notation underneath the signature notes that He Fu received an advance of eight silver dollars to be deducted from his future wages. This contract, along with the *cedula* of José Puchal, numbers among Ripley's meticulously collected papers from her residence in Cuba (see figures 1.3 and 1.4).

Unlike black chattel slaves, Chinese laborers, Ripley observes, "were intelligent, and it seems almost incredible that any people could be reduced to such abject poverty as would lead to selling themselves or some member of their family into servitude, but such is the fact" (112). "Each man, before embarking from China," she continues, subscribed to a printed contract, one page in Spanish and the other in Chinese characters, setting forth that Ah Sin (Christian name José), province of Macao, is contracted with his own free-will and consent to—"La Alianza y Co."—to do field-labor, to be granted one day in seven for rest, two full suits of clothing, one blanket and one overcoat annually, twelve ounces of meat and two and a quarter pounds of vegetables—yams or rice—per day; medical attendance and medicines; comfortable living quarters, and four dollars in gold monthly; the privilege also of complaining to the captain of the partido, in case of non-compliance with these terms. (113)

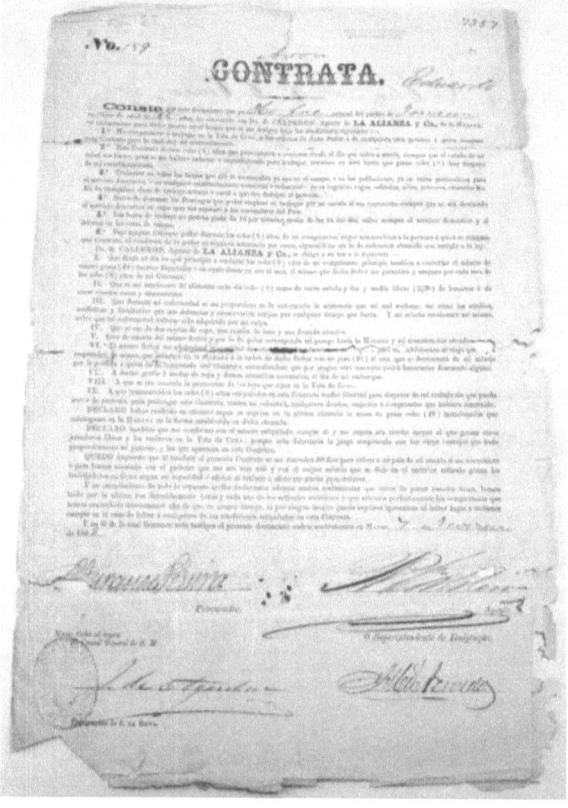

Figure 1.3. Contrata for He Fu (Eduardo), number 159, Macao, 1868 (Carton 10, Thomas Hubbard McHatton Family Papers; courtesy of the Hargrett Rare Books and Manuscript Library, University of Georgia Libraries)

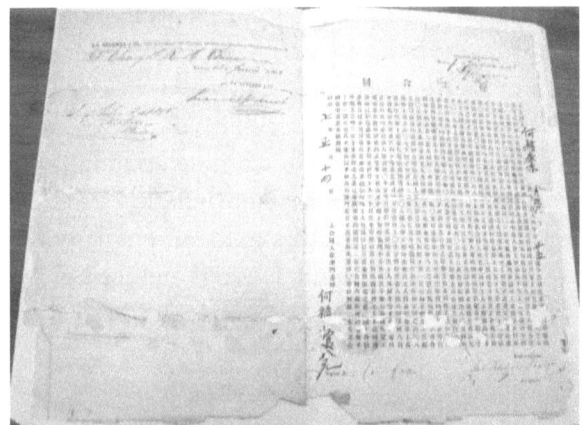

Figure 1.4. Chinese translation of Contrata for He Fu (Eduardo), number 159, Macao, 1868 (Carton 10, Thomas Hubbard McHatton Family Papers; courtesy of the Hargrett Rare Books and Manuscript Library, University of Georgia Libraries)

And while the contract bound the Chinese to servitude, Ripley wryly notes that Chinese laborers also attempted to use the contract to delimit the bounds of their exploitation and assert the few contractual rights that they were entitled to by law. The Chinese laborer kept his copy of the contract "on his person for the duration of his servitude" for identification, while the other was transferred to the *patrón* from the contracting agency upon purchase.[131] The "poorest, lowest coolie," Ripley writes, "carried his contract on his person, and never hesitated to assert his rights; and it generally happened that each new lot arriving on a plantation had to be interviewed by the captain of the partido two or three times, to reduce them to a proper regard for the discipline of a well-managed estate" (113). The Chinese, forced to subject themselves to a disagreeable lockjaw-preventative coal-oil application to the feet, Ripley recalled, grumbled that "the oft-referred to *contract* did not include that ceremony," and "it was always attended with remonstrances and threats" (116). Such anecdotes reveal Ripley's careful attention to plantation management in preventing a painful bacterial infection that also impedes labor, while she renders comical and insignificant Chinese efforts to use the contract to negotiate asymmetrical power relations.

As in her account of Delia in Mexico, Ripley often diffuses instances of racial insubordination through racialist humor. Her wry anecdotes emphasize her domestic guardianship over her extended plantation household. They also relegate the pervasive danger of violent Chinese labor rebellion as epiphenomenal of Chinese acclimatization to Cuba and not constitutive of the coercive labor relation itself. However, on occasion, Ripley's efforts at narrative containment falter. For example, she recounts how the new Chinese laborers mount a full-scale revolt against her parsimonious domestic economy:

> The Chinese were in full rebellion: stripped to the middle, their swarthy bodies glistening in the hot sun, they rushed with savage impetuosity up the road, leaped the low stone fence that surrounded the cluster of plantation-buildings, of which the massive dwelling-house formed the center, brandishing their hoes in a most threatening manner, and yelling like demons, as with hastily grasped rocks from the fences they pelted the retreating overseer. Ramon [another Chinese indentured laborer nearing the end of his contract] rushed from his bench at the carpenter-shop, and did his best to stem the tide; but they brushed him by in their determined assault upon the overseer, who, while issuing them full rations, would not yield to their demand for an unlimited supply of food. (110)

Such labor revolts numbered among the quotidian struggles that "lay at the heart of the social relations of sugar production" in both Cuba and the U.S., according to Jung.[132] Ripley's racialist humor cannot contain the threat of organized Chinese noncompliance, and she turns to coercive police power to reestablish her authority, giving the alarm signal for the local authorities. After quelling the riot, the Capitan reasserts the legal subjection of the coolies through a ritualized reading of their contract, which binds them to Ripley's authority. "He then read their contract to them," writes Ripley, "Ramon repeating it sentence by sentence in Chinese. They stood in a double row—thirty-five of them—sullen but somewhat defiant, straight upright and a bit arrogant" (111). The legal text of the contract fuses with the coercive discipline of slavery as the Capitan orders his soldiers to cut off the laborers' queues. The shorn queue was considered an act of treason punishable by death; it forever severed the Chinese subject from China.

By representing this thwarted Chinese labor rebellion as an isolated incident, Ripley sought to contain the near-daily occurrence of Chinese intransigence and protest that she faced as mistress of Desengaño. An endless enumeration of runaway and recalcitrant "chinos" fills the pages of the McHattons' Desengaño 1866–1869 account book. The Chinese "have been of late out of line and not disposed to do well," reads an entry dated August 21, 1866, soon after the McHattons took possession of Desengaño—possibly a reference to the rebellion Ripley recounts in the book.[133] Another entry reads, "Chinese unsettled—put two in the stocks," and five days later that number had risen exponentially: "Have had for past few days 21 Chinese in irons and stocks."[134] Entries recounting the McHattons' frustration with runaway Chinese laborers run throughout the account book. "2 Chinos new . . . ran off," "Caught Chino Adolfo No. 2," "2 Chinos run off (Carlos 104 and Elizio 529)," and "Chino Carlos caught tonight," reads one series of entries across a short ten-day span in November 1867. In addition, these notations also counter the former Cuban slave Esteban Montejo's claim (recorded by Miguel Barnet in 1963) that "the Chinese didn't fly."[135] Effaced from the published account of Ripley's narrative, the account book's meticulous economic record of Chinese resistance, escape, and recapture reveals the racial coercion and violence entailed in Ripley's strained efforts to reconstitute her old plantation life on Cuban soil. Such instances of Chinese noncompliance were unusual but not uncommon features of American accounts of the "coolie trade." For example, Edgar Holden's elaborately illustrated 1864 exposé "A Chapter on the Coolie Trade," published in *Harper's New Monthly Magazine*, portrayed Chinese coolies both as abject victims of latter-day slavery and as vengeful, mutinous insurgents out to destroy innocent whites.[136] Woodruff's 1871 travelogue also describes a thrilling encounter with a runaway coolie who had twice attempted suicide after recapture. She recalls how the "Chinese glowered like a spark of fire amid gray ashes; his usual expression of sullen insubordination being sharpened by the pressure of physical suffering." He was "the very incarnation of impotent hate and rage," Woodruff continues, and "felt himself at war with the whole tyrannous universe and especially resented the indignity of being exhibited and commented upon as if he had been a wild beast."[137]

In Ripley's extended descriptions of Cuban plantation life, she notes that the Chinese "did not mingle with the negroes, either in their work or socially, though subject to the same rules and regulations in regard to their hours of labor and hours of rest" (120). In constructing the Chinese and blacks as culturally opposite and antagonistic, Ripley's narrative manages by effacing fears of cross-racial collective resistance.[138] One of the greatest threats to Cuban planters lay in the specter of a Chinese-and-black alliance precipitating a "horrible servile war," in which "the Asiatics would be[come] the means of casting off the chains of Slavery that now appear so firmly riveted on the unfortunate Africans," declared one newspaper.[139] However, the same did not hold true with Ripley's American slaves whom she tasked with managing and training Chinese laborers. Martha spent hours transforming a "tidy Chinaman" named Ciriaco into the household's cook, replacing "the black woman, in a dirty, low-necked, sleeveless, trailing dress, a cigar in her mouth," whom Ripley found repulsive (95).[140] Ripley also tended to individuate Chinese laborers from her black Creole slaves, using the rhetoric of dehumanized, mechanistic labor to tout the advantages of Chinese over black enslaved labor. Ciriaco, she describes, "was like a machine wound up when he kindled the morning fire, and run down when he turned the key in the court at night" (117). However, she suppresses the detail that Ciriaco, like other coolies and Creole slaves, also challenged her authority by running away from Desengaño. A terse entry from another plantation diary, dated September 11, 1870, reads, "Martin and Ciriaco run off today." Four days later, another entry announced with relief, "Ciriaco and Martin Piña were caught near Union. We paid $21.25 for their arrest."[141]

In this fashion, Ripley's 1889 travelogue, published shortly after the end of slavery in Cuba, responds as much to ongoing U.S. debates over Chinese "cheap" labor and immigration regulation as to literary reconfigurations of the Old South and race relations in the wake of the Civil War. Ripley's anecdotes about her Chinese coolies, particularly the ones involving her former American slaves, Martha and Zell, attempt to reimbue the Cuban plantation with the "patriarchal character" lost with the passing of the Old South. Her book differentiates Chinese labor from the degraded forms of black Creole slave labor on the island and characterizes it in terms of the dependent relations of the old plantation household. For example, the narrative often pairs Zell and Ciriaco in humorous escapades, from the hunting of feral cats to the capture of snakes, in an effort to mask the plantation economy's exploitative relations of racialized unfree labor (127, 129). In one anecdote, the good-natured Zell costumes himself as a haunt with the aim of "skeer[ing] dem Chinese": "fur dey done got dat bad we can't get no decent orange outen dat garden now" (125). In a fashion reminiscent of Joel Chandler Harris's popular *Uncle Remus* tales, Ripley mixes forces and guile in portraying Zell's enforcement of her plantation authority against the Chinese and their predatory raids on the family orchard.

These depictions allow Ripley to reassert a narrative of patriarchal benevolence associated with the plantation romance. "Nostalgia," she writes, "was frequent among the newly imported. Like all diseases of a purely mental and emotional nature, its symptoms varied, usually tending to distressing melancholia, though sometimes to the desperation of suicide" (113). She relates "one case of nostalgia which deeply touched our sympathies," involving "a tall, well-made, robust Chinaman" named Epifanio (listed as no. 548 in the 1868 account book) who "gradually faded away to a shadow, . . . never speaking, or taking any interest in his surroundings" (114).[142] Ripley's sense of isolation in Cuba may have facilitated her identification with Epifanio's plight. Even after the family's nearly ten-year residence, Desengaño, according to Ripley, remained "a home that was ever strange to us," even though she took pains to differentiate her American sense of time management and efficiency from the indolence of the Cuban women surrounding her (177). In this, Ripley was not so different from other American women travelers to Cuba. Both Julia Ward Howe and Julia Woodruff also wrote disapprovingly of Cuban domestic management and gender norms, claiming narrative authority through national difference.[143]

Epifanio allows Ripley to portray herself as an idealized plantation mistress whose careful custodianship secures the coolie's undying fidelity. Of course, Epifanio's deteriorating health also put Ripley's monetary investment at risk, since importers received an outlay of $400 for each coolie. "[I] had the melancholy creature brought daily under the shed of the sugar-house near the window of our room, and by his bedside, with books and work, we sat a portion of every day," Ripley recounts (114). This "patient care" eventually revived Epifanio, who then became a skilled technician of "sugar-boiling," capable of telling "'to a turn' when the bubbling sirup had reached the granulating point and was ready to be thrown into the coolers" (114). Ripley notes that the patriarchal bond forged with Epifanio—as in the case of Martha and Zell—was so strong that he "voluntarily remained at *Desengaño* long after his term of service had expired, though he had the option of returning to the home for which he had suffered and pined so long" (114). Of course, she makes no mention of the policy of forced recontracting that structured Chinese labor in Cuba and most likely influenced Epifanio's "voluntary" decision to remain on a familiar plantation rather than risk imprisonment and forced labor at a depot. Ripley's favorable portrait of Chinese contract labor, as with her loving depictions of Martha and Zell, allows her to assert a nostalgic narrative of patriarchal benevolence that minimizes her participation in the regimes of racialized unfree labor in Cuba that continued after her return to the U.S.[144]

Composed while Ripley resided in the heart of the industrial North, *From Flag to Flag* clings to a world in which sympathy and benevolence mediated labor relations. Ripley's sentimentalized portrayal of Chinese contract labor (a harbinger of the modern wage system that she was to experience in New York) refuses to acknowledge the logic of commodification structuring the contract relation. However, Ripley took full advantage of how market exchange and the commerce in labor (as opposed to bodies) under contract produced a far less morally objectionable—but equally pliable—alternative to slavery. In an otherwise meticulously recorded account, Ripley suppressed many details of her life leading to her departure from Cuba and resettlement in New York. In 1868, anticolonial struggles broke out on the eastern end of Cuba, which developed into the First War of Cuban Independence, or the Ten Years' War.[145] The McHattons risked this "lawless condition of affairs" and remained on Desengaño, thinking that the "insurrection" would soon be put down (132). Ripley remained unconvinced that the rebellion would amount to anything, given her low regard for Cubans, whom she deemed in correspondences as "totally unfit for freedom."[146] However, insurgency and counterinsurgency transformed the sociopolitical landscape of Cuba far beyond Ripley's imagination. In 1870,

Spain adopted a formal plan of gradual abolition called the Moret Law, which freed slave children born after 1868 and slaves over sixty years of age.[147]

During the latter years of the McHattons' residence, the family, facing heightened restrictions against the coolie importation and slave labor on which sugar cultivation depended, foresaw the end of their way of life on the island: "The gradual emancipation of slaves was enforced, the importation of coolies prohibited, and, as an inevitable sequence, an untold number of valuable estates were abandoned by their impoverished owners" (188).[148] However, Ripley's *From Flag to Flag* portrays her return to the U.S. in the sentimentalized terms of familial reunion, repressing the fact that she remained the absentee part owner of Desengaño until 1877. "Henry's departure [for New England boarding school] had already sundered one of the ties that bound us to the Cuban home that the boy loved so well," Ripley announces. She continues, "It was easy for us to break away after that" (188). She superimposes a narrative of familial reunification and overwhelming longing for return to the American "fatherland" on the political-economic restructuring of the Cuban sugar economy and the diminishing profitability of sugar cane cultivation. Ripley also omits mention of her husband's unexpected death while on business in St. Louis in 1872. The following year, she married Dwight Ripley, a lawyer. They settled in New York City (and later Brooklyn), where she began composing the reminiscences that became *From Flag to Flag*, steeped in the nostalgia for an Old South and a slaveholding Cuba that no longer existed.

In suppressing these details from her narrative, Ripley resisted the conventionalized closure of the plantation romance, which often figured North-South reconciliation through the trope of marriage between a Yankee and former Confederate. Instead, she devotes the final pages of *From Flag to Flag* to her two American slaves and ends with Zell's matrimonial union with a black Creole Cuban, a "dusky Maud Muller, who raked cane in the field," as Ripley wryly puts it, referencing a popular John Greenleaf Whittier poem (187). In the era of emancipation, the marriage contract, according to Stanley, had come to figure the self-sovereignty and possessive individualism that had long been denied to slaves such as Zell.[149] In acknowledgment of Zell's faithful service to the family, Ripley finally furnished her former slave with the "necessary papers of United States citizenship," ending her prolonged circumvention of slave emancipation and enfranchisement in Cuba (189). Black American citizenship becomes thinkable for Ripley at the precise moment when she can no longer lay claim to Zell's unwaged labor. As a parting gift, Ripley provides Zell with "several hundred dollars, the accumulated amount of his savings" (189). Up until his death, the ever-grateful Zell, according to Ripley, dictated numerous letters to her: "giving all the neighborhood news of interest, and messages from the Chinese and negroes, among whom we had lived and labored almost ten years—invariably subscribing himself 'Your devoted and faithful *slave*'" (189). And before leaving Cuba, Ripley prided herself on binding Zell with a "favorable contract" to the new owner of the plantation—not unlike the Chinese coolies whom Zell had labored alongside during the McHattons' tenure at Desengaño (189).[150]

It is perhaps not surprising to discover that Ripley's published narrative provides a far more romanticized account of her relationship with her beloved former slaves and Chinese coolies than the one revealed in letters she traded with her brother Richard Chinn, who managed the plantation after McHatton's death and until the sale of Desengaño in 1877.[151] The struggles between mistress and slave are recorded at length in the voluminous personal correspondences between Ripley and Chinn, her nephew Charles Jackson, and son Henry, who returned to Cuba to assist "Uncle Dick" in 1875.[152] Ripley's private correspondences reveal a mistress desperate to maintain authority over domestic servants who were no longer legally her slaves. According to Cuban law, Ripley could not compel Martha and Zell to continue in her service against their will, as they had been admitted to temporary residence in Cuba as U.S.-born foreigners.[153] Ripley withheld this information, and Martha and Zell remained unaware of their legal rights as U.S. subjects (and citizens after the Fourteenth Amendment) until the accidental revelation of this information in 1874. In early 1871, after the passage of the Moret Law, Ripley's Cuban friend and adviser Anastasio Millet responded to her inquiries about Martha and Zell, informing her, among other things, that "both are considered by the laws here as foreign negroes,— they are free. . . . They can at any time claim the protection of the U.S. Consul under the plea of being included in the decree—now law in the American Union—which declares free all persons from there."[154]

After Ripley's departure from Cuba, Chinn wrote U.S. Secretary of State Hamilton Fish for further information in the matter of Martha and Zell. Fish wrote back declaring that the two "are free and free American citizen paper will be granted them upon application, unless they have been made citizens of another country."[155] On his sister's behalf, Chinn sought to circumvent this mandate by claiming that Martha and Zell had been made "citizens and peons of Mexico" previous to their arrival in Cuba and therefore were not entitled to U.S. citizenship.[156] "Consequently," avers Chinn, the U.S. consul in Cuba, Henry Hall, "had no business to give them certificates [establishing that] they were American citizens and put the devil in Martha's head as big as a mountain."[157]

Read in this context, Ripley's generous dispensation to Zell might be viewed as an informal settlement to placate a former slave with legal claims against her. Contrary to her published account, Ripley had left Martha in Cuba when she remarried and resettled in New York. In March 1874, Chinn informed Ripley, "Zell and Martha are yet here, the former partially satisfied—the latter I don't know, she has done nothing but sit in her room and sew for the Chinese—I don't think she will . . . be of any value to you and certainly not to me. Mr. Brown and Mr. Millet advised strenuously sending her off—Hall sent them their free papers and Mr[s.] B said if I did not write to you she would that she knew they were going to sue you for $25 each per month for all the time on the island and Hall first put them up to it."[158] Significantly, the struggle that ensues takes the form of a wage dispute over Ripley's exploitation of Martha's free labor in Cuba. Chinn's letters go into detail about Martha's discovery of Ripley's long deception. "Your note concerning Martha has been received," writes Chinn. "I will give you some account of her since your departure":

> Upon Zell's return from Havana and telling her what Mr. Hall had said it appeared to upset her completely. . . . She asked for a cart to take her traps away. . . . I need not say that she was very insolent. . . . I am perfectly willing Martha should have the balance of her expenses paid to leave the country as it seem if she remains she will give trouble Zell informs me. In former days she was a good servant to you, but certainly has been a great relief to me [now that] she is off. . . . Her tongue certainly had become too flippant of her past and future and those connected with her.[159]

In an effort to placate the nettled Martha, Ripley wrote Chinn requesting the he send Martha to the U.S. As Delia had done in Mexico, Martha, now the mother of two daughters—another detail omitted from the narrative—rejected Ripley's offer, refusing to leave Cuba. In a note accompanying this missive, Chinn informed his sister, "Since mailing this, Martha and her two children have been here on horseback. I asked her what she wanted. She said she wanted to see me. I had sent her word I would pay her way to the North—yet—that was not what she was after she wanted her pay from the day she landed here. . . . You will have no fear of her falling in the hands of *bad white men*—She is there, and has been for some time."[160] The following weeks saw the infuriated Martha seeking out the U.S. consul in Havana to lay claim against Ripley for the accumulated back wages that had been due to her as a free laborer.

After several months of bickering and threatened legal action, Martha finally agreed to return to the U.S. with her Cuban-born children. As they departed, Chinn offered a final warning to Ripley: "Be careful Martha does not sue you in some of the Circuit Courts in the states . . . as I have had some intimation of the kind, as she claims you brought her here and deserted her by going to N.Y. to live. . . . She's far more shrewd than anybody . . . give[s] her credit for."[161] Pasted into this letter is a clipping from a newspaper announcing the departure of "Sres. Dona Marta Mc Ratton [sic] y sus hijas Natalia y Luisa" for New York (see figure 1.5). Ironically, the published travelogue transforms these rancorous struggles over labor and wages into a moving eulogy to a beloved family servant:

> Martha returned to the United States with us, and, when she married, her savings were found sufficient to purchase a lot and pay for the building of a comfortable house in Virginia, near enough for us to see her almost every year, when she could take our daughter, already taller and larger than herself, in her loving arms, and call her "my Mexican baby."
>
> Now that tender, faithful soul, who ministered to our comfort, not as slave but helpful companion during those trying years, has gone "where change shall come not till all change end"—thus severing one of the few remaining links that bound us to the old, old life. (189–190)

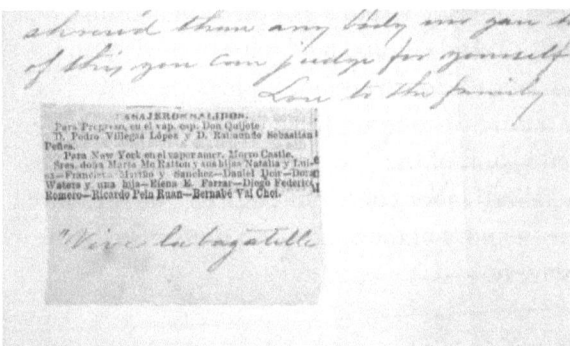

Figure 1.5. Newspaper clipping pasted into letter from Richard H. Chinn to Eliza McHatton Ripley, July 9, 1874 (Series 13, Carton 10, File 149, Thomas Hubbard McHatton Family Papers; courtesy of the Hargrett Rare Books and Manuscript Library, University of Georgia Libraries)

Like Zell, Ripley emphasizes Martha's marriage and homemaking on U.S. soil as evidence of her freedom from bondage. Martha's death marks the decisive break between antebellum slavery and postbellum freedom, even though Ripley had struggled to artificially extend her "old, old life" in Cuba. Like Ripley's account of the loyal Chinese Epifanio, her depiction of Martha seeks to rewrite so-called free labor contract relations in the filial language of slaveholding paternalism and personal dependence. These were, citing Ann Laura Stoler, "tense and tender ties," marking domestic arrangements in which race, gender, and labor relations were defined and defied.[162] In this enlarged context, Ripley's characterization of Martha as an archetype of the loyal plantation slave, symbolized by the servant's possessive claim on Ripley's daughter as "my Mexican baby" (and the erasure of Martha's Cuban-born daughters), marks the mournful passage of the world of Atlantic slavery into contract freedom. This nostalgic narrative of declension must elide the figures of runaway coolies such as Ciriaco and an "insolent" Martha battling her mistress for accumulated back wages. Ripley sought to re-create in narrative the world that she had lost with the fall of the Confederacy. "I am no apologist for slavery," she wrote in her final year, "but we were born to it, grew up with it, lived with it, and it was our daily life."[163] *From Flag*

56 | "COSA DE CUBA!"

to Flag offers a fantastic structure of racial imaginings that refracts the changing political and cultural landscape of the U.S. in the aftermath of the Civil War and Reconstruction. Ripley's narrative is as much about the illusory nature of contract freedom as it is about memorializing a romanticized vision of the Old South that sought to mask continuing forms of racialized labor coercion—indeed, the brutality of free labor itself—in the memory of the benevolent mutualism of the bygone era of plantation slavery.

The Contract Coolie: The *Cuba Commission Report*

In summer of 1874, resident and nonresident sugar planters such as Eliza McHatton Ripley and Richard Chinn discussed the probable outcomes of the official Chinese commission sent to investigate the conditions of Chinese contract labor in Cuba. The end of Chinese contract labor would blight the siblings' economic prospects now that it had become the cheapest labor source in Cuba after the suppression of the contraband African slave trade.[164] Two months after the commission's departure from the island, Chinn addressed a concerned letter to his sister in New York. "The English Consul had a good deal to do with the Chinese Commission sent out here last month," he writes. "They told him they would not recommend their government to renew the Contract just expired with Spain to allow any more to come onto here."[165] Chinn moved quickly to claim as much of the dwindling supply of Chinese labor as possible, motivated in part by speculation that China would halt the transport of laborers to Cuba. By 1874, Ripley and Chinn held over a hundred Chinese under contract in various aspects of sugar cultivation and processing—a substantial increase from the nineteen Chinese and eighty-one black Creole slaves they had begun with in 1866.[166] In the year that the commission arrived to the island, the Spanish colonial government had begun subjecting the Chinese—many of whom had participated in the anticolonial rebellion of the Ten Years' War—to even greater surveillance under threats of imprisonment in depots and deportation.[167] This section builds on and extends Lisa Yun's comparative study of the *Cuba Commission Report*, which emphasizes the collective transformation of a state inquiry process into an expressive form of Chinese subaltern resistance to bondage.[168] The report offers a significant record of Chinese testimonial voices structured through the complexities of East-West diplomatic relations and U.S. colonial interests in Cuba. In charting some of these relations of influence, this section illuminates how the contradictions of contract captured in the report refracted and further complicated Reconstruction-era debates over Chinese immigration, black citizenship, and free labor.

During the Cuba Commission's three-month inquiry, 2,841 Chinese laborers testified in speech and writing to their experiences of practical, if not formal, enslavement. In 1873, the Chinese government, in consultation with ministers from the five Western Powers (Russia, the U.S., Britain, France, and Germany), authorized the formation of a three-member commission, which included two European representatives—A. MacPherson, the British commissioner of customs at Hankow, and A. Huber, the French commissioner of customs at Tianjin (both of whom were fluent in Mandarin)—to investigate the conditions of coolies in Cuba.[169] The Commission was formed in China during a period of heightened anti-Western protests against foreign incursion, which had intensified in the wake of the Opium Wars. The Chinese government began to pay more attention to its subjects abroad, and it exerted pressure on the coolie trade centered in Portuguese Macao, taking sterner measures to suppress kidnapping. The Cuba Commission was the culmination of these more vigorous attempts to end the transport of Chinese to the Spanish Caribbean.[170] Gathered in 1874 while Ripley and Chinn remained the coproprietors of Desengaño, the Chinese testimonies formed the basis of the 1876 *Report of the Commission Sent by China to Ascertain the Condition of Chinese Coolies in Cuba*. An invaluable document in nineteenth-century migration and labor history, the report's vivid accounts of labor control, abuse, and coercion eventually led to the end of Chinese labor recruitment and transport to Cuba with the ratification of a treaty to that effect in 1887, according to Yun.[171]

Chen Lan-Pin (Chen Lanbin), who had been posted to Connecticut as the commissioner of the first Chinese Educational Mission to the U.S., led the commission. His work did not go unnoticed in the U.S. The elite women's magazine *Harper's Bazaar*, for example, noted that "a distinguished Chinese gentleman, has come to this country to join a commission which is to proceed to Cuba to look after the condition of the coolies in that island." "The object of the commission," it continued, "is to ameliorate, if possible, the present deplorable condition of the coolies."[172] The Connecticut *Hartford Daily Courant*, likewise, reported that "the object of the trip is to gather accurate information concerning the condition of the coolies on the island—the current reports of their almost slave-like state having apparently reached the home government."[173] Chen Lan-Pin traveled with a staff of Chinese teachers and translators who, like him, had been based in the U.S. along with two Americans, "Messrs. [Luther] Northrup and [Henry] Terry," according to one report.[174] Information gleaned from their private correspondences to American friends and colleagues often found their way into local newspapers. During the commission's brief stop in New Orleans en route to Cuba, the *Daily Picayune* sent a reporter to interview the men, given that all matters concerning "the Chinese Government and the coolie trade" were "destined in the future to exert considerable influence on the condition of our laboring classes."[175] Like many others, the *Daily Picayune* saw the "Labor Question" as tightly bound to the future of Chinese contract labor in Cuba.

The commission launched its eight-week investigation in Havana. It charted an itinerary that was not unlike those touted in popular travelogues of the day, moving from the "dépôt, prison, and the plantations" in Matanzas, Cardenas, Cimmarones, Colon, Sagua, Cienfugoes, and Guanajay and returning to Havana by way of San Antonio with a final visit to Guanabacoa, the Regla, and the Santa Catalina sugar warehouses (*Cuba Commission Report* 32–33). Some Spanish officials and planters went to great lengths to prevent their laborers from appearing before the commission.[176] In October, the jointly authored report was completed (with MacPherson and Huber providing English translation) and submitted to the Chinese government. In the face of Spanish protest, China forwarded the *Cuba Commission Report* with supporting documents to the ministers of the Five Powers.[177] Again, U.S. newspapers followed these developments. The antislavery periodical *Friends' Review* reported, "In consequence of unfavorable reports from Cuba as to the condition of the coolies, the Chinese government has peremptorily forbidden the further departure of emigrants. This has caused a difficulty with the Spanish Charge d'Affairs at Peking, who pronounced it a violation of the treaty, and efforts at arbitration by diplomatic corps had failed."[178] As the *Cuba Commission Report* began circulating globally,

China and Spain struggled over a new treaty that included sixteen new provisions for the protection of current and future Chinese emigrants to Cuba. It was eventually signed in 1877, shortly after Ripley and Chinn sold Desengaño, and ratified in 1878.[179]

The testimonies included in the report reveal the complex ways by which contract—specifically, the labor contract—became a legal mechanism to conceal new forms of bondage and servitude in a globalizing economy.[180] The labor contract did not mention or specify disciplinary correction; consequently, the coercive power of Cuban law was required to safeguard all contractual obligations.[181] Recontracting policies were often based on "renewal" clauses built into labor contracts that effectively denied freedom to laborers who completed their original contracts.[182] Such compulsory and successive recontracting practices blurred the distinction between indentured and enslaved labor, anticipating similar forms of racial subordination that "continued under the aegis of contract" during Reconstruction in the U.S. South.[183] Indeed, the Chinese interviewed by the commission repeatedly represented themselves as "sold into slavery" regardless of the legal form of their labor bondage. "I was decoyed to Cuba, and sold to a sugar plantation," asserts the petition of Chêng-chiu, emphasizing, like the many other testimonies, the logic of commodification underlying the free-labor ideology of contract (*Cuba Commission Report* 36). Other testimonies such as the petition of Hsieh Shuang-chiu and eleven others relate how upon "landing, four or five foreigners on horseback, armed with whips, led [them] like a herd of cattle to the barracoon to be sold," while the petition of Yeh Fu-chun and fifty-two others describe how they were "offered for sale in the men-market" (48). These depositions also reveal that most laborers "signed their contracts under compulsion," asserting almost univocally, as in the petition of Lo A-pao, "I was compelled to sign the contract" (39). Indeed, the commission concluded that "8 or 9 of every 10 [Chinese] have been conveyed there against their will" and "brought there by fraud or violence in order to the sold" (38, 39).

In a regulatory context where *patróns* held legal documents and their interpretations, the contract became a racializing mechanism of power, for it could be virtually enforced against anyone who appeared Chinese regardless of the original signee.[184] Moreover, contract terms were often unenforceable or easily circumvented by planters legally vested with the power to construe the conditions of the contract as they saw fit.[185] In addition, only the Spanish text of the contract was permitted in testimony before Cuban courts, even though the Chinese translations often differed in small yet significant details. Some planters levied fines and wage deductions for "lost time" not enumerated in the original contract and forced laborers to make all purchases from the estate shops where merchandise was both costly and of poor quality (56).[186] Similar to the emerging system of black sharecropping and debt peonage in the New South, Chinese laborers often ended their terms either indebted to planters or accruing a mere fraction of their contracted wage. A Chinese laborer, Wang A-jui, testified before the Cuba Commission, "My master did not furnish me with food. He issued to me orders for edibles to be handed to the plantation shop. These orders were regarded as money, and their amount being placed to my debit, my earnings for the entire eight years were thus deducted" (51). After abolition in the U.S. South, American planters had begun their own experiments with labor contracts.[187] Chinese contract labor in Cuba provided an ideal model for the New South's search for an effective legal system of black labor control.[188] Like the Chinese in Cuba, black freedmen came to view the labor contract negatively as a "device to bind them to the land and to ameliorate the effects of abolition on the planter class," according to Guterl.[189]

Given the official charge of the Cuba Commission, the report expressed a deep preoccupation with the meaning of the labor contract and the "contract coolie" that it created. Section 30 of the report reads, "The contract coolie is a man who had pledged himself to work according to contract for a term of years: he is not a slave. Is he treated as a man who has consented to be bound by a contract, or as a slave?" (88). The commission set out to evaluate Chinese labor migration against a Western contract paradigm based on volition and consent that ramified in the U.S., where, as Yun points out, "rival understandings of the free contract" were jostling for hegemonic ascendancy.[190] In fact, the tenets of voluntariness and consent at the heart of contract ideology later defined the fundamental difference between voluntary Chinese immigration and banned coolie importation in the embattled context of the "Chinese Question" in the U.S.

By conjuring the likeness between coolie transport and the Atlantic slave trade, the *Cuba Commission Report* appealed to English-language readers by positioning the plight of Chinese laborers in relation to the abolition of slavery in the U.S. and British Caribbean, as Sean Metzger notes.[191] It parsed the differences between enslaved and contract laborer at length, concluding that the lawless transport and exploitation entailed in contract labor located the Chinese in a position no "different from that of the negroes whose servitude has so long existed in the island" (89):

> The distinction between a hired labourer and the slave can only exist when the former accepts, of his own free will, the conditions tendered, and performs in a like manner the work assigned to him; but the lawless method in which the Chinese were—in the great majority of cases—introduced into Cuba, the contempt there evinced for them, the disregard of contracts, the indifference as to the tasks enforced, and the unrestrained infliction of wrong, constitute a treatment which is that of "a slave, not of a man who has consented to be bound by contract." (88–89)

Neither a free laborer nor a slave, the contract coolie represents a racialized labor form homologous to yet legally differentiated from black chattel slavery. "Slaves can make no contract," wrote the abolitionist William Goodell in *The American Slave Code in Theory and Practice* (1853).[192] However, slaves, according to Orlando Patterson, were not simply fungible things or transferrable property but carefully construed, if degraded, persons in law.[193] Cuban law acknowledged Chinese laborers as free persons so as to establish their perfect legal submission to the operations of contract. Like the relations of slavery, Chinese labor in Cuba involved similar forms of legal dominion and subjugation, revealing the enduring ambiguities of the contract relation.

For Chinese laborers on plantations such as Desengaño, contract did not chart the passage of labor from (racial) status to the wage system.[194] Recontracting policies ensured that laborers who entered into contracts entered a life of perpetual servitude. Failure to recontract was punished by incarceration in depots, where authorities forced laborers to work on public projects without wages—ostensibly to cover the costs of their upkeep until they accumulated enough for return passage to China. New legislation also stipulated that all Chinese entering Cuba must renounce their civil rights "which may not be compatible with the accomplishment of the obligations" entailed in the contract.[195] In other words, Spanish law established what Colin Dayan terms "civil death" or "dead in law" as a fundamental condition of Chinese contract labor in Cuba.[196] The petition of Ch'iu Tê-i summarized this collective condition: "We are now more than 100,000 Chinese in this island, whose daily existence is that of criminals confined in jail" (*Cuba Commission Report* 70). These imprisoned laborers effectively became "slaves of the state," in Dayan's formulation.[197] Forced recontracting became a defining characteristic of Chinese labor in Cuba. It enforced perpetual submission while sustaining the idea of lawful contracts of a limited period, at the end of which free laborers, according to contract ideology, might find another employer of their choosing. Through both law and exploitative practice, Chinese laborers, as the commissioners observe, are "deprived of freedom of choice," given the "withholding of the certificates of completion by employers, the compulsory renewal of contract and the detention in depots" (75, 77).

Mandatory recontracting reveals the illusion of volition or free will associated with the idealized form of contract. It also resembled the vast "apparatus of labor compulsions" constructed in the New South to punish so-called criminal vagrants with imprisonment and forced labor in the convict leasing system.[198] In the final years of Ripley's ownership of Desengaño, her son Henry increasingly relied on coercion to secure the recontracting of their Chinese laborers, especially in the case of their cook Ciriaco, whose humorous escapades Ripley recounts at length in *From Flag to Flag*. "The Chinese all but Ciriaco and Apolinar said that they would stay," writes Henry, "so we sent Ciriaco and Apolinar to the field so as to get a little work out of them before they left—they both came up that night and said that they would stay. We are to give $25 (paper) a contract all the year—are going to contract for a year—the terms of the contract are not settled yet."[199] Henry's letters recount similar punitive measures meted out to any Chinese refusing to recontract. He later complained of the "slave Chinese" who "refused to take another stroke of work till they had their contracts and papers."[200] He eventually called on the local authority for assistance: "The Captain came down at twelve, and we had all the Chinese up signing their contracts. I have been all evening filling them up. It was lots of work as there were over hundred and four in number." However, such difficulties did not prevent Henry from receiving a "new gang of Chinese" the following week and further augmenting the plantation's labor pool.[201]

The findings of the *Cuba Commission Report* challenged fundamental ideas about the meaning of contract, and the circulation of the English-language report in the U.S. helped transform the popular idea of "the Coolie" as "essentially a slave" into a widely accepted fact of Cuba. "Such is the report of the Chinese commission . . . which was made up of one Chinaman, one French and one Englishman," concludes one New England newspaper.[202] During the period of Union military occupation of the South, the federal government began establishing voluntary wage labor on southern soil, and the labor contract symbolized this new postwar freedom.[203] However, conflicting accounts regarding the nature and form of Chinese contract labor in Cuba, from popular travelogues and the *Cuba Commission Report* to the narrative of a "fugitive coolie" recorded by the controversial Chinese American newspaperman Wong Chin Foo continued to shadow and unsettle this American vision of contract freedom.

The Fugitive Coolie: The Narrative of Chun Young Hing

The tale of the "fugitive coolie" Chun Young Hing is the earliest known English-language publication of the Chinese American journalist Wong Chin Foo. An enigmatic figure from early Asian American print history, Wong was an outspoken critic of Chinese exclusion, best remembered as the founder of the first Chinese American newspaper in New York and the Chinese Equal Rights League (1892), studied at more length in chapter 2. Wong published the "Story of Chun Young Hing's Sufferings as a Slave in Cuba" in the *New York Times* just months after the Cuba Commission concluded its investigation in 1874. Wong's account transformed Chun's narrative of kidnap, forced contracting, and escape into a representative text of Chinese migrant life in the West.[204] The escaped coolie's tale of suffering, according to Chicago's *Inter-Ocean*, "attained publicity through the instrumentality of an educated countryman, Wong Chin Foo."[205] Wong's tale was widely reprinted with variations in a range of regional periodicals, including the *Milwaukee Daily Sentinel*, the *Chicago*

Daily Tribune, the *Inter-Ocean*, the *New Hampshire Patriot*, the *Ticonderoga Sentinel*, the *Sacramento Daily Union*, and the *Prairie Farmer*.[206] And, in the following year, the *New York Evangelist* took notice of other Chinese such as Chun, "refugees from Cuba, having escaped from the cruel bondage to which they were subject there as coolies."[207]

One of Wong's earliest known publications, his account of Chun's escape from contract labor took advantage of the publicity surrounding the Cuba Commission to protest the exploitation of Chinese laborers and to criticize the Chinese government for its failure to protect its subjects abroad. Arriving in San Francisco in 1873, Wong reportedly fled China as a political refugee for his alleged role in a revolutionary plot against the Chinese emperor.[208] Wong interviewed Chun in Boston and used his story as an opportunity to publicly attack the corruption of the Chinese government.[209] Given China's dearth of global political power, it could do nothing to prevent the tragic plight of men such as Chun who cannot "enjoy freedom to its fullest extent" but must "depend solely on national charity or political influence" for protection.[210] By emphasizing the vexed relationship of the Chinese migrant to China, Wong also provides a counter to the "stable and continuous notion of Chineseness" often on display in the *Cuba Commission Report*.[211] Fusing aspects of the popular antebellum slave narrative with the American travelogue of Cuba, Wong weaves, in the words of the *Prairie Farmer*, a "pitiful story of the horrors of the Chinese coolie system in Cuba." "From his account," the newspaper continues, "it appears that the condition of the Chinese laborers in Cuba is much worse than that of the negro slaves. The poor Chinaman is held for a limited period; his owner has paid a good price for his term of bondage, and he must get all that he can before coolie freedom comes."[212]

Newspapers noted the unprecedented nature of Chun Young Hing's narrative, for "it is the first account given by one of the victims himself—all our previous knowledge on the subject having been mainly derived from blue books and dispatches."[213] As amanuensis and translator of Chun's oral account, Wong, in the fashion of the amanuenses of past slave narratives, prefaces the autobiographical tale with an attestation of veracity that serves a dual function. It mitigates Wong's involvement in the narrative while emphasizing his agency in establishing its truth value:

The following is the story of one of my countrymen who arrived in Boston recently from Cuba, where he was held in bondage by Panto Francisco, the owner of a sugar plantation, situated in the country, a few hours' journey back from Cienfuegos. I have questioned him closely, and am convinced of the truth of his narrative. I give it just as it was related by him, suppressing only the name of the bark on which he arrived and the Captain who kindly assisted him. This Chinaman was placed on shore by the Captain, and being unable to speak English, was taken by a policeman to the store of Ar-Show, the Chinese tea merchant, who kindly took him in charge. His appearance serves to prove the truth of his statement.[214]

Wong's decision to suppress the name of the captain, whom the *New Hampshire Patriot* specifically describes as a "Yankee captain," and the vessel that transported Chun again harks back to the strategic silences that once structured the fugitive slave's narrative of escape—perhaps most famously in Frederick Douglass's 1845 *Narrative*, which withheld the "facts connected with" the escape and chastised "the very public manner in which some of our western friends have conducted what they call the *underground railroad*, but which . . . by their open declarations, has been made most emphatically the *upperground railroad*."[215] Wong again draws tighter the implied comparison between present-day Chinese coolieism and antebellum black chattel slavery by locating Chun Young Hing's "coolie freedom" in Boston, the oft-mythologized origins of American antislavery radicalism. In the narrative, Chun recounts suffering the plantation discipline of one hundred lashes for the paltry offense of returning late from a walk in the woods, and Wong calls attention to the "marks of that whipping" still on the coolie's body. Chun's pitiful "appearance," like the severely lacerated slave Gordon placed on spectacular display in antislavery print culture, serves to further authenticate the truthfulness of his narrative.[216]

Chun's pathetic tale begins in Canton in 1869, when he was inveigled by promises of work to travel to Amoy, a major entrepôt on China's southeastern coast and the site of the first "coolie trade" center.[217] Once in Amoy, the promises of work disappeared, and the penniless Chun, unable to return home, agreed to "go over the water" for "$10 a month." He along with 368 other men were loaded into the dark "between decks" of a French vessel. Those who resisted "were thrown down, and the hatches closed." Three months later, Chun arrived "at Havana in the island of Cuba," where the men were "led out and examined and [their] strength tested." Panto Francisco purchased Chun's contract, along with forty-nine others to "work on his plantation" in the mountains "a few hours' journey back from Cienfuegos." Once on the isolated plantation, Chun is ordered to "cut cane" and quickly learns the brutal nature of field labor. Granted only four and a half hours of rest a night, he is starved, "compelled to work," and "watched continually by a driver, who, with long whip in his hand, would walk behind and if anyone lagged he would received fifty lashes." Whippings were meted out to sick men unable to work, and the Chinese, according to Chun, "were not allowed to speak to each other in our native tongues" to prevent organization and collective action in a language incomprehensible to overseers and *patróns* alike.[218]

Chun makes little mention of the African slaves he toiled alongside, yet his narrative emphasizes the extreme exploitation of Chinese contract labor in a comparative manner, revealing how *patróns* calculated the costs-benefits of Chinese contract labor over slave ownership. In words recalling the testimonies of the *Cuba Commission Report*, he relates in great detail his experiences of slavery by another name:

> We were used worse than the negroes, for the masters said that while they owned the negroes for life, they owned us for eight years only. Panto Francisco, my master, had 150 Chinamen in his employ. Part of this number were working on a new contract, having served their eight years. I learned that when their term had expired they had no money, and were compelled to make a new contract for a number of years or starve, for no one would hire them by the month, it being contrary to the custom of the owners of the plantations. Not one in twenty-five of the Chinamen at work in Cuba ever returns to China, for if they are strong enough to survive their toils for six or seven years, the last year or two they are worked night and day without rest, and in a short time they are able to work no longer. All hope is given up, and many die. Those who survive find that the little money they had saved to return has been used to pay for food and care while sick, and they have no alternative but to make a new contract.[219]

After "five years' slavery," Chun seized on a stray opportunity to escape and "ran into the woods early in the morning before the hour of work, while the driver was absent." Subsisting on berries and fruit, Chun traveled for five days, often "compelled to stop and hide on account of the barking of the dogs" until he arrived at Cienfuegoes. There, while walking the wharves, Chun recounts meeting a sympathetic American captain: "[he] took what money I had ($32), and hid me on the brig."[220]

Wong explicitly addresses the narrative to an American audience, urging it to place political pressure on China to end the coolie trade to Cuba. His commentary marshals a sentimentalized appeal—in the fashion of Harriet Beecher Stowe's famous injunction to "feel right," encouraging U.S. political intervention in the name of moral duty. "The cry of anguish that comes from the Chinese in Cuba ought to move the heart of the most cruel savage," admonishes Wong.[221] He seizes on the testimonial structure of the popular slave narrative to craft an eyewitness account of Chinese suffering in Cuba. In this story calculated to elicit the sympathetic response of American readers, Wong answered Williams's call "for a Harriet Beecher Stowe, to write a Chee-Chow-Wang romance upon the cruelty to this deluded people," which began this chapter. Like Stowe before him, Wong adapts an African American literary form—the slave narrative—to humanize the Chinese coolie. He centers Chun as the agent of his fugitive freedom from the bondage of contract and inserts his narrative into Reconstruction-era debates over labor versus capital.

The anomalous figure of the "contract coolie" embodied the contradictions of contract freedom as an episteme of U.S. political modernity. The oft-repeated question "What is a coolie?" designates a "global conjunction," in Lowe's formulation, that ramified deeply in the literature, political discourses, and practices of contract freedom, yet the coolie remains "illegible in the history of modern freedom."[222] The earliest English-language coolie narrative published in the U.S. explicitly drew on the genre of the black-authored slave narrative to transform a labor migrant's story of kidnap, forced contracting, and escape into a representative text of Chinese life in the Atlantic world. Cuba's experiment with Chinese labor facilitated new forms of comparative knowledge production as the "contract coolie" became renominalized as the "coolie-slave" in U.S. popular literature and political discourses on the

"Chinese Question." This genealogical excavation of the Chinese coolie lays the groundwork for the following chapter, which examines how the racial analogy embedded in the "coolie-slave" came to dominate public discussions over black political rights and Chinese immigration after emancipation.[223]

2

From Emancipation to Exclusion

Racial Analogy in Afro-Asian Periodical Print Culture

After the abrupt end of Reconstruction, the analogical bridges between African Americans and Chinese immigrants became more vexed as Pacific Coast legislators and labor agitators began drawing more heavily on the figure of the coolie-slave to devise a federal policy for Chinese exclusion. Anti-Chinese advocates found growing eastern support for their position as mainstream newspapers such as the *New-York Herald* and the *New York Sun* shifted from favoring Chinese immigration (and the labor competition it stimulated) to limiting it, according to John Kuo Wei Tchen.[1] While respectable politicians continued to distance themselves from the demagoguery of anti-Chinese "hoodlums" such as Denis Kearney and his Workingmen's Party in California, they happily seized on the specter of unfree coolie labor (and its degradation of free white or "American" labor) to mobilize support for Chinese exclusion. The Republican presidential nominee James Blaine, for example, made explicit the linkages between black chattel slavery and Chinese immigration as he identified Chinese restriction with the ideals of American freedom. Blaine, the popular Republican from Maine who helped oversee the Reconstruction Amendments, became one of the most forceful eastern advocates of Chinese exclusion before his appointment as secretary of state in 1881.[2] In 1879, Blaine began publicly supporting the anti-Chinese "fifteen passenger bill," restricting the number of Chinese immigrants on any U.S.-bound vessel to fifteen. A precursor to the 1882 Chinese Exclusion Act, the bill passed Congress, although President Rutherford B. Hayes later vetoed it. The controversial bill helped transform Chinese labor immigration from a regional concern into a topic of national news and debate.[3]

"In the Chinamen," Blaine proclaimed before the Senate, "the white laborer finds only another form of servile competition—in some respects more revolting and corrupting than African slavery."[4] Chinese immigration to the U.S., he warns in alarmist tones, "had the worst and most demoralized features of coolyism."[5] The conditions of Chinese labor in the U.S. were often exploitative, yet this misleading identification of Chinese immigration with the defunct institution of "African slavery" allowed moderate Republicans such as Blaine to portray Chinese exclusion as consistent with abolitionism's egalitarian principles. "Whoever contends for the unrestricted immigration of Chinese coolies," he continues, "contends for that system of toil which blights the prospects of the white laborer—dooming him to starvation wages, killing his ambition by rendering his struggles hopeless, and ending in a plodding and pitiable poverty."[6] Such duplicitous forms of analogical equivalence between Chinese labor migrants and black chattel slaves facilitated the presentation of Chinese exclusion as an "antislavery, pro-immigrant measure" in a country committed to universal equality and democratic inclusion, according to Moon-Ho Jung.[7] By eliding the legal, social, and economic histories that shaped the racial particularization (and subsequent conflation) of blacks and Chinese, immigration restriction advocates such as Blaine harmonized Chinese exclusion with the ideology of universal egalitarianism espoused in radical Reconstruction. As it was once America's moral imperative to abolish black chattel slavery, it becomes, according to such logic, America's duty as a free nation to abrogate the Burlingame Treaty (1868) encouraging Chinese immigration to the U.S, for China violates it with the "vicious immigration of Chinese coolies."[8]

First printed in the pages of the *New-York Tribune*, Blaine's widely reprinted vitriolic exchange on the "Chinese Question" with an aged William Lloyd Garrison just months before Garrison's death shaped the tenor of the immigration debates to come, leading to the passage of the first of several Chinese exclusion laws. Blaine's championing of the fifteen-passenger bill reveals the deepening ideological rifts within Republican ranks as the party grew more conservative with the end of Reconstruction.[9] The "Chinese Question" divided Republicans as moderates such as Blaine found themselves urging exclusionary protectionism against China despite the party's commitments to economic liberalism and free immigration.[10] The *New-York Tribune* introduced Blaine's lengthy letter defending his support of the bill as one of the strongest presentations of the "anti-Chinese view," pronouncing it as free from the regional partisanship marking much of the anti-Chinese agitation from the Pacific Coast.[11] The editor stood assured that "Mr. Blaine's letter to *The Tribune* on the Chinese question will command universal attention."[12] And indeed it did, eliciting the immediate approbation of numerous northeastern newspapers, which praised it as a "powerful . . . exhibition of the evils and dangers of an unrestricted and immense immigration from China."[13]

Blaine's studied ten-point defense of the bill summarized all aspects of the anti-Chinese position, deftly attributing the effects of prevailing legal violence as the consequence of the failings of Chinese moral character. Indeed, his arguments illuminate how religious differences — specifically, the discourse of Chinese heathenism — had come to define the parameters of acceptable and unacceptable racial difference in the U.S. In a tautological gesture, Blaine, for example, cites the disproportionate immigration of adult males and lack of Chinese home life as evidence of the failure of Chinese "domestication and assimilation" to American norms rather than as the consequence of the 1875 Page Act, which prohibited the immigration of so-called immoral Chinese women.[14] Presented as an antiprostitution measure, the Page Act created further gender imbalance in Chinese emigration while strengthening perceptions of Chinese men as unnatural bachelors. Anti-Chinese agitators often portrayed Chinese sexual perversion and alienation as the causes for rather than the effects of such exclusion policies.[15] By discouraging Chinese marriage, reproduction, and home life in the U.S., the Page Act ensured an exploitable class of temporary male laborers or sojourners. The regulation of gender and sexuality under the aegis of Christian morality was the first step in Chinese immigration restriction.

After the passage of the Reconstruction Amendments, anti-Chinese political discourse began overtly emphasizing the inassimilable religious otherness of Chinese immigrants, recoding Asiatic racial difference in terms of "heathenism." As with the Page Act, anxieties over gender, sexuality, and domesticity became central to the characterization of Christian and heathen as opposed social systems in the Chinese immigration debates that followed. In the context of the "Chinese Question," heathenism often took on additional Orientalist significance, although it racialized both non-Christian Chinese and Native Americans as antagonistic to the nation's manifest destiny.[16] Indeed, Pacific Coast states such as California had long denied Chinese and Native Americans the right to legal testimony, claiming that so-called heathens did not understand the oath. Moreover, this racializing discourse of heathenism often intersected with and drew from widely circulated "racial scripts" of African American lasciviousness and amorality that justified slavery and Jim Crow.[17] The Reconstruction Amendments and the extension of nominal citizenship rights to black freedmen did not break the constitutive link between whiteness and citizenship. However, it underwent modification as Republicans such as Blaine began defending Chinese racial exclusion as ideologically consistent with the ideals of abolition and black political inclusion. Racialization found increasingly powerful expression through an exclusionary discourse of white Christian civilization, and it continued to define U.S. citizenship and national identity in the tumultuous decades after Reconstruction.

Blaine, for example, deftly marshaled an Orientalizing discourse of heathenism to portray Chinese immigration restrictions as a defense of American civilization. As vectors of physical, moral, and sexual contagion, the Chinese constituted an inassimilable race. Blaine's argument advancing the "religious sentiment opposed to the Chinese" struck a chord with numerous political commentators, including one who pithily distilled the debate on the anti-Chinese bill as a question of "Christ or Confucius."[18] Blaine's reasoning also complemented evangelical missionary discourses, which saw China as a land in desperate need of Christian salvation.[19] More than thirty years of Chinese immigration to the West—"nearly an entire generation," as Blaine notes—has proven the vast majority of Chinese incapable of forgoing the ways of heathenism. "Under what possible sense of duty any American can feel that he promotes Christianity by the process of handing California over to heathenism, is more than I am able to discover," he insists, citing the failure of Chinese conversion to Christianity.[20] In particular, this statement drew Garrison's ire for its mobilization of so-called Christian civilization to vilify the Chinese as irredeemable heathens and thus inassimilable to America. Garrison queried, "Has he forgotten that, long before the advent of Christ, it was from the lips of Confucius came that Golden Rule which we are taught in the Gospel to follow as the rule of life all our dealing with our fellow-men."[21] Indeed, these words later inspired the opening salvo of the Chinese journalist and activist Wong Chin Foo's blistering polemic, "Why Am I a Heathen?," studied later in this chapter.

Blaine's analogical efforts to re-present Chinese labor immigration as coolie importation tantamount to "African slavery" and consequently Chinese restriction as a continuation of antebellum abolitionism set the tone for Garrison's spirited replies. In the two letters published in the *New-York Tribune*, Garrison soundly condemned Blaine for advocating a new form of "caste proscription." He accused Blaine of hypocritically defending black citizenship and suffrage while denying those same rights to Chinese immigrants. In other words, Garrison attacked Blaine for espousing the dialectic of black inclusion/Chinese exclusion, declaring, "the gifted and eloquent Senator from Maine . . . who, for himself and in behalf of the Republican party, is ready to stand by this once unutterably hated class in the assertion and defence of every right and privilege that he claims for himself, while he indulges in the most contemptuous and derogatory language toward the Chinese laborers in California!" Blaine, continues Garrison, professes a "vulgar assumption of superiority of race" that was no different from those "formerly made in disparagement of our colored population."[22] This bitter exchange between Blaine and Garrison anticipated how the "Chinese Question" would become one of the most politically divisive issues facing the nation. It too marked the end of the hard-fought Republican consensus of radical Reconstruction, which the German American illustrator Thomas Nast captured with satirical aplomb in a series of political cartoons that he inked for the popular illustrated magazine *Harper's Weekly*.

Blaine's attempt to identify Chinese restriction with abolitionism's egalitarian ideals provided the satiric fodder for Nast's elaborate front-page cartoon "The Civilization of Blaine," bearing the familiar catchphrase of organized abolitionism. "Am I Not a Man and a Brother?" cries "John Confucius" in mimicry of the beseeching slave who once dominated the political imagery of organized abolitionism (see figure 2.1). In Nast's satirical composition, Chinese exclusion both shapes and undermines the significance of U.S. political modernity in the aftermath of Reconstruction. A stern Blaine with hand outreached in a preemptory gesture functions as the dividing seam of the image, which positions (perhaps unintentionally) Blaine's white American manhood as

74 | FROM EMANCIPATION TO EXCLUSION

Figure 2.1. Thomas Nast, "The Civilization of Blaine," *Harper's Weekly* (March 8, 1879) (Courtesy of the Mark Twain Collection, University of California–Berkeley)

emerging from the tense interplay between the "Negro Problem" and the "Chinese Question." With ballot in hand, a caricatured childlike black figure leans joyous into Blaine's protective—indeed, paternalistic— embrace, while a Chinese merchant stands among other transpacific commodities—tapestries, vases, and silks—in the background. The

Burlingame Treaty lies crushed underneath Blaine's heel. The illustration offered a satirical prolepsis of the future of U.S.-China relations. President Hayes's veto of the fifteen-passenger bill did not dissuade anti-Chinese forces in Congress. They refocused their efforts on the modification of the treaty in 1880 and later passed the 1882 Chinese Exclusion Act, banning the immigration of Chinese laborers over the next ten years and reclassifying Chinese in the U.S. as "aliens ineligible to citizenship."

Nast satirized the dialectical configuration of black inclusion / Chinese exclusion, taking particular umbrage at what he viewed as Blaine's betrayal of Republican ideals in endorsing Chinese immigration restrictions. However, the cartoon's caricatured black-citizen-as-child also alludes to the belated temporality of black racial equality in social, if not strict legal, fact.[23] The rapid resurgence of antiblack violence and Jim Crow in the wake of Reconstruction revealed that inclusion into the category of formal citizenship did not mitigate black racial inequality or racially subordinated American identities. The Chinese exclusion movement further exposed the tenuous status of black citizenship in the era leading to *Plessy v. Ferguson* (1896). By the 1870s, popular media and political commentary had begun linking the so-called Negro Problem and the Chinese Question, and the prominence of this racial analogy fueled black and Chinese efforts to assert their racial-legal distinctiveness as nonwhite subjects.[24] "Racialization in the United States," observes Joshua Paddison, "was always comparative, and nineteenth-century observers constantly juxtaposed Indians and the Chinese with each other and with African Americans, Mexican, the Irish, and others."[25] Such juxtapositions among racialized minority populations often took an analogical form. This chapter tracks the early discursive history of what literary scholars such as Colleen Lye have begun to critique as the "Afro-Asian analogy."[26]

The remainder of this chapter explores the varied responses of African American and Chinese American writers to the heated national debates over the "Chinese Question." In attending to largely understudied forms of early periodical print culture, this chapter begins to chart some of the cross-racial connections that shaped and challenged the course of national politics.[27] By broadening Reconstruction to encompass the West and its "Chinese Question," this chapter draws on a diverse range of contemporaneous writings and oratory by James Williams, William H. Newby, Frederick Douglass, Yan Phou Lee, and Wong Chin Foo to investigate the analogization of blacks and Chinese in popular political discourse and how these writers negotiated and contested these homogenizing racial representations. Their varied experiments with the periodical form chart dynamic circuits of cultural translation and knowledge production that gave rise to new modes of racialized subjectivity.

Black writers from the West such as Williams and Newby remain overlooked despite ongoing African American print culture recovery work. In their multiform western writings, Williams and Newby, like their more prominent contemporary Douglass, drew on their experiences of eastern slavery as critical reference points.[28] This chapter places these writers into critical dialogue with equally understudied Chinese American writers from the East. A leader in the struggle for Chinese citizenship and suffrage, Wong, like Douglass, was a prolific writer; he embraced the periodical form and assumed editorship of the earliest bilingual Chinese American newspaper published in the East. Wong composed more than 140 different short-form writings, nearly all of which appeared in English-language periodicals. Wong and Lee, in their varied print journalism, sought to dismantle the racializing discourse of heathenism, which helped sustain the dialectical configuration of black inclusion / Chinese exclusion embraced by the likes of Blaine. The interactive, dialogic quality of the newspaper form—its invitation to participate and respond—appealed to these various writers and gave shape to their complex racial politics, which took place alongside and through efforts to understand other racial and ethnic histories unfolding in the U.S. By emphasizing the relational character of U.S. racial formations, this chapter explores how these writers refashioned the ideas of America and Americanization as Reconstruction began to reformulate the foundational narratives of white racialized citizenship and national identity.

From East to West: James Williams's *Life and Adventures*

During California's economic depression in the 1870s, Philip Alexander Bell's San Francisco–based black weekly, the *Elevator*, began expressing open support for Chinese exclusion.[29] In the face of intensifying labor competition, Bell, a former abolitionist and editor of the New York City–based *Colored American*, spoke out in "self-defense" against "the hordes of Chinese who are flocking to our shores and sapping to the foundation our mechanical and labor interests," and he urged his black readers "to withhold ... any encouragement to them to come among us."[30] The end of the Civil War returned Democrats to power in California, and some black leaders in the West, such as Bell, began to publicly separate their condition from that of Native Americans and Chinese immigrants as a matter of political expediency.[31] However, the *Elevator*'s endorsement of Chinese exclusion ran against the political grain of the nineteenth-century black press, which voiced almost unanimous opposition to a race-based immigration exclusion that harked back to slavery's past, namely, the 1790 Naturalization Act limiting naturalization to "any alien, being a white person."[32] The African Methodist Episcopal Church's *Christian Recorder* denounced the *Elevator* as it offered a lesson in far-too-recent history: "Only a few years ago the cry was, not 'The Chinese must go,' but 'The niggers must go.'"[33] In another issue, it struck out against the "revived spirit of proscription ... [against the Chinese] in perpetuating an outrage like to that the Nation often witnessed before the war."[34] At the height of the anti-Chinese movement, the *Christian Recorder* marshaled the contradiction of Chinese exclusion in the wake of black legal inclusion as it brought the past to bear on the geopolitics of race, labor, and sexuality in the postemancipation West. "Having felt this fire ourselves," it admonished, "we would be exceedingly ungrateful were we not to extend the hand of sympathy toward the Chinese."[35] Editorials such as the ones from the *Christian Recorder* often condemned the perpetuation of Jim Crow policies against the Chinese in California as they endeavored to arouse African American sympathy and outrage on behalf of a differently "proscribed" race.[36]

By intensifying nonwhite racial differentiation and conflict, the Afro-Asian analogy, particularly as it emerged in the Chinese exclusion debates, provoked black periodicals such as the *Christian Recorder* to think more expansively about black identity formation in a comparative racial context. The *Christian Recorder* editorial highlights how the "lives of racialized groups are linked across time and space" by publicly recognizing what Natalia Molina terms the "racial scripts" that once marginalized African Americans and were now revived and recycled to disenfranchise the Chinese.[37] It also adapted "sympathy"—a powerful organizing trope of sentimental reform studied at length in chapter 4—to seek common ground with another racialized nonwhite minority. Rather than evidence of black identification with Chinese racial difference, the *Christian Recorder*'s profession of political sympathy, emerging as it did from a critique of state violence and institutionalized slavery "before the war," sought to account for the shifting dynamics of Reconstruction racial formations within a comparative framework. Such attentiveness to political similarities did not efface the incommensurability of divergent racial histories. In reasoning from the known to unknown and from the visible to speculative, such forms of comparative racialization—with its stress on relations of similarity or resemblance in the face of differences—hold the potential to foster political analyses that are responsive to structural inequalities and capable of producing forms of ethical subjectivity.[38]

This section focuses on one largely underexamined text, Williams's once-popular postbellum slave narrative *Life and Adventures of James Williams* (1873), to tease out an emergent analytic of comparative racialization—one that became explicitly politicized in Douglass's "Composite Nationality" speech studied in the next section. A controversial figure, Williams arrived in California in 1851 at the height of Chinese immigration into the state, and he witnessed the earliest campaigns to ban what anti-Chinese ideologues styled as the "threatening hordes" of "Asiatic slaves."[39] In 1873, he published the first edition of his narrative in San Francisco as the last great Indian Wars were being fought and the Chinese exclusion movement gained momentum, leading to the ratification of the first in a series of race- (and gender-) specific immigration laws in 1875 with the Page Act. This section reads Williams's *Life and Adventures* alongside the key legal and political contexts that gave it narrative shape (and to which Williams addressed his text), including California Governor John Bigler's anticoolieism campaign (1852), the California Supreme Court ruling in *People v. Hall* (1854), and the widely publicized Modoc War (1872–1873). It builds on the analytics for articulating racial difference—indeed, differential thinking—honed in U.S. race and ethnic studies to help illuminate Williams's literary efforts to formulate an early politics of comparative racialization.[40] By disarticulating the racial logics that underlie the Afro-Asian analogy,

Williams provides a critical alternative to the analogical model of racial comparison popularized by legislators such as Blaine in the national debates over Chinese immigration. Writing during and in the immediate wake of radical Reconstruction, Williams sought to understand the paradoxical structure of black political inclusion by way of comparison to Chinese exclusion and Native American removal. In *Life and Adventures*, Williams brings these uneven, multiple, and often competing racial histories within a single comparative framework to investigate the contradictions of citizenship and national inclusion in the West.

Frontier California—after the discovery of gold near Sutter's Mill— held the possibility of new beginnings for self-emancipated blacks when the 1850 Compromise dashed their hope for slavery's end. Just days after the Fugitive Slave Bill became federal law, California—among the vast lands acquired in the Mexican-American War—entered the Union as a free state. Williams, a fugitive, joined the black exodus from the East, fleeing the new federal law. Many sped northwards to the safety of British Canada, but Williams struck out for California, where warmer climes and better economic prospects beckoned. He numbered among the early black pioneers, and his account of black life in the West offers us an opportunity to revisit Houston Baker's early claim that "tales of pioneers enduring the hardships of the West for the promise of immense wealth are not the tales of black America."[41] Born John Thomas Evans, the slave of William Hollingsworth of Elkton, Maryland, Williams escaped to Philadelphia in 1838, searching for his mother, Abby, who "had run away years before."[42] By the age of sixteen, Williams was a self-identified "abolitionist" and, in his words, "commenced [his] labors with the Underground Railroad" (4). As a fugitive in Philadelphia, Williams witnessed the many antiblack riots that broke out in the city, and these eastern experiences later shaped his responses to the anti-Chinese movement in California. The many trials that Williams suffered over the course of his westward journey serve as evidence of "what a man that had made his escape from the blood-hounds hath to undergo to reach the shores of California, where he could be free and safe from all danger of being apprehended" (22). Williams's voyage led him from Philadelphia across Panama to California and later to Mexico and British Columbia for a time.[43] The complex contours of these itinerant experiences remap the conventional pathways of south-to-north fugitive flight even as they participated in the transnational flows of racialized labor migration that facilitated the incorporation of the American West.[44]

Like Williams, black pioneers, including Peter Anderson, Mifflin Wistar Gibbs, Mary Ellen Pleasant, Jeremiah Burke Sanderson, and William H. Newby, had participated in organized abolition in the East and continued their activities in the West. The abolitionist John Jacobs, the brother of Harriet Jacobs, had shared the antislavery platform with the likes of Douglass and Garrison, and he "concluded to go to California" on "the day President Fillmore signed the Fugitive Slave Bill into law."[45] A self-identified abolitionist, Williams filled the first half of his narrative with vignettes of those fugitive slaves whom he assisted while a member of the Philadelphia Vigilance Committee. He reportedly participated in William and Ellen Crafts's well-publicized stand-off in Boston against Georgia slave catchers before fleeing the East himself. Once in California, Williams continued to intercede on the behalf of those slaves brought within the bounds of the newly admitted free state, using the indeterminacy of state law to his advantage. "Be it known," informs Williams, "that about this time there was a number of slaves brought into California by their masters, one of which was a woman. . . . I went there, taking a white man with me at the time, and took her away" (24). Williams also recounts assisting in Archy Lee's defense in the only federal fugitive-slave case to come before California courts.[46] "I was the first man in the fray," recalls Williams, "which occurred on the night of the attempted arrest," and "we succeeded in rescuing the man . . . and . . . Archy, is now a resident in Sacramento" (27).[47]

Williams charts these oft-neglected histories of black westward migration in an autobiographical narrative that he began in 1869, published in 1873, enlarged in 1874, and reprinted in 1893. The San Francisco Women's Union Print published the first four editions of the autobiography, while the Philadelphia-based printers A. H. Sickler brought out a fifth edition two decades later in 1893. According to an inscription in the fifth-edition copy held at the Historical Society of Pennsylvania, the Quaker genealogist and local historian Gilbert Cope had originally "purchased [it] from the author 3-30-1897," indicating that Williams was still living in 1897 and had authorized this final edition (see figure 2.2).

Williams's postbellum slave narrative was neither impelled by the political imperatives of organized abolitionism nor produced for its

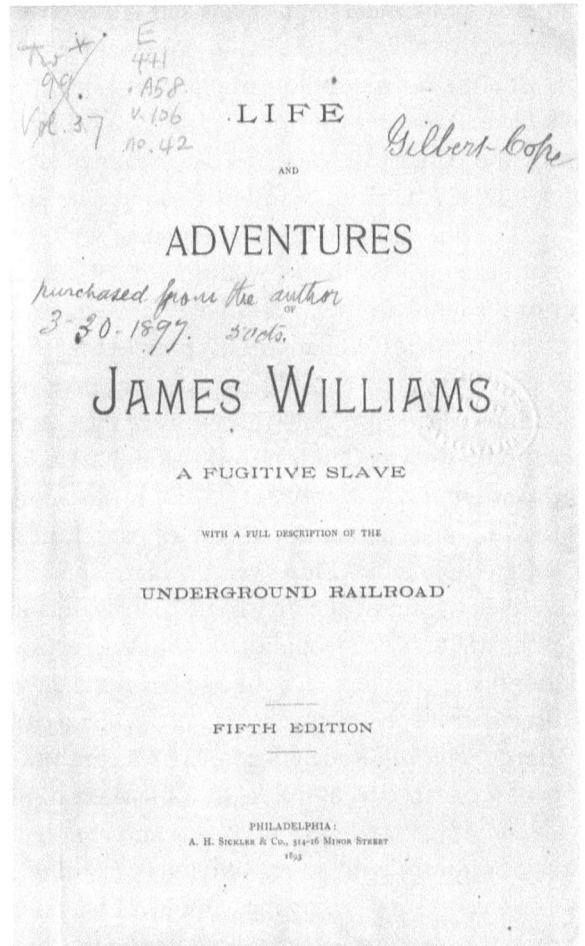

Figure 2.2. Title page, *Life and Adventures of James Williams, a Fugitive Slave* (Philadelphia: A. H. Sickler, 1893) (Courtesy of the Historical Society of Pennsylvania)

audiences. It begins as a conventional slave narrative, yet the testimonial form falls away as Williams moves westward. Resisting the teleological trajectory of the slavery-to-freedom narrative, all editions end, not as expected with Williams's emergence as a modern black political subject—marked by the passage of the Fifteenth Amendment—but rather with sketches exploring the political condition of "The Chinese in California" (in the original) and "The Modocs" (in the enlarged edition).

Thus, the autobiography understands black self-knowledge and narration as both productive of and produced by comparative racialization.

Like the masculine self-mythologizing at work in the black frontiersman Nat Love's *Life and Adventures* (1907), Williams embraced the freedom of the American West, yet he remained deeply skeptical of the ideology of American Manifest Destiny. The lawlessness of the frontier—"the wild and free life of the plains," in Love's words—appealed to both men, particularly given the identification of slavery with "the law of the land" in their narratives.[48] "We had no law in the country at that time," writes Williams of his prospecting experiences in "Nigger Hill," and "we miners constituted a law for ourselves" (23).[49] In this, both men intervened in racialist accounts of the western frontier popularized in books such as Charles Howard Shinn's *Mining Camps: A Study in American Frontier Government* (1884), in which mining-camp life revealed the Teutonic "hereditary fitness" of American pioneers for democratic self-government.[50] Moreover, Williams specifically adapts the slave narrative's hallmark skepticism of the law and its ability to administer justice to the racial geopolitics of the American West.

Short epigrammatic chapters recounting tales from slavery times—some lifted directly from the black abolitionist William Still's recently published *Underground Rail Road* (1872)—are roughly yoked together with accounts of western adventure. With a focus on topical controversies and a blend of national news and local and regional items with popular history, scripture, and song, Williams's *Life and Adventures* mimes the periodical form—the primary mode of textual production in the early black West, as Eric Gardner notes.[51] In this, Williams's narrative draws on and experiments with the periodical form embraced by the other writers studied in this chapter. The autobiography's wide-ranging, nonchronological first-, second-, and third-person narrative voices form the ligaments of a comparative critique of the racial ideologies that helped constitute and sustain the idea of a unified national polity. The narrative is, to borrow Williams's mining metaphor, "honeycombed" with observations on African enslavement, Chinese exclusion, and Native American removal as the failures of radical Reconstruction illuminated the similarly undermined firmament on which U.S. political modernity was built.

Debates over Chinese immigration played a critical role in the development of black understandings of life in the West and immediately shaped the comparative racial contexts of Williams's narrative.[52] These early debates help us understand Williams's approach to comparative racialization, particularly as they informed his "Chinese in California" chapter and its efforts to disarticulate the logic of racial analogy that became established in the popular and political discourses of Chinese exclusion. Arriving in 1851, Williams joined the growing black and sizable Chinese, Native American, and Spanish-Mexican (Californio) populations already in California, although he soon discovered that multiethnic California was far from free of the "colorphobia" that had dogged his life in the East. Concerns over mining monopolies employing slave labor rather than high-minded principles compelled California lawmakers to endorse an antislavery constitution, which neither ended efforts to extend slavery into the West nor quelled concerns over the immigration of black and Chinese laborers into the newly established free state. Proslavery southern emigrants, for example, demanded the reconstruction of the West into a free North and slave South at the 36° 30' parallel of the Missouri Compromise. This proposition was laid repeatedly before the California legislature, and in 1852, the *Frederick Douglass' Paper* eagerly reported "the defeat of the Bill for the division of the gold State" with "its intent . . . to devote Southern California to slavery."[53] Bills restricting black and Chinese immigration, often resembling those statutory restrictions—from slave codes to black exclusion and registration laws—that continued to police free and enslaved blacks in the South, where control over mobility was essential to the logic of white mastery, continually found their way before California legislatures.[54] This early regional history of racialized restrictions reveals the contested processes by which "Chinese" became reelaborated as a racial category analogically equated to legal "blackness."

Williams's antebellum California became the staging ground for the subsequent national debates over Chinese immigration. As the slavery controversy raged in the East, California, under the leadership of its Democratic governor, John Bigler, launched its earliest campaign to prohibit Chinese immigration into the state. By the end of his first term,

Bigler had helped reconfigure "Chinese" into a racial category subject to legal restriction, taxation, and intimidation, culminating in the California Supreme Court's infamous ruling in *People v. Hall*, which barred Chinese from the right to testify against whites in court. In 1852, shortly after Williams's arrival, Bigler delivered a "Special Message" before the state legislature urging it "to prevent or discourage shipments of vast bodies of 'Coolies'" into the state.[55] Breaking from his predecessor's proimmigration policy, Bigler cast nonwhite Chinese immigrants as "coolies" and racially ineligible to partake in the "civil and political privileges of citizens of the United States."[56] Chapter 1 examined how U.S. involvement in the Spanish Caribbean helped popularize this racializing discourse of Chinese coolieism. As the black press began advancing the question of "whether a colored man can be a citizen or not" in the East, Bigler's anti-Chinese campaign in California began recentering the citizenship debate on the "yellow or tawny races of the Asiatics."[57] Addressing the question of "whether Asiatics could, with safety, be admitted to the enjoyments of all the rights of citizens in our Courts of Justice," Bigler argued that it would be "unwise to receive them as jurors or permit them to testify in courts of law," and the subsequent California Supreme Court case of *People v. Hall* established this in law.[58] Bigler reasoned that "under the laws of the United States"—specifically, the 1790 Naturalization Act—the Chinese could not "become American citizens" and should remain subject to the civil disabilities that had long beleaguered free blacks in the country.[59] In this, Bigler anticipated the arguments of anti-Chinese politicians in the East, such as Blaine, seeking to devise a federal policy against Chinese immigration in the 1870s.[60]

The black press joined the chorus of protest that erupted from California's Chinese communities contesting these legislative attempts to map political status onto racial identity. Douglass's New York–based *Frederick Douglass' Paper* was one of the earliest newspapers to criticize how California lawmakers analogically translated racial restriction laws from East to West and from blacks to Chinese. "We can by no means sympathize with Gov. Bigler," it reported, "recommending the passage of laws prohibiting Chinese emigration, and putting the emigrants under the disabilities of the African, or expelling them from the country."[61] Bigler's "pretence is," it explained, "that the Chinese are a people of color, and he enters upon a labored law argument . . . to show that they are not *white* men within the meaning of the statute of the United States, and therefore may not be citizens thereof; and that their emigration may be burdened with any amount of taxation and oppression, *alamode* Georgia and Carolina."[62] The Washington, DC, *National Era* also weighed in against California legislators as it simultaneously utilized and resisted the racial mandates of slave law with sardonic aplomb: the Chinese "are not white, certainly, and just as certainly they are not black; and *partus sequitur ventrum*! (which is Latin for cursing a nigger) these barbarians are free born, and cannot be legally reduced to chattel slavery."[63] Taking up the metaphor of the national polity as "one family of people," the editorial revealed the underlying, shared racial logic of both proslavery and proexclusion advocates: "You may exterminate the Indians, and hold the Africans in chattel slavery, but you cannot put . . . [the Chinese] . . . under the ban of barbarism or of color" or "reduce them to slavery" for "white in slave-law language does not mean color, but descent."[64] Both the *National Era* and *Frederick Douglass' Paper* protested the fusing of race with status and the subsequent realignment of Chinese nonwhiteness with the subordinate political status of black chattel slaves.

By identifying the Chinese in California as "Asiatic slaves," the Joint Committee tasked to review Bigler's recommendations further strengthened the analogical bridges by which questions over black citizenship and Chinese immigration became linked in the popular mind.[65] Najia Aarim-Heriot has shown how this Afro-Asian racial analogy subsequently shaped the law and jurisprudence of the state in critical ways, especially in the infamous ruling in *People v. Hall* (1854). California law had long denied blacks and Native Americans legal defense in cases where there were no white witnesses, and jurists soon encumbered the Chinese population with similar legal disabilities. As Williams notes, "the colored people were not allowed their oath against a white man" (27). This prohibition against legal testimony had long been a cornerstone in California's racial legislation (and a long-standing source of black protest), and it underwent expansion in *People v. Hall*. Convicted and sentenced to death for the murder of Ling Sing, a Chinese miner in Nevada County, George Hall, a white man, appealed his case, claiming the inadmissibility of the Chinese witnesses who had testified against him.[66] In reversing the judgment against Hall, the California Supreme

Court effectively barred Chinese subjects, as it had for blacks and Native Americans, from securing legal retribution for the violation of their rights. The California civil and criminal codes stipulated, "No Black, or Mulatto person, or Indian, shall be allowed to give evidence in favor of, or against a white man." In *People v. Hall*, the California Supreme Court struggled to expand by way of analogical reasoning the "already existing framework of 'legally defined' racial groups," namely, black, white, and Native American, to encompass Asiatic difference.[67]

A jurist whom the *Frederick Douglass' Paper* excoriated as the most "unjust and oppressive . . . of all the [state] Supreme Court Justices," Chief Justice Hugh Murray, seized on *People v. Hall* as an opportunity to extend his judicial efforts to another nonwhite population.[68] In a turn to racial taxonomy (or "ethnology," in his words), Murray began by tracing back Native Americans to the "Mongolian, or Asiatic" (who had made the passage across the Bering Strait to the New World) in order to align Chinese with Native American racial difference. He then broadened the category of "black" to encompass "all races other than the Caucasian": "We are of the opinion that the 'White,' 'Negro,' 'Mulatto,' 'Indian,' and 'Black person,' wherever they occur in our Constitution and laws, must be taken in their generic sense, and that . . . the words 'Black person,' . . . must be taken as contradistinguished from White, and necessarily excludes all races other than Caucasian."[69] In the face of racial multiplicity, Murray resurrected the dichotomous logic of the black-white binary to redefine the existing legal nomenclature, claiming "black" as the "generic" term for all nonwhites. By jumping from one racial meaning and context to another, Murray exploited the arbitrary relatedness inherent within analogy to argue that "Mongolian" difference was consistent with *either* black *or* Native American racial identity (as all were equally nonwhite). On the basis of analogical resemblance, Murray drew legal inference from one (racial) classification and applied it to another, transforming divergent U.S. racial formations into homogeneous sameness: Chinese is black (or Native American) by another name. Thus, *People v. Hall* illuminates analogy's potential to mislead as it slides into equivalence, equalizing heterogeneous domains of racial meaning while radically expanding the racial-legal category of "black" to ban nonwhite Chinese as it had blacks, mulattos, and Native Americans from forms of legal redress.[70]

Codified and extended to civil cases in 1863 by the California legislature, *People v. Hall* helped deepen the ideological gulf between white and nonwhite, paving the way for additional anti-Chinese laws in the period.[71] Murray's paranoid vision of Chinese with "all the equal rights of citizenship" also serves as the springboard into Pierton W. Dooner's *Last Days of the Republic* (1880), the earliest U.S.-based Chinese invasion novel, studied in chapter 3. Like Bigler's "Special Message," *People v. Hall* was also met with protest in the black press, which viewed it as yet another outgrowth of the racial proscriptions that blacks suffered under the regime of chattel slavery. The "Americans at length decided," reported the Canadian *Provincial Freeman*, "that the Chinese shall be treated like Indian and negroes, and not allowed to give evidence in a court of justice."[72] In response to Murray's ruling, the black nationalist Martin Delany concluded, "The Chinese stand in the same political position as the black man. He too is degraded to the level of a slave."[73] Garrison's *Liberator* also denounced *People v. Hall* as a regressive "stride towards slavery," reminding readers, "There is no more abominable and oppressive law in the whole slave code than that which prevents its victims from testifying in a court of justice."[74]

After *People v. Hall*, public discussions over black citizenship published in *Frederick Douglass' Paper* denouncing various "black law[s] upon the statutes" drew attention to California, "now subjecting the Chinese to the enormous odium which has been engendered against colored people, and the Supreme Court of that State has decided, that they are included under the head of Negroes, Mulattoes, Colored people, etc."[75] Many of the leading black periodicals of the day had long criticized the importation of antebellum black codes against the Chinese as "a people of color."[76] Anticipating the racialized logic of Taney's *Dred Scott* ruling, Bigler's anti-Chinese campaign helped establish the discursive terrain of the Afro-Asian analogy (and the analogical equivalence of Chinese with black legal status), which later facilitated the application of antiblack case law including *Dred Scott* to Chinese populations in the West. Even the proexclusion *San Francisco Elevator*, which professed "no sympathy with the Chinese" found itself provoked to respond in kind as it likened California's anti-Chinese measures to the presumptive racial logic at work in *Dred Scott*, asking readers, "Have Chinese Any Rights Which Americans Are Bound to Respect"?[77]

Williams addressed his brief yet revealing "Chinese in California" chapter to this highly volatile and as-yet-unfolding national debate. In it, he suggests that legal subjection forms the basis of racial citizenship. The abolition of slavery and extension of citizenship to black Americans neither mitigated this fundamental contradiction nor lessened the nativist anxieties of those who were so recently assimilated to the national narrative of "We the People."[78] "Some of our true Americans," he writes in reference to the growing popularity of Yellow Peril discourse, "say they don't want them [the Chinese] here; that they will get so numerous that we Americans can't live" (92). Williams's use of the first-person plural "we Americans" dramatizes the paradoxical structure of his political inclusion. He refuses to be excluded from the American polity that he names, yet he acknowledges his inclusion in an agonistic and historically conscious way. His "Chinese in California" chapter ridicules the contradictory logic of a wide spectrum of exclusion advocates from the Sand Lot agitator Denis Kearney to the presidential hopeful Blaine who embraced free labor yet insisted on its degradation by Chinese "cheap" labor.[79] "What would we do in the State of California but for the Chinamen?" asks Williams. "The rich people couldn't get along without them," he notes, "for servants and cooks, whether white or colored, it is difficult to hire; therefore, they must have Chinamen as house servants. But, they say, we must drive the Chinamen out of California, for they work so cheap. As cheap as they work, they pay more for rent, and are taxed more than any other race of people" (93). Williams shifts narrative voice to address exclusion agitators in second-person form to heighten the impact and challenge of his critique. He remarks with sarcasm, "Drive them out? Ah, my learned friends, are you not aware that California is a free country? It is part of the United States of America, and America throws open her doors for all nations" (93). Williams asserts a historical relationship between these uneven processes of Americanization and racialization that produced, in his ironic words, the "true Americans, white and black" (93).[80] Immigration policies shaped American understandings of national membership through specific forms of racial exclusion. Chinese exclusion—the exception that proved the rule—helped America redefine itself as a free nation in the wake of racial slavery.[81]

Williams links anti-Chinese agitation in California not only to earlier and ongoing forms of antiblack violence but also to the cries initially raised "among the true American people against the Irish people" (93). Memories of antebellum Philadelphia, where labor competition intensified the need to reestablish racial distinctions between white and non-white, temper his account of the Chinese in California. He drew from these experiences to formulate a politics of comparative racialization that went beyond the limits of the Afro-Asian analogy. In 1849 on election night, the Irish Catholic street gang known as the Killers (allied to the Moyamensing Hose Company and sometimes referred to as the Moyamensing Killers) attacked a black-owned business, the California House—provoked by rumors that the mulatto proprietor was living there with a white wife—and instigated a violent two-day riot.[82] In Williams's efforts to extinguish the fire that destroyed the California House, he received a buckshot wound to his right thigh and "a blow over . . . [his] left eye—the mark of which is there until this day," and he later thrashed an officer who attempted to arrest him (7, 8).

The Philadelphia native Mifflin Wistar Gibbs—a contemporary of Williams in California—also recalled the "ravages of what was known as the 'Moyamensing Killers,' who burned down the churches and residence of the colored people and murdered their occupants."[83] In his memoir, *Shadow and Light: An Autobiography* (1902), Gibbs remarked on the forces, both social and economic, that propelled Irish racial differentiation: "The Irish, having fled from oppression in the land of their birth, for notoriety, gain, or elevation by comparison, were nearly all pro-slavery."[84] Williams also reminds readers of the ethnic antipathies that once greeted these immigrants on U.S. soil and fueled the need for racial differentiation and conflict. He recalls those angry accusations once levied against the Irish and now redirected against the Chinese: "The damned Irish are all immigrating here from Ireland; that we, the American people, would be starved, and couldn't get work on account of the Irish" (93). Many of the trade unionists who joined Kearney's Workingmen's Party of California in rallying popular support for Chinese exclusion were, like Kearney, Irish immigrants. These Irish immigrants, argues Paddison, "increasingly staked their claim to Christian whiteness on their opposition to Chinese immigration, successfully portraying themselves as potential allies to white Protestants in a common struggle against debasing pagan outsiders."[85] The "Irish and the Niggers," Williams remarks dryly, "have outlived that sentiment, and now it is the Chinamen" (93). In thus disarticulating nativity, ethnicity, and race, Williams limns, as he contests, the violent processes by which one becomes a racialized subject of America.

Writing against the pervasive rhetoric of analogical equivalence, Williams, like his contemporary Newby (studied in the next section), registers how existing restrictions against Chinese immigrants drew on and revised those disciplinary technologies once directed against black migrants in antebellum California. In the fashion of the *Christian Recorder*'s profession of cross-racial political sympathy, he reminds his postbellum audience "that in 1855, in Sacramento, there was a bill introduced into the Legislature to prohibit colored men from immigrating to the State of California, and that those that were here should leave, and those that did not leave should be taxed heavily, and should wear tags" (93). In 1858, another "Negro Exclusion Bill" came before the California State Assembly, and a bill prohibiting the entry of "Mongolians" soon followed. While a technicality prevented the passage of the black exclusion bill, the Chinese exclusion bill passed the state legislature and was enacted into law.[86]

Such repressive racial legislation in free California mimicked the regime of spatial control that black pioneers such as Williams and Newby had sought to escape by westward migration. "This is a white man's government," Williams wrote, paraphrasing *Dred Scott*—"A 'colored man has no rights that a white man is bound to respect'"—as he joined Archy Lee and nearly six hundred blacks emigrants to British Columbia in protest of the proposed "Negro Act" (36–37). Williams's dream of freedom on British rather than American soil proved to be as elusive as the one that propelled him westward. With wry reference to the landmark British civil case *Somerset v. Stewart* (1772), William recalls, "Thinking, with a number of my colored friends, that I would like to breathe purer air, I, with a number, emigrated to Vancouver Island, where we thought the air was more pure; but, on arriving there, finding the air somewhat tainted, I returned . . . to Sacramento" (27). Williams thus inflects his accounts of black westward migration through the complex dynamics of racialization—the combination of law, prejudice, and economic forces that fueled increasing racial differentiation and conflict between whites and nonwhites and between Chinese and blacks in the West.

Williams's reflections on the political condition of Pacific Coast Chinese and Native Americans shape the larger story that he seeks to tell about the contradictory processes of his American citizenship and inclusion. In charting the discursive and historical processes that transform race into a "crime of status," Williams further widens his framework of comparative Chinese and black racializations to encompass another history of coerced dislocations—state-sanctioned expropriation and removal—by which Native American populations were forced from their ancestral lands and driven into the western territories.[87] His final chapters on the Modoc Indians further illuminate the multiple and overlapping forms of racial violence that constituted U.S. political modernity after slavery. Williams substantially enlarged these final chapters in his later revised edition, and this extended account calls to mind the deployment of black Civil War veterans in the Tenth Calvary of the U.S. Army—the famed "Buffalo Soldiers"—to the southwest borderlands and Great Plains to fight in the Indian Wars from 1866 to 1890.

Williams's Modoc chapters, however, do not share in the nationalist sentiments of other black frontier narratives such as Love's *Life and Adventures*, Henry Flipper's unpublished memoir of his experiences in the American Southwest and Mexico (1916)—the sequel to his *Colored Cadet at West Point* (1878)—and James Beckwourth's dictated (to Thomas Bonner) *Life and Adventures* (1856), to which Williams's narrative might be compared.[88] Predicated on the seizure of indigenous lands, western incorporation and regional economic growth intensified the need for cheap and plentiful labor, for as Love writes, "with the march of progress came the railroad."[89] His narrative fashions the "iron horse" as the harbinger of western industrialization, yet it is the encroachment of the law that deals the deathblow to the "wild and free life" that once lured men such as Love, the self-proclaimed "Deadwood Dick," and Williams westward: "Laws have been enacted in new Mexico and Arizona which, forbid all the old-time sports and the cowboy is almost a being of the past."[90] In a far more polemical vein, Williams brings this skepticism of the law—a convention of both the masculine frontier narrative and slave narrative on which he draws—to bear on the variegated histories of racial formations in the American West.

Williams's chapter "The Modocs" acknowledges the coercive role of law in the legacy of white supremacy, and it condemns the law and legal process in the arbitration of racial justice. The revised edition recounts the execution in California of the captured Modoc Indians who had violently protested their relocation to southern Oregon in the Modoc War (1872–1873)—the last great Indian War in the area. "I have traveled this part of the country for more or less than twenty-five years, among the Indians," Williams recounts, "and I have never been molested by them, I have also visited the camps by myself, been in the caves with them, and witnessed the war-dance, and never was molested yet" (99). The federal government formalized its policy of indigenous containment with the Removal Act (1830), yet ongoing territorial appropriation required further and further westward tribal resettlement. Racial particularization again found an unlikely articulation with liberal agendas as politicians, bureaucrats, writers, and settlers began to represent forced removal as necessary to aboriginal preservation. They sought both to "legitimate and mystify removal" in the trope of the vanishing Indian as they embraced what Renato Rosaldo describes as "imperialist nostalgia" in their longing for "forms of life they intentionally altered or destroyed."[91]

Rather than the fulfillment of a conservationist program, Indian removal, for Williams, recalls the mismanaged Reconstruction of the South and the pledges that went unfulfilled to the black freedmen. From 1869 to 1872, President Ulysses S. Grant began reforming federal Native American policy to promote Christian "civilization and ultimate citizenship" for Native Americans, now redesignated as "wards of the state." The subsequent Modoc War served as evidence not only of the failure of Grant's Peace Policy but of the innate savagery of Native Americans, who, like the Chinese, were incapable of Christian civilization.[92] Williams's "The Modocs" chapter places black identity formation in yet another comparative racial context to further elaborate, in literary terms, what Claire Jean Kim describes as the "field of racial positions," in which subordinate groups are at once "differently racialized" and "racialized in comparison with one another."[93]

Espousing little of the romantic racialism that characterized many contemporaneous accounts of Native Americans, Williams casts a critical eye on the state-sanctioned execution of the captured rebel warriors as he places himself in the position of a witness to "this horrible crime" (98). Now a citizen of the national polity and thus, as he self-mockingly asserts in the "Chinese in California" chapter, a "true American, white and black," Williams again emphasizes the ambiguities of his racial citizenship as both witness to and participant in this federal execution. The rebel Modoc leader, Kientpoos (or Kintpuash), popularly known as Captain Jack, led a small band to Tule Lake in protest of the U.S. government's failure to supply adequate rations to the tribe after its relocation in 1864. The U.S. Army sent troops to return the rebel Modocs to the reservation. The celebrated former Union general E. R. S. (Edward Richard Sprigg) Canby led the force of three hundred troops and numbered among the killed once peace talks failed.[94]

The unexpected resistance from the outnumbered Modocs spurred sensationalized accounts of the six-month "Indian War in Oregon," which appeared on the front pages of the nation's leading newspapers, including the *San Francisco Chronicle*, *Philadelphia Inquirer*, and *New York Herald*. In contrast to these lurid reports of "hostile redskins," Williams insists that the U.S. government's betrayal provoked the Modoc attack.[95] "I believe," he wrote, "that they were trying to deal with Captain Jack like they dealt with the freedmen down South, but Jack didn't see the point; they used to send out agents to collect money for freedmen and distressed soldiers during the war, and they would stick the money in their pockets; they would also bring great donations of clothing and provisions . . . but . . . those poor freedmen . . . had to . . . go without" (99). The "freedmen," reports Williams, "told me so down South," and this was "what they were playing on Captain Jack, but he would not stand it, and you hung him" (99). Williams compares the false promises the federal government extended to the Modocs with the suffering of black freedmen as southern Democrats began regaining by gunpoint and Jim Crow legislation the power they had lost under radical Reconstruction.

Williams's deep ambivalence toward law and legal process as an arbiter of racial justice—voiced earlier in his Philadelphia and early California chapters—emerges most forcefully in these Modoc chapters. He writes, "it was wrong to hang him [Captain Jack], because there was no law established by Congress to hang him" (99). Williams further reasons, "no law to hang Jeff Davis, according to Congress," even though he was the "cause of thousands of lives being lost, and widows distressed to-day in our land; cause of our President of the United States being assassinated" (99–100). "If he had been a poor Indian," remarks Williams, plying yet another comparison, "he would [have hung]" (100). In posing this counterfactual claim, Williams interrogates the unequal protection of abstract individual rights under the law. Again, challenging the reader with second-person address, Williams's account of another Native American warrior illuminates the execution's crude parody of legal process. "You are the law-giving party," acknowledged the convicted Indian from the gallows. "You say I must die. I am satisfied if the law is correct" (101). Williams interpolates the reader as both addressee and witness to the execution, and his strategic use of second-person form—a feature common to periodical writings—reveals the constitutive violence of U.S. assimilation from the point of view of the Indian warrior.

His first-person voice oscillates between aggrieved black citizen and condemned Indian, expanding both the historical and ethical compass of the crime. "Where they got the law from to hang the first Indians in the United States of America," asks Williams, "I do not know" (98). In "Force of Law," Jacques Derrida argues that there is no law without enforceability and no enforceability of the law without force; violence both inaugurates and preserves the law.[96] As the "law-giving party," the federal government possesses the exclusive power to delegate what it chooses to define as justice. In these final sketches, Williams questions whether law can indeed become a tool of racial amelioration in the reunified nation. Indeed, the comparison between failed southern Reconstruction and forced Native American resettlement finds powerful expression in the expropriation of Captain Jack's corpse as private property. Williams notes, "Some one offered $2,000 for Jack's body" as the Native American leader was transformed into a commodity to be bartered and traded, as Williams had once been as a slave in antebellum Maryland. "I have seen more law in California than any other part of the world which I have traveled in," wrote Williams from the vantage of 1873, "but, according to my belief, *little justice*" (51).

A Composite Nationality: Frederick Douglass and William H. Newby

The "Chinese Question" provoked the first major national debate over immigration regulation and control. The public contestations that ensued constructed Chinese racial difference in relational ways—specifically, in correspondence to already existing racialized minority groups and their political struggles. As much as the Union-occupied South, the multiracial West of Williams's text emerged as a key "battleground in the national struggle to define citizenship that followed the Civil War," according to Paddison.[97] Williams placed the "Chinese Question" within the context of comparative racial formations to develop more variegated understandings of U.S. nationality—which found critical amplification in Frederick Douglass's oft-cited "Our Composite Nationality" speech, in which he championed the right of migration as a universal "right . . . [that] belongs to no particular race" (252).[98] Of Douglass's extensive repertoire of oratory and print journalism, "Composite Nationality" offers his most candid views on Chinese immigration, expanding on his various editorial remarks on the subject. This section focuses on Douglass's speech as a critical response to the overlooked role that the "Chinese Question" played in Reconstruction-era debates over black citizenship and suffrage. In "Composite Nationality," Douglass explores the more expansive forms of national inclusion and political membership that radical Reconstruction opened to public debate but legislative compromise subsequently foreclosed. As in the case of Williams's *Life and Adventures*, the emerging black western press and regional coverage of Indian removal and Chinese exclusion informed Douglass's radical stance on immigration and naturalization, which found expression in the pages of the *Frederick Douglass' Paper* and his lyceum speeches.

Douglass began giving his now-famous "Our Composite Nationality" speech in the late 1860s and early 1870s as part of his lyceum lectures. Newspapers from Connecticut, New York, New Jersey, Pennsylvania, and Illinois advertised the "lecture by the talented and distinguished Fred. Douglass, . . . the theme chosen being 'Composite Nationality,' one upon which, from the peculiar stand point the orator occupies, he is presumed to be fully posted."[99] With James Redpath as his manager, Douglass, who had first honed his oratorical skills as a speaker for the

American Anti-Slavery Society, numbered among the most popular of the lyceum celebrities, a select group that included Wong Chin Foo.[100] On December 7, 1869, Douglass delivered the earliest version of the speech with the title "Composite Nation" as part of the Parker Fraternity Course in Boston.[101] Lyceum lectures addressed topical matters, and Douglass's speech proved especially timely given the recent news coverage of the Chinese diplomatic mission to the U.S. led by Anson Burlingame and the treaty that he brokered for China.[102] The Burlingame Treaty encouraged Chinese immigration to the U.S. by extending protections to "the citizens or subjects of" China as a "most favored" nation.[103] The speech consolidated Douglass's stray comments on Chinese immigration into a full-throated public endorsement. It even went so far as to advocate extending the rights of citizenship and suffrage to the Chinese. Douglass declared in no uncertain terms, "Do you ask, if I favor such immigration, I answer *I would*. Would you have them naturalized, and have them invested with all the rights of American citizenship? *I would*. Would you allow them to vote? *I would*. Would you allow them to hold office? *I would*" (252). Douglass's position was a radical one even among radical Republicans.

Douglass first began delivering "Composite Nationality" as Congress concluded its discussions on the last of the three Reconstruction Amendments, which extended suffrage to newly enfranchised black freedmen. Anxieties over the growing presence of Chinese immigrants in the West seeped into these congressional debates and subsequent discussions on the Civil Rights Acts and the 1870 Naturalization Bill.[104] According to the legal scholar John Torok, the "deliberate and careful choice of language in the Reconstruction amendments and laws, regarding words such as 'citizens,' 'aliens,' or 'inhabitants,' was made with these immigrants in mind and is particularly significant given the continuing debate on immigration" over the next decades.[105] While legislators limited certain constitutional provisions such as suffrage to "citizens," other conditions, including the Fourteenth Amendment's due process and equal protection clauses, referred more broadly to "persons" and "inhabitants." As a consequence, later Chinese immigrants facing severe restrictions and deportation brought thousands of largely successful habeas corpus suits challenging Immigration Bureau decisions. Chapters 3 and 4 examine in more depth the complex legal processes by which Chinese immigrants laid claim to Fourteenth Amendment protections, both as U.S. citizens and as aliens and subjects of China.[106] In the speech, Douglass elaborates on the more expansive but ultimately failed arguments for granting citizenship to Chinese and Native Americans (in the Fourteenth Amendment debates) and banning discrimination in suffrage and officeholding on the basis of "race, color, nativity, property, education, or religious belief" (in the Fifteenth Amendment debates) urged by radical Republicans such as Senator Charles Sumner of Massachusetts.[107] A former abolitionist, the uncompromising Sumner urged the extension of political rights to Native Americans and Chinese in addition to black freedmen.[108] In subsequent debates over amending the Naturalization Act, Sumner also proposed striking the word "white" so that the right of naturalization might be made available to all, regardless of "race or color."[109] His proposals were all soundly defeated, and Congress amended the naturalization law to include only "aliens of African nativity and to persons of African descent" in addition to "free white persons," limiting citizenship to a black-white binary.

Reconstruction radicalism "was first and foremost a civic ideology, grounded in a definition of American citizenship," writes the historian Eric Foner.[110] And while black citizenship and suffrage served as the centerpiece of its legislative efforts, radicals such as Sumner went even further in their proposals to expand political membership in the nation. By 1869, when Congress began discussing the Fifteenth Amendment, the recently signed Burlingame Treaty strengthened the resolve of Pacific Coast legislators to oppose any extension of citizenship and voting rights to Chinese immigrants, and they resisted all provisions that might be construed as potentially favorable to the Chinese.[111] For example, Republican Congressman William Higby of California found the Chinese unfit for naturalization and citizenship, claiming that they "are nothing but a pagan race," while Republican Senator Edgar Cowan of Pennsylvania feared the consequences of even admitting children born in the U.S. to Chinese parents to citizenship, anticipating the 1898 federal case against Wong Kim Ark (studied in the following chapter).[112]

These legislative debates continued the racialization of Chinese immigrants that had begun in California with Bigler's anticoolieism campaign and *People v. Hall*. However, it underwent a significant modification as Republicans came under attack for opposing Chinese immigration while supporting African American citizenship and suffrage in the name of racial egalitarianism. In response, statesmen such as Blaine began emphasizing the moral unfitness of Chinese and Native Americans as heathens—unlike black freedmen—and consequently unsuited to participating in the political future of the Christian nation. Moderate Republicans, especially those representing Pacific Coast states, began espousing a new political hierarchy in which the longstanding racial limitation against citizenship became recoded as an exclusionary discourse of Christian civilization and selectively expanded to include African American men as a matter of political expediency.[113] This line of reasoning refashioned Native American and Chinese racial differences in the charged Christian rhetoric of "heathenism," deeming them morally unfit for citizenship.[114] By re-presenting forms of racial otherness as failures of moral conviction (and thus detrimental to home life and the national polity), Republicans of various stripes, as Paddison argues, invited "northerners, southerners, and westerners; Protestants, Catholics, and Jews; whites and African Americans—to unite around what they were not: heathens."[115] Thus, the benefits of Reconstruction became limited to suitably Christianized black and white men, with non-Christian nonwhites as the categorically excluded.

"Composite Nationality" provided Douglass with the occasion to publicly establish his position on the "Chinese Question" while critiquing the limitations of mainstream Republican ideology in the postwar reconstruction of citizenship and national identity. The *New York Herald* commented on the radical import of Douglass's Boston lecture. Douglass had gone "over his old argument for suffrage for his own ebony race" and then "went a step or two further by demanding it for the noble red man and the Oriental Chinaman. Our trouble, he said, was not because republicanism was a experiment, but the mistake was in hesitating to give absolute equality in every direction."[116] In the speech, Douglass called on universal "human rights" as justification for his radical position on immigration, citizenship, and suffrage (252). In alluding to William Blackstone's influential *Commentaries on the Laws of England*, Douglass argued that any racial restriction on immigration violated the "rights of humanity," namely, "the right of locomotion; the right of migration" (252). "It is this great right," he continues emphatically, "that I assert for the Chinese and Japanese, and for all other varieties of men equally with yourselves, now and forever" (252).

For Douglass, Americanization does not require assimilation to dominant racialized norms. His exposition on the "character and mission of the United States" addressed the "question [of] whether we are the better or the worse for being composed of different races of men" (241). It sought to disarticulate nationality from racialization and the deployment of categories of ethnicity, civilization, and religion to mark the boundaries of national membership. In this fashion, Douglass forcefully articulated what Williams enacts in the experimental form of his autobiographical narrative. For Douglass, individual self-knowledge derives from contact with others: "Men only know themselves by knowing others, and contact is essential to this knowledge" (255). Difference is essential to Douglass's understanding of national culture for it serves as a catalyst for national development. In his words, "It is said that it is not good for man to be alone. This is true, not only in the sense in which our women's rights' friends so zealously and wisely teach, but it is true as to nations. The voice of civilization speaks an unmistakable language against the isolation of families, nations and races, and plead for composite nationality as essential to her triumphs" (254). Lest we forget, Douglass reminds his audience, "Europe and Africa are already here, and the Indian was here before either" (245). The United States, he continues, is "a country of . . . extremes, ends and opposites; the most conspicuous example of composite nationality in the world" (245). Racial differences figure centrally in the making of this modern America, and an analytics of comparative racialization is essential to understanding and facilitating this national progress: "It is by comparing one nation with another, and one learning from another, each competing with all, and all competing with each, that hurtful errors are exposed, great social truths discovered, and the wheels of civilization whirled onward" (241).

For Douglass, honing such forms of comparative thinking in a multiracial U.S. would also begin to address the seemingly insurmountable differences between East and West. He advances the theory of monogenesis—the thesis of the single origins of humanity—expounded in an earlier speech, "The Races" (also known as "The Races of Men" or "The Brotherhood of Man"), that became, like "Composite Nationality," a mainstay in his repertoire of lyceum speeches.[117] "Contact with these yellow children of the Celestial Empire," reasons Douglass, "would convince us that the points of human difference, great as they, upon first sight, seem, are as nothing compared with the points of human agreement" (254). Thus, the incorporation of the foreign into the national body politic does not erase differences but creates the conditions for the recognition of shared similarities. This orientation toward "otherness" expresses what Robert Levine describes as Douglass's antiracist "transnational humanism."[118] In later addresses, including "The Future of the Negro" (1884), Douglass again emphasized this "transnational humanism," for "the tendency of the age," in his words, "is unification, not isolation, not to clans and classes but to human brotherhood."[119] Shortly after assuming editorship of the *New National Era* in December 1870, Douglass again extolled the "composite character of the nation" in publications aimed at dismantling the polygenesist environmentalism—what he dismissed as "the doctrine of the diversity and inferiority of races"—associated with the likes of Louis Agassiz, Josiah Nott, George Gliddon, and Samuel George Morton.[120]

As early as 1854, shortly after the infamous *People v. Hall* ruling, Douglass had already begun to formulate this theory of the composite character of national life, rooting his understanding of comparative racialization in an early awareness of the "Chinese Question" unfolding in the West. His radical stance on Chinese immigration was informed, in part, by the writings of William H. Newby, who, like James Williams, numbered among the earliest black pioneers to California. The son of an enslaved father and a free black mother, Newby, like Williams, came of age in Philadelphia and struck out West in 1851, shortly after the passage of the new Fugitive Slave Act.[121] He settled in San Francisco and became politically active in its small but growing black community. As Eric Gardner notes, Newby, along with Jonas Townsend, Peter Anderson (the *Pacific Appeal* editor), and John Jamison Moore, later established California's first black newspaper, the short-lived *Mirror of the Times*; he staffed the *Mirror* as a writer, editor, and traveling agent until 1857, when he relocated to Haiti for a time.[122] Shortly after settling in the West, Newby wrote to Douglass in 1854, offering his services as a California correspondent.[123] "Your not being in the receipt of any regular correspondence from California, and knowing your great interest in all that concerns the welfare of 'our people,' had induced me to pen this epistle," reads Newby's published letter.[124] Writing under the penname "Nubia," Newby served as the *Frederick Douglass' Paper*'s San Francisco correspondent. He provided Douglass with a yearlong series of letters describing the welfare of "the colored people" in California.[125] Like Williams's *Life and Adventures*, Newby's varied accounts of black life in the West also addressed the deteriorating conditions for Native Americans and Chinese in the state, particularly after *People v. Hall*.

In 1855, Douglass published Nubia's correspondences at regular intervals as a (often front-page) feature of the *Frederick Douglass' Paper*, thus integrating a western perspective into its generally eastern-based content and concerns. Nubia's reports on Chinese restrictions, Indian removal, and Spanish-Mexican land disputes in California became woven into the periodical's coverage of the slavery controversy engulfing the East. This material insists that western regionalism should be included in scholarly discussions of Douglass's national and global networks of discursive circulation and exchange. In fact, Nubia's San Francisco serves as a microcosm for the "composite nationality" that Douglass later endorsed in his 1869 speech. "Its population is composed of almost every nation under heaven," informs Nubia. "Here is to be seen at a single glance every nation in miniature. The Chinese form about one-eighth of the population."[126] Newby's later correspondences to Douglass also began to demystify the freedoms popularly associated with the West by addressing the growing hold of white power and hegemony in recently established states. "The Americans here, as every where," Nubia informs, "have succeeded in imbuing them [Spanish-Mexicans] with a proper amount of prejudice against colored people for it seems to be the settled policy of the people of this country, in their intercourse with foreigners, to fill them with their beastly and disgusting prejudices."[127]

The terms of the Treaty of Guadalupe Hidalgo conferred the full rights of U.S. citizenship to Spanish-Mexicans in the annexed territories. In fact, the treaty imposed ascriptive U.S. citizenship on the conquered population, and the 1849 California constitutional convention later granted Spanish-Mexicans the same citizenship rights as white people.[128] The racialization of Spanish-Mexicans as legally white later exempted them from twentieth-century immigration bans based on the rule of racial ineligibility to naturalization and citizenship.[129] For Nubia, the induction of Spanish-Mexicans into the socially constructed category of legal whiteness entailed interiorizing white racial identity as both privilege and property. In California, legal whiteness became the basis for the allocation of formal rights and societal benefits. However, this did not halt the periodic violence that erupted between Spanish-Mexicans and white settlers. In retaliation against "Mexican banditti," white settlers in Amador and Calaveras Counties "commenced a war of extermination against the Spaniards. Some thirty Mexicans have been hung without judge or jury," according to another Nubia dispatch.[130] As legally white, Spanish-Mexicans were not subject to the racial legislation affecting blacks, Native Americans, and Chinese in California, yet they continued to suffer forms of violence that indicated their ongoing racialization as nonwhites.

Subsequent letters enumerate in great detail legislative efforts to establish a system of racial legislation aimed to remake California into "a white man's country." In relating a new mining bill preventing "Chinese and *all others* not eligible to citizenship" from holding mining claims, Nubia insists, "The Chinese have taken the places of the colored people, as victims of oppression. The poor Chinese are, indeed, a wretched looking set; that they are filthy, immoral and licentious according to our notions of such things is unquestionable. But these vices do not justify the whites in oppressing them."[131] Like a number of his black contemporaries, Newby racializes the Chinese as non-Christians or "heathens" lacking in moral fitness; however, more significantly, black political sympathy for the Chinese continues to flourish in the face of this perceived difference. The immoral "vices" of the so-called heathen Chinese do not justify white racial domination.

While Newby's accounts often figured the Chinese as grotesquely foreign to Christian norms, resembling what Helen Jun provocatively calls "black Orientalism," they also illuminate how the structural violence of white hegemonic power created the conditions for cross-racial connections across these seemingly insurmountable differences.[132] "The whites are greatly alarmed at their rapid increase," continues Newby's report on the Chinese. "They are very badly treated here. Every boy considers them lawful prey for his boyish pranks. They have no friends, unless it is the colored people."¹³³ For Newby, racial affiliation proceeds from an understanding of white structural violence. Like Williams's *Life and Adventures*, Newby's letters also meditate on the continual expropriation of Indian lands in the name of American Manifest Destiny. Newby praised the "fruits of Yankee industry and enterprise" in changing California's "desolate wilderness" into "well stocked and beautifully laid out farms," yet he also sought to understand the magnitude of these changes from the perspective of the indigenous population: "The poor natives can hardly realize the change, so recently the lordly possessors of thousands of acres, and so suddenly wrested from their grasp, and this so quietly, so legally, so easily effected. Truly, these Americans are a strange people; they as effectually destroy nations by their civilization, as [by] their fixed bayonets."¹³⁴ Such ambivalence positioned Newby both within and without the compass of American identification, as he embraced American modernization while deploring its racialized violence and expropriation. As in Williams's *Life and Adventures*, Newby positions the "colored people" of California in a comparative framework, and his complexly structured references to "these Americans" reveal simultaneous desires for racial autonomy *and* for inclusion. These critical accounts of multiracial California informed Douglass's understanding of comparative racialization in "Composite Nationality."

Douglass advocated unfettered immigration and racial heterogeneity as essential to U.S. nation building, as he diverged from many of his former abolitionist associates and fellow Republicans such as Wendell Phillips on the issue of Chinese immigration. As Douglass lectured on "Composite Nationality" in 1869, Phillips began endorsing a far more equivocal position on the "Chinese Question" as news of the controversial importation of Chinese strike breakers from California to Massachusetts and New Jersey began turning eastern public opinion against Chinese labor. In addition, periodic reports of antiforeign rebellions sparked by the Opium Wars in China and attacks on Western missionaries further polarized U.S. public opinion. Reformers such as Phillips began to view the "Chinese Question" as more than a matter of "labor versus capital" but as a vast struggle over the destiny of America as a Christian civilization.¹³⁵ For example, Phillips's 1870 editorial "The Chinese," published in the *National (Antislavery) Standard*, gives voice to the "melting-pot" theme of American nationality, in which assimilation to homogeneous U.S. (racial) norms must precede and facilitate inclusion into the national polity. For Phillips, the unrestricted immigration of Chinese would overwhelm the nation's capacity to domesticate such threatening difference in ways detrimental to American home life and the sexual division of labor. The importation of Chinese laborers, he argues, represents an attack on the "American home," for capitalists, in artificially lessening wages "with barbarous labor, are dragging down the American home to the level of the houseless street-herds of China."[136] In the face of this imminent danger, Phillips, in apocalyptic tones, insists that we must find "in the armory of the law some effectual weapon to prevent it, [or] our political and social future, for fifty years, is dark indeed."[137] Phillips shared Douglass's expansive vision of U.S. citizenship and suffrage unbounded by racial exclusion, yet he, like many other Republicans, faltered on the subject of Chinese immigration.

In contrast, Douglass embraced difference in formulating an understanding of Americanization as a nonassimilative process that entails a reciprocal diversification and expansion of national life. In his earlier "The Races" lecture, Douglass emphasized the significance of a composite nationality, offering fulsome praise for "the marked differences in colour, forms and features of men." Moreover, he condemns the violence of race making in the course of Western empire and the rise of the modern world systems, from the U.S. annexation of Mexican territory to the English colonization of Ireland: "It is strange, passing strange, that mankind should have ever made a difference in Color, or in any mark of variety, an apology for oppression."[138] In thus arguing against the racialized "ethnology" popular at the time (and exploited by the likes of Justice Murray in *People v. Hall*), Douglass insisted that the "necessity for diversity among beings of the same species needs no argument."[139] "Difference is [as] essential as likeness, and we have both," he proclaimed.[140] "Eternal wisdom," Douglass continued, "was sufficient to produce likeness, without destroying Individuality, and difference without producing confusion."[141] Indeed, Douglass imagines the U.S. as a microcosm of the globe, in which all the "different races of men," "whether from Asia, Africa, or the Isles of the Sea," might be drawn together for "the same national ends," united under a single national destiny ("Composite

Nationality" 259). In Douglass's words, "We shall mould them all, each after his kind, into Americans; Indian and Celt, negro and Saxon, Latin and Teuton, Mongolian and Caucasian, Jew and gentile" (259). Contrary to many critical accounts of this speech, Douglass saw no antagonism between difference and unity. He envisioned a national culture that is continually enhanced and reconstituted through the heterogeneity of new immigrants, as Angela Ray argues.[142]

Douglass's speech gave powerful early expression to an "American pluralist ethos" that functioned as much as a critique of racial nativism as of Americanization as homogenizing assimilation to an Anglo-American racial norm.[143] Moreover, Douglass anticipated the expansive, global vision of race relations that later characterized the political writings of W. E. B. Du Bois, especially *The Souls of Black Folk* (1903), which proclaimed, the "problem of the twentieth century is the problem of the color-line, the relation of the darker to lighter races of men in Asia and Africa, in America and the islands of the sea."[144] For Douglass, the struggle against white racial hegemony at home extends beyond the black-white binary to encompass the larger global relations between white and nonwhite. He writes, "the fact that only one-fifth of the population of the globe is white and the other four-fifth are colored, ought to have some weight and influence in disposing of this and similar questions" ("Composite Nationality" 252). In this, Douglass did not simply dismiss Yellow Peril fears of an Asiatic invasion of the U.S.; he inverts the dynamics of the invasion trope to argue for Chinese citizenship and suffrage. Given the inevitability of "Mongolian invasion," as Douglass styles it, "we shall be stronger if we receive them as friends and give them a reason for loving our country and our institutions," rather than repeating the "race pride" of past governmental policies, which had sown "the dangerous seeds of discontent and hatred" into "the Indian . . . [and] . . . the negro" (248, 253, 245).

Perhaps most significantly, the American "civilization" that Douglass imagines in "Composite Nationality" is not the hegemonic Christian civilization that a range of political figures from Blaine to Phillips enumerated in support of Chinese immigration restrictions. The Chinese, writes Douglass, "may, like the negro, accept Christianity," but the Christian religion is not a precondition for their Americanization

(249). "In disposing of this question whether we shall welcome or repel immigration from China, Japan, or elsewhere," Douglass continues, "we may leave the differences among the theological doctors to be settled among themselves" (257). In this fashion, Douglass disarticulates the racialized discourse of heathenism as a rationale for Asiatic and indigenous exclusion from citizenship and suffrage; he saw no threat in "Mongolian civilization."

On the contrary, Douglass invited religious differences and satirically criticized those who objected to the "heathenism" of Chinese immigrants. In an extended passage toward the end of the lecture, Douglass exclaims with notable wryness,

> This is the last objection which should come from those who profess the all-conquering power of the Christian religion. If that religion cannot stand contact with the Chinese, religion or no religion, so much the worst for those who have adopted it. It is the Chinaman, not the Christian, who should be alarmed for his faith. He exposes that faith to great dangers by exposing it to the freer air of America. But shall we send missionaries to the heathen, and yet deny the heathen the right to come to us? I think a few honest believers in the teachings of Confucius would be well employed in expounding the doctrines among us. (258)

In this playful call for a "heathen missionary," Douglass anticipated the cultural work of the Chinese activist Wong Chin Foo (studied in the following section). For Douglass, differences remain essential to national progress and the continual production of new knowledge, and this understanding of national heterogeneity runs counter to Waldo E. Martin Jr.'s early claim that "Douglass's assimilationism was thoroughly integrationist" and derived from his "belief in miscegenation."[145] In contrast, the Douglass of the 1869 lecture describes the nation as "composite," signifying a compound structure made of various parts and elements (rather than "amalgamated" or "miscegenated," with its connotations of mixture and combination in forming a homogeneous whole). By bringing the "Chinese Question" to bear on the Reconstruction Amendment debates, Douglass's "Composite Nationality" emphasizes an understanding of Americanization that does not entail the loss of differences or "unlike elements."

From West to East: Wong Chin Foo and Yan Phou Lee

As black pioneers such Williams and Newby sought to forge links between East and West in their various writings, the Chinese newspaperman Wong Chin Foo (1847–1898), in a reciprocal gesture, began shifting the regional axis of the "Chinese Question" (as it became a subject of increasing national debate and concern) from the West to the East. Wong did not address comparative racialization with the intensity of Williams and Douglass, yet his print journalism, including his critical adaptation of the African American slave narrative in the 1874 fugitive coolie narrative of Chun Young Hing (studied in the preceding chapter), became increasingly politicized along these lines, as he prioritized the struggle for Chinese citizenship and suffrage in his later life. Wong, alongside his contemporary Yan Phou Lee (Li Enfu, in Pinyin translation), focused his early print activism toward disarticulating the racializing discourse of heathenism that helped sustain the dialectical configuration of black inclusion / Chinese exclusion during Reconstruction. At the time, Wong and Lee numbered among the few Chinese in the U.S. writing and lecturing in English. Wong went on to become the most broadly published Chinese American writer in the nineteenth century, although his long-overlooked writings have only recently elicited sustained critical study.[146] Literary scholars such as Hsuan Hsu have begun recovering Wong's periodical writings, while Scott D. Seligman published in 2014 the first critical biography of this elusive public figure.

Hsu notes that Wong's writings "do not fit comfortably into the current geographical or formal frameworks of Asian American cultural history, which have tended to privilege west coast centers of publication and protest as well as the literary genres of fiction and autobiography."[147] In the overlapping roles of lyceum lecturer, freelance journalist, and newspaper editor, Wong courted the public gaze and used it as a reformatory force, constructing alternative representations of China and the Chinese. His countless speeches and journalistic pieces in prominent periodicals and daily newspapers sought to demystify Chinese religious practices and, specifically, Confucianism—or heathenism, as it was popularly styled—for Christian American audiences in a period of heightened racial and legal violence against Chinese immigrants.[148] As a self-fashioned exiled Chinese nationalist, Wong utilized forms of self-Orientalism, juxtaposing the Chinese "heathen" against the American "Yankee" in the rhetorical effort to transform the unknown from being unknowable. These commoditized acts of self-revelation demonstrated that Asiatic foreignness might be made familiar and hence knowable. In fact, Wong's representational medium of choice, the periodical, was predicated on the constant reinvention of the new and unknown—indeed, the very concept of "the news"—ordered and represented according to generic conventions that related it to the familiar and made it available for consumption.[149] Like Douglass, Newby, and Williams, Wong and Lee were drawn to the periodical form as a vital outlet for counterrepresentational political contestation. The two took a prominent role in these public debates over the "Chinese Question" as they struggled to reshape how Chinese immigrants were imagined in relation to the U.S. national polity.

Wong dedicated his long print career to the comparative theorizing of East-West relations, and he took advantage of the heterogeneity of the periodical form to do so, experimenting with different genres of short- and serial-form writing, from travelogues of American Chinatowns, editorials, manifestoes, satirical sketches, and correspondences to essays on various topics. Wong also serialized two "Chinese historical novels," *Wu Chih Tien, the Celestial Empress* and *Poh Yuin Ko, the Serpent-Princess*, in the prestigious literary magazine the *Cosmopolitan*; *Wu Chih Tien* became the first novel published by a Chinese American. In these varied publications, Wong repeatedly crossed the line between so-called high culture and popular culture and on occasion plunged headlong into sensationalism, as in his provocative manifesto "Why Am I a Heathen?" His comparative essays often exploited Orientalist misconceptions of a fundamental opposition between East and West. The "dichotomy between *Chinese* on one hand and *people* on the other," according to Alexander Saxton's classic study, lay at the heart of white workingmen's anti-Chinese ideology in the West.[150] This concept of "fundamental differentness" increasingly centered on the opposition between Chinese heathenism and American Christianity. In response, Wong sought to represent the structural relation between East and West, China and the U.S., as a complementary "affinity of opposites."[151] Essays such as "The Chinese in New York" allowed Wong opportunities to deconstruct East-West dichotomies in an elaborate narrative tour of

New York's Chinatown, which he satirically described as a diverse "little world composed of every variety of Christians, heathens, Irishmen, and other savages."[152]

Unlike Lee, his younger Christianized contemporary, Wong famously manipulated the complex dynamics of the discursive marketplace in which he circulated as a curiosity. As Hsu notes, Wong "made a name for himself by creating and manipulating controversy in the periodical press," and he carefully honed an "official" narrative of his life in print.[153] Seligman's biography tracks Wong back to Jimo, Shandong province in northern China, where he was born in 1847 as Wong Sa Kee, son of a once-prosperous tea merchant.[154] Wong and his impoverished father were taken in by Baptist missionaries who later financed Wong's education abroad in the U.S. in 1867, in preparation for a life of missionary service in China. In 1870, Wong returned to China after three years of peripatetic studies at the Preparatory School of Columbian College in Washington, D.C., and Lewisburg Academy in Pennsylvania.[155] He resumed his association with the Baptists, married a Chinese student from the mission school, and secured work as an interpreter for the imperial customs house in Shanghai.[156] However, Wong's growing involvement in subversive activities against the Qing government forced him to flee China. A sympathetic former American consul, Charles Shepard, arranged him safe passage to San Francisco, where he disembarked in 1873 as Wong Chin Foo, the name by which he was to become known in U.S. print.[157]

Once in the U.S., Wong struck out in the "Yankee way," traveling eastward and lecturing on the topics on which he styled himself an expert: China and the Chinese. In 1874, the Circuit Court for the County of Kent in Michigan granted Wong's petition for naturalization to U.S. citizenship, although controversy followed him on his eastward route as a "tramping lecturer," including allegations of miscegenation that again stressed how sexuality was used as a way of making meaning for race.[158] In these lectures, Wong performed as a "'red-button' mandarin" "attired in his rich native costume"—"a blouse and a garment . . . made of dark-blue stuff; . . . a little skull cap and queue ornamented his head"—to accentuate his Chinese difference, although he gained entry into Protestant churches by representing himself as a Christian convert.[159] However, the content of his lectures shifted radically once he arrived in the

East. Wong refashioned his religious identification in response to the politicized discourse of heathenism that had begun to justify the racial exclusion of Chinese immigrants in Reconstruction America. "Religion and race were mutually constitutive systems, at times blending, at times conflicting, each capable of acting as a metalanguage for the other," argues Paddison.[160] As Blaine's so-called Christian argument against the Chinese gained in popularity, expressions such as "heathens," "pagans," "idolaters," and "celestials" came to designate the specificity of Chinese racial difference in the U.S. In lectures and periodical writings, Wong continually tested the limits of the nation's professed toleration of religious difference in his long-standing efforts to disarticulate race and religion as vectors of Chinese political exclusion.

In the move from small western churches to the crowded public auditoriums of Boston's Parker Memorial Hall and Philadelphia's Academy of Music, Wong radically transformed himself from Christian convert to staunch advocate of "the Life and Doctrines of Confucius."[161] One account describes Wong's Philadelphia lecture "as heathen to the core; a heathen mission, as if in retaliation of our Christian missions."[162] In these lectures, Wong honed the rhetoric skills that he later deployed in print. His performance of Confucianism turned him into "a lively curiosity," and eastern auditors flocked to "hear what a 'heathen Chinaman' can have to say in defense of his own religion as against Christianity."[163] In this, Wong embraced his fellow lyceum lecturer Douglass's suggestion that "a few honest believers in the teachings of Confucius would be well employed in expounding his doctrines among us" ("Composite Nationality" 258). From 1875 to 1878, Boston's Redpath Lyceum Bureau arranged Wong's speaking engagements, alongside those of Douglass.[164] During this time, Wong may have crossed paths with Douglass, especially given their popularity as lyceum lecturers and their work in periodical print culture as representative spokesmen for their respective races. By 1876, Wong's lectures had already begun to emphasize the "problem of Chinese immigration" as "one of great importance."[165] (Indeed, the topical nature of the "Chinese Question" might be deduced in Redpath's inclusion of James Blaine, Thomas Nast, and Wong as lecturers in his 1877 list.)[166] Wong's talks on Confucianism and the domestic manners of China remained the most popular of all his lectures.[167]

Wong took advantage of the diversity of nineteenth-century publishing practices and served as a self-appointed cultural translator of all "subjects connected with his native land" for his American audiences, even though his cultural diplomacy turned critical and even outright aggressive on occasion, as Hsu notes.[168] As Christian rhetoric became a key axis for forms of racial differentiation and political exclusion, Wong's various writings sought to make Chinese difference, particularly Confucianism, knowable to his American readers. He attempted to rectify virulent misrepresentations of Chinese inassimilability circulating at the time while insisting on his Asiatic difference; he publicly embraced his so-called heathenism. In 1887, Wong retooled the content of his popular lectures "explain[ing] the religious systems of Buddha and Confucius and compar[ing] them and their teachings with Christianity and its teachings" into his controversial essay "Why Am I a Heathen?," which first appeared in the *North American Review* in a multiyear series of essays exploring comparative religions in the U.S.[169] Expanding on this framework, the *Atlantic Monthly* published the Sioux Indian Zitkala-Sa's "Why I Am a Pagan?" (1902)—later revised as "The Great Spirit" (1921)—which denounced the coercive religious education she encountered in Indian boarding schools. And while Zitkala-Sa's essay has become widely anthologized, Wong's vitriolic polemic remains largely forgotten, even though it was widely excerpted and republished at the time.

Hsu argues that this publication marked a turning point in Wong's print career, for it provided Wong with a "secular outlet to voice a more direct attack on missionary discourses concerning the Chinese."[170] The essay issues a searing rebuke against the practice of Christianity as a constitutive component of Western modernity. Wong takes pains to explain his earlier, failed attempt at Christian conversion while claiming his moral fitness for American citizenship and suffrage as a so-called heathen follower of Confucianism: "Born and raised a heathen, I learned and practiced its moral and religious code."[171] As a child, Wong recalls being abruptly "transferred to the midst of . . . Christian civilization": "at this impressible period of life Christianity presented itself to me at first under its most alluring aspects" (169). Under the "spell" of "would-be soul-savers," Wong contemplated a life of missionary service in China (169). However, his careful study of the Christian religion as it was practiced in the U.S. revealed a "multiplicity of Christian sects," and the dogmatism and narrow-mindedness of such sectarian strife undermined Wong's faith (169). "The more I studied Christianity in its various phases, and listened to the animadversions of one sect upon another," he relates, "the more it all seemed to me 'sounding brass and tinkling cymbals'" (170). Wong saw no justice in the "New Dispensation" or the Christian precept of salvation through conversion and repentance of sins. He explains with biting sarcasm, "The idea of coming into daily or hourly contact with cold-blooded murderers, cut-throats, and other human scourges, who had but a few moments of repentance before roaming around heaven, was abhorrent" (172).

Perhaps Wong's most insightful criticism of America's Christian civilization lies in his linking of "the restless Christian doctrine of ceaseless action" to a relentless mode of capitalist exploitation in what the sociologist Max Weber later theorized as the classic "Protestant Ethic and the 'Spirit' of Capitalism" (172). In charting the relation between religious belief and social practice, Weber suggested that the Protestant injunction to disciplined achievement recast the biblical doctrine of a calling, casting all work as God's work. Consequently, the acquisition of wealth became an unintended consequence of such ceaseless striving to exult God's glorification. "As the spiritual framework faded and accumulation became more acceptable," explains Jackson Lears, "the Protestant Ethic became the Spirit of Capitalism—a set of moral and psychological sanctions for systemic moneymaking."[172] However, anti-Chinese agitators often portrayed the tireless activity of Chinese laborers—stripped of its associations with a Protestant ethos—as a menacing force undermining the moral tenets of sexuality, home life, and free labor in the U.S.

In "Why Am I a Heathen?," Wong cites the Opium Wars as an example of this racialized Christian spirit of commerce: "When the English wanted the Chinamen's gold and trade, they said they wanted 'to open China for their missionaries.' And opium was the chief, in fact, only, missionary they looked after, when they forced the ports open" (176–177). Wong charges that, "the Christian's only practical belief appears to be money-making (golden-calf worshipping); and there is more money to be made by being 'in the swim' as a Christian than by being a heathen" (173). In juxtaposing Confucianism against so-called Christian civilization, Wong paraphrases the Fifteenth Amendment to claim the Chinese to be "so far heathenish as to no longer persecute men simply on account of race, color, or previous condition of servitude, but treat them all according to their individual worth" (175). Moreover, Wong, as in Douglass's "Composite Nationality" speech, calls the U.S. to task as a republic founded on religious liberty. Unlike Christian Americans, so-called heathen Chinese, writes Wong, "do not organize into cowardly mobs under the guise of social or political reform, to plunder and murder with impunity; and we are so far advanced in our heathenism as to no longer tolerate popular feeling or religious prejudice to defeat justice or cause injustice" (175). Wong makes reference to the vigilante-led anti-Chinese pogroms of the 1880s, which sought to purge from the Pacific Coast the many small communities that had managed to establish themselves into Chinatowns, as Jean Pfaelzer has documented.[173] Wong's essay offers a penetrating critique of the recoding of Chinese racial difference in the rhetoric of heathenism and the violent exclusion of Chinese from the nation on the basis of this supposed moral unfitness.

Wong's outspoken denunciations of Christianity distinguished and alienated him from other Chinese American writers such as Yan Phou Lee who spoke out against Chinese restrictions with the authority and support of the Protestant church. Like Wong, Lee sought to combat anti-Chinese agitation in print, authoring numerous essays on China and the Chinese, albeit from a Christianized Chinese perspective and with the elite imprimatur of Yale, where he received his degree.[174] Lee numbered among the handful of Chinese students who traveled to the U.S. to study under the auspices of the short-lived Chinese Educational Mission (1872–1881) in Hartford, Connecticut. Supported by the Chinese government and directed by Chen Lan-Pin (who also oversaw the Cuba Commission in 1874), the Chinese Educational Mission began with 120 young Chinese students dedicated to the study of Western science and engineering as part of a larger effort to modernize China.[175] Notable Americans including Mark Twain and Ulysses S. Grant championed the Chinese Education Mission, and they protested the Chinese government ending the experimental program in 1881 after prolonged conflicts over the direction of the mission and the extent to which the Chinese students had become Americanized by host families, nearly all of whom were members of the Congregational church.[176] Chinese Americans such as Lee who joined Protestant churches "gained access to a potentially powerful political and cultural discourse," according to Paddison.[177] Conversion enabled them to use Christian rhetoric and theology to challenge nativism, racism, and political inequities.[178] In adapting Christian discourse, Lee embraced a rhetorical strategy of mollification, while Wong took a more aggressive tact; yet both men shared in broader print efforts to dispel damaging misconceptions regarding the Chinese in U.S. popular culture. "I still continually find false ideas in America concerning Chinese customs, manners, and institutions," Lee remarked in his widely reprinted reminiscences of China.[179]

In the subsequent issue of the *North American Review*, Lee published a spirited rebuttal to Wong, titled "Why I Am Not a Heathen," that defended Christian universalism and its fundamental principle of broad, cross-racial acceptance in the idea of "Christianity is one."[180] Lee's earnest epistle takes Wong's satirical diatribe to task in its efforts to distinguish the Christian faith from the discourses of Christian civilization used to justify Western imperialism and economic exploitation in the Opium Wars. "So the perversion of Christian teachings has produced many poisonous weeds," admits Lee.[181] However, Lee's defense of Christianity and American Christians also inadvertently bolstered Wong's powerful critique. In referencing the work of prominent ministers such as Henry Ward Beecher and Joseph Cook who advocated for the Chinese, Lee writes, "If there was no Christianity in this land, things would be too hot, not only for the Chinese, but for all who form the base of the social pyramid."[182] As depicted in the racialized ethnology of the day, African Americans, Native Americans, and Chinese were among those at the base of America's "social pyramid." The Chinese, as K. Scott Wong notes, "were frequently compared with black Americans and white Americans—comparisons that stressed racial hierarchies, and the perceived immorality of the Chinese, their supposed cultural inferiority, and their ultimate unassimilability into American Society."[183]

In defamiliarizing Christianity for his American audiences, Wong sought to illuminate how the discourse of Christian commonality and universalism helped align the political agendas of anti-Chinese Irish ideologues such as Kearney with respectable mainstream Protestant Republicans such as Blaine. In particular, Blaine utilized Christian religious commonality to maintain the logic of political exclusion against morally unfit Indians and Chinese well after the formal inclusion of properly Christianized African Americans. In the West, the discourse of heathenism more immediately cast the Chinese population as the religious and racial other against which Irish Catholics (who were themselves subject to virulent Protestant bias) contrasted their own Christian whiteness, helping new Irish immigrants establish their own claims to racial and moral citizenship in the U.S. Furthermore, the anti-Chinese extremism of Kearney's Workingmen's Party allowed more restrained voices such as Blaine's to depict their anti-Chinese arguments as benign and even compassionate in comparison.[184] Wong's biting sarcasm in "Why Am I a Heathen?" illuminates the centrality of religious discourse in the reformation of race and citizenship after Reconstruction.

The nationalization of the regional Pacific Coast anti-Chinese movement helped facilitate the provisional unification of diverse interest groups behind a reinvigorated Christian white supremacy.[185] For politicians such as Blaine, the discourse of heathenism helped mitigate the contradiction of continued Chinese disenfranchisement after black political inclusion; it helped purify Chinese restriction of its crude racial biases, transforming it into a moral as well as economic good for the nation. By recoding racial as religious and cultural difference, politicians such as Blaine defused post-Reconstruction anxieties over Republican race radicalism while engaging "in anti-Chinese race-baiting without espousing blatant white supremacy, which they still denounced as un-Christian and Democratic," argues Paddison.[186] In response, Wong publicly embraced the title of "heathen missionary," noting of course the irony of this position, given earlier efforts in China to make him into a Baptist missionary. "You send your missionaries to us and we have listened to them," read Wong's correspondence to the *New York Herald*. "Is it unfair for me to ask them to hear what we have to say?"[187] Wong infuses such reversals of ethnographic perspective and inversions of East-West relations with his unique brand of ironic humor in the fashion of a classic picaresque hero. Indeed, the satirical *Puck* quickly picked up on Wong's performative rhetoric in summarizing the import of his lectures, for now "the boot is on the other leg; we are really the outer barbarians, and those jolly almond-eyed celestials are the models of refinement, intellect and goodness."[188]

In this fashion, both Wong and Lee embraced evolving postbellum commercial print practices to reshape the meaning of China and the Chinese in U.S. culture.[189] In so doing, they acknowledged the key role of U.S. print culture in facilitating forms of acculturation and "the flow of ideas and expressions that create communities of thought and feeling," in a manner analogous to Kirsten Silva Gruesz's study of earlier Hispanophone periodical print practices in the U.S.[190] Moreover, "print capitalism," as Tchen argues, played "a major role in nationalizing the "Chinese Question" as a "newly empowered republic of readers and voters" in the era after Reconstruction began to receive and reinterpret "locally produced representations of Chinese in the print media."[191] Wong and Lee inserted themselves into U.S. political culture by way of print, and their work as journalists and editors might also be understood as a form of "cultural ambassadorship," to borrow from Gruesz, pledged to combat racist stereotypes and convince readers that Chinese Americans, regardless of their religious affiliations, were capable of citizenship and political participation in the nation.[192]

In 1883, newspapers began announcing with much fanfare the "first number of the first Chinese newspaper ever published in this city," with Wong as the editor in chief.[193] A notice for the newspaper even appeared in the AME church's *Christian Recorder*.[194] Wong's *Chinese American* was the first Chinese newspaper in the East, and Wong was active in all aspects of his newspaper venture and even found himself transcribing copy for the lithographing print process on occasion.[195] For Wong, the *Chinese American* was to serve a political goal. "I wish to teach the Chinamen their true position in this country," he asserted to a *World* reporter.[196] Like Newby's California correspondences for the *Frederick Douglass' Paper*, Wong's *Chinese American* pledged to publish "news from China and the western part of America," as it sought to bring together the transnational (China) and regional (American West), giving literary shape to the heterogeneous racial identifications, forms, and flows of Chinese immigration to the U.S.[197] Print culture, as Yumei Sun argues, "was not only an integral part of the lives of the Chinese in America, [but] it also played a leading role in shaping the thinking of the Chinese community."[198] Printed almost entirely in Chinese, Wong's initial issues offered English translation of only the title and editor's salutatory; however, the *Chinese American* soon underwent, according to one account, "a rapid evolution toward becoming wholly an English paper," as it attempted to negotiate more fluidly between Chinese readers and mainstream U.S. society.[199] The financial failure of the *Chinese American* in September 1883 did not end Wong's career as a newspaperman.[200] In 1888, he established an illustrated weekly titled the *New York Chinese Weekly News*; in 1893, he began publication of the Chicago-based *Illustrated Chinese Weekly News* (or the *Chinese American*); in 1896, he put out the first edition of the Chicago biweekly *Chinese News*.

Lee also ventured into commercial print just as Wong ended the *Chinese American*, taking advantage of the vacuum created by the now-defunct newspaper to propose publication of a Chinese weekly called the *Chinese Evangelist* in its stead. Lee's weekly continued his predecessor's progress toward an English-Chinese bilingual print discourse. Slated to appear in New York the following spring, Lee's *Chinese Evangelist* (to be coedited with Guy Maine and J. Stewart Happer) aimed to assist "teachers in the hundred or more Chinese Sunday-schools throughout the country" with printing "a Bible lesson in English and Chinese, with explanatory notes; hints to teachers and short sentences in English, with a Chinese translation. To assist pupils in acquiring the English language."[201] In addition to the *Chinese Evangelist*, Lee wrote regularly for Christian-affiliated periodicals and gained prominence for a series of popular essays on China that he wrote for the *Wide Awake*, a Christian children's magazine, which he republished as an autoethnography titled *When I Was a Boy in China* (1887). Lee's book was also advertised in the AME church's *Christian Recorder*.[202] As in Wong's case, the end of the *Chinese Evangelist* did not end Lee's print career. According to Amy Ling, Lee cobbled together freelance journalism, lecturing, and stray jobs until he settled into full-time English-language newspaper editing in the East.[203]

Wong began toward the end of his life to strategically disarticulate the political issue of Chinese immigration from Chinese American citizenship and suffrage. He saw citizenship (and the political participation and protection of group interests that it enabled) as the key to solving the purported "problem" of Chinese immigration. In response to the Geary Act, Wong helped establish the Chinese Equal Rights League, serving as the organization's official spokesman.[204] The league held its first mass meeting at Cooper Union in New York City, which drew a racially mixed audience of over twelve hundred people. Newspapers noted the presence of "two colored men," one of whom Seligman identifies as Rev. William B. Derrick, an Antiguan immigrant and bishop of the AME church, sharing the stage with Wong.[205] In Wong's refocusing of his attention on Chinese citizenship and suffrage, he also embraced a more comparative frame of analysis. He insisted that Chinese Americans simply wanted "a share in this government, and to have the same privileges as the negroes and Italians, or any other foreign-born citizen."[206] In his print campaign for Chinese citizenship, Wong explained, "We want Illinois, the place that [Abraham] Lincoln, [Ulysses S.] Grant, and [John A.] Logan called their home, to do for the Chinese what the North did for the Negroes. Why should we not have a voice in the municipal and national affairs like other foreigners?"[207] In calling on these historical figures, Wong, like Douglass and Williams before him, begs the question of Reconstruction's failed vision of racial egalitarianism as he challenges the Orientalizing discourse of heathenism sustaining the dialectical configuration of black inclusion / Chinese exclusion. However, on occasion, his writings also utilize this well-worn racial dialectic for dramatic effect, as in the 1897 circular issued from the Chicago chapter of the revivified Chinese Equal Rights League: "We feel grieved and humiliated every time we behold our colored brethren, even from the wilds of African jungles, sit and eat from the National family table, while we, the descendants of the oldest race on earth, are not even allowed to pick up the crumbs from under the table!"[208]

While Lee embraced Christianity, Wong's experiences in the U.S. reanimated his conviction in Confucianism, which remained constant even after he moved from lyceum lecturing and freelance writing to political organizing. Later in life, Wong cut his queue and advocated Chinese assimilation, including the adoption of Western dress and the English language, as preconditions for political participation in the nation; however, he continued to reject Christian conversion as a necessary aspect of Americanization.[209] Like Douglass's "Composite Nationality," Wong understood Americanization as an inclusionary process of "each after his kind." For Wong, Americanization did not entail the adoption of all things purportedly American, including the Christian religion. Put another way, Wong begged the question of whether Christianity need be a constitutive element of Americanization, especially given the nation's profession of religious liberty. He marshaled the Republican ideologies of America's promise to argue for Chinese inclusion within the national polity, deftly attributing his unfavorable criticisms of "English and American missionaries, the Christian religion, and our glorious Republic itself" to his deep affiliation for America and its founding principles.[210] "I love my newly adopted country and countrymen so well that I have almost forgotten the way to China," Wong asserted in one Chicago lecture.[211]

Wong's consistent position on Confucianism is especially significant given how the formal and financial exigencies of freelance writing for niche audiences prevented him from "sustaining any single argument or genre through the years," as Hsu argues.[212] Wong's sustained defense of Confucianism lay at the heart of his critique of the racialization of America as a "Christian civilization." Indeed, he was invested in disarticulating American civilization from its intimate associations with Christian religion—of the kind on display in Blaine's letter and satirized in Nast's cartoon, which began this chapter. Wong's efforts to establish the moral and social legitimacy of Confucianism (and its compatibility with American identity) continued throughout his life, and he helped establish a Confucian Temple for Americans in Chicago in 1896 two years before his death.[213] Taken together, the varied periodical writings of Wong and Lee span the spectrum of Chinese American responses to the "Chinese Question" in the 1880s and attest to the coercive force with which the racializing discourse of heathenism had come to restructure the debate over Chinese immigration and black citizenship and suffrage in the wake of Reconstruction.

Against Analogy

In juxtaposing lesser-known figures from early African American and Asian American cultural histories, this chapter has sought to illuminate how popular discourses imagined these racialized groups in relation to each other and how these writers imagined these relations in oratory and print journalism. After the radical Reconstruction of citizenship and suffrage, the hegemonic discourses of Christian civilization modified the Afro-Asian analogy to racialize African Americans, Chinese, and Native Americans in ways that justified their continued social and/or political exclusions from the imagined national polity. The alternative racial histories limned in this chapter reveal how U.S. racial formations functioned as a set of highly relational as well as dialectical processes between institutions of power and among differently racialized and ethnicized groups. Black writers such as Williams, Newby, and Douglass critically acknowledged the complex political histories (and futures) that they shared with indigenous and other racialized groups in the U.S., even as Chinese American writers such as Wong and Lee struggled to disarticulate the powerfully racializing discourse of heathenism that helped sustain the dialectical configuration of black inclusion / Chinese exclusion in the wake of Reconstruction.

The chapter began with Williams's *Life and Adventures* to emphasize the role of other racial histories in African American identity formation; his accounts of slavery, political activism, and western adventure resist cohering into a first-person narrative of American inclusion and success. Like the Chinese American writers who followed him, Williams parses together the complex ways in which these racialized figures—black, Chinese, Indian, and Irish—relate in his narrative adaptation of the periodical form to encompass his life in multiracial California. In 1869, Williams took advantage of the newly opened Transcontinental Railroad on an eastward journey (reversing his trailblazing outward voyage) to witness firsthand the ratification of universal black male suffrage. Built largely by black and Chinese and Irish immigrant labor on land forcibly seized from the Plains Indians, the Transcontinental Railroad facilitated the rapid industrialization of the American West as it bound together the Atlantic and Pacific coasts. In 1870, Williams marched in Philadelphia "in the first procession of the celebration of the passage of the Fifteenth Amendment," even though white rowdies later attacked him, cursing, "Get out of the way, you damned black Fifteenth Amendment" (*Fugitive Slave* 40). Citizenship asserts and derives its authority through the law—wielded, as Williams remarks in "The Modocs" chapter, by the same "law-giving party" that had once relegated him to chattel slavery.[214] Williams's emergence as a modern political subject further reinforced the liminal racial-legal status of the Chinese, whose nonwhiteness no longer made them "black" in the "generic sense" (according to *People v. Hall*), for they remained ineligible for the citizenship and suffrage that the U.S. Constitution extended to former black bondsmen. Williams's narrative begins to disarticulate this complex structure of state violence and white supremacy by positioning his racial citizenship in a comparative relation to the ongoing processes of indigenous appropriation and Chinese exclusion.

In 1873, Williams published the first edition of *Life and Adventures* just as Wong Chin Foo and Yan Phou Lee arrived in San Francisco—that "paradise of self-exiled Chinese," as Lee recalled later.[215] The thirteen-year-old Lee arrived with the second detachment of Chinese students selected for the Chinese Educational Mission. Wong and Lee made their way eastward along separate yet parallel tracks. By the time Wong arrived East, he had undergone naturalization to U.S. citizenship and renounced Christian conversion to embrace his new public identity as the "heathen missionary." Lee's journey proved equally transformative. Like Williams, Lee looked forward to his eastward journey aboard the Transcontinental Railroad—indeed, it represented the Western technological modernization that he was to master under the auspices of the Chinese Educational Mission and embody upon his return to China. However, this journey, like his return to China, became hopelessly interrupted.[216] As in the case of Williams, Lee's experience of the American West demonstrated that "the protection of the American eagle" offered little assurance of the condition of his future welfare in the country (106). With subtle humor, Lee recalls, "Nothing occurred on our Eastward journey to mar the enjoyment of our first train ride on the steam-cars—excepting a train robbery, a consequent smash-up of the engine, and the murder of the engineer."[217] Peeking through the car windows, Lee was shocked to behold "two ruffianly men" with "a revolver in each hand . . . taking aim at [the passengers] from the short distance of forty feet."[218] "Five men, three of whom, [were] dressed like Indians," recalls Lee, had robbed the train of its gold and the passengers of their valuables.[219]

Lee recounts this experience in the penultimate pages of his autoethnography, and it captures the wonderment, terror, and uncertainty of his new American life. The adolescent Lee comes face to face with America's racialized legacies in the form of bandits "dressed like Indians" who revisit on the motley passengers the nation's founding act of violent expropriation. Grant's Indian Peace Policy and its unprecedented federal commitment to evangelism faltered with the onset of the Modoc War as so-called wild Indians fiercely resisted coercion onto reservations to undergo the civilizing process.[220] As in the racialization of Indian difference, the heathen beliefs of Chinese immigrants became an integral part of their supposed racial inferiority, and politicians such as Blaine couched their most compelling anti-Chinese arguments in terms of spiritual contamination as well as economic and political threats.[221] Over a decade later, after Christian conversion and the renunciation of the Chinese Empire, Lee looked back on this encounter as his ambivalent introduction to the U.S. "One phase of American civilization," he writes, "was thus indelibly fixed upon our minds."[222]

From opposite sides of the continental U.S., Williams, Newby, Douglass, Lee, and Wong sought to make sense of their liminal subject positions across diverse discursive registers, from the political, legal, and historical to psychological. Taken collectively, their varied writings took advantage of early periodical print culture to intervene in and redirect the wide-ranging national debates over race, representation, and the law in Reconstruction America. Their observations help recalibrate our own cross-racial understandings of immigration, citizenship, and national identification in the period. For Williams, African enslavement, Chinese exclusion, and Indian removal are tragic expressions of the constitutive violence of Americanization and western incorporation. White supremacy and state violence—immediately figured in his narrative's introductory statement, "I, John Thomas, was . . . born a slave"—are the comparative standards against which Williams evaluates and responds to Chinese and Native American racial formations (1). Like his contemporaries Newby and Douglass, Williams wrote against the Afro-Asian analogy that pervaded the popular and political discourses of the 1870s and was given graphic form in the well-known political cartoons that Nast inked for *Harper's Weekly* linking the so-called Negro Problem with the Chinese Question (see figure 2.3). Williams's comparative mode of establishing and negotiating racial meanings and contexts also revises the "discourse of provisional black inclusion / Chinese exclusion" that black newspapers such as the *San Francisco Elevator* marshaled to construct black Americans as politically modern U.S. subjects.[223] Thus, Williams's autobiography as much as Douglass's "Composite

Figure 2.3. Thomas Nast, "The Nigger Must Go" and "The Chinese Must Go," *Harper's Weekly* (September 13, 1879) (Courtesy of the Mark Twain Collection, University of California–Berkeley)

Nationality" and Wong's "heathen mission" might "point the way," to borrow the title of Sutton Griggs's 1908 novel, to reading practices that makes difference and heterogeneity of historical experience the basis for cross-racial connection and political critique, anticipating the current scholarship on comparative racialization.[224]

3

American Futures Past

The Counterfactual Histories of Chinese Invasion

As industrializing Europe and the U.S. turned away from legalized black chattel slavery, demands for "cheap labor" facilitated the migration of Chinese laborers to the New World and the Pacific Rim, where they toiled in the mines and railroads of the American West, cultivated sugarcane in Cuba and Hawaii, harvested the Peruvian guano islands, and quarried the Australian goldfields. The Burlingame Treaty first encouraged Chinese immigration to the U.S. by granting China most favored nation status in recognition of "the mutual advantages of the free migration and emigration of their citizens and subjects for purposes of curiosity, of trade, and, or as permanent residents."[1] However, by the final decades of the nineteenth century, as discussed in chapter 2, the notion of Chinese immigration as a national threat had become established in American culture. "Either we must drive out the Chinese slave," opined the California Workingmen's Party's anti-Chinese propaganda, "or we shall soon be slaves ourselves. There is no other solution of the problem. It is death or victory."[2] Originating in the Pacific Coast states, anti-Chinese interests demanded the abrogation of the Burlingame Treaty (1868) as it cast Chinese labor migrants as "coolie-slaves" whose unfettered entry presaged the rise of monopolies, corporate slavery, and the end of white power. From heated Senate-floor debates and populist diatribes against "coolieism" to Supreme Court test cases brought by Chinese activists, public anxieties over major shifts in the American industrial landscape and class relations became displaced onto the racialized figure of the male Chinese labor migrant.[3]

In the 1870s, Pacific Coast anti-Chinese interests coalesced into a coherent political movement during a prolonged global economic depression, which intensified labor competition in the West. By constructing Asiatic difference "as fundamentally 'foreign'" and "antipathetic to . . . modern American society," the Chinese exclusion movement united disparate interest groups behind the idea of a homogeneous white Christian nation.[4] It also created a popular market for the varied cultural materials that formed the now-familiar tradition of American Yellow Peril. The figurative threat of Asiatic conquest has a long discursive history stretching back from Genghis Khan's Mongol invasion of the European continent to the British novelist Sax Rohmer's wildly popular criminal mastermind Fu Manchu. In vicious populist campaigns against Chinese immigrants, Pacific Coast propagandists began investing this powerful trope of Asiatic invasion with a distinct literary form. Sensational futuristic plots of Chinese invasion first began appearing in American print and visual culture in the 1880s. The counterfactual forms and complex temporal schemas of Chinese invasion fiction made the subgenre especially conducive to political propaganda. As cautionary tales, these fictions promoted the virtues of Chinese exclusion and white supremacy, paradoxically, through their antithesis. Set in a future in which the Chinese Empire has subjugated white America, invasion fiction tested the possibility of unity within the nation as industrial capitalism began to dissolve, in Fredric Jameson's words, "the fabric of all cohesive social groups."[5] As histories oriented toward future action, Chinese invasion fiction helped constitute Yellow Peril as a powerful object of racial fear, one of those "werewolves," in the haunting language of Max Horkheimer and Theodor Adorno, that "exist in the darkness of history and keep alive the fear without which there can be no rule."[6]

This popular subgenre serves as a literary antecedent to the pulp tradition from which modern American science fiction arose after 1926 with the launch of Hugo Gernsback's science fiction magazine, *Amazing Stories*. Characterized by the purposive violation or estrangement of realism (in time and space), invasion narratives model complex forms of temporal extrapolation, tracing aspects of the present into the future.[7] The subgenre offers a largely understudied episode in the social history of American race relations, let alone in the history of literary form. It receives but brief mention in I. F. Clarke's catalogue of "future war" fiction and remains absent from more recent work on "allohistory" or the alternate history genre.[8] Literary critics such as Catherine Gallagher date the explosive popularization of alternate history fictions to the military histories of the 1960s, overlooking earlier subgenres such as Chinese invasion fiction in the formal development of mainstream alternate histories.[9] Cultural historians including Gary Okihiro and John Kuo Wei Tchen have identified the significance of Chinese invasion narratives to Asian American racial formations; however, the science fiction author William Wu's pioneering *Yellow Peril: Chinese Americans in American Fiction, 1850–1940* (1982) remains the only extended literary study of these early narratives.[10] This chapter recovers a number of stories not included in Wu's compendium and explores how Reconstruction-era debates over black citizenship and suffrage influenced the imaginative structures of this influential subgenre. By reintroducing readers to these key earlier texts, the chapter investigates the varied political uses of a subgenre that powerfully expanded and limited historical sense. It concludes by charting the radical transformation of the form into a critique of white supremacy and nativism at the turn of the twentieth century.

In these popular fictions, Chinese exclusion serves as a pivotal turning point in American history, providing the historical premise for a range of conjectural speculations. From legal discourse—most infamously in the Supreme Court case of *Chae Chan Ping v. U.S.* (1889), also known as the Chinese Exclusion Case, which upheld the Chinese Exclusion Acts—to the once-popular but largely forgotten novels of Pierton W. Dooner, Robert Woltor, Arthur Dudley Vinton, and Marsden Manson and the short stories of more recognized writers, including Jack London, James Corrothers, and Vachel Lindsay, published in a range of literary magazines from the California-based *Overland Monthly* and *McClure's Magazine* to the NAACP's *Crisis*, the invasion trope came to dominate U.S.-China relations and public discussions of and federal policies on the so-called Chinese Question. Advertisements, notices, and reviews for all of the full-length novels (and even a few of the short stories) made their way into regional newspapers and a range of literary magazines, including the *Critic*, the *Californian*, the *Nassau Literary Magazine*, and the *Literary World*. A highly opinionated, if largely regional, audience consumed these fictions, with the exception of Vinton's *Looking Further Backward* (1890), which rode the literary coattails of Edward Bellamy's best-selling utopian romance to some national acclaim.

In combating negative portrayals of white lawlessness and anti-immigrant violence, Chinese invasion fiction projected the anxiety of white displacement from labor markets to displacement from the country. "This process of the displacement of the Caucasians and the planting of the Chinese instead," cautioned G. B. Densmore's anti-Chinese polemic *The Chinese in California* (1880), "has here begun, and it is going on, slowly it may be, but steadily, with that silent inexorable movement of time."[11] However, such anti-Chinese discourse often found itself struggling to reconcile conflicting representations of Chinese labor migrants as both abject coolie-slaves *and* villainous agents of foreign aggression. Animating American Yellow Peril, this ambivalence was fueled, in part, by the unresolved status of Chinese labor in the U.S. Unlike the British and Spanish Caribbean, discussed in chapter 1, the U.S. did not institute a legal system of indenture. Political commentators on both sides of the "Chinese Question" made contradictory claims about the nature of Chinese labor migration to the U.S. Did the credit-ticket system constitute a form of voluntary migration or debt bondage (in the form of "servile labor contracts") to hiring agencies such as the San Francisco–based Chinese Six Companies that held Chinese laborers in a state of racial semislavery or "coolieism"?[12] According to Moon-Ho Jung, the coolie embodied "a conglomeration of racial imaginings" that threatened to collapse the distinction between past and present, slavery and contract freedom.[13] This racialized discourse of servile labor came to mark all forms of Asiatic immigration to the U.S., as anti-Chinese advocates sought to rename Chinese immigration as "coolie" importation.[14]

In linking industrial modernization to national dissolution, these invasion fictions offered a nonteleological vision of American history as they imagined China as the horizon of capitalist markets. They projected the contradictions and disjunctive temporalities of American modernity onto the malleable figure of the Chinese labor migrant. Early stories such as "The Battle of the Wabash" (1880), published in the *Californian* magazine, tied U.S. industrialism to Chinese infiltration as it imagined the U.S. in the year 2078, in which "villages had become cities . . . threaded by a net-work of railroad lines" yet densely populated by "pig-tails" and filled with "Asiatic architecture, with the queer gables and pagoda-shaped tops."[15] As aesthetic vehicles for political propaganda, Chinese invasion fiction transformed America into an unbounded Chinatown to frighten readers with the devastating consequence of the country's shortcomings on the "Chinese Question."[16] These fictions imagined Chinese immigration to the U.S. as covert espionage and prelude to military colonization, with San Francisco's Chinatown as the epicenter of China's new "American kingdom."[17] Hence, invasion fiction heightened the affective impact of anti-Chinese political ideologies and provided mass cultural instruction by negative example. And by stimulating and exploiting racial fears, the subgenre sought to reestablish white political hegemony as industrial capitalism, wide-scale immigration, and class antagonisms restructured the postbellum social order.

To that end, the sensational plots of Chinese invasion also powerfully reworked the historical tensions of American settler colonialism and chattel slavery, projecting them onto the future threat of white expropriation and enslavement by hostile Asiatic aggressors or, in the graphic prose of one novel, "the white man and the yellow man in their death-grip, contending for the earth."[18] In thus imagining the tragic consequences of unfettered Chinese immigration, invasion fiction absorbed and refracted growing anxieties over the end of western expansion—indeed, of American Manifest Destiny—and the changing composition of the national polity in the wake of black citizenship and suffrage. In championing Chinese exclusion, Republican John P. Jones of Nevada asked his fellow senators, "What encouragement do we find in the history of our dealings with the negro race or in our dealings with the Indian race to induce us to permit another race-struggle in our midst?"[19] In preparing readers for the dangers to come, the subgenre professed a disinterested concern for the national future as it marshaled Yellow Peril to restabilize the hierarchy of white racial power. The popularity of these fictions well into the twentieth century emphasized both the soundness of the federal Chinese exclusion policy and the cultural resiliency of the Asiatic invasion trope.[20] The following sections offer a genealogical history of this largely understudied popular subgenre that conveys, albeit in a historically transformed way, collective anxieties over the racialized "Other" that continue to menace American society today.

Counterfactual Histories

The emergence of Chinese invasion fiction in the U.S. coincided with the wide popularization of what I. F. Clarke calls "future war fiction" from the 1880s to 1914, when the onset of World War I eclipsed the desire for imagined ones.[21] The founding text of future war fiction was the former British general George Chesney's "The Battle of Dorking" (1871), serialized in *Blackwood's Magazine*. By the 1890s, future war stories had become a stock feature of the popular press in England and Europe and increasingly in the U.S., where they helped facilitate political consensus on the "Chinese Question."[22] While fin de siècle American writers imagined a variety of national threats from countries such as Mexico, Canada, Spain, and England, the racialized threat of Asiatic invasion gained especial prominence, as Chinese exclusion became a national issue. Japan's stunning success in the Russo-Japanese War (1904–1905) further intensified fears over America's economic future in the Pacific, fears that took shape in Yellow Peril anxieties over a militarily ascendant Japan absorbing China to form an Asiatic "combination" against the West.[23] For example, Marsden Manson's *The Yellow Peril in Action* (1907) envisions the unstoppable "Allied Asiatic fleet" of Japan and China "wiping out ... American trade and commerce on the Pacific Ocean."[24] British variants of Chinese invasion fiction, including the mixed-race West Indian Matthew Phipps Shiel's *Yellow Danger* (1898), *Yellow Wave* (1905), and *The Dragon* (1913; reissued in 1929 as *The Yellow Peril*) and George Griffith's *Angel of the Revolution* (1893), often portrayed China acting in concert with Japan, yet these Asiatic villains often remained safely outside the imagined bounds of the British Isles. In contrast, U.S. writers, responding to concerns over Chinese immigration and naturalization, envisioned the Asiatic threat as emerging from within the imagined community of the nation. The earliest American example of the subgenre, Dooner's *Last Days of the Republic* (1880), was the first such novel to structure its narrative around the device of an internal foreign enemy erupting from within the nation.[25]

Dating from the 1880s, American variants of Chinese invasion fiction eschewed the sentimentalism and linear model of historical progress found in other popular regional subgenres such as the plantation romance studied in chapter 1. However, the catastrophic dystopias envisioned in the invasion subgenre expressed a shared anxiety over the racial integrity of the United States as the nation emerged from the Civil War and Reconstruction into a period of prolonged economic instability.[26] For example, Dooner's novel imagines how lingering sectionalism after the Civil War precipitates Chinese invasion. Past history divides into new possibilities as Dooner relates how "partisan spirit which had settled down upon the popular understanding, at the close of the rebellion of 1864, [had] never, for a moment, lifted its baleful influence from the affairs of the nation," for it plunged the country headlong into a hostile Chinese takeover.[27] A largely masculine subgenre, Chinese invasion fiction also defined itself against Christian missionary literature, which initially embraced Chinese immigration to the U.S. in the ecumenical mission to Christianize the "heathen Chinee," as Wong Chin Foo sardonically styled it.[28] Female-authored narratives ranging from Eliza Bridgman's nonfictional *Daughters of China; or, Sketches of Domestic Life in the Celestial Empire* (1852) to Mary Bamford's novella *Ti: A Story of San Francisco's Chinatown* (1899) rehearsed, according to Hsuan Hsu, "the conventions of antebellum domestic fiction" and its "plot of the civilized, converted, tested, and redeemed [Chinese] orphan" to advance its missionary labors both at home and abroad.[29] In contrast, the invasion subgenre depicted Chinese immigrants as irredeemably heathen and incapable of Christian civilization, while it cast the white family-as-nation as tragically doomed by the error of its collective folly on the "Chinese Question."[30]

In the backward-looking diegesis of Chinese invasion fiction, a narrator—often a history professor from the future—recounts the historically possible before the fact. In these retrospective frameworks, the invented historian narrator sets out to tell the "history of the future" (Dooner 84). The narrative moves backward in order to move forward, which allows the narrator to envision for the reader the historically possible before the fact. In forcing readers to become aware of how the past might be used to effect a vital transition from present to future, the historian narrator of Chinese invasion fiction enjoins readers to act in the present to forestall invasion and secure a white national future.[31] Dooner prefaced his ingenious 1880 novel as a "history written for the Twentieth, and not for the Nineteenth Century," casting the denouement of his historical tale far into the future: "But the present generation must, in the ordinary course of nature, pass into the grave before the curtain shall have fallen upon the last act of this national drama" (3). To enhance the didactic effect, Chinese invasion fiction also derived its plots from a broad substratum of uncontroversial facts, which often included the historical details of the Burlingame Treaty.[32] In this, they professed to cleave to the truth, avoiding the fabulous at all costs, yet their plots eventually diverge from the historical time line to imagine the proliferating contingencies in a world without federal restrictions on Chinese immigration and naturalization.[33] Like contemporary alternate history fictions, these Chinese invasion fictions base their counterfactual speculations on the assumption that the reader knows the premise to be false. In other words, they ask readers "to consider the probable, plausible, or possible consequences of an admittedly false condition," as Gallagher explains.[34] In this fashion, Chinese invasion fictions expressed a deep investment in the problem of historical knowledge as modern documentary history began establishing itself according to standards of evidentiary empiricism, seeking to gain a specific "explanatory affect," borrowing from Hayden White, in charting alternate historical processes and the cause-effect of future catastrophe.[35]

Framed as a historical lesson from the future, Chinese invasion fiction addressed the production of historical knowledge itself—exemplified in the subtitle to Manson's novel *The Yellow Peril in Action*: "a possible chapter in history." Published in San Francisco just as the Chinese Exclusion Act became federal law, Woltor's *Short and Truthful History of the Taking of California and Oregon by the Chinese in the Year A.D. 1899 by Robert Woltor, a Survivor* (1882) took the form of a historiography by a self-described "survivor" of Chinese invasion. Five months after the capture of California and Oregon by Chinese forces, the narrator sets out to chronicle "a brief, unprejudiced, and connected history of the Mongolian invasion of California, from the time the influence of the Chinese became felt in the different branches of industry, up to the time of the occurrence of the fearful calamity which threatened to overwhelm this great country."[36] In this fashion, Woltor's story, like others in the subgenre, eschewed its own fictional or imaginative conditions of possibility in fashioning the narrative as an authoritative historical record of the distant (and not-so-distant) past. Set in 1899, the novel forgoes a teleological narrative of historical progress to proclaim in a past conditional or conjectural tense: "paradoxical as it may appear, though some fifteen years ago the expulsion of the Chinese would have been salvation to California, [but] it was now too late" (35–36). The invasion subgenre purported to mediate history—indeed, to draw "aside the veil of the future," in the words of one reviewer, and prophesize it.[37] The preemptive temporalities of these counterfactual histories defamiliarize and restructure the experience of the present, encoding the present in the form of some future's remote past.[38] By emphasizing the idea of historical mutability, Chinese invasion fiction challenged the idea of U.S. historical progress and the interpretation and knowledge of the American past.[39] Ignatius Donnelly's best-selling *Caesar's Column: A Story of the Twentieth Century* (1891), for example, envisions a Chinese professor challenging the collective memory of an American founding father: "Then came the news that a Manchurian professor, an iconoclast, had written a learned work, in English, to prove that George Washington's genius and moral greatness had been much over-rated by the partiality of his countrymen."[40]

These fictions exploited the bifurcating power of counterfactual thinking—the cleaving of the present into parallel and simultaneous tracks—in their fantastical efforts to reinvigorate race's explanatory power as foreign immigration, industrial capitalism, and overseas empire began to transform the racial legal categories of "white" and "nonwhite," citizen and alien. These texts employed a technique of counterfactual conjecture that also permeated the legal contests over Chinese immigration, naturalization, and citizenship, from *Chae Chan Ping v. U.S.* (1889) and *Fong Yue Ting v. U.S.* (1893) to *U.S. v. Wong Kim Ark* (1898). Counterfactuals are conditional statements that pertain to or express, according to the *Oxford English Dictionary*, "what has not in fact happened, but might, could, or would, in different conditions."[41] "A counterfactual supposition allows one, in literary analysis," as Stephen Best explains, "to imagine what a text from the past would mean if it were being reauthored in the present" and, in legal analysis, "to make inferences regarding causation, to infer not merely what happened or will happen, but, in addition, 'what *would* have been the case if some actual event, which in fact happened, had not happened.'"[42] The counterfactual's conjectural syntax of what might have been structures these narratives; it asks readers to imagine how altered relations of racial power might produce alternate historical paths.

In the interest of prevention, Chinese invasion fiction imagined the chilling consequences of a future without Chinese restriction laws. Their futuristic plots, particularly in those tales such as Dooner's published before the first Chinese Exclusion Act (1882), offer justification for state and federal anti-Chinese law and legislation by casting a range of punitive racialized restrictions, from the bans against Chinese legal testimony and naturalization to outright exclusion, as prophylaxis against an invasion that was certain to come. Kearney's Workingmen's Party of California similarly defended its anti-Chinese vigilantism in terms of the future legislation that would lend it legitimacy after the fact: "We will not violate the law. We will execute it."[43] Likewise, Chinese invasion stories drew their animating power from elaborate conspiratorial plots, which served as explanatory fictions for anti-Chinese law. In other words, an invasion that does not come to pass might be attributed to the success of anti-Chinese law in preventing the outbreak of hostile invasion. In this, the subgenre's experimentations with historicism and historical determinism offer up new ideas about the relations between contingency and causality in narrative form.[44] The remainder of this section limns the general contours of this heterogeneous subgenre by way of two representative examples. It focuses on Dooner's *Last Days of the Republic* (1880), the earliest of the Chinese invasion novels published in the U.S., and tracks the evolution of the form in the complex narrative structure of Vinton's *Looking Further Backward* (1890).

Like subsequent texts in the subgenre, Dooner's *Last Days* sheathes its anti-Chinese ideology in the garb of a historiography that sets out to "trace the causes"—in the language of economic and health security— of "the poison that is slowly corroding the vital principle of our national life" and "arrest the disease, before the power so to do shall have passed, forever, beyond the reach of political regeneration" (9). The novel was published after the long economic crisis of the 1870s brought the anti-Chinese zealot Denis Kearney and his Workingmen's Party to power in California. An amateur novelist, Dooner drew on his background in newspaper editing and the law in composing *Last Days*. He served as

Figure 3.1. George Frederick Keller, "San Francisco A.D. 1900," *Wasp* 5 (August–December 1880) (Courtesy of the Bancroft Library, University of California–Berkeley)

editor of the *Tucson Arizonian* in 1870 and later worked for the *Weekly Arizona Miner*, although his print career was cut short when he ran afoul of divisive partisan politics over the reelection of ex-governor Richard McCormick as Arizona's territorial delegate.[45] By 1873, Dooner was in Los Angeles practicing law in the firm of Wilson and Dooner, although he continued writing on regional topics.[46] Dooner published *Last Days* by subscription, and he spared no expense in its production. He collaborated with the prominent illustrator George Frederick Keller to produce original illustrations for the novel—Keller's only book work in his career.[47] A former Civil War soldier, Keller became acclaimed for his political cartoons in Ambrose Bierce's anti-Chinese satirical weekly the *Wasp*, and his illustrations for Dooner were an extension of this magazine work. In a pictorial analogue to the novel, the *Wasp* published an elaborate two-page color-tinted Keller illustration titled "San Francisco A.D. 1900" (1880), which counterfactually imagined San Francisco conquered and colonized by the Chinese (see figure 3.1).

Dooner's novel begins in 1848 with the discovery of gold in California, and the narrative moves forward in time, exceeding the temporal confines of the past to offer an apocalyptic vision of the U.S. "at the dawn of the Twentieth Century" (258). After taking the narrative up to the date of writing and publication in 1880, the omniscient historian-narrator proceeds to offer an account of the future—thus providing the *frisson*, citing Gallagher's work on allohistories, "of alternate realities" inside a bilinear structure.[48] "The preceding chapters have brought the history of the Chinese immigration down to the date of this writing," he relates, "but it does not, for that reason, become necessary to close this volume, or to abridge the subject which it proposes to treat,—simply because the future interposes an obstacle to the recordation of occurrences that have actually taken place" (83). In drifting away from realism toward counterfactual imagining, the novel proceeds to "deduce a comprehensive history of the future . . . extending over, at least, a period of time equal to that from which the data has been collected" (84). The text subsequently yokes the historical account up to 1880 (the publication date) to the counterfactual one that follows it "to forecast . . . the general outline of the events that remain to be enacted upon the world's stage" (85).

The idea of a deep-laid Chinese conspiracy—a scheme initiated at the end of the Civil War—propels Dooner's counterfactual history and becomes the interpretative framework for all subsequent events. It recasts Chinese labor migration as "a most elaborate . . . scheme which, in the course of a few years, swelled the Mongolian population of the Pacific States and Territories from a few thousand to more than one hundred thousand souls" (18). The novel incorporates verbatim text from the 1858 Treaty of Tianjin and the 1868 Burlingame Treaty that amended it, yet it reinterprets them through the prism of a fictional conspiracy. Dooner's performance of documentary empiricism—represented in the faithful citation of primary source materials—shapes the historical revisionism that follows leading to Chinese invasion. In circling back to the idea of "foreign conspiracy," Dooner begins to reshape the significance of past events recounted in the novel, as historical figures such as Anson Burlingame and Denis Kearney emerge alongside invented characters. China's political ambition was to gain "control of the Western Hemisphere," and "the introductory act" in this stratagem involved the "transport [of] her surplus population to America and to have them learn to maintain themselves there" (24). To this end, the "cunning statesmen of China" manipulated Burlingame to secure a favorable U.S.-China treaty with more lenient immigration provisions, thus ensuring the success of China's "scheme of invasion" (27). So began, according to Dooner, the "Coolie" invasion of the Pacific Coast (28).

Partway into Dooner's counterfactual history, the narrative abruptly shifts away from the impending political crisis at hand to offer an alternate chronicle of the controversial California Supreme Court ruling in *People v. Hall* (1854) banning Chinese legal testimony in state courts (examined at length in chapter 2). By drawing the legal text of *People v. Hall* into the fictional world of the novel, Dooner sought to illuminate "the difference of sentiment then and now." The nine chapters leading to this moment recontextualize the now-defunct *People v. Hall* (as of 1870) within the novel's diegetic frame of an alternate past, establishing the novelistic reality of Justice Murray's "hypothetical condition" of Chinese political power:

> The Chief Justice had no thought that the time should ever come when the premises which he had conceived should be actually presented in the United States. His picture was intended simply as a figure, to illustrate a principle. But now, after the lapse of less than half a century, that hypothetical condition was established; and it remains to be seen whether his deduction will be faithful to his premises, in the logic of actual experience. He says: "The same rule that would admit them to testify would admit them to all the equal rights of citizenship, and we might soon see them at the polls, in the jury-box, upon the bench, and in our legislative halls.
>
> "This is not a speculation which exists in the excited and overheated imagination of the patriot and statesmen, but it is an actual and present danger." (186–187)

Murray's counterfactual conjecture—his paranoid vision of the Chinese with "all the equal rights of citizenship"—becomes the springboard into the fictional Asiatic America of *Last Days*. "And all this had come to pass," continues the novel, "not only in California, but in the East and South as well" (187). In this alternate future, discriminatory anti-Chinese laws explicitly draw their explanatory power from fiction. Dooner's counterfactual history envisions a future that unfastens history from the law—specifically anti-Chinese restriction and exclusion measures—in order to produce the fictional evidence for their ongoing political and social necessity. The novel thus imbues Murray's counterfactual postulates with a powerful (if fictional) historical life even as it decontextualizes *People v. Hall* from a complex history of racial legislation—one that had targeted black Americans as well as Indians residents in the state. After the fall of the "Pacific States of the Great American Republic," the novel reorganizes itself into a military history tracking the relentless march of the "Asiatic invader" against allied American forces and toward Washington City, until the "Imperial Dragon of China . . . floated from the dome of the Capitol" (219, 232, 256). "The very name of the United States of America," concludes the narrator, "was thus blotted from the record of nations and peoples" (256–257).

Numerous invasion novels and short stories saw publication in the decades after the appearance of Dooner's novel and the subsequent passage of the first Chinese Exclusion Act. Of all these texts, Vinton's *Looking Further Backward* (1890) offers the most sophisticated refashioning of the subgenre's narrative form. Its complex structure of temporal extrapolation further complicates the political arguments and social tensions around Chinese exclusion. By revealing how the imaginings of Chinese invasion reconfigured the relations among history, law, and literary practice, the novel illuminates the centrality of literary discourse to the political project of destabilizing Chinese legal claims. Vinton's story overlays its plot of future Chinese invasion onto the characters and fictional settings drawn from Edward Bellamy's influential utopian novel *Looking Backward 2000–1887* (1888). Advertised as "an answer to and continuation of Edward Bellamy's famous novel," *Looking Further Backward*, Vinton's second novel, garnered some laudatory reviews yet appears not to have fared well commercially.[49] Like Dooner, Vinton was also a lawyer by trade and a frequent contributor to literary magazines, including *Godey's Lady's Book*, *Ballou's Monthly Magazine*, and the *Magazine of Western History*. In 1884, he joined the *North American Review* as an assistant editor.[50] Vinton imagined his novel as an homage and sequel to fellow lawyer-novelist Bellamy's famous narrative utopia. In 1887, Bellamy's original man-out-of-time Julian West falls into a deep hypnotic trance and reawakens 113 years later to discover the U.S. transformed into a modern utopia, governed by a collective form of government referred to as Nationalism.

Vinton's *Looking Further Backward*, wrote the *Daily Alta California* review, "may be said to be practically a continuation of 'Looking Backward,'" which takes "advantage of Bellamy's statement that China, alone of all nations, has retained her ancient form of government and civilization" to test "the Nationalistic system by supposing it to be submitted to the strain and trial of war—war between China and the United States."[51] Vinton's fictional sequel condemned Bellamy's celebration of cooperative life and deemphasis of individualism, which ran against the grain of anti-Chinese propaganda and its promulgation of the specter of Chinese masses. This racialized contest between American individualism and what Woltor styled as the "drones of the Orientalist hive" overrunning America was later given powerful figurative shape in "The American Gulliver and Chinese Lilliputians," the oft-referenced frontispiece of the American Federation of Labor pamphlet *Some Reasons for Chinese Exclusion* (1902), advocating for the indefinite extension of earlier Chinese Exclusion Acts (Woltor 30).[52] By bringing anti-Chinese discourse to bear on Bellamy's socialist utopia, Vinton's *Looking Further Backward* envisions the end of Bellamyite Nationalism and its diminution of American individualism in Chinese invasion and colonization.

Like Dooner, Vinton offers a meditation on counterfactual history and how it reshapes the future in the telling of the (as yet unrealized) past.[53] Written well after eastern manufacturers had begun experimenting with Chinese labor in the 1870s, Vinton's complex narrative framework interweaves the first-person perspectives of three narrators from different times and from opposite sides of the Chinese-American conflict.[54] Set after the Chinese capture of the U.S. in 2023, the novel takes the form of a series of historical lectures delivered by Chinese Professor Won Lung Li, who succeeds Julian West as chair of the Historical Section at Boston's Shawmut College. Speaking at the end of the great war, Vinton's Professor Won explains to his audience of American college students the causes for China's successful colonization of North America. Mindful of the "unpleasant task" before him, the professor acknowledges the scene of instruction as an extension of military conquest. "I have no doubt that there may be some persons among you who look upon me not only as a man of alien race," he begins, "but as an instructor placed over you by the force of arms, a director of your thoughts, a guide to your historical studies, forced upon you by the physical supremacy of an alien nation."[55]

In charting the historical "causes" for present calamity, Professor Won fashions a narrative of moral and legal culpability that holds Bellamy's Nationalistic system of government, which made "individual initiative" and self-reliance obsolete, largely responsible for American defeat. "In my lectures to you," declares the professor, "I shall endeavor to direct your attention, not only to events and to results, but also to causes; because until you know the cause you cannot rightly measure the result. The study of causes enables us better to appreciate results; it greatly broadens the scope of our knowledge, and greatly develops the reasoning powers of our mind" (17). The professor's use of the second-person form heightens the "explanatory affect" of this novel's historical lesson.[56] In his lectures, he addresses the reader along with the freshman students of Shawmut College. "It was because your ancestors did not understand history," warns Professor Won, "that they failed to be forewarned by its obvious teachings, or to appreciate the omens that foretold the coming catastrophe" (18). The full state regulation of the economy combined with a too liberal immigration policy under the American Nationalist system facilitated the astounding success of the Chinese invasion.[57] As the professor explains, "owning to the short-sightedness of your remote ancestors you had permitted your country to be over-run with emigrants from the slums of other nations; they had been given equal rights, socially and politically, and they had intermarried with your native stock until it became so debased that, one hundred years ago, your ancestors were as ready as the Frenchmen of the eighteenth century to abandon every thing for the sake of an idea" (31).

Professor Won leavens his historical account with quotations from the recovered manuscript diary of the now-dead Julian West (who was killed in battle in 2022) and the intercepted personal papers (partly written in cipher) of his son Colonel Bartlett Leete West chronicling the ongoing American resistance to Chinese invasion. Heeding Leopold van Ranke's dictum that modern history be constructed from "the accounts of eyewitnesses," the Wests' personal narratives form the ligaments of a social history that supplements Professor Won's depersonalized political history of the flawed governing system of Nationalism.[58] In fact, the lectures call attention to the important differences between these two forms of historical knowledge: "The news which he [Julian West] sets out therein for the most part correct, so far as it goes, but it is meager. Of the important events that were almost hourly taking place, *we* know now far more then *he* knew then. His diary is of inestimable value as contemporaneous history, and of no small value as literature" (82). The inclusion of the Wests' personal narratives also offers Professor Won an opportunity to portray the human agents, both American and Chinese, involved in the "Chinafication of the United States" (176). "I have quoted thus at length from this manuscript," admits the professor, "because the episode which it narrates shows that the Chinese officers, to whom was confided the task of conquering, had tender and sympathetic hearts. . . . As servants of our gracious Emperor, they had duties to perform, some of which were necessarily distasteful to their humane hearts. . . . They shed many tears over the sufferings of the captive nation" (176). Professor Won co-opts Colonel Bartlett Leete West's words—the words of the American resistance—for the contrary end of crafting a more compelling history of Chinese invasion: "That they [the Chinese] may be judged less harshly, is my excuse for quoting at such length from his manuscript" (176). In thus marshaling the tropes of sentimentalism, "hearts" and "tears," Vinton's Chinese invasion novel appears to stand apart from Dooner's *Last Days* and other antisentimental predecessors in the tradition of Yellow Peril. Duty bound, the Chinese, according to Professor Won, had carried out the laws of their sovereign, even though these acts of violence against Americans conflicted with their refined moral sensibilities. He represents the Chinese as the unwitting functionaries of legal violence (rather than as the recipients of it).

However, the objectivity of this "historical lesson" is merely an effect of the novel's dialogical framework, which beguiles readers into accepting the lectures as the disinterested counterpart to West's impassioned and "purely personal narrative" (151). The novel encourages readers to forget that Professor Won is also a duty-bound subject of the Chinese emperor. "There was no fear," he explains in his final lecture, "that her expatriated people would become less loyal subjects of her Emperors. The desire possessed by every Chinaman, high or low in estate, rich or poor in this world's goods, is that his dust may repose in the soil of China, and the history of the race had shown that this desire is sufficient to prevent the absent sons of China from becoming other than transient citizens of foreign lands" (181). The novel's final moments return us to the ideological context of the present-day "Chinese Question" in its depiction of Chinese immigrants as perpetual sojourners and "transient citizens of foreign lands," even though the U.S. is now Chinese territory. Lest we forget, the novel ends with the reminder—in the form of counterfactual conjecture—that the Chinafication of the United States requires the consent of the governed, for "if the United States was to be held by China, then the people of the United States must be willing subjects of China—or, at least, such a majority of the people as to render all attempts at resistance individual, and not National" (179). In thus "looking further backward" from an Asiatic America—indeed, from the perspective of a Chinese narrator—Vinton positions the reader, like Bellamy's original Julian West, to see "the past and present, like contrasting pictures, side by side."[59] While Dooner inaugurated the subgenre with a novel vested in the garb of (future) historiography, Vinton transforms fictional historiography into a didactic lesson in future history, interpolating the reader into the dystopian Asiatic future it seeks to circumvent. In this fashion, Chinese invasion fiction occupied a fabricated historicity that sought to forestall the future perfect tense of an Asiatic America in the making.[60]

The Chinese Exclusion Case and the Plenary Power Doctrine

For Pacific Coast anti-Chinese interests, the intensification of their efforts to end Chinese immigration increasingly placed the sovereignty of state governments into conflict with federal power. As subjects of the emperor of China, Chinese immigrants were protected under the provisions of the Burlingame Treaty, even though they remained subject to the laws of the individual states in which they resided. Thus, the exercise of state police powers often came into conflict with federal powers over foreign commerce and treaties. Self-identified "Representative Chinamen in America," officials from the Chinese Six Companies, for example, addressed an 1876 memorial to President Ulysses S. Grant, reminding him, among other things, that "the Chinese people are now here under solemn treaty rights" and "hope to be protected according to the terms of this treaty."[61] In the 1880s, anti-Chinese interests began the discursive transformation of the "Chinese Question" from a regional to a national concern, seeking a permanent solution to their Pacific Coast Chinese problem in the federal government. Chinese invasion fiction played a key role in popularizing the idea of Chinese labor immigration as a national security threat and to be excluded for that reason.[62] Initially honed in such nativist propaganda and fiction, the trope of invasion began to shape the legal imaginary and rhetoric of Chinese immigration in critical ways. Specifically, jurists began invoking the subgenre's tropes and narrative structures in rulings that helped establish the plenary power doctrine of American immigration law. First developed in the context of Chinese exclusion, the plenary power doctrine holds congressional and executive-branch decisions on immigration and naturalization as largely exempt from normal constitutional constraints and judicial review.[63] Plenary power is based on the idea that immigration involved the question of sovereignty, relating to a nation's right to define and police its borders.

This section charts the dynamic influence of such Chinese invasion fictions on the courts to reveal how immigration regulation became embedded in the concept of absolute sovereignty. The complex temporal schemas and tropes of Chinese invasion fiction began to find their way into the Chinese immigration case law of this period, especially in two Chinese test cases, *Chae Chan Ping v. United States* (1889) and *Fong Yue Ting v. United States* (1893). *Chae Chan Ping v. U.S.*, or the Chinese Exclusion Case, challenged the Scott Act (1888), modifying the original Chinese Exclusion Act. The Scott Act explicitly violated the terms of the U.S.-China Treaty by retroactively canceling the re-entry certificates of the roughly twenty thousand Chinese resident noncitizens who were then traveling outside the U.S. without granting them the means to recover the personal property they left in the country.[64] Earlier revisions to the U.S.-China Treaty had restricted but not ended Chinese immigration to the U.S. Teachers, students, merchants, tourists, and returning laborers with proof of residence numbered among those exempted from exclusion. *Chae Chan Ping* was followed by *Fong Yue Ting*, which contested the additional anti-Chinese restrictions enacted under the subsequent Geary Act (1892). In these Chinese test cases, the Supreme Court upheld discrimination against immigrants on the basis of race and granted federal immigration law an unusual immunity from judicial review. At the end of the twentieth century, as the legal scholar

Gabriel Chin argues, *Chae Chan Ping* and *Fong Yue Ting* "continue[d] to be cited in modern decisions of the Supreme Court; because all constitutional immigration law flows from these cases, even decision that do not cite them must rely on cases that do."[65]

Chae Chan Ping first arrived in the U.S. in 1875. On June 2, 1887, he departed on the steamship *Gaelic* for a voyage to China. Before embarking, he secured a reentry certificate, as required by the 1882 Chinese Exclusion Act and the 1884 statute amending it, to facilitate his immigration processing upon return. After a yearlong sojourn abroad, Chae Chan Ping boarded a California-bound vessel in Hong Kong on September 7, 1888, before the Scott Act was even introduced into Congress. However, during his month-long Pacific passage, the Scott Act became law. The new statute had dire implications for Chae Chan Ping, who was divested of his "right of return" when he attempted to land in San Francisco in early October. As in the case of Ju Toy, examined in the following chapter, Chae Chan Ping petitioned for a writ of habeas corpus while detained aboard the vessel. Assisted by the San Francisco Chinese Six Companies, Chinese litigants such as Chae Chan Ping initiated a number of test cases challenging the constitutionality of the various Chinese Exclusion Acts. The Six Companies was an executive council for the various family and district associations that served as an "instrument of social and labor control within the community as well as its representative to mainstream society and voice of protest to the government," according to Mae Ngai.[66] Thomas Riordan served as counsel for the Six Companies. He represented Chae Chan Ping before the U.S. Supreme Court and Wong Kim Ark before circuit court and arranged the *Fong Yue Ting* test case.[67] *Chae Chan Ping* was appealed to the U.S. Supreme Court after the circuit court ruled against the Chinese immigrant.[68]

By the end of the decade, exclusionists had succeeded in advancing the idea that Chinese immigration posed a danger to the nation. In both literature and law, Chinese invasion (or the imagined threat of it) facilitated a claim to the natural right of (national) self-preservation that existed outside or "above" the existing legal order. Anti-Chinese pamphlets such as Densmore's *The Chinese in California* (1880) noted that while President Hayes vetoed earlier restriction legislation such as the "fifteen-passenger bill" (studied in chapter 2), he also "admitted the right of the legislative power to modify a treaty in the face of a pressing danger, calling for immediate relief."⁶⁹ In upholding the Scott Act in *Chae Chan Ping*, Justice Stephen Field's unanimous opinion argued similarly that the nation held the sovereign power to maintain "absolute independence and security throughout the entire territory." It focused on the scope of federal power over immigration, concluding, "That the government of the United States, through the action of the legislative department, can exclude aliens from its territory is a proposition which we do not think open to controversy."⁷⁰ Field's opinion responded to the contention that the Constitution did not mention immigration among the enumerated powers granted to Congress, and it recognized this authority as inherent in national sovereignty. Moreover, Field, like Dooner's *Last Days*, invoked the politically charged rhetoric of "an Oriental menace" to portray Chinese immigration (and its threat to free white labor) as an incipient form of "foreign aggression and encroachment":

> To preserve its independence, and give security against foreign aggression and encroachment, is the highest duty of every nation, and to attain these ends nearly all other considerations are to be subordinated. It matters not in what form such aggression and encroachment come, whether from the foreign nation acting in its national character or from vast hordes of its people crowding in upon us. . . . If, therefore, the government of the United States, through its legislative department, considers the presence of foreigners of a different race in this country, who will not assimilate with us, to be dangerous to its peace and security, their exclusion is not to be stayed because at the time there are no actual hostilities with the nation of which the foreigners are subjects. The existence of war would render the necessity of the proceeding only more obvious and pressing. The same necessity, in a less pressing degree, may arise when war does not exist, and the same authority which adjudges the necessity in one case must also determine it in the other.⁷¹

Field resorts to Yellow Peril imagery to affirm congressional authority to limit and exclude the entrance of "foreigners of a different race," especially if they endanger the "peace and security" of the nation. He regards Chinese exclusion as a kind of "war measure" as he counterfactually postulates race war as the inevitable consequence of Chinese labor immigration, revealing the figurative forms and counterhistorical causation involved in legal meaning making. The trope of invasion restructures Chinese immigrants into a national security threat, turning exclusion (and the abrogation of the U.S.-China Treaty) into a "necessary" measure to ensure U.S. sovereignty.

By portraying "vast hordes" of Chinese "crowding in upon us" as a hostile act tantamount to war, Field's ruling assigns counterhistorical causation in an elaborate counterfactual mode. Before his appointment as an associate justice in 1863, Field, a unionist Democrat, served six years on the California Supreme Court (1857–1863), and the regional politics of Chinese immigration shaped his judicial career. Field's ruling in *Chae Chan Ping* marks the success of anti-Chinese interests in transforming the regional issue of Chinese immigration into a national concern. Advocates of Chinese immigration had warned against such attempts "to frighten a nation of well-nigh fifty millions of people into a proceeding unprecedented in its history."[72] However, by 1889, Chinese exclusion had become a "necessary" measure to the federal judiciary even when "war does not exist" and "at the time [when] there are no actual hostilities with the nation." Field wrested the language of sovereignty—"the natural law of self-preservation"—from states'-rights discourse (where it had long rested) and applied it to the national government. He departed from past holding to root immigration regulation in "a doctrine of inherent sovereign powers," which delegated to the legislative and executive branches plenary power or absolute authority over immigration.[73] This doctrine of inherent sovereign powers, according to the legal historian Lucy Salyer, "expanded . . . to bolster the absolute power of the federal government to control immigration and to diminish the rights of aliens and the participation of courts in immigration decisions," both limiting judicial review of immigration decisions and leading to the growth of immigration administration—indeed, the rise of the modern bureaucratic state.[74]

In *Chae Chan Ping*, the federal judiciary legitimized the trope of Chinese invasion and transformed it into a legal rationale for the abrogation of the U.S.-China Treaty and the termination of the few remaining privileges secured to Chinese immigrants in the U.S.[75] Four years after Chae Chan Ping's deportation in 1889, *Fong Yue Ting v. U.S.* (1893) brought before the Supreme Court the Geary Act's new registration mandate (tantamount to an internal passport system), which made noncompliance punishable by a maximum one-year term of imprisonment at hard labor followed by deportation. Justice Horace Gray's controversial majority (6–3) opinion in *Fong Yue Ting* affirmed a virtually unlimited congressional discretion in legislating all aspects of the nation's immigration policy, including the rules and procedures for alien registration and deportation.[76] By confirming the federal plenary power to exclude as inherent in sovereignty, *Chae Chan Ping* laid the groundwork for the summary deportation of permanent legal residents upheld in *Fong Yue Ting*.[77] In order to make Chinese exclusion consistent with "republican principles," Field, like the anti-Chinese writers who preceded and followed him, invokes what Giorgio Agamben, building on Carl Schmitt, describes as the "state of exception": no system of law is fully complete unto itself but relies on an "exception"—a suspension of the norm—that exists both within and outside the juridical order that it helps constitute.[78]

Chinese invasion fictions had long disseminated such elaborate counterfactual histories of this racialized state of exception, which figured Chinese labor migrants as national security threats. "It should," reads Woltor's *Short and Truthful History*, "have been granted that the national and unwritten law of nations demands, when circumstances unexpectedly arise which oblige a nation to diverge from its general course for its own lawful advantage and future safety, that any necessary steps taken on such occasions should be, as in the only instance in which the United States could ever be called upon to act against their fundamental law of 'equity to all,' not only excusable, but warranted in the opinion of the world" (37). Appealing to the higher law of "self-preservation," Woltor marshals Chinese invasion as a legitimate "excuse" for the U.S. to act against its "fundamental law 'of equity to all.'" Vinton's novel, likewise, portrays a future U.S. government so limited by its Constitution (indeed, one divested of military and police powers) that when faced "with an invader not only at [its] gates but on [its] soil," it cannot act to protect its own citizens against violent expropriation (129). His incredulous Julian West challenges the president, "You tell me that your powers are limited, and that it would be treasonous to assume such vast authority, But what limits your authority?—the Constitution. But what is the object of the Constitution? Is not its sole purpose to secure the lives, liberties and happiness of the people? How then in fulfilling the plain purpose of the Constitution do you override it?" (129–130). In appealing to the higher or natural law of self-preservation against a Chinese enemy, West urges the president to exceed constitutional mandates in the name of the Constitution (and, indeed, to preserve the Constitution itself), limning the duality central to the "state of exception." The suspension of law coincides with and depends on its invocation and enactment. By the turn of the century, the counterfactual imaginaries of Chinese invasion had laid the foundation for the enduring American tradition of Yellow Peril. In giving form to the legal and literary struggles over Chinese immigration, the invasion subgenre helped forge a post–Civil War idea of absolute national sovereignty, laying the groundwork for the modern plenary power doctrine.

Reimagining U.S. Settler Colonialism

By imagining the U.S. colonized and enslaved by the Chinese Empire, the Chinese invasion subgenre energized forms of nativism—racialized political xenophobia—as it positioned white Americans as an indigenous people facing violent foreign expropriation. The violent pasts of U.S. settler colonialism and black chattel slavery shaped the speculative premises of this cautionary subgenre. Specifically, the form refracted growing anxieties over the end of American Manifest Destiny. The subgenre often reimagined the brutal past of U.S. settler colonialism and Indian relations in terms of the Chinese expropriation of white American occupied lands. It positioned white Americans (in lieu of Indians) as the true natives of the continent holding a rightful—and, indeed, original—title to the territory. While anxieties over Chinese immigration led the federal government to assume regulatory power over immigration, comparable developments in relation to Indian removal and resettlement also allowed the federal government to assume plenary power over all Indian affairs. Indeed, the violation of treaty rights in Chinese exclusion recalls the similar legal encroachments on treaties ensuring indigenous or tribal sovereignty. Two years before *Chae Chan Ping*, the Supreme Court ruling in *United States v. Kagama* (1886), a California case involving a murder on the Hoopa Valley Indian reservation, established broad federal power over Native Americans on the basis of the "right of exclusive sovereignty which must exist in the National Government."[79] According to the doctrine of discovery, Native Americans retained only a "right of occupancy" to indigenous lands, over which the U.S. exerted absolute control and authority. This section focuses on two early Chinese invasion stories, "The Battle of the Wabash: A Letter from the Invisible Police" (1880) and Woltor's *Short and Truthful History* (1882), to explore the invasion subgenre's complex relations to these interrelated questions of treaty rights, U.S. sovereignty, and plenary power so often raised in the adjudication of Native American as well as Chinese immigration case law at the time.

Invasion fiction often moved in two opposed yet complementary directions: the subgenre's progressive orientation toward an Asiatic future erased the African American presence from the U.S., while its retrogressive orientation toward an invented past vanished the Indian. The imagined community, as Priscilla Wald reminds us, "requires the act of remembering, even if, as in [Benedict] Anderson's formulation, it is the deliberate act of remembering, collectively, what to forget."[80] By establishing the primacy of white American nativism and racial self-preservation, these fictions envisioned an alternate chronicle of the founding violence of American settler colonialism and the racialized histories of Indian removal, expropriation, and political disenfranchisement. In this, the subgenre modified the anti-immigrant ideologies of the Know-Nothing political movement from the 1830s to 1860s, which resisted the early influx of ethnicized Irish Catholic and German immigrants to realign the conflict along a white and nonwhite (yet nonblack) racial line. The "Chinese Question" disarticulated and recomposed the ethnic and racial nativisms that shaped, in largely underexplored ways, the Progressive-era projects of racialized "Americanization." For example, Walter Benn Michaels's *Our America* posits the primacy of anti-black Progressivist racism to the "reinvention of the American state," even though the "Chinese Question" had first begun to link the nativist racialization of inassimilable foreign immigrants with an idea of American culture redefined as white racial inheritance.[81]

In envisioning a dystopian Asiatic America, invasion fictions also rooted their catastrophic futures in invented pasts of aboriginal whiteness. The violent history of U.S. settler colonialism animates the story that "The Battle of the Wabash" tells about America's Asiatic future.

Published in the *Californian* (later revived as the *Overland Monthly*) under the pseudonym Lorelle, "The Battle of the Wabash" takes the form of an anonymous letter discovered in 1880 yet dated from the future, 2080, warning America of its eventual colonization and destruction by Chinese invaders. The story derives its enigmatic title from one of the bloodiest battles in American settler colonialism and long considered the greatest defeat of the U.S. Army by Native Americans. In the Battle of the Wabash (also known as St. Clair's Defeat), a confederated force of Miamis, Shawnees, Delawares, and Potawatomis routed the American forces led by General Arthur St. Clair along the banks of the Wabash River in 1791. Lorelle's story limns a repetition crisis of this frontier violence. Its tale of fictional race war and the end of white American dominance is also set along the banks of the Wabash River. Early U.S. continental expansion had utilized treaties (and the abrogation of them when necessary) to systematically extinguish Native American titles to western lands, calling to mind similar legislated infringements on U.S.-China treaties in statutes such as the Scott Act. An epistolary tale, Lorelle's story recounts the experiences of a white time traveler "liv[ing] in the future as well as the present" (364). Framed as a final lesson in a "course of comparative history," his letter sets out to offer an account of "the period of American history elapsing between the years 1870 and 2080," leading to the great "Americo-Mongolian conflict" (365, 364). Once the gateway to the western territories, St. Louis is now the new U.S. capital after the fall of the Pacific Coast. Outnumbering whites three to one, the Chinese in this alternate future have "celestialized California," in all industries, the arts, and even the courts (366). Bewildered by these changes, Lorelle's time traveler seeks out a "noted historian," the Chinese Professor Hap Lee—the literary predecessor of Vinton's Professor Won Lung Li—for a "short *résumé* of the last two hundred years of American history" (366).

The subgenre's desire for a different future facilitates the narrative transformation of the collective past. "The Battle of the Wabash" calls attention to the fantasy of discovery as it recasts the contest between Chinese colonization of U.S. territory and Anglo-American claims to the same land. A menacing variant of an unreliable narrator, Lorelle's Professor Lee casts Chinese arrival on American shores as discovery of terra nullius (land belonging to no one), "sparsely inhabited by [white] aborigines," to be secured through colonial conquest and occupation (366). Chinese sovereignty claims have their origins in discovery. Like the precolonial North American Indians, the white aborigines whom the Chinese encounter may have a "right of occupancy" but not ownership of these lands, for they inhabit a prenational state. From a detached, ethnographic perspective, Lee describes (with intended irony) how the white "aborigines, the ancestors of the present Melicans of this land," were "sprung from a small tribe known originally as Diggers . . . because they were all given to digging in the hills and mountains for precious metals" (366). This wry reference to the California Gold Rush also forges an imagined white link to the soil, displacing the stereotype of the "Digger Indian" with the fantasy of aboriginal "Melicans." According to Professor Lee, it was only a matter of time before the Chinese conquered the primitive "Melicans," beginning the processes of industrialization and modernization of the land. In this alternate colonial framework, white Americans are cast as the dominated indigenous peoples of now Chinese colonized lands. Jack London later marshaled a similar idea of white American indigeneity in his proletarian novel *Valley of the Moon* (1913) by having a white character proclaim, "We're the last of the Mohegans."[82] Such fictions illuminated the ideology of white entitlement to the resources of the West that often erupted into violence against Indians and Spanish-Mexican (Californio) settlers as well as against Chinese immigrants.[83] According to Lorelle's Chinese historian narrator, these "native barbarians" assisted in their own defeat: "the aborigines showed a want of knowledge of our people that surprised us no little, but they entirely failed to see what was going on before their faces," for they blindly held onto the "theory that we [the Chinese] had as much right here as they or any other people—that we were entitled to the benefits of certain principle, that declared all men brothers" (367, 368).

In this fashion, Chinese invasion fiction conjured complex fantasies of the colonial appropriation of indigenous lands, which figured the U.S. as the eastern horizon of Chinese imperialist venture in a parallel yet inverted course from American Manifest Destiny. In *A Short and Truthful History*, assimilation of Western historical knowledge catalyzes Chinese imperial aggression toward the U.S. The fictional author and "survivor" of invasion, Robert Woltor, explains that isolationism had made the Chinese "ignorant of the history of other nations" until

"British guns" opened their ports and forced "modern civilization" on them (45). The Chinese applied themselves diligently to the study of Western history, taking particular interest in the violent course of Western imperialism:

> They had not been slow in studying the history of past foreign events, and particularly noting those referring to government and war. They noticed that the most civilized nations had sometimes availed themselves of wholesale treachery and massacre for the gaining of some great aim. They had read the fascinating blots of blood which stain the pages of the history of Greece, Italy, France, Spain, Britain, and America, and imagined those events had happened in our very age—and indeed some have. The Conquest of Peru greatly interested them; and Pizzaro's treachery to Atahualpa particularly impressed them as a masterpiece of duplicity. (45)

Thus, having "learned all they wished to learn" about the course of Western empire, the Chinese, according to Woltor, "had now come to teach their tutors a lesson" (46). In capturing the U.S., the Chinese simply embraced the lesson of Western history. The "clever Mongolian," according to the novel, "asserted what his cultivated tutor, the Caucasian, has, in practice, seldom hesitated to do—'a great and successful end justifies the most damnable means'" (73).

As Woltor's dystopian tale draws to a close, it reveals among its "ultimate facts" the long-term strategy of the Chinese to conquer the rest of the continental U.S., from west to east. *A Short and Truthful History* imagines the horrifying inversion of the westward course of American Manifest Destiny: "The Europeans displaced the red Indians by driving them first to the west of America, thence back to a point midway between the Atlantic and Pacific oceans, and, at last, to the corner of their fate—extermination. Just such a fate seems to await the Caucasian race in America at the hands of the alien Mongolian, now irredeemably engrafted on her shore" (79). The novel ends with an uncanny historical homology as Chinese forces gathering on the Pacific Coast prepare to repeat the course of U.S. settler colonialism in the opposite direction. The Chinese invasion of the U.S. is contingent on the very "fact" of America: its constitution as a colonial state and the westward course of its continental expansion. In the dénouement of Woltor's historical tragedy, the conquering Chinese force demands "all surviving Americans and Europeans to vacate California and Oregon immediately," thus reversing the oft-repeated refrain of anti-Chinese propaganda in "You Americans must go" (58–59).

By revising the founding acts of invasion and indigenous expropriation that constituted America's founding, Woltor makes white Americans into the innocent victims of rapacious Chinese territorial aggrandizement. The penultimate pages of Woltor's novel express most forcefully the specter of U.S. settler colonialism and the repressed violence of national origins haunting the spatial and temporal imaginaries of the subgenre. Writing from the Pacific edge of America's western frontier, Woltor's tale lends a false sense of cohesion to the U.S.—a union that had almost foundered with Confederate secession and Civil War—by mourning the loss of a white America in Chinese colonization. As in Lorelle's tale, the rhetoric of white racial extinction in the U.S. repurposed the figure of the vanishing Indian. Fears of so-called Anglo-Saxon "race suicide" threatened in the precipitous decline in white marriage and reproduction toward the end of the century further augmented these anxieties over white national unity in the wake of Reconstruction.[84] By centering plots on the dialectical movement between Chinese invasion and American resistance, invasion fiction helped forge a sense of white Christian America unified against the threats of racial miscegenation and loss of U.S. sovereignty. This binary structure facilitated white national identification and belonging by emphasizing its vulnerability to racialized attack.[85]

In imagining a parallel case of colonial invasion and occupation, Woltor's anti-Chinese fiction adapted a satirical structure drawn, in part, from Washington Irving's earlier speculative fiction "The Men of the Moon" (1809), which imagines armed "aerial voyagers" from the moon, known as Lunatics, who descend on Earth and revisit on Christian Americans the cultural arrogance and violence that they had inflicted on the Indians.[86] In this, Irving, like Woltor and Lorelle after him, modeled the figure of the white aboriginal American on the Indian, revealing the cultural amnesia and racial surrogation involved in the politics of nativism. The threat of unfettered Chinese immigration refracted anxieties over the diminishment of the western frontier and the changing composition of the national polity in the wake of black political enfranchisement. In arguing for Chinese exclusion, western politicians depicted their constituencies, in the words of Senator Eugene Casserly of California, as the "outposts of civilization" and envisioned the end of American Manifest Destiny in the Asiatic colonization of the Pacific Coast.[87]

Chinese invasion fiction absorbed and refracted nationalist anxieties over the so-called closing of the American frontier by depicting its end in Asiatic occupation and colonization. In 1893, the historian Frederick Jackson Turner proposed the end of the fantasy of continuous westward continental expansion into lands emptied of indigenous populations, in his famous frontier thesis. Later invasion fictions such as London's sardonic short story "The Unparalleled Invasion: Excerpt from Walt. Nervin's 'Certain Essays in History,'" written in the wake of the Spanish-American War and U.S. overseas empire, inverted the dynamics of Chinese invasion to envision the continued westward course of American Manifest Destiny onto the Asian continent.[88] Also told from the perspective of a future historian, London's tale plots the arc of Chinese labor migration in terms of a global race war led by the Chinese emperor, albeit one that results, in an ironic twist, in the "racially motivated invasion of China" by Western nations.[89] Signifying on the republic's founding moment, London's tale, published in *McClure's Magazine* in 1910, begins in 1976 with the "celebration of the Bi-Centennial of American Liberty" and resolves its invasion plot in a genocidal germ warfare, borrowed from M. P. Shiel's *Yellow Danger*, that transforms China into "a howling wilderness" decimated of its multitudes—indeed, a new frontier—to be colonized "according to the democratic American program."[90] Such imagery draws on and defamiliarizes Progressive-era discourses of disease and contagious outbreak that were so often levied against the overcrowded tenements of San Francisco and New York Chinatowns, stigmatizing their Chinese residents as menaces to American public health.[91] Unloosed on China on May 1—International Workers' Day, London's American-engineered plague roughly yokes together labor activism and empire, mapping an earlier paradigm of white settler colonialism onto U.S. neocolonial relations with China, in which exploitation of overseas markets—Secretary of State John Hay's so-called Open Door policy—had begun to replace continental expansion.[92]

Reimagining Black Citizenship and Suffrage

Chinese invasion fictions sought to assuage anxieties over the closing of the frontier as well as the changing racial composition of the national polity in the wake of radical Reconstruction. They projected the threat of black citizenship and suffrage onto Chinese labor immigration and replotted the history of Indian removal as white American dispossession. In the face of disorienting forms of fin-de-siècle economic and territorial expansion, these imaginative efforts to solidify the nation's shifting racial boundaries betrayed a desire to reassert an idea of race derived from antebellum slavery in which racial identity determined political status.[93] From the perspective of anti-Chinese ideologues, the dependency of U.S. industrialization on the importation of transnational Chinese labor—facilitated in part by a new phase of U.S. capital expansion into the Asia Pacific—smacked too much of the long-defunct African slave trade.[94] These anti-Chinese discourses simultaneously identified Chinese laborer migrants with new forms of monopoly finance as well as with the now-archaic past of black chattel slavery.[95] This Janus-faced representation of Chinese labor migrants as both abject coolie-slaves and villainous agents of military (and economic) invasion—inciting both pathos and fear—lay at the heart of these racializing discourses of exclusion, mediating explicit forms of Afro-Asian similarity and difference.

This section charts the connected racial histories and temporal structures modeled in early anti-Chinese polemics and given fantastical literary form in the Chinese invasion subgenre. Specifically, it focuses on the productive tensions surrounding the figure of the "coolie-slave" who embodied both the threatening future of "Capital" writ large and the past error of black chattel slavery. Jack London helped popularize the idea of alien, premodern Chinese difference, yet he too praised the Chinese for grasping "the Western code of business," specifically the "radically new idea" of "contract," which lay at the heart of post–Civil War American industrial modernization, as examined in chapter 1.[96] This contradictory presentation, in Colleen Lye's words, "of the economic modernity of America's Asia" as both national progress *and* regression was refracted through the disjunctive temporalities of Chinese invasion fiction and its investment in simultaneous notions of structural transformation and continuity. The push-pull of hope and fear, the desire to teach and warn, shaped this ambivalent imagination of the "Chinafication of the United States."[97]

Such conflicted representations produced a range of formal tensions in the Chinese invasion narrative as Reconstruction politics redefined the freedom of the white laborer under capitalism. Early anti-Chinese polemics such as Milton B. Starr's *The Coming Struggle; or, What the People on the Pacific Coast Think of the Coolie Invasion* (1873) insisted on defining Chinese labor immigration as outgrowth and repetition of the history of American chattel slavery: "As the features of a child resemble its parents, so the coolie traffic resembles the traffic in chattel slaves."[98] Like other anti-Chinese ideologues, Starr subsumed Chinese labor immigration to the historical framework of black chattel slavery and retailored the past of slavery, like the fiction it influenced, to tell an apocalyptic story of an invasion to come.[99] By casting Chinese immigration as "coolie invasion," Starr drew a portrait of race war as the inevitable consequence of the "free migration and emigration" enumerated in the Burlingame Treaty. For Starr, America's early "experiment" with the African slave trade provides the interpretative framework for understanding the present and future dangers of Chinese labor immigration. Chinese "cheap labor," like the African chattel slavery that preceded it and with which it is identified, threatens the free republic "with another revolution more bloody and costly than the first" (39). Starr's narrative of U.S. exceptionalism depicts the capitalist importation of "unlimited... heathen [Chinese] men and women" as another spiritual test—as African slavery had once been—of the Christian nation (13).

In the Chinese labor migrant, Starr saw the old specter of caste-based society—supposedly expunged with the abolition of the "traffic in African coolies"—rather than the promise of a free post–Civil War society premised on contract (65). In thus "judging the future by the past," Starr envisions the nation teetering on the edge of a repetition crisis, one that would plunge it back into the days of African slavery (68). By remapping the Old South onto the newly settled Pacific Coast, Starr's anti-Chinese polemic takes the form of a redemptive liberal narrative of American history that understands black chattel slavery as an anachronistic anomaly—a throwback to "the old English feudal system"—that was destined to be overcome in the nation's teleological march toward progress and the democratic ideal (81). Indeed, Starr anticipates the revisionist histories associated with the so-called Dunning school of Reconstruction historiography, which was sympathetic to white southerners and viewed black suffrage, among other things, as a corrupt stratagem for Republicans to seize power in the South. In Starr's polemic, the Old South and plantation slavery becomes a didactic "warning by the past" against an Asiatic future (83). The Chinese labor migrant is both remnant of a feudal mode of production and the consequence of U.S. industrial capitalism and its unceasing labor demands. As a "doubled or doubly mediated figure," the Chinese labor migrant, as Eric Hayot argues, has been "forced to bear on its surface the mutually intermediating concepts of racial otherness and industrial modernization."[100] The trope of Chinese invasion gave powerful expression to this figural ambivalence as it justified racialized violence in the name of national progress. By linking the anti-Chinese campaign with abolitionist ideals, Starr aligns Chinese exclusion with black freedom, giving form to the dialectic of black inclusion/Chinese exclusion studied at length in the previous chapter.

From the earliest example of Dooner's *Last Days*, invasion narratives saw no contradiction in portraying Chinese labor migrants as innocent victims of economic exploitation or "human slavery" and as strategic military agents in control of their destiny. Chinese labor migrants appear as abject "coolie-slaves," yet Dooner's invasion plot hinged on their transformation into hostile foreign aggressors. The "Coolie traffic" was an essential element of the "deep conspiracy" by Chinese aggressors to colonize the country (51, 56). The narrative informs us that "the so-called Free Immigration was false in its representation and false in practice," for "Asiatic Coolieism is a form of human slavery" (50–51). Labor immigration functions as an elaborate cover for the Chinese exportation of advance soldiers, and the dire conditions of so-called Chinese cheap living in the U.S. serve as military training in preparation for attack. Bereft of familial ties and able to subsist solely on rice, these "Coolie laborers" serve as ideal soldiers in the "battle of the Chinese conquest" of the U.S. (123). In a similar fashion, *A Short and Truthful History* suggests that the Chinese concentrated themselves into urban ghettoes for strategic military purposes rather than as the consequence of anti-Chinese legislation, which allowed incorporated communities in California to segregate Chinese immigrants into Chinatowns.[101] Both novels vacillate between pity for the Chinese coolie and fear of the Chinese invader.

Of all of these fictions, Dooner's *Last Days* most closely aligned itself with Starr's neoabolitionist argument, retailoring it to the fictional form of the invasion narrative. After the inundation of the Pacific Coast states, the Chinese begin colonization of the "territory known as the Slave States" (130). Southern landowners, according to Dooner, "were delighted" to find in Chinese labor "a substitute for" black labor: "the Coolie . . . was . . . so servile, that the Southern land-owners once more imagined themselves the masters of a race of slaves,—but this time of willing slaves,—and a prospect of permanence to the institution" (131). Aping the form of voluntary or free labor, the "coolie," in fact, represents a regressive movement backward to the "race-labor hierarchies" of institutional slavery.[102] Dooner aligns southern landowners with Pacific Coast monopolists in their shared desire to relive the "barbaric" fantasy of mastery over a racially subject population without the unseemliness of coercion. Chinese labor was desirable precisely because it was an exploitable racialized labor force that had yet (or so it seemed) to forge a political identity like black Americans. "The Coolie," according to Dooner's narrative, "had not, as yet developed a taste for politics; while the . . . [Negro], growing from bad to worse, had finally advanced to a stage of political development . . . in the fruitless effort to ape the partisan intrigues of his white exemplars" (96). Dooner marshals the specter of coolie slavery forged in the Spanish Caribbean (studied in chapter 1) to emphasize the anachronism of Chinese labor in postemancipation America. The Chinese coolie represents an untenable contradiction in terms: a voluntary or contractual slave.

In a similar fashion, Vinton's *Looking Further Backward* also identifies Chinese arrival with a return to the long-defunct forms of industrial capitalism and chattel slavery banished from Bellamy's future America. By depicting the Chinese deportation of white Americans to Europe, where they are sold as chattel slaves, Vinton heightens the affective impact of this association of Chinese arrival with the human exploitation of Capital writ large. In fictionally recasting Starr's polemic, Vinton depicts the American resistance against Chinese invasion as a struggle against white slavery. In Bellamy's original collectivist utopia, the nation had become the "sole corporation" and "sole employer," while "all the citizens, by virtue of their citizenship, became employees."[103] In Vinton's tale, Chinese conquest and occupation results in the destruction of Bellamy's Nationalist system, followed by the reinstatement of banks, paper currency, private property, and wage labor. By aligning the Chinese invaders with the now-defunct system of capitalism, Vinton also reframes Bellamy's original metaphor of wage slavery as a race war between China and the U.S. In Bellamy's final chapter, a "horror struck" West analogizes the squalor and dehumanizing conditions of the largely immigrant laboring masses of the South Cove tenement district to the stultifying cargo holds of slave ships that once transported Africans to the New World: "The streets and alleys reeked with the effluvia of a slave ship's between-decks."[104] In Vinton's sequel, Chinese officials begin implementing a policy of mass white American deportation as a prelude to Chinese occupation, which calls to mind the atrocities of the Middle Passage and the African slave trade:

> The condition of those who were exported was indeed pitiable in the extreme. On board ship their feet were manacled to lessen the danger of insurrection. The vessels that carried them were necessarily overcrowded. The confined quarters, the vitiated air, the unavoidable discomforts of an ocean passage, and the dejection of mind of the unfortunates, all combined to generate diseases which decimated their numbers. And when they disembarked in France or China their condition was not much improved. Strangers in a strange land, not knowing the tongue of their masters, sold at private sale and public auction as laborers to whosoever would hire them, they became practically slaves. The mortality among them is frightful to contemplate, but we may well doubt if those who died were not more fortunate than those whose existence continued for a longer term of years. This wholesale deportation was then, and is now, considered excusable only as a frightful necessity of war. (86–87)

By associating Chinese rule with the return to nineteenth-century slave labor and the capitalist system, Vinton emphasizes the pathos of the American plight while identifying anti-Chinese resistance as an anticolonial and antislavery movement. In this fashion, Vinton's novel incorporates blackness metaphorically in a Chinese invasion plot that otherwise banishes black Americans from its imagined future.

Like Dooner, Vinton depicts the Chinese as a fifth-column enemy from within for, as West observes, the Chinese "invaders have made the main features of our Nationalistic theory serve the ends of their own government" (149). The novel reiterates—via Professor Won Lung Li's lectures and Colonel Bartlett Leete West's letters—scenes of white enslavement to convey the "full meaning of this Chinese invasion" and to reinforce the idea of racial otherness through the threat of physical violence (100). Boston awakens to the gravity of its situation when "armorers of the war vessels appeared and carts containing chains and shackles were driven up" to Boston Common, beginning a new era of American enslavement (101). The grand scheme of Chinese colonization paired American deportation with expanded Chinese immigration to the U.S. "to solidify the hold of China upon the country": "Every American deported was one less enemy to fight, while at the same time the place that he had filled was opened to a Chinese" (180). Thus, Vinton's novel makes the Chinese colonial resettlement of North America coterminous with the reestablishment of a long-defunct foreign slave trade aimed to depopulate the U.S. of its native white American citizenry. Chinese arrival presages a return to a feudal era of chattel slavery, but with a terrifying new twist in the specter of white deportation and slavery.

Such analogical constructions produced future imaginaries that erased the African American presence in the effort to contain the threat of racial multiplicity and black political power in the wake of radical Reconstruction. The idea that black chattel slavery—in the guise of Chinese coolieism—had yet to be fully expunged from the annals of the nation helped facilitate the discursive alignment of the anti-Chinese movement with antebellum abolitionism. Thus, the temporal architecture of Chinese invasion fiction was at once diachronic and regressive, resulting in plots that necessitated the erasure of blacks from the Asiatic future of the U.S. Dooner, for example, roughly yokes the arrival of the Chinese in the South to the sudden disappearance of black freedmen. "Throughout the Slave States," writes Dooner, "the presence of the Mongolian was the signal for the departure of the African; and of these latter, such as were not transferred to the land of their ancestors by emigration societies and private enterprise, were scattered about among the cities of the Union and fast striding toward extinction" (134). In this racialized imaginary of servile labor regimes, black freedmen and the archaic system of chattel slavery that they represent gradually disappear before the modern advance of Chinese coolieism.

The coming disaster of the Chinese invasion also facilitates the removal of black citizens from the national polity at large. "The Negro," continues Dooner, "faded before this invasion, and gradually, but rapidly and noiselessly disappeared—perished, it seemed, by the very fact of contact, and scattered, none knew whither, beyond the fact that many of them were transported back to the home of their ancestors. At this point it was estimated that out of the four millions of Blacks that were emancipated through the war of rebellion, less than half a million remained" (173–174). Just as Thomas Dixon Jr. once imagined the "negro" as a "vanishing quantity in our national life,"[105] Chinese invasion fiction such as "The Battle of the Wabash" manipulates demography to effect the disappearance of blacks from the U.S.: "Of blacks, in 1880, they had 4,327,341, which had gone down to 1,843,734 in 1900, and in 2000 to 320,453" (370). Thus, the "Mongolian question," according to the narrator, presents a "rather pure problem of race contests," with "the negro becoming in the clash of these Titans, nearly extinct" (365).

In these narratives, the imaginative expulsion of blacks from America precedes the devastating race war that leads to the Asiatic subjugation of the U.S. The system of chattel slavery had sought to make black men and women into things without a past, barring them from the technologies of literacy and public record. After the legislated end of slavery, representations of a "temporally arrested blackness," as Stephen Best writes, sought to heal the divisiveness of the Civil War by resituating black Americans in the regional past; blackness became increasingly incompatible with the idea of the economic future of free (white) labor.[106] Thus, Donnelly's *Caesar's Column* envisions a multitudinous future New York underworld composed of "all nations commingled," yet the comprehensive list that follows reveals the striking absence of black Americans: "the French, German, Irish, English—Hungarians, Italians, Russians, Jews, Christians, and even Chinese and Japanese; for the slant eyes of many, and their imperfect, Tartar-like features, reminded me that the laws made by the Republic, in the elder and better days, against the invasion of the Mongolians hordes, had long since become a dead letter."[107] Donnelly even imagines Anglo-European colonists repopulating the African continent emptied of its black inhabitants. In this fashion, Chinese invasion fiction reveals the deeply relational processes involved in the production of American racial meanings. It conjures the black slave as a figure for Old World hierarchy and feudal serfdom to be replaced by Chinese "coolies" or "blackened" European immigrants (as metaphors for white wage slavery). Identified with the past of slavery, black Americans had no place in the future capitalist world order depicted in these tales of Chinese invasion and race war.

Reconstruction-era fears of black political power heightened the emotional undercurrents structuring these fictions of the "coming struggle" between the U.S. and China. Their conspiratorial imaginations marshaled the threat of an "impending anarchy" that would engulf the nation if the Chinese, like black freedmen, were given "the privilege of the ballot-box, with seats in legislative assemblies," in the words of Starr's polemic (9). Dooner's *Last Days*, for example, envisions Chinese political organization as the first stage in military aggression against U.S. sovereignty. The Chinese successfully organize to challenge the racial dictates of U.S. naturalization law and "to procure for the Coolie the exercise of the elective franchise" (Dooner 100). According to assimilationist ideology, immigrants became Americans by participating in the political, economic, and social life of the U.S. Well aware of their population's numerical strength, these enfranchised Chinese exploit the representative nature of U.S. governance to "place the politics of California largely in the hands of the Chinese Mandarins" (100). Despite intimidation by white militias, including the Ku Klux Klan, the Chinese "availed themselves of their great numbers and the high privilege of American citizenship; and at the general election voted themselves into power" (175). In the South, racial antipathy explodes into armed conflict when white incumbents refuse to cede their positions to the newly elected Chinese, and the southern states rise up in rebellion under the banner of "State Sovereignty and white supremacy" (192). As the democratic expression of the "will of the majority," the election of Chinese officers forces the president to abide by the rule of law and declare the southern states in a state of rebellion against the Union. In considering the possibility that the Chinese might have the capacity for democratic rule, Dooner toys with an idea that he must eventually disavow. Chinese enfranchisement sets the stage for a catastrophic repetition crisis, plunging the nation into a second Civil War. The federal regiment dispatched to assist in subduing the southern rebellion, unable to bear the slaughter of its white countrymen, turns on the Chinese, realigning the conflict between state sovereignty and federal authority into a "war of races."

Dooner retailors the threat of "Negro domination" at the polls and casts Chinese political assimilation to the U.S. as a precursor to invasion and colonization, intensifying the calculus of Asiatic otherness in proportion to their imagined political participation in the nation. In the decades before *Plessy v. Ferguson*, Dooner had begun to explore a concept of racial citizenship that did not entail social assimilation to the nation. By imagining the Chinese as "Asiatic citizens," Dooner depicts Chinese inassimilability not as a consequence of denied political equality with white citizens, as Chinese activists such as Wong Chin Foo argued, but as a consequence of inherent racial difference or "Asiatic civilization" and "Chinese ideas in morals and government."[108] Despite the "exemplary conduct of the Asiatic citizens, in every sphere of industrial life," citizenship does not bind them to the U.S. nation-state, for their allegiance remains with the Chinese Empire (122). The extension of formal or political citizenship to Chinese immigrants does not alter the terms of Dooner's impending race war. In fact, exclusion politicians argued that Chinese labor involved the imposition of "Chinese conditions, social and political," on American life. Thus, the Chinese imperiled "America" itself, threatening to colonize the Christian nation from the inside out.[109] Invasion fictions such as Dooner's *Last Days* gave figurative shape to the continued racialization of citizenship after Reconstruction in its construction of the Chinese as immutably foreign even after political assimilation and to be preemptively ostracized on this basis.[110] In the invasion plot, the Chinese labor migrant appeared as an "internal enemy" who mimes the appearance of national loyalty while plotting to destroy it. Assimilation to U.S. political values in the exercise of citizenship rights and suffrage in a representative democracy does not alter the "essential" (or racialized) allegiance of Chinese immigrants to China.

The landmark U.S. Supreme Court case of *U.S. v. Wong Kim Ark* later marshaled, in a slightly revised form, this racialized trope of an "internal enemy" in its effort to denationalize U.S. citizens of Chinese descent. Born in 1873 to Chinese parents domiciled in San Francisco,

Wong embarked on a yearlong visit to China in 1894, presumably to visit his parents, who had returned to China in 1890. Prior to departure, he secured the requisite "certificate of identity," bearing his photograph and the signatures of three white witnesses attesting to his birth in California. However, when Wong attempted to land in San Francisco in 1895, immigration officials denied him permission to enter the country, claiming that his birth in the U.S. did not make him a citizen. Detained aboard the steamship, Wong petitioned for a writ of habeas corpus, and the U.S. District Court for the Northern District of California later released him from custody, basing its decision on Wong's birthright citizenship. However, the U.S. attorney appealed the case to the Supreme Court. The federal government, which prosecuted the case against Wong, alleged that his birth on U.S. soil did not make him a citizen, for his parents as "subjects of the Emperor of China" had remained under Chinese jurisdiction even while in the U.S.[111]

In the subsequent Supreme Court ruling, the majority opinion favored the common law interpretation of the doctrine of *jus soli*, or "right of soil," which held that all children born within U.S. territory were citizens with the exception of those born of foreign ambassadors or of alien enemies (although historical exceptions to this rule had been made for African Americans and Native Americans). In fact, the government analogized Wong's case to *Elk v. Wilkins* (1884), in which the Supreme Court ruled that Native Americans, even those who had assimilated to U.S. society, were not citizens under the Fourteenth Amendment because their native tribes (as quasi-foreign nations) remained outside full U.S. jurisdiction. Moreover, the racial logic the Court brought to bear against Wong was a formal feature of Chinese invasion fiction, which cast all Chinese in the U.S. as "alien enemies" or enemy subversives whose racial affinities to the Chinese Empire were severed by neither migration nor political assimilation. Formal citizenship does not alter Chinese racial inassimilability; they remain, in Lisa Lowe's words, as "foreigners-within" living among yet plotting against loyal white citizens.[112] This idea of Asiatic difference later helped justify Executive Order 9066, authorizing the evacuation and internment of roughly 120,000 persons of Japanese descent during World War II. In *Wong Kim Ark*, the 6–2 ruling upheld Wong's citizenship claim, yet it did not address the racialized logic that underwrote the case against him, which argued citizenship according to jus sanguinis ("right of blood"), to emphasize the radical alterity of Asiatic racial difference in the essentialized language of blood and descent.

In this fashion, Reconstruction-era debates over black citizenship and suffrage shaped the Chinese invasion plot and its structure of imaginative possibilities, for the "Chinafication of the U.S." entailed the threat of Chinese citizenship and suffrage in the nation. For example, "The Battle of the Wabash" imagines U.S. defeat as a direct consequence of Chinese enfranchisement, for the nomination of a Chinese presidential candidate espousing Mongolian "supremacy" and the disenfranchisement of white "Melicans" presages the bloody race war that concludes Lorelle's tale (373). Manson's *The Yellow Peril in Action* also marshaled the fear of Chinese citizenship, and it presented racial disenfranchisement as essential to the preservation of the democratic process.[113] In the cheaply printed tale, "Allied Asiatic Powers" defeat the "once powerful and rich United States," forcing the country into an armistice that provided, among other things, "that the Constitution and Laws of the United States should be so amended so as to extend to all aliens equal rights of citizenship" (20). This provision, according to the future narrator, "set the whole country ablaze—that Asiatic powers should dictate the terms upon which the right of citizenship should rest was too unbearable to consider for an instant" (20). To ensure the "purification of the ballot box" after the treaty, Congress "amended the Constitution of the United States, absolutely prohibiting foreign immigration from all countries for ten (10) years; and FOREVER DENYING TO ANY PERSON THE RIGHT OF FRANCHISE UNLESS BORN AND EDUCATED ON AMERICAN SOIL AND BENEATH THE FLAG" (24–25). The humiliation of defeat thus becomes the crucible from which white Americans emerged racially purified and prepared to remake the U.S. in the originalist image of "what the forefathers made it" (25). Such racial nativism continued to efface black citizenship and political participation in the guise of defending the U.S. from an Asiatic aggression that emanated from inside (as a threat to citizenship) and outside the nation (as a threat to Pacific commerce).

By projecting Reconstruction's "bottom rail on top" onto the "Chinese Question," invasion fictions channeled anxieties over the changing economic landscape and the expansion of black political power in

Figure 3.2. George Frederick Keller, "A Fresh Eruption of the Pacific Coast Vesuvius," *Wasp* 8 (January–June 1882) (Courtesy of the Bancroft Library, University of California–Berkeley)

the nation. A number of invasion narratives, including Dooner's *Last Days*, imagined this Yellow Peril threat of Chinese political power as a "slumbering volcano" threatening to engulf the nation (143). In a similar fashion, Vinton depicted unsuspecting America as "a people dwelling on the hillside of a volcano" (58). In the *Wasp*, Keller pictorially analogized Chinese immigration to an erupting Vesuvius (in the conical shape of a Chinese hat), raining down destruction on the Pacific Coast (see figure 3.2). The oft-repeated image of Chinese immigrants as a "slumbering volcano" harks back to the use of this complex metaphor by a range of earlier black and white writers, including Frederick Douglass, William Lloyd Garrison, and Herman Melville, to warn the U.S. of the dangers of incipient black slave revolt.[114] The novelist Sutton Griggs later recast Dooner's trope of the racialized "internal enemy" in the elaborate black conspiracy plots of *Imperium in Imperio* (1899) and the *Hindered Hand* (1905). Written in the wake of the Spanish-American War, Griggs's *Imperium* envisions a secret, underground black shadow government working in concert with unnamed "foreign allies" and cultivating the "foreign enemies of the United States," while *Hindered Hand* features a similar conspiracy of "mixed bloods" passing into the white world to "lay hold of every center of power that could be reached" in the interests of the "Negro race."[115] These radical visions hark even further back to Martin Delany's serialized *Blake; or, The Huts of America* (1859–1862) and its conspiratorial imagination of an incipient hemispheric black revolt joining together southern slaves and anticolonial black Cuban revolutionaries. Dooner's *Last Days* first wedded the trope of the Asiatic "internal enemy" to the threat of black political mobilization, and it helped establish a popular subgenre that found critical reelaboration in a variety of later fictions and specifically in the stories that James Corrothers and Vachel Lindsay published in W. E. B. Du Bois's *Crisis* magazine, studied in the following section.

Counternarratives of Chinese Invasion

"The possibility of race adventure has not passed away," wrote Jack London in response to the rising "menace" that Asia represented to the West and specifically to the U.S. "Why may not the yellow and the brown start out on an adventure as tremendous as our own and more strikingly unique?" he inquired.[116] The "great race adventure" is London's euphemism for the course of Western empire and colonization—a violent history, as he admits, mitigated only by the "colossal fact" that the Anglo-Saxon, unlike the "yellow and brown," is a "preeminently religious race, which is another way of saying . . . a right-seeking race."[117] In his infamous "Yellow Peril" essay, London acknowledges the radical possibility of an alternate, Asiatic course of imperial conquest (for "brown" refers to the Japanese), yet he quickly proceeds to disavow it, citing among other things that the "Western world will not admit the rise of the yellow peril."[118] The trope of Asiatic invasion often provoked responses that took the form of disavowal, expressing an attitude or perspective toward the future of American modernity that acknowledged the very thing that it sought to deny.[119] Writing from Manchuria during the Russo-Japanese War (1904–1905), London continues to insist, perhaps a bit too strenuously, "The ultimate success of such an adventure the western mind refuses to consider."[120] However, the continued popularity of Chinese invasion fiction and its vision of a catastrophic American future well after the indefinite extension of Chinese exclusion (1904) appeared to indicate otherwise. The Chinese invasion plots studied in the preceding pages elaborated complex anxieties and fears about the potential for the Asiatic conquest and colonization of the U.S. that subsequently required management and control. Thus, London's protestations to the contrary, the "western mind" appeared excessively preoccupied with imagining the "Chinafication of the United States," the menacing future condition that London's essay introduces in order to deny.

Motivated by a different set of aims, later American writers began pushing the counterfactual imagination of future Chinese invasion to its limit, plying the disruptive potential of an Asiatic threat in their various efforts to challenge the meaning of whiteness and existing racial power hierarchies. In diverging from both the racial logics and political aims of the anti-Chinese movement, James Corrothers and Vachel Lindsay seized on the Chinese invasion narrative's counterfactual form to craft fictions that challenged and critiqued the structure and ideology of white supremacy in a world reshaped by Jim Crow. On the eve of World War I, Corrothers, a former Chicago newspaperman turned Methodist minister, serialized his two-part short story "A Man They Didn't Know" in the December 1913 and January 1914 issues of Du Bois's *Crisis* magazine.[121] Discussed at more length in the conclusion, Corrothers's adaptation of Chinese invasion explores black identifications and interests inimical to the imperial mission of the U.S. nation-state. It resists the idea of black Americans as willing agents of white Western civilization and empire.[122] Set in an unspecified future, the story depicts revolutionary struggles erupting across the Texas-Mexico borderlands and the Pacific Islands, as it remapped the hemispheric and transpacific political economic structures entailed in U.S. expansion.[123] Corrothers envisions a future in which the subjects of domestic racism join forces with the subjects of U.S. imperial foreign policy.[124] "Negro soldiers" unite with anticolonial Mexican revolutionaries and dissident Nisei and Chinese Americans in a transnational alliance against U.S. white supremacy and colonial incursions. Unlike earlier Chinese invasion fictions, "A Man They Didn't Know" identifies the racist structures of U.S. foreign and domestic policies as the provocation for Asiatic invasion, and the invasion plot allows Corrothers to counterfactually imagine the radical possibility of black political progress in the era of legal segregation. The *Crisis* followed the serialization of Corrothers's story with the poet Vachel Lindsay's lesser-known adaptation of Chinese invasion fiction, "The Golden-Faced People: A Story of the Chinese Conquest of America" (1914).[125] Both Corrothers and Lindsay hailed from the sparsely settled "old Northwest," and they self-identified as "western" writers.[126]

This final section explores Lindsay's likeminded adaptation of the Chinese invasion narrative into a self-professed "study" of the "Negro Problem" and Progressive-era race relations. Like Corrothers, Lindsay experimented with counterfactualism and its potential, in Nancy Bentley's words, to "reopen received histories" and produce alternate narratives of the past.[127] Lindsay found himself energized by reading Harriet Beecher Stowe's *Uncle Tom's Cabin* and Du Bois's *Souls of Black Folk*, and he crafted the story in response to the brutal 1911 Coatesville, Pennsylvania, lynching of the black steelworker Zachariah Walker, who was accused of killing a white policeman.[128] In composing "The Golden-Faced People," Lindsay recalls the long list of literary and historical materials that he reworked into the narrative structure and plot of this Chinese invasion tale. "Then I had in my list some of the things 'Uncle Tom's Cabin' meant, and the emancipation proclamation," he writes. "I had in mind the affairs of Coatesville, Pa., and the other burnings alive of Negroes, some of them guilty Negroes, many of them innocent. I put in my list the songs of Stephen Collins Foster. I put in the list my memories of 'The Souls of Black Folk,' that beautiful tragic book by the black leader W. E. B. Du Bois."[129] Witnessing the brutal 1908 Springfield anti-Negro riots had sensitized the young Lindsay to the history of U.S. race relations. "Those riots," he wrote, "shook my young soul then as much as the war in Europe has done. It was my first revelation of the savagery of white men."[130] In "The Golden-Faced People," Lindsay brought an exploration of white supremacy and black-white race relations to bear on the overlapping yet divergent histories of another proscribed race. As critics note, Lindsay's interest in China and the Chinese often found expression in his poetry and prose, although he declined numerous invitations to visit China, where his sister Olive Wakefield and her husband settled as Christian missionaries. In 1914, Lindsay published "The Golden-Faced People" and composed what he considered his most successful poem, "The Chinese Nightingale," which utilized Orientalized tropes also found in the short story.[131] Lindsay observed that these Chinese writings garnered especial praise among African American readers who had previously found fault with his other self-identified "Study of the Negro Race." In a 1916 letter to NAACP chairman Joel Spingarn, Lindsay lamented that his earlier poems, namely, "Congo" and "Booker T. Washington Trilogy," had "been denounced by the Colored people," although they had "published with great approval [his] story of the Golden-Faced People."[132]

While living in New York, Lindsay reportedly entered a Chinese laundry in a fruitless attempt to interest the Chinese man working there in the dream poetry that he was composing, and this curious incident may have provided imaginative fodder for his later writings on Chinese topics.[133] Partaking of a grotesque minstrel humor, Lindsay's tale begins as a racial comedy in which the unnamed white narrator, in rushing to retrieve his week's washings to dress for "Lincoln's birthday banquet," comes to blows with his Chinese laundryman—a variation on Chang, the Chinese laundryman of "A Chinese Nightingale"—who aspired, in the narrative's words, "to be something more than a coolie" (36). A scuffle ensues when the irate laundryman refuses to hand over the laundry without the narrator's half of the "red ticket." After sustaining a particularly heavy blow to the head, Lindsay's narrator, in a playful reference to Mark Twain's *A Connecticut Yankee in King Arthur's Court* (1889), realizes that he has been "knocked . . . into the next millennium" (37). Lindsay's narrator reawakens in a future world, in which the Chinese reigned supreme over the "white man" (37). The narrator realizes that the blow had also "knocked the Chinese language into . . . [his] head," along with the idea "that a Chinaman is so infinitely superior to a white man [that] there is no comparison" (37). Now endowed with an august majesty, the Chinese laundryman presides over the one hundredth anniversary of Lin-Kon, the "emancipator of the white man" and Chinese avatar of Abraham Lincoln, born exactly one millennium later "on the hardy plains of central China where the people have a rough sort of equality, being all one race" (37). Growing up in central Illinois just blocks from the Abraham Lincoln Home, Lindsay had felt deeply the influence of Lincoln, which found expression in many of his works, including "Abraham Lincoln Walks at Midnight" in the antiwar section of *The Congo and Other Poems* and in the Chinese invasion plot of "The Golden-Faced People."[134]

Lindsay's retailoring of Chinese invasion fiction shares Corrothers's critique of white supremacy, yet it does so through a white narrator whose self-consciousness suffers the painful "twoness" or dividing experience of what Du Bois described as "double-consciousness." In addressing the psychic life of racial segregation, Du Bois proposed the theory of double consciousness: the "peculiar sensation . . . of always looking at one's self through the eyes of others, of measuring one's soul by the tape of a world that looks on in amused contempt and pity."[135] In this alternate racial-social order, the Chinese have subjugated and rendered servile white America. Suddenly in possession of a manuscript containing a history of the "Chinese conquest of America," Lindsay's terrified narrator finds himself escorted before an audience composed of Eurasian "half-breeds," "half yellow, half white," who express open contempt for the "pure and pale" Anglo-Saxons seated among them in an empty show of racial egalitarianism (39, 37). As in *A Short and Truthful History*, the Chinese embrace of Western knowledge, particularly scientific knowledge in this tale, had impelled the once-antiquated Chinese Empire rapidly forward into modernity. In consequence, the political and social strength of the Chinese in the U.S. gradually increased until it "became an ingenuous tyranny," leading to the enslavement of all white Americans (Lindsay 38).

In the fashion of Vinton's *Looking Further Backward*, Lindsay draws on the iconography of black chattel slavery and projects it onto a vision of a "Chinafied" U.S. in the next millennium. Appalled by the horrors of the new American slave trade, Lin-Kon led the "celestial abolitionists," who were "resolved to make them [Americans] equal with themselves or destroy the reigning dynasty in the attempt" (39). They eventually "secured," in the narrator's words, "through bloody revolution an equal place for us before the Law" (39). Lindsay then proceeds to transpose a critique of black-white racial equality into his fictional world. He depicts his white protagonist advocating a programmatic racial amelioration reminiscent of Booker T. Washington: "There are no fatherly Chinese reformers watching over us. Lin-Kon is fifty years dead, and the Abolitionists are under the sod, and all that generation. We must not ask for social equality, nor to have the color-line rubbed out. Our highest dream must be, by patience and dignity, by more care for ethics and ceremony, by a sweeter Christianity to attain to a sort of *spiritual rank* with the conservative, everlasting race that still dominates" (39). The narrator's advocacy of self-help and accommodation as the "watchword of reconstruction" between the races elicits the admiration of his former laundryman, now a dignified official (40).

Lindsay's story explores the psychic dimensions of racial hegemony in an alternate future world structured according to a racial hierarchy that inverts and defamiliarizes the black-white color line. Lindsay's apocalyptic racial fantasy drew its animating logic from *Plessy v. Ferguson* (1896), which upheld the constitutionality of de jure racial segregation in public accommodations under the doctrine of "separate but equal." In the 7–1 majority opinion, Justice Henry Billings Brown dismissed the idea that segregation constituted a "badge of inferiority," speculating, "if . . . the colored race should become the dominant power in the state legislature, and should enact a law . . . relegat[ing] the white race to an inferior position, . . . we imagine that the white race, at least, would not acquiesce in this assumption."[136] In this turn to the "imagination," Brown invoked the counterfactual to test the consistency of the law's equity under a different set of historical conditions, namely, the inverted racial order once prefigured in Reconstruction's "bottom rail on top." Yet the conclusion that he draws—the constancy of white supremacy—exists in a formal vacuum removed from the historical circumstance that it purportedly seeks to explore.[137] In yoking *Plessy* to the Chinese invasion narrative, Lindsay amplified the destabilizing potential of Brown's racial counterfactual to investigate the "stigmatization" of racialized citizenship. By identifying whiteness rather than blackness with slavery's inherited racial caste status, Lindsay asks readers to imagine how altered relations of racial power produce alternate historical paths. In this alternate future, the narrator is filled with a despairing sense of his "white and ghastly skin," and the racially superior Chinese laundryman's efforts to publicly recognize the narrator as a social equal sends him into a panic, as they transgress the racial rule of segregation holding white and Chinese apart (40). "I was the cynosure of a thousand reproving and astonished glances," confesses the anguished narrator (41). The fantasy turns violent when the narrator, overcome with terror, accidentally strikes the laundryman in his panicked efforts to flee, calling forth the violent wrath of a Chinese mob on the whites.

Unlike the escapist Oriental fantasy of "The Chinese Nightingale," the vision of the future in "The Golden-Faced People" purposively returns the reader to the historical violence of black chattel slavery, its racial ideologies, and its legacy in Jim Crow. On the point of death at the hands of the Chinese, the narrator awakens from his terrifying dream to rediscover "the white still supreme" (41). An angry white mob lynched four men while the narrator was unconsciousness. The body of the Chinese laundryman dangled alongside the bodies of a Japanese, a Greek, and "a nigger," hung, according to one southerner, simply because the mob "did not want to burn him alive on Lincoln's birthday" (41–42). Indeed, the Lincoln festivities proceed calmly, and the southerner ends the evening with a speech on Lincoln that "did not touch on the race question or the question of equality at all" (42). The conclusion of "The Golden-Faced People" channels in a more qualified fashion the elegiac sentiments expressed in the final stanza of "Abraham Lincoln Walks at Midnight," which reads, "It breaks his heart that things must murder still, / That all his hours of travail here for men / Seem yet in vain. And who will bring white peace / That he may sleep upon his hill again?"[138] In emphasizing the need for the living to complete the work of the dead—to bring "white peace" to the world, Lindsay's poem pays homage to both the spirit and tropes of Lincoln's famous "Gettysburg Address" (1863), in which he enjoined, "It is for us, the living, rather, to be dedicated here to the unfinished work which they who fought here have thus far so nobly advanced."[139] In the short story, however, the graphic extralegal violence of Anglo-Saxon nativism depicted in the four lynched men frames the story's commemoration of Lincoln. It offers a far more cynical reflection on his thwarted legacy as the "Great Emancipator" in the early decades of the twentieth century. It too limns the extent to which triumphalist narratives of antebellum abolitionism diverged from later struggles against slavery's racial legacies in Jim Crow America. "How far this Republic has departed from its high ideals and reversed its traditionary policy," condemned the Chinese American writer Yan Phou Lee, "may be seen in the laws passed against the Chinese."[140] By ending "The Golden-Faced People" with the lynching of the Chinese, Japanese, Greek, and African American men, Lindsay renarrativizes the occultation of blackness from earlier Chinese invasion to reveal the articulation of antiblack violence with nativist attacks on foreign immigrants.

By projecting contemporary anxieties onto a specifically contrived future and an equally invented past, the Chinese invasion narrative both limited and expanded readers' sense of the possible while intensifying the incoherence at the heart of U.S. fictions of race and nation.[141] This chapter ends by way of two recastings of the subgenre that turned "Yellow Peril" on its head, revealing its buried racial histories and ideological forms. Motivated by different aims, Corrothers and Lindsay pushed the counterfactual imaginary of Chinese invasion to its limit, plying the disruptive potential of an Asiatic threat in their literary efforts to challenge the meaning of whiteness and existing racial hierarchies. In an analogous manner, Jing Tsu notes that Chinese invasion fiction also circulated in China through adaptive translations that re-created Yellow Peril according to a vision of a strong China, offering Chinese readers a self-affirming and empowering "prospect of regeneration and resilience" in the face of Western incursion.[142] This chapter suggests how the counterfactual imaginaries of Chinese invasion fiction mined the histories of U.S. settler colonialism, slavery, and Reconstruction for its persuasive tropes and arguments even as its narrative forms and temporal schemas began to find their way into the legal debates over immigration and citizenship in the age of Jim Crow. At the end of the century, the rise of monopoly capitalism had begun to restructure U.S. relationships to China and the Chinese, and Chinese invasion fiction gave narrative expression to these new forms of American historical consciousness in ways that complemented and departed from the aesthetics of Progressive-era realism and naturalism. Galvanized by a sense that the literary might provoke action in the present, these fictions cast the Chinese labor migrant as an ambivalent representation of the possibilities and perils of national progress and modernization. In this fashion, Chinese invasion narratives experimented with temporal mutability and extrapolation—hallmarks of science fiction—and with forms of historical knowledge and interpretation, giving unexpected wry new meaning to the British novelist L. P. Hartley's oft-cited line, "The past is a foreign country: they do things differently there."[143]

4

Boycotting Exclusion

The Transpacific Politics of Chinese Sentimentalism

At the end of the nineteenth century, U.S. relations with China underwent a shift as the need for overseas consumers began to replace earlier demands for Chinese "cheap" labor. U.S. foreign policy refocused on the "great China market," imagining the country's vast population as a solution to surplus overproduction and the periodic recessions that beleaguered the post–Civil War economy.[1] During the Progressive era, Chinese exclusion became a key aspect of U.S. overseas empire. Colonial expansion into the Asia Pacific extended the geographical compass of Chinese exclusion from the U.S. mainland to the newly acquired territories of Hawai'i and the Philippines, exacerbating national tensions over the "much vexed Chinese question" and endangering the country's commercial ambitions in China. The extension of Chinese exclusion into the Asia Pacific further defined assimilable European immigrants and American citizens against the Asiatic aliens plaguing the U.S. and its Pacific territories.[2] It also laid bare the contradiction between an "insular policy of benevolent assimilation" abroad and a domestic policy of excluding "undesirable" Asiatic immigrants from the U.S., as the legal historian Mae M. Ngai notes.[3] In 1904, Congress extended Chinese exclusion in perpetuity (in both the U.S. and its territories), as it permanently supplanted the expansive notions of membership in the U.S. polity once made possible by the 1868 Burlingame Treaty.

These measures did not go unchallenged. In the U.S. and abroad, Chinese protests erupted into a wide-scale global boycott of U.S. goods. Although short-lived, the 1905 boycott remains one of the largest antiforeign movements to take place in China after the Boxer Uprising and before the May Fourth Movement of 1919. As discussed in chapter 3, Chinese immigrants also turned to the courts to challenge these new laws until the U.S. Supreme Court ruling in *United States v. Ju Toy* (1905) effectively ended the judicial review of Immigration Bureau admission decisions, granting immigration officials final authority over all Chinese immigration cases. This chapter explores Chinese exclusion and the transpacific protests that it catalyzed as underexamined facets of Progressive-era immigration control and its increasing regulation of Chinese immigrant home life. These protests found expression in a range of analogous cultural forms spanning the English-Chinese language divide, from the Chinese translator Lin Shu's 1901 adaptation of Harriet Beecher Stowe's antislavery masterpiece *Uncle Tom's Cabin* and the Chinese boycott novel *The Bitter Society* (1905) in partial English translation (by June Mei and Jean Pang Yip) to the self-identified Chinese American Edith Maude Eaton's English-language writings on the North American Chinese. These writings, products of their specific locations and imagined audiences, exhibit a variety of agendas—sometimes contradictory to each other—yet together they begin to delineate something that might be called a transpacific politics of sentimentalism.

The wide dissemination of Yellow Peril and its depictions of Chinese immigrants as labor-saving machines incapable of feeling, domestic attachments, and home life helped center sentiment as a politicized idiom in these transpacific literary struggles. For Lin, Stowe's vision of black chattel slavery became a touchstone for a sentimentalized politics of Chinese nationalism against Western power, which took specific literary form in what became known as the boycott novel. Like Eaton's Chinatown stories, the boycott novel drew its plot structures, tropes, and characters from the legal text of Chinese exclusion. The tragic representations of Chinese subjection to U.S. power were calculated to spur a sense of profound national injury and to galvanize readers toward passionate collective identification based on a shared racial pain. As Jing Tsu argues, these sentimentalized narratives of racial victimization enabled the articulation of a regenerative Chinese cultural identity in the face of Western colonial hegemony.[4] This chapter concludes by resituating Eaton's familiar Chinatown stories in this broader transpacific framework to reveal understudied aspects of her literary politics and experimentation with sentimentalism in the era of its waning popularity in the U.S. By reinventing sentimentalism's imaginative orientation toward human connection and its persuasive strategies of sympathetic identification and of making political problems legible by their effects on the household, these analogous—yet divergent—literary formations contested the racial epistemologies and political paradigms of U.S. power in the Asia Pacific.[5]

The Case of Ju Toy and U.S. Immigration Administration

In forging Chinese exclusion, legislators had sought to placate labor agitators who saw Chinese labor as a threat to "free white labor" without damaging U.S.-China foreign relations in light of the growing significance of the China market to American industry. Such a balancing act led to restriction laws that offset racial exclusion by class. Common laborers were prohibited, while the "superior classes" of merchants remained exempt from exclusion. Chinese exclusion case law later established that the wives and children of merchants were also exempt, as it followed the classical wage doctrine defining men as breadwinners and wives as dependents.[6] Proexclusion agitators later cited the merchant exception as evidence of the judiciousness of Chinese exclusion. It was an immigration policy attuned to public good rather than racial animus, they reasoned, even if it controverted the idea of America as a classless society.[7] "It has never been the purpose of the Government to exclude persons of the Chinese race merely because they are Chinese, regardless of the class to which they belong," insisted Jewish American Oscar Straus, the new secretary of the Department of Commerce and Labor.[8] However, Immigration Bureau inspectors often disregarded distinctions of rank as they reestablished the racial category of the banned Asiatic in practice. The Immigration Bureau enforced a narrow interpretation of the new U.S.-China Treaty, which limited the skilled occupations qualifying for exemption, effectively expanding the prohibited class of so-called dangerous Chinese laborers. As Ng Poon Chew, editor of the influential San Francisco–based Chinese-language newspaper *China West Daily* (*Chung Sai Yat Po*) noted, "Chinese traders, salesmen, clerks, buyers, bookkeepers, bankers, accountants, managers, storekeepers, agents, cashiers, interpreters, physicians, proprietors of restaurants and laundries, employers, actors, newspaper editors, and even preachers and missionaries of Christianity" had undergone redefinition as prohibited laborers after admission into the U.S., making them illegal aliens and subject to deportation according to exclusion laws.[9] Contrary to

Immigration Bureau proclamations, Chinese racial difference continued to serve as the fundamental baseline for exclusion.

In 1888, the anti-Chinese *San Francisco Evening Bulletin* offered a "brief history of the operation of the [Chinese Exclusion] Acts of 1882 and 1884," opining that the "future historian will find one of the most interesting chapters on the jurisprudence of the American Republic to consist in a description and analysis of the writ of habeas corpus as applied to landing Chinamen in violation . . . of the Restriction Acts in the United States Courts of California."[10] In numerous legal test cases, Chinese in the U.S. took to the courts to challenge the new Immigration Bureau and its abusive administration of the federal exclusion laws.[11] Over a twenty-five-year span, Chinese petitioners such as Chae Chan Ping (studied in the preceding chapter) deluged the U.S. District Court for the Northern District of California with habeas corpus suits challenging the admission and deportation decisions of San Francisco immigration inspectors. A satirical illustration by the *Wasp* illustrator Solly Walter, titled "There's Millions in It" (1888), lampoons Judge Lorenzo Sawyer of the San Francisco–based U.S. circuit court for abetting in the Chinese inundation of the West (see figure 4.1). In 1905, the landmark Supreme Court ruling in *United States v. Ju Toy* ended the judicial review of Immigration Bureau decisions. It revoked the precedent set in an earlier case, *In re Jung Ah Lung*, which ruled in favor of the immigrant, holding that a Chinese person claiming U.S. residency should be entitled to habeas corpus and due process in presenting relevant evidence in court, regardless of the Exclusion Act.[12] In 1888, the Supreme Court upheld this ruling on appeal; however, subsequent rulings in Chinese immigration cases marked the gradual retreat of federal courts from judicial review of Immigration Bureau decisions, culminating in the infamous *U.S. v. Ju Toy*, decided just days before news of the Chinese boycott of U.S. goods broke newspaper headlines.[13]

In 1903, a twenty-seven-year-old Chinese American named Ju Toy embarked on his first visit to China. Before departure, Ju Toy took the precaution of securing a notarized affidavit with photograph verifying that he was "a native born" American citizen (see figure 4.2). In China, Ju Toy married and, after an eleven-month sojourn, returned to San Francisco. He remained on board the transpacific steamer *Doric* while he waited for the Immigration Bureau to process his application

Figure 4.1. Solly H. Walter, "There's Millions in It," *Wasp* 21 (July–December 1888) (Courtesy of the Bancroft Library, University of California–Berkeley)

to land. He presented his affidavit as evidence of his right to admission, but he had no residence certificate, as required by the 1892 Geary Act. Three days later, Ju Toy—identified as ticket number 36—underwent a lengthy interrogation with Immigration Inspector John Dunn. Thus began the legal saga that was to end before the Supreme Court and with the deportation of Ju Toy in November 1906.[14]

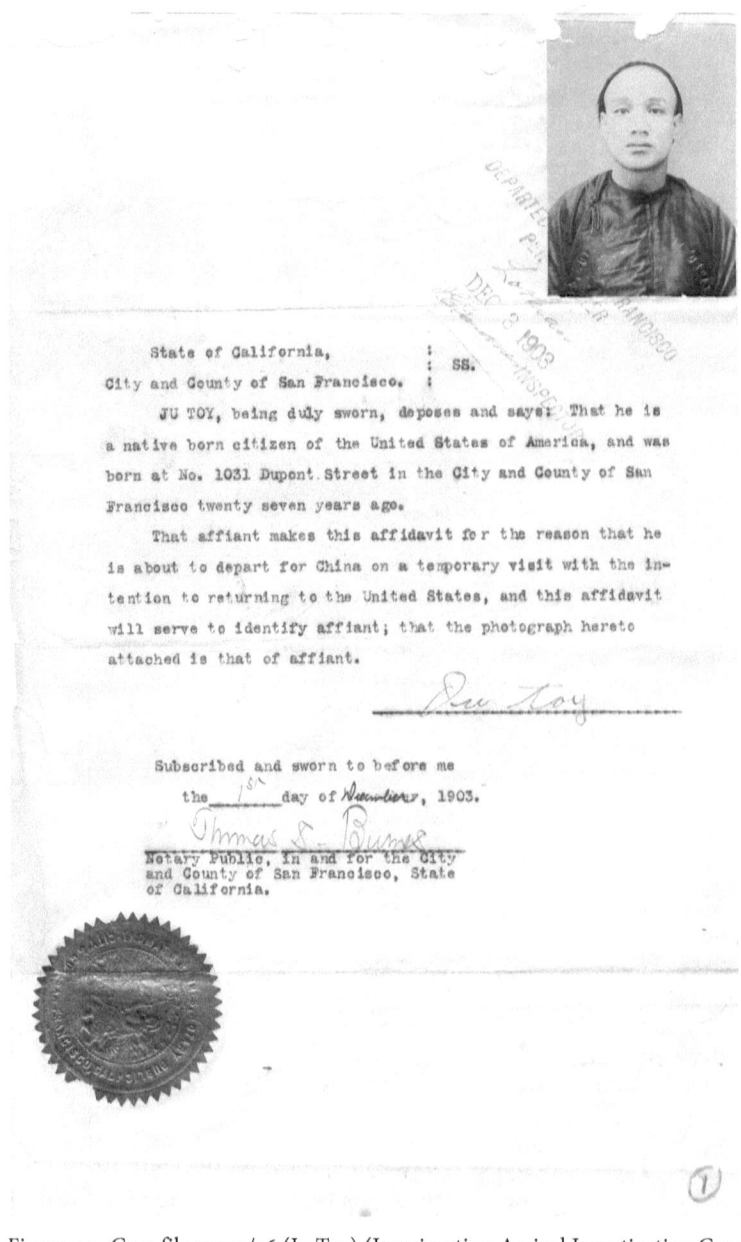

Figure 4.2. Case file 10025/36 (Ju Toy) (Immigration Arrival Investigation Case Files, 1884–1944, Records of the San Francisco District Office of the Immigration and Naturalization Service, Record Group 85; courtesy of the National Archives at San Francisco)

When questioned about the missing residence certificate, Ju Toy explained, "Some of my friends told me I did not need to register because I was born here." The Chinese Exclusion Acts generally applied to Chinese aliens—not to natural-born citizens such as Ju Toy. In the subsequent interrogation, Dunn challenged this claim of birthright citizenship, largely basing his suspicions on Ju Toy's account of home life. Fluent in English, Ju Toy had no need for a translator. Born in the U.S., Ju Toy was an only child. His father had been a salesman and solicitor with a now-defunct general-merchandise firm in San Francisco. He had fallen ill, and clansmen urged him to return temporarily to China with his wife to recover his health. Both parents died in China while Ju Toy remained in the U.S., leaving him in the permanent care of a business partner named Ju Sing Foon, the firm's bookkeeper who had since returned to China. The typewritten transcript of the interrogation reads,

Q: How old were you when your father and mother went to China?
A: Five years old.
Q: Do you mean to say that both your father and mother went away and left you alone when you were a child of five years of age?
A: Yes, they left me in the care of Ju Sing Foon.
Q: Is Ju Sing Foon living or dead?
A: He returned to China in KS 14 [1888].
Q: What part of the year?
A: Beginning of that year, I don't know what month.
Q: Do you know what vessel he went on?
A: I don't know the name of the steamer.
Q: Was this man married?
A: I don't know. He was not married in this country.
Q: Then you had no woman to look after you when you were a little child of five years old?
A: No.

Dunn posed similar questions to the two Chinese men, Ju Sing and Ju Fung, named in Ju Toy's interrogation.

The first witness, Ju Sing, had been an acquaintance of Ju Toy's father. Speaking through the Chinese translator, Ju Sing confirmed Ju Toy's birth in the U.S.; it had taken place shortly after Ju Sing's arrival to the

U.S. in 1877. He had attended the traditional shaving feast celebration one month after Ju Toy's birth.[15] In examining Ju Sing, Dunn again expressed open disbelief and incredulity when he received answers corroborating Ju Toy's account of home life:

> Q: How old was the applicant when his parents went to China?
> A: Four or five years old.
> Q: Do you mean to say that the father and mother of the applicant went to China and left in this country their child of four or five years old?
> A: Yes. Applicant's father was sick himself, and a clansman advised him to go to China.
> Q: Whom did they leave the applicant in the care of?
> A: Ju Sing Foon.
> Q: Did no woman take care of him at all?
> A: No. Sometimes the wives of some of his clansmen looked after him a little, but he was left in charge of Ju Sing Foon at the store.
> Q: Did any of the partners of this store have families here at that time?
> A: Ju Haw Dip is the only one that had a family here.[16]

Both Chinese witnesses signed an affidavit affirming Ju Toy's birthright citizenship, "for the purpose of assisting . . . Ju Toy in establishing his nativity and to facilitate his landing."[17]

Dunn remained unconvinced. In a letter to his superior, John Endicott Gardner Jr., he denied Ju Toy's application, citing among other things a minor discrepancy over Ju Toy's address (1031, as opposed to 1301, Dupont Street, as reported by Ju Sing).[18] However, it was Ju Toy's failure to give an account of himself that conformed to Dunn's idea of normative domesticity and mother love that provided the rationale for rejection. "It does not seem reasonable, however, to credit his story," wrote Dunn, "as it would be hard to find a mother, Chinese or otherwise, who would have so little humanity as to go away and leave for good her mere babe of a few years, not even entrusting the care of the child to some woman."[19] Dunn refuses to accept the alternate domestic arrangements presented in Ju Toy's case and, further, in a tautological gesture, expresses moral indignation at the idea of a mother unwilling to find a female surrogate when immigration law largely banned the entry of Chinese women into the country, with the exception of the dependent wives of merchants.[20] Of all the partners associated with the firm, only one man, according to Ju Sing's testimony, had managed to establish a household in the U.S. Indeed, both witnesses for Ju Toy were unmarried men. Thus, the applicant in failing to conform to a normative home life, in the words of Dunn, "has failed to prove beyond a reasonable doubt that he is a native of the United States," as he inverted the language of the due process clauses of the Fifth and Fourteenth Amendments, which established the presumption of innocence and the burden of proof as cardinal principles of U.S. criminal justice.[21] After the Geary Act, immigration procedures assumed all Chinese to be illegal aliens until the right to enter the U.S. was proven "beyond a reasonable doubt."

Inspectors moved Ju Toy into the detention shed at the Pacific Mail Dock, where he remained a "U.S. prisoner" while he awaited the results of an appeal to the secretary of the Department of Commerce and Labor, who oversaw the Immigration Bureau.[22] In early December, Assistant Secretary Lawrence Murray upheld Inspector Dunn's decision in the case, maintaining that Ju Toy's "birth in this country has not been satisfactorily established."[23] Ju Toy faced immediate deportation. His advocates went into action and secured a writ of habeas corpus releasing him from custody pending trial of his case. In 1905, the case came before the U.S. district court, which affirmed Ju Toy's claim of birthright citizenship and released him from detention.[24] However, Ju Toy's case was not yet resolved. The assistant attorney general of the United States urged Marshall Woodworth, the U.S. attorney in San Francisco, to bring Ju Toy before the U.S. Supreme Court as a test case for recent amendments to the Chinese Exclusion Act.[25]

While Ju Toy was abroad, China withdrew from the Gresham-Yang Treaty pending the renegotiation of its terms, at the insistence of the Chinese foreign minister, who cited, among other wrongs, the Immigration Bureau's overzealous administration of existing exclusion laws.[26] Congress took advantage of this lapse in the treaty to pass new anti-Chinese legislation, extending the Chinese Exclusion Act in 1904 with no time limit and maintaining this policy in the new territories. In an effort to close off the courts to Chinese, legislators also placed alleged birthright citizens of Chinese descent, such as Ju Toy, under the control of immigration officials, "specifying that the agency had the power to decide their right to enter."[27] It was this last provision that came under direct contestation in the case of Ju Toy.

As in *U.S. v. Wong Kim Ark* (1898), the federal government prosecuted the case against Ju Toy.[28] In writing for the majority, Justice Oliver Wendell Holmes evaded Ju Toy's citizenship status in a ruling that sought to make this case consistent with legal principles established in earlier Chinese exclusion cases that dealt specifically with alien *noncitizens* seeking admission into the U.S. The legal scholar Neil Gotanda has shown how the juridical categories of included citizen and excluded alien derived their meaning from the racialized social distinction between "American" and "foreign."[29] Based on nonwhite racial status, this ideological presumption of "foreignness" influenced judicial outcomes in the nineteenth and twentieth centuries, particularly in immigration cases involving petitioners from various Asian national backgrounds. In *Ju Toy*, Holmes strategically blurred the distinctions between citizen and alien to uphold what Gotanda refers to as the "racial association of Other non-Whites with foreignness."[30] He affirmed the enduring association of Chinese racial identity with perpetual foreignness.

In the effort to make past Chinese exclusion case law consistent with the ruling in *Ju Toy*, Holmes asks his fellow jurists to reimagine the actual conditions of the case at hand. He hypothetically casts Ju Toy outside the geopolitical bounds of the nation-state in which he was born, ignoring the lower court's ruling. By turning to the counterfactual, Holmes reformulates as speculation the fact of Ju Toy's citizenship and his right to constitutional protections, including habeas corpus and due process under the Fifth Amendment: "If, for the purpose of argument, we assume that the Fifth Amendment applies to him and that to deny entrance to a citizen is to deprive him of liberty, we nevertheless are of the opinion that with regard to him due process of law does not require a judicial trial."[31] The ruling reveals the extent to which U.S. citizenship and the rights that it conferred were made intelligible through exclusionary racial categorizations.[32] Holmes turns to the imagination to remake a birthright citizen into an illegal alien. In this fashion, *Ju Toy* serves as a restrictive corollary to the doctrine of *jus soli*, or birthright citizenship, established in *U.S. v. Wong Kim Ark* (studied in chapter 3). This judicial act of counterfactual deterritorialization also establishes the white/nonwhite color line, in Nikhil Pal Singh's words, as "an internal border," revealing the legal liminality of U.S. citizens of Chinese descent.[33]

The contested 6–3 ruling in *U.S. v. Ju Toy* marked a fundamental shift in the federal interpretation and application of constitutional law in relation to all immigrants to the U.S. Before *Ju Toy*, immigrants had regularly secured writs of habeas corpus for judicial review of executive-agency decisions affecting their claims to U.S. residency and citizenship. The legal historians Lucy Salyer and Charles McClain Jr. have extensively documented how Chinese immigrants successfully fought the enforcement of the Exclusion Acts through writs of habeas corpus and used the courts to challenge the authority of the Immigration Bureau. By limiting the jurisdiction of federal courts over immigration cases, the Supreme Court made the decisions of field agents final. In a vigorous dissent from the majority, Justice David Brewer (with Justices Rufus Peckham and William Day concurring) found the ruling to be "appalling," for it vested a low-ranking immigration official such as Inspector Dunn with the authority to impose on a "a free-born American citizen" who is "guilty of no crime" "a punishment . . . of the severest sort": banishment from his native country.[34] Among the many so-called Chinese cases decided by the *Plessy*-era Supreme Court, *Ju Toy* marked the radical expansion of the discretionary authority vested in the Immigration Bureau. It set a dangerous precedent derived from a racialized statute—Chinese exclusion—that became a procedural norm in general immigration administration.[35] After *Ju Toy*, immigrants seeking admission into the U.S. became subject to the power of immigration officials such as Inspector Dunn, who were transformed from "law-enforcers" into "self-constituted, law-maker[s]," in the words of the immigration reformer Max Kohler.[36] Ju Toy, a U.S. citizen, was deported in 1906.

By unmooring immigration procedures from constitutional principles, *Ju Toy* radically expanded the power of the Immigration Bureau, allowing its functionaries to denationalize U.S. citizens without judicial review or oversight.[37] Thirty-five Chinese petitioners claiming to be birthright U.S. citizens and denied entry by immigration officials awaited the decision in *Ju Toy*; all were deported.[38] After *Ju Toy*, habeas corpus petitions filed by Chinese in the U.S. circuit court at San Francisco fell precipitously from 153 cases in 1904 to 9 cases in 1906, and the

Chinese Six Companies later addressed a memorial to President Theodore Roosevelt, asking him "to recommend to Congress the enactment of laws eliminating from jurisprudence the pernicious doctrine laid down by the Supreme Court of the United States vs. Ju Toy, 198 United States, 253."[39] *Ju Toy* catalyzed concerns over the potential abuse of new administrative power, and American critics funneled their fears into a vociferous critique of "bureaucratic tyranny."[40]

In the wake of *Ju Toy*, angry protests against the racializing logic of U.S. immigration administration and foreign policy also erupted across the Asia Pacific. Reports of an impending Chinese boycott of U.S. goods broke newspaper headlines just days after Holmes rendered his ruling, and many commentators quickly noted the "inconsistency of directing the efforts of the Department of Commerce and Labor to the extension of American trade in China while the same Department was creating indignation among Chinese merchants."[41] The boycott crisis marked a significant shift in public discourses surrounding Chinese exclusion. One editorial channeled the language of another notorious U.S. Supreme Court ruling, *Dred Scott v. Sandford* (1857), to denounce the "outrageous treatment" of the Chinese "by both the people and Government of the United States," for under "the dictation of the sand lot politicians we have treated the Chinese as if they had no rights we were bound to recognize."[42] Across the political spectrum, commentators began reviewing the legal history of Chinese exclusion, citing it as just cause for Chinese economic retaliation: "If in consequence of this ignorant and prejudiced legislation against Chinamen, American merchants find their goods boycotted in China they deserve no more pity than is expressed in the comment, 'Served you right.'"[43]

Closing the "Open Door": The Chinese Boycott of U.S. Goods

In an effort to claim a larger sphere of influence in China, the U.S. issued two diplomatic messages—U.S. Secretary of State John Hay's so-called Open Door Notes (1899, 1900)—asking that the imperial powers already established in China (Britain, France, Portugal, the Netherlands, Germany, Russia, and Japan) respect the autonomy of China and the right of equal access to its trade.[44] The U.S. touted the virtues of this policy of nonterritorial appropriation, fashioning itself as China's protector and "greatest friend."[45] However, long-standing Chinese exclusion policies and territorial aggrandizement in the Asia Pacific, superadded to the deployment of the U.S. military in the Boxer Uprising (1899–1901) and the invasion of Beijing (in the so-called China Relief Expedition), facilitated a radical shift in Chinese perceptions of the U.S., culminating in the 1905 boycott.[46] Chinese merchants and English-speaking compradores (local commercial agents) in collaboration with Chinese in Singapore, the U.S., Hawai'i, the Philippines, British Columbia, and Japan launched a two-month boycott of U.S. goods coming into China to protest both the extension of Chinese exclusion to Hawai'i and the Philippines and the Immigration Bureau's abusive treatment of Chinese in the U.S.[47] The protection of overseas Chinese had become a serious foreign-relations issue for China, especially after the Burlingame Treaty began encouraging Chinese immigration to the U.S. Chinese officials extended initial support to the mass movement, but concerns of its inciting hostilities against the Chinese government accelerated state intervention in an edict banning the boycott. However, the boycott continued in certain regions such as Guangdong and Fujian with high outward migration and with the financial backing of overseas Chinese until 1906.[48] Such forms of mass action had a long history in Chinese challenges of Western hegemony. For example, Chinese in the U.S. organized a highly publicized registration boycott protesting the implementation of the Geary Act. And Amitav Ghosh's *Ibis* trilogy, fictionalizing the Opium Wars, also makes playful reference to the Chinese "tactic that has since become their favourite weapon against the Europeans: a boycott."[49]

In the U.S., fears abounded that the boycott signaled the end of America's "Open Door" to China. The boycott crisis, arriving just days after the *Ju Toy* controversy, also furnished American illustrators with satirical fodder as they lampooned the iconography of the "Open Door" in political cartoons. In the humor magazine *Puck*, an illustration titled "The Chinese Boycott" depicts an oversized vault door barring the entry of a frustrated Uncle Sam. Chinese onlookers watch as a Chinese mandarin leans over the Great Wall of the "Open Door" to present Uncle Sam the "new combination" carrying the demand: "Fair Treatment of China."[50] Such political commentary drew attention to the obvious conflict between U.S. domestic policies on the Chinese and its economic aspirations in China. Anti-Chinese agitators had long promulgated

Yellow Peril specters of monstrous coolie masses in league with monopolistic corporations, but the actual transpacific coordination of Chinese collective action took most U.S. commentators by surprise.[51] "Never before has there been such unanimity of action on the part of the Chinese," exclaimed one editorial.[52] Major newspapers from the *Atlanta Constitution*, the *San Francisco Chronicle*, the *St. Louis Post-Dispatch*, and the *New York Times* to the *Chicago Daily Tribune* reported continuously on all aspects of the threatened boycott, from its potential impact on U.S. manufacture, particularly on the southern-based cotton textile trade, and ongoing U.S.-China diplomatic negotiations, including President Theodore Roosevelt's much-publicized efforts to mitigate the abusive administration of existing exclusion laws. Increasingly, major newspapers such as the *Chicago Daily Tribune* began to view the boycott crisis as an opportunity for the country to reform its "inconsistent and confusing" system of Chinese exclusion.[53]

The Chinese boycott revealed the extent to which U.S. racial policies at home influenced its foreign relations abroad. U.S. newsprint accepted as common knowledge the idea that the Chinese initiated the boycott in "retaliation" against the "old Chinese exclusion law," and the American Peace Society's *Advocate of Peace* went so far as to ponder why "the Chinese government ha[d] not retaliated long ago, and put in force [just such] a counter exclusion measure."[54] As one of the largest antiforeign movements to take place in China after the Boxer Uprising, the 1905 boycott pressed for more liberal U.S. domestic and foreign policies on Chinese immigration and expressed, in the words of the newspaperman Ng Poon Chew, "the bad feeling which had arisen between the two countries because of the violation of the treaty and the accumulated sense of injustice."[55]

Widespread U.S. media coverage of the boycott spurred public debates over current anti-Chinese immigration laws, their administration, and the newly empowered Immigration Bureau. In the South, modification of Chinese exclusion became a particularly "live question," given that "southern farmers, particularly along the coast, are seriously considering the Chinese as a substitute for the negroes in the cane and rice fields," alongside general fears that the boycott would "cripple the growing cotton manufacturing business in the southern states."[56]

Roosevelt made a point to address these concerns, assuring one audience in Charlotte, Virginia, that "he was doing all he lawfully could as executive to spare the Chinese needless humiliation" in the effort to avert the boycott.[57] And once the boycott began, Roosevelt sent his secretary of war and the former governor of the Philippines (1901–1903) William Howard Taft to Canton and Amoy "in the endeavor to put a stop to the boycott."[58] He was later joined by Alice Roosevelt, who served as private envoy for her father and as an ambassador of American goodwill.[59] By repeatedly insisting that "existing exclusion laws must be interpreted leniently," Roosevelt and Taft carefully distinguished the corpus of long-standing racial exclusion laws from its abusive administration by overzealous state functionaries, such as Inspector Dunn in the recent case of Ju Toy.[60]

U.S. reportage of the boycott crisis also tapped into growing public concerns over the bureaucratization of the U.S. given the expansion of administrative power and rise of new agencies. In 1903, the Immigration Bureau had undergone substantial enlargement when it was transferred from the Treasury Department to the newly created Department of Commerce and Labor. Editorials blamed the foreign-relations impasse on the newly empowered Immigration Bureau and its "asinine immigration inspectors" and their tactless enforcement of Chinese exclusion law.[61] Even the generally anti-Chinese *Los Angeles Times* accused immigration officials of having "gone beyond the line of commendable vigilance, and hav[ing] themselves become violators of the law."[62] Secretary of Labor and Commerce Victor Metcalf (whom Straus replaced) publicly defended his immigration inspectors, contending that "the trouble is with the law and not with its enforcement."[63] The uncooperative Metcalf even suggested the further expansion of his agency's authority by sending "immigration bureau officers to China to examine the merchants and students who claim the right to enter the United States" to save "some of them the expense of a trip."[64] The boycott crisis revealed deep tensions within the executive branch as state functionaries vied to delineate the power and purview of new administrative agencies.[65]

The growing tide of U.S. public opinion sympathetic to the Chinese and urging for the easing of Chinese exclusion restrictions prompted the immediate response of labor unions, which alleged the boycott to be a conspiracy engineered in the U.S. "between capitalists here opposed to union labor and Wu Ting Fang," now head of the recently established Chinese Ministry of Foreign Affairs.⁶⁶ A former Chinese diplomat, Wu was an outspoken advocate of the boycott and had warned of growing Chinese resistance to exclusion policies.⁶⁷ As a corrective to Roosevelt's plea for more liberal administration of Chinese exclusion, labor agitators led by Samuel Gompers, the English-born president of the American Federation of Labor, argued that "unless there is a return to the harsher methods of enforcing the exclusion and immigration laws 'the yellow peril' will become an actual menace to the prosperity of the American working-man."⁶⁸ Furthermore, proposals to placate China with the repeal of Chinese exclusion in Hawai'i and the Philippines gave Pacific Coast agitators additional cause for alarm. They viewed these Pacific territories—once free of exclusion laws—as breeding grounds for a Chinese invasion of the mainland. Such paranoid visions reveal deep-seated anxieties over the attenuation of U.S. borders by overseas expansion. The *San Francisco Chronicle* declared that China, leagued together with monopolistic "sugar and tobacco trusts," had engineered the trade crisis with the aim of "turning Hawai'i and the Philippines into coolie colonies."⁶⁹ Such alarmist editorials reinforced the conspiracy theories of labor agitators such as Gompers and added fuel to anti-imperialist arguments. "The people of this country are not wedded to the idea of retaining the Philippines," argued the *San Francisco Chronicle* in the language of economic rationalization, if the islands "are to be converted into places where cheap coolie labor may be brought into sharp competition with the dear white labor of the mainland."⁷⁰

The *San Francisco Chronicle* was not alone in adapting Yellow Peril to cast the Chinese boycott's economic threat to U.S. manufacture as a form of military aggression. For example, the *St. Louis Post-Dispatch* wryly commented, "The yellow peril just now is the Chinese boycott. It has even scared Mr. Roosevelt."⁷¹ In assessing the impact of the Chinese boycott, the *Advocate of Peace* speculated that "the boycott in the hands of the Chinese masses may prove to be more potent than armies and navies, and it is an instrument against which the biggest 'expeditions' would be perfectly helpless."⁷² The cartoonist Fred Morgan of the *Philadelphia Inquirer* depicted these pervasive anxieties in a lurid illustration of animated consumer commodities "Made in the United States"—a canned good, an alarm clock, and a roll of cotton fabric—fleeing from a Chinese mandarin atop a fire-breathing dragon.[73] In this fashion, sensationalist reports conflated these informal Chinese economic sanctions with military antagonism against the U.S., and such depictions drew their animating logic from Chinese invasion fiction and its Janus-faced characterizations of Chinese as villainous military agents and abject coolie-slaves (examined at length in chapter 3). For example, Marsden Manson's *Yellow Peril in Action* (1907) imagined a second boycott as the precursor to the Chinese declaration of war on the U.S., leading to the loss of the Hawaiian Islands and the end of U.S. global power.

Historians of the Chinese boycott, such as Wong Sin Kiong and Guanhua Wang, note that the actual volume of U.S. trade with China was relatively small at the time. However, the boycott was launched just as the U.S. began to embrace a more deterritorialized form of economic neocolonialism in the Asia Pacific region, particularly in its foreign relations with China.[74] The boycott crisis unsettled a powerful future fantasy of U.S. economic dominance in the Pacific.[75] U.S. editorials expressed anxieties over the continued viability of U.S. economic relations with China, specifically in the futurity of the "great and growing trade with that country."[76] For example, one editorial opined that the "gravest question before the country to-day . . . is this 'Chinese question'": "trade with China's 400,000,000 inhabitants in the future, when the awakening, of which many think they see the signs, shall have come, is likely to be of stupendous importance."[77] Among the political cartoons commenting on the Chinese boycott, one illustration, titled "Fearful Finale of the Great Chinese Boycott" and published in the satirical *Puck*, conjured the dystopian vision of an economically underdeveloped U.S.—so defamiliarized as to resemble a Chinatown—to emphasize the threat occasioned by the boycott.[78]

Economic opportunism on the part of Chinese merchants may have played a part in the initiation of the boycott, but it rapidly developed into a broad-based popular movement with far more ambitious goals.[79] It received widespread support both within and without China and across political lines.[80] "An anti-American sentiment is developing among Chinese not only in China but in other parts of the world," noted one editorial.⁸¹ By late June, U.S. newspapers reported that the roughly six thousand Chinese in British Columbia had begun "working energetically to aid the boycott," and a subscription had been raised "to aid in reimbursing coolies who lose wages at Chinese ports by their refusal to unload steamers carrying United States goods."⁸² In Manila, the Chinese chamber of commerce "by a unanimous vote" decided to "stand in line with the treaty ports of China in boycotting American merchandise in retaliation for the American exclusion laws," while reports from Honolulu carried similar news of a "Chinese mass meeting . . . called . . . to endorse the efforts being made in China to effect a boycott of American goods on account of the operations of the exclusion laws."⁸³

In the U.S., conservative groups such as the Society for the Preservation of the Emperor (the political party of many wealthy San Francisco Chinese merchants) along with progressive students, laborers, and reformers, including Sun Yat-sen and K'ang Yu-wei, supported the boycott.⁸⁴ One U.S. newspaper reported that "six local Chinese firms" in San Francisco had "held a meeting and endorsed a movement to boycott American goods until the exclusion act is modified or repealed," and a report was to be "sent to China to aid in conducting the boycott."⁸⁵ Chinese sailors aboard steamers temporarily docked in San Francisco learned of the boycott from "notices in Chinese . . . tacked up all over [their] . . . ship[s]" and refused to "buy any wares offered for sale" by American peddlers.⁸⁶ Chinese in the U.S. helped shape the goals of the boycott through telegrams, letters, and the publication and republication of articles in Chinese-language periodicals such as Ng's *China West Daily* and the Shanghai-based *Shibao*.⁸⁷ A cornerstone of U.S. domestic and foreign policies, the racializing imperatives of Chinese exclusion created the conditions of possibility for collective identification that cut across the divisive lines of class and caste in the Chinese diaspora. At the dawn of the modern era, decades of foreign encroachment and the steady decline in Chinese imperial sovereignty at home and abroad lent urgency to these protests. As the following section argues, these emerging forms of Chinese national consciousness and resistance against the U.S. gravitated toward a sentimental idiom, given its powerful imagination of community and correspondence of feeling in a transpacific context.

Lin Shu's *Uncle Tom's Cabin* and the Boycott Novel

The 1905 Chinese boycott against U.S. goods illuminates the complex ways by which Chinese in diaspora mobilized networks of communication, commerce, and support to challenge U.S. power and racial hegemony in the Asia Pacific. In China, the boycott movement took advantage of the telegraph, expanded market conditions, and the daily press as it disseminated its anti-American message through an unprecedented outpouring of cultural materials, ranging from handbills, songs, poems, pamphlets, and essays to short stories and novels. Popular boycott novels including titles such as *Tongbao shounue ji*, or *A Story of the Ill Treatment of Chinese Brethren* (1905); *Ku xuesheng*, or *A Wretched Student* (1905); *Ku shehui*, or *The Bitter Society* (1905); *Juyue qitan*, or *The Bizarre Tale of the Boycott* (1906); *Huangjin shijie*, or *The Golden World* (1907); and *Jie yu hui*, or *Ashes after the Catastrophe* (1908), sought to forge new forms of Chinese national consciousness given the dispersed geographies of transpacific migration.[88] After the Burlingame Treaty, writings about the U.S. became increasingly popular in China, as Chinese officials began publishing accounts of their travels to the U.S., including the report of Chen Lan-Pin, the commissioner of the first Chinese Educational Mission to the U.S. who also led the investigative Cuba Commission studied in chapter 1. The boycott novel often took pains to portray a modernizing China, acknowledging the institutional reforms initiated under the Self-Strengthening Movement, which sought to place China on an equal technological and economic footing with Western nations. These novels often gave sentimental form to nascent Chinese nationalisms and refracted these broad changes taking place in China at the turn of the century.

The historian Guanhua Wang first studied these novels and their transpacific networks of production and dissemination, but they remain generally overlooked in the U.S. This critical neglect stems as much from the unavailability of English translations as from the nation-based frameworks conventionally brought to bear on the study of Chinese exclusion, U.S. immigration law, and racial formations. This section maps some of the reciprocal effects of Chinese exclusion in the U.S. and in China to achieve a more textured understanding of the literary politics of Chinese resistance to the racializing imperatives of U.S. immigration law and foreign policy. In detail-laden scenes of Chinese subjugation to U.S. power, the boycott novel emphasized sympathetic identification through a shared sense of racial pain and Western victimization in ways that resembled yet departed from analogous developments in U.S. literary sentimentalism. The boycott novel's pathos-inducing plots and settings of Chinese immigration to and exclusion from the U.S. delineate a literary politics of resistance against Western racial hegemony and economic neocolonialism. This section sets out to investigate what the politics of literary sentimentalism looked like in this multilingual and transpacific context.

Lin Shu's radical translation and recontextualization of Harriet Beecher Stowe's *Uncle Tom's Cabin* serves as a touchstone for the transpacific sentimental politics of the boycott novel. In the U.S. and China, reform-minded Chinese writers began repurposing the complex "racial signifying systems" of U.S. imperial governance, particularly after the annexation of the Philippines.[89] The history of American slavery and abolition offered Chinese writers a powerful archive of images, texts, and arguments by which to challenge Chinese exclusion and its Asiatic racial formations. Writers such as Lin looked to the influential cultural work of *Uncle Tom's Cabin* (serialized 1851–1852), which had catalyzed the popular mass movement to end black chattel slavery on U.S. soil. "No book in American history," writes David S. Reynolds, "molded public opinion more powerfully than *Uncle Tom's Cabin*."[90] In 1901, the prolific Chinese translator Lin Shu (1852–1924) with the assistance of Wei Yi translated *Uncle Tom's Cabin* into classical Chinese as *A Black Slave's Cry to Heaven* (also translated as *A Record of the Black Slaves' Plea to Heaven* and *A Record of the Black Slaves Lamenting, "Heaven!"*).[91] Marking the original's fiftieth year, 1901 saw a resurgence of interest in *Uncle Tom's Cabin*. In the U.S., an outraged Thomas Dixon Jr. began penning his best-selling novel *The Leopard's Spots* as a corrective to what he viewed as the "gross misrepresentation of Southern life" promulgated by Stowe's antislavery masterpiece and the Tom plays that it popularized.[92]

In China, Lin Shu began translating *Uncle Tom's Cabin* shortly after U.S. involvement in the "China Relief Expedition," during the later years of the Boxer Uprising. Lin had just completed his first translation of the popular *The Lady of the Camellias* (1848) by the mixed-race

French novelist Alexandre Dumas, which inaugurated a popular style of Chinese sentimental romance known as Mandarin Duck and Butterfly fiction.[93] Over the course of two decades, Lin collaborated with twenty different readers trained in various languages to translate over 180 novels into Chinese, introducing Western literature to China. The translations involved a two-part process of "tandem translation" from the original into spoken Chinese and from the aural to the written in ancient-style prose.[94] Lin's unorthodox tandem translations gave full expression to the dynamic cultural mediations and borrowings in the practice of translation and its "double process of appropriating and replacing what is foreign while keeping its foreignness in view," to borrow the words of Vicente Rafael.[95] Stowe's novel was Lin's second translation and the first full translation of an American novel in Chinese.[96] Completed in sixty-six days, Lin's translation secularized Stowe's novel by removing its overt Christian tropes and themes—indeed, the very elements that distinguished Stowe's antislavery politics from the anti-institutional radicalism of William Lloyd Garrison.[97] A noted essayist and novelist in his own right, Lin included a preface and an afterword that explained the political goals involved in his translation of the novel. For Lin, excessive sentiment was a self-conscious mode of self-fashioning, marking his aesthetic and moral sensibilities, according to Haiyan Lee.[98] In *A Black Slave's Cry to Heaven*, Lin explicitly politicized sentiment, emphasizing racial pain as the foundation for an emergent Chinese nationalism. His paratextual materials delineated this transpacific politics of literary sentiment and influenced the form of the boycott novel that followed.

Lin's translation provides one example among many of the significance of sentiment and sentimentalism in Chinese literary protests against U.S. law and colonial hegemony. A detailed comparison between *A Black Slave's Cry to Heaven* and the original *Uncle Tom's Cabin* lies beyond the scope of this book, although Chinese literature and translation studies scholars, including Martha P. Y. Cheung, Michael Gibbs Hill, and Jing Tsu, have begun this important work. In particular, Hill's comprehensive biographical study *Lin Shu, Inc.* (2012) illuminates the powerful cultural and political work performed by the translation in the making of modern Chinese culture.[99] Lin's translation of *Uncle Tom's Cabin* exhibited a range of contradictory desires. He detested racial slavery, yet he was fascinated by the New World civilizations that had emerged from the African slave trade. Lin also utilized and rejected the political analogy between Chinese and black Americans, as he fashioned an emergent Chinese national consciousness from George Harris's impassioned championing of black resettlement to Liberia. In this, Lin's *A Black Slave's Cry to Heaven* expresses a complex psychology of utopian yearnings to change the condition of Western oppression (by colonizing another territory and starting anew), which aligned it with other narratives of colonization from the late Qing period. These narratives established sympathy on the basis of shared racial suffering in what Tsu translates from Chinese as the term "kumen" (or "guwen"). Associated with Chinese literary modernity, the concept of "kumen," according to Tsu, "encompassed a sense of social suffering that included while exceeding individual affliction."[100] It revolutionized pain, especially of individual psychic anguish, channeling it toward social enlightenment and criticism. In this chapter, sentimentalism emerges as more than a U.S. literary genre. It helps name multilingual articulations of racial pain and forms the foundation for a transpacific literary politics with varying local expressions, from Lin's translation of *Uncle Tom's Cabin* and the boycott novel to Eaton's Chinatown stories.

At the end of the century, Stowe's novel reappeared in a Chinese context far different from the antebellum one in which the sentimental reform novel first gained its cultural and political prominence.[101] Meg Wesling reveals how the complex politics of U.S. overseas expansion first brought *Uncle Tom's Cabin* to the Asia Pacific. In the days after the U.S. seized the Philippines, *Uncle Tom's Cabin* served as powerful cultural touchstone for understanding the colonial situation, as the history of slavery and ongoing racial conflict in the U.S. was retailored to the circumstances of the Philippines-American War, the racial character of freedom, and the uncertain legal status of Filipinos.[102] U.S. imperial governance utilized such literature as a privileged vehicle for extending American republican values and middle-class sensibilities from the domestic nation-state to its "foreign" territories, according to Wesling.[103] As the exemplary U.S. literary object, Stowe's *Uncle Tom's Cabin*, argues Wesling, helped justify U.S. rule through the dissemination of Anglo-Saxon tradition as it recast "the exceptionalism" of "U.S. sovereignty in the islands . . . as an extension of U.S. republicanism."[104] In this fashion, U.S. colonial administrators conscripted *Uncle Tom's Cabin* into the project of colonial rule in the Philippines.[105] The transformation of *Uncle Tom's Cabin* into a tool of colonial administration was perhaps not surprising given that even moderate Reconstruction Republicans such as James Blaine (studied in chapter 2) depicted Chinese exclusion as consistent with the moral values of abolitionism and essential to the preservation of U.S. freedom, especially after the acquisition of the Pacific territories.

Unlike in the Philippines, Lin's translation of *Uncle Tom's Cabin* served as politicized response to—rather than an ideological vehicle for—U.S. racial hegemony and economic encroachment in the Asia Pacific. For Hill, this translation provides the key to understanding how Lin and his collaborators established lasting aesthetic and political relevance for their works. Lin's translation challenged the racialization of Chineseness as a category for exclusion in the U.S. and its newly acquired territories, galvanizing public protest against Chinese exclusion through a sentimental idiom. According to Hill, it was the "earliest attempt to imagine through fiction how the problem of race might map on to the territory of the Chinese empire."[106] Fifty years earlier, Stowe had written *Uncle Tom's Cabin* to combat another infamous U.S. federal law, namely, the 1851 Fugitive Slave Act. In crafting characters such as Senator Bird, who (at his wife's urging) transgresses the law that he helped pass, Stowe encouraged readers to embrace the "higher law" over legal statute and the Constitution. For Lin, the racial histories of black enslavement depicted in *Uncle Tom's Cabin* offered a stark presentiment of one possible course of Chinese relations with the U.S.—one that might yet be forestalled.[107] Emancipation, according to Amy Dru Stanley, "cleared the way ideologically" for comparing a range of oppressive relations to black chattel slavery, as postbellum reformers transformed slavery into a powerful metaphor for illustrating the urgency of their particular political needs.[108] This also held true within the transpacific context of Lin's translation. His preface relates the founding of the American republic in 1619 with the "enslavement of the blacks in Virginia . . . when the Dutch transported twenty African blacks in a warship to Jamestown and sold them."[109] "This was the beginning of the enslavement of blacks by whites," reads the preface, and "it was not until Lincoln's time that the slaves were fortunately emancipated."[110]

"Recently," Lin concludes, "the treatment of blacks in America has been carried over to yellow people."[111]

Lin transforms Stowe's account of antebellum slavery and race relations into an illustrative "precedent" for the current condition of Chinese in the U.S. His afterword emphasizes that the most salient feature of sentimentalism lies in its forging of what Tsu describes as intersubjective pain alliances, in which shared Western oppression facilitates the transpacific politicization of Chinese readers:

> In translating this book, Mr. Wei and I did not strive to describe sorrow for the purpose of eliciting useless tears from readers. It was rather that we had to cry out for the sake of our people because the prospect of enslavement is threatening our race. In recent years the American continent has severely restricted the immigration of Chinese laborers. A stockade has been erected at the landing place where hundreds of Chinese who have come from afar are locked up. Only after a week do they begin to release one or two people, and some people are not released even after two weeks. This is [like] what is referred to in this book as the "slave quarters." . . . As we can read in George's letter to his friend, a person without a country will be treated like a barbarian even by civilized people. So if in the future we Chinese become material for slaves, will this not be the basis?[112]

In referencing Harris's letter, Lin gravitates toward what most literary critics consider the least sentimentalized passage in the novel. However, Lin's identification of Chinese immigrants with black chattel slaves emphasizes a statelessness tailored to elicit from his Chinese readers a shared sense of racial injury. His goal is a didactic one: to foster a Chinese national consciousness based on a shared sense of Western victimization. "Do we Chinese have a nation or not?" Lin demands.[113] By focusing on Harris, Lin fashions a sentimentalism that finds expression along a horizontal axis—ideally, in the form of racial nationalism—unlike the racially hierarchized appeal found in the original, which asks white readers to sympathize with black suffering.

In *Uncle Tom's Cabin*, Harris stands as a figure for the statelessness of the black racialized subject in the U.S. In an exchange between Harris and Mr. Wilson, a northern manufacturer who attempts to dissuade him from escape, Harris retorts, "*you* have a country, but what country have *I*, or any one like me, born of slave mothers? What laws are there for us? We don't make them, — we don't consent to them, — we have nothing to do with them; all they do for us is to crush us, and keep us down."[114] According to Chang-fang Chen, the English translation of Lin's version of the scene reads, "Where is my country? You are brought up from a decent family. It is proper for you to respect your country. I am the scion of ugly slaves. What country should this person belong to?"[115] Lin's afterword further analogizes Harris's powerful expression of racial statelessness to the current condition of Chinese under Western power; however, this racial resemblance is structured along the axis of temporal difference, for it is the (as yet to be realized) "prospect of enslavement" that threatens the Chinese race. Hence, this act of interracial sympathy enables differentiation, for the past of American slavery serves as a caution against one possible future for China. Lin turns racial statelessness and denationalization into a rallying cry for a reinvigorated Chinese nationalism in the face of a weak China incapable of protecting its subjects from Western oppression.[116] "Our country's power is weak," reads his preface, "and our envoys are cowardly and afraid of arguing with the Americans."[117] Lin fuses outrage against U.S. dominion with shame over China's passivity, presenting his translation as a "warning" to readers who "favor the white race . . . under the erroneous illusion that the Westerners are generous with vassals."[118] In this fashion, Lin adapts Stowe's novel to the context of Chinese immigrant life in the U.S., likening the plight of Chinese migrants to black slaves and detention sheds to slave quarters in the didactic effort to forestall the future realization of this racial analogy.[119]

Lin's translation of *Uncle Tom's Cabin* redirected attention away from the strong religious piety of Uncle Tom to focus on the heroic struggles of Eliza and George Harris to protect their home life from the incursions of slavery and slave law. Unlike the southern plotline depicting the trials and tribulations of Uncle Tom, Stowe's northern plotline explicitly addressed the injustices of the new Fugitive Slave Act as it charted the Harris family's escape, reunion in the North, and immigration to Liberia.[120] This plotline held particular resonance for Lin. His afterword references Harris's oft-quoted letter from the penultimate pages of the novel, which features Harris's mastery of Western knowledge and its application to Liberia. In it, Harris makes an eloquent proclamation of "African *nationality,*" rejecting the U.S. to cast his family's lot with the "African race" and in the future young republic of Liberia. "I want a people that shall have a tangible, separate existence of their own," Harris exclaims. "Let me go and form part of a nation, which shall have a voice in the council of nations, and then we can speak," he continues. "A nation has a right to argue, remonstrate, implore, and present the cause of its race" (610). Lin translates Harris's strident call for an "African nationality" into a new form of Chinese nationalism, emphasizing China's need to establish itself as a peer nation to the U.S.[121] Late Qing Chinese sentimentalism had begun to reorganize the nation in "emotive terms, emphasizing horizontal identification, egalitarianism, voluntarism, and patriotic sacrifice," according to Lee.[122] Given this, Lin reads a powerful call to racial-national empowerment out of the Liberian ending, which numerous literary critics have criticized as Stowe's "segregationist resolution."[123] For Lin, the separatist conclusion may have added to Harris's appeal, given the open hostility toward racial amalgamation voiced in other Chinese nationalist novels, as noted by Tsu.[124] The translation ends quickly, some 750 characters after the end of Harris's letter, which reads like the "real conclusion," according to Hill.[125]

The unexpected success and wide dissemination of Lin's translation reveal seemingly analogous East-West developments in the politicization of literary sentiment and its role in shaping Chinese understandings of American racial formations in the Progressive era. Countering "Open Door" discourses of U.S. benevolence and friendship with China, Lin's preface sets out to inform readers of the long histories of U.S. racial violence and their enduring legacies in current immigration policies. Citing Harris's example of "African nationality," Lin's preface embraces a language of racialized nationalism—"us yellow people"—to assert a collective sense of Chinese identity, one that bridges the geopolitical cleavages between his readers in China and Chinese subjects abroad.[126] For Lin, the novel's depiction of black chattel slavery and the racial ideologies it established serve as an interpretative framework to understand the condition of Chinese migrant life and as a caution against the future. Undoubtedly, Lin was drawn to the didacticism of Stowe's sentimental idiom: its famous injunction to "feel right," which emphasized the authenticity of feeling, specifically of love and suffering, as a universal solution to structural forms of injustice and oppression. It modeled a sentimental pedagogy promoting "individual acts of identification based on collective group memberships," which bound "persons to the nation through a universalist rhetoric not of citizenship per se but of the capacity for suffering and trauma at the citizen's core," argues Lauren Berlant.[127] Lin's afterword explicitly embraces sentiment as a pathway to modern China and political reform: "Fittingly, this book has been completed just as we are beginning to reform the government. Now that people have all thrown away their old writings and are diligently seeking new knowledge, this book . . . may still be of some help in inspiring determinations to love our country and preserve our race."[128] Given this, Lin's criticisms of China might also be read in relation to the English-language writings of Wong Chin Foo, particularly in his translated "fugitive coolie" narrative of Chun Young Hing (studied in chapter 1), which likewise condemned China for a failure of sentiment in its inability to protect Chinese laborers in Cuba. Thus, Lin reformulates sentimentalism into a literary template for a new China.

As part of an understudied literary history of transpacific protests against Chinese exclusion, *A Black Slave's Cry to Heaven* invested the sentimental politics of *Uncle Tom's Cabin* with powerful new meanings. By the time of the threatened 1905 boycott, U.S. readers had begun to remark on the literary curiosity of these "Oriental translations" of popular American novels. In an article titled "Uncle Tom in Other Tongues!" (1905), one commentator compared the differences among the Chinese translation and a "Persian version" and a "Turkish ballad" version.[129] By 1911, U.S. newspapers proudly touted *Uncle Tom's Cabin*, alongside British novels such as *The Adventures of Sherlock Holmes* and *Robinson Crusoe*, as "the most popular of the translated novels" in China, with no recognition of the translation's anti-American politics.[130] Recent studies of Lin's translation have also acknowledged its profound influence on Chinese aesthetics and political culture. In 1906, the Chinese Ministry of Education approved it as one of forty textbooks for its newly established schools.[131] Like the original, this translation was also adapted to the stage.[132] In 1907, the prominent Chinese dramatist Zeng Xiaogu's five-act play was first staged by an organization of dissident Chinese students in Tokyo called the Spring Willow Society in protest against the Qing government's inadequate protection of Chinese in the U.S.[133]

No play script has yet been found, but a short synopsis reveals that the play, like Lin's translation, focused on Harris, who kills his master in the struggle for freedom. Moreover, this full-length staged drama departed from traditional Chinese opera and inaugurated a new spoken-drama movement in China. At the dawn of the twentieth century, as *Uncle Tom's Cabin* came under attack in the U.S. and traveling theater troupes performing adaptations of the novel were banned or prohibitively taxed in states such as Kentucky, Arkansas, Georgia, Texas, Florida, and Maryland, the novel's liberation plot came to figure the possibility of political and cultural transformation in modernizing China.[134]

The paratextual frame of *A Black Slave's Cry to Heaven* provided a template for a transpacific politics of literary sentimentalism that sought to arouse readers to collective identification and action. In Lin's words, the translation does not "describe sorrow for the purpose of eliciting useless tears from readers." In exploring the enormous popularity of such late-Qing sentimental literature, Haiyan Lee charts the "reconceptualization of identity and sociality in emotive terms" in Chinese modernity.[135] Lin's call prefigured the 1905 boycott and the outpouring of cultural materials associated with it, including what became known as the boycott novel. Progressive Chinese writers drew inspiration from Lin's sentimental politics in didactic novels emphasizing shared racial pain and victimization as the foundation for a reinvigorated nationalism against bellicose U.S. policies toward China and the Chinese. By turning the experiences of overseas Chinese into story, the boycott novel acted as a "catalyst for sympathetic response . . . producing intense emotion" in readers fearful of China's survival in the modern era.[136] Novels such as *The Bitter Society* and *The Golden World* depict the arduous transpacific journeys of Chinese laborers to the West and their subsequent legal subjection to U.S. immigration law. For example, *The Golden World* tells the intersecting story of three different sets of Chinese migrants, both voluntary and coerced, who become ardent critics of the West after confronting the racializing force of Chinese exclusion. In *The Bitter Society*, the complex portrayals of home life and community support networks offer a powerful counterpoint to Yellow Peril depictions of inassimilable Chinese incapable of feeling or domestic ties, in a fashion analogous to the aesthetic politics of Eaton's English-language stories of North American Chinese life.

Critics surmise that Chinese writers (most likely based in Shanghai) and Chinese returnees from the U.S. collaboratively produced the boycott novels, given the wealth of detailed information they contain about the condition of Chinese migrant life in the U.S. Written in classical Chinese, these novels, like Lin's works, remain largely unavailable in English translation, with the exception of *The Bitter Society*, which was partially translated into English by June Mei and Jean Pang Yip and published in 1981 by the *Amerasia Journal*. The Shenbao Publishing House, a leading Shanghai publisher during the Chinese boycott of U.S. goods, first published the anonymously authored novel, and it had an initial press run of three thousand copies. The novel suggested a sequel, which did not see publication.[137] According to Wang, Shenbao ran advertisements for *The Bitter Society* over the course of many weeks, starting on July 10, 1905, as the boycott crisis gripped U.S. headlines.[138] According to the translators, the novel takes the form of a collective autobiography charting the vicissitudes of five young Chinese migrants traveling to work abroad in Peru and the U.S. Only four of the five men survive their journeys abroad and return to China. Bound by a "coolie" labor contract, one dies of illness and abuse aboard a Peru-bound steamer. The intersecting plotlines incorporate a dizzying array of stories from the perspectives of overseas Chinese whom the remaining four men encounter while in the West. Committed to making known the abuses suffered by Chinese in the U.S., *The Bitter Society* ends with the men returning to Shanghai with the intention of organizing a boycott of U.S. goods so that the Americans, in the words of one protagonist, "may change their stand and abolish some of these harsh regulations to accommodate the Chinese."[139]

In following the paths of Chinese migrants, the boycott novel, as Wang notes, contributed to the consciousness of a vast Chinese diaspora, ranging from Guangdong to Peru and the U.S. in *The Bitter Society*, from Guangdong to Cuba and the U.S. in *The Golden World*, and from Guangdong to Singapore, the Philippines, Hawai'i, and San Francisco in the short story *Qiaoming lei*, or "The Tears of the Overseas Chinese."[140] Thus far, only the sections of *The Bitter Society* set in San Francisco have been translated into English, yet these ten chapters illuminate the complex ways by which U.S. immigration law mediated and shaped early North American Chinese households and transpacific identifications.

In charting the events that befall three Chinese merchants, Li Xinchun, Wang Bofu, and Gu Zifeng, in San Francisco, the chapters reveal the cumulative impact of anti-Chinese laws on the formation of Chinese immigrant communities and home life. For example, *The Bitter Society* publicizes the Immigration Bureau's interrogation techniques that took place largely behind closed doors, revealing the intimidation and violence of immigration procedures. In lieu of numbered immigration case files, *The Bitter Society* transforms Chinese subjects, such as Ju Toy, into sympathetic figures who invite reader identification. These chapters also reveal the growing regulation of Chinese home life as a main feature of Progressive-era immigration control. A proper home life figured significantly in how the Immigration Bureau determined the eligibility of an applicant to enter and participate in the nation. Questions regarding the parentage, marital status, and community relations formed the basis of U.S. immigration inspectors' interrogations. As Ju Toy's interrogation transcript reveals, inspectors privileged a particular configuration of family and rejected applicants charged with perversions of normative home life.

The San Francisco chapters of *The Bitter Society* do not feature a main protagonist; they are loosely organized around the episodic events that befall the three Chinese merchants. They acclimate to life in the U.S. and face increasing anti-Chinese harassment, including periodic raids on Chinatown searching for "illegal immigrants." News that the Chinese government "signed the treaty excluding Chinese laborers" adds to the immigrants' growing unease (38). Soon thereafter, a local commission "alleged" that a majority of Chinese labor migrants in the U.S. were "here illegally and ordered deported" (38). By 1894. when the Gresham-Yang Treaty was signed, registration and deportation was already an established feature of Chinese exclusion.[141] *The Bitter Society* depicts how policemen were sent "to check registration papers" and "careless workers who happened to lose their papers were arrested" (39). The police arrest Wu Ashuang, the "registered foreman" at Li Xinchun's store, when he fails to show his identification papers. Wu's imminent deportation facilitates a domestic crisis, for it also entails separation from his wife and children, who are domiciled in the U.S. The novel charts the social impact of *Ju Toy* in Li's discovery that the "courthouse" was "truly not accessible" to the Chinese (39). In the failure of law, Li arranges for the return of Wu's family on the same China-bound vessel on which he was to be deported. Upon return to the store, Wang Bofu and Li Xinchun face yet another crisis of impending familial separation. In this case, the exempt status of He Jintang, a wealthy merchant, does not protect his household from the arbitrary enforcement of Chinese exclusion. After a visit to China, He's wife is denied reentry to the U.S. (although their son is admitted) because the frightened woman had given "an inconsistent answer" during the interrogation (42). Like Wu's family, He Jintang is forced into self-deportation as the only alternative to familial separation.

Subsequent chapters chart the social impact of additional anti-Chinese regulations, including the Bertillon system of bodily measurements (later replaced by fingerprinting) to police Chinese immigrants and the construction of detention sheds to house arriving Chinese for further questioning (44). Immigration inspectors often initiated lengthy investigations into the claims made by Chinese seeking admission into the country. Ranging in duration from days to months, these investigations held the private steamship companies responsible for lodging and upkeep of immigrants until the conclusion of their cases. To prevent delays, steamship companies built cheap wooden sheds—often cramped and unsanitary—on their docks for detained Chinese.[142] Before the removal of shed detention to Angel Island Immigration Station, it served to racialize Chinese upon arrival to the U.S. Detained immigrants found the promiscuous mixing of gender and class especially offensive. Conversely, the shared conditions of shed detention also enabled powerful forms of Chinese racial consciousness that cut across the generally divisive social lines of class and gender. In the U.S. and in China, one of the most condemned abuses of Chinese exclusion was shed detention—what Lin referred to as "slave quarters" in his translation of *Uncle Tom's Cabin*—and it became a potent symbol of U.S. violence against the Chinese.[143] These detention sheds were located within U.S. bounds, yet immigration law regarded the Chinese person housed within them, in the language of Holmes's *Ju Toy* ruling, "as if he had been stopped at the limit of our jurisdiction and kept there while his right to enter was under debate."[144] They refracted the legal liminality of Chinese personhood: subject to U.S. laws yet entitled to few—if any—of its protections. Shed detention thus became a powerful chronotope for

Chinese racialization on U.S. soil, which often called forth the claustrophobia of containment associated with coolie transport, as depicted in Joseph Conrad's serialized novella *Typhoon*.[145]

The 1892 Geary Act explicitly redefined Chinese racialization as a form of criminalization, for it held "any Chinese person or person of Chinese descent arrested under" its provisions "to be unlawfully within the United States, unless such person shall establish, by affirmative proof, to the satisfaction of such justice, judge or commissioner, his lawful right to remain in the United States."[146] In *The Bitter Society*, the wife and nephew of another merchant, Zilan, a twenty-year resident of San Francisco, become the first occupants of these poorly constructed, pestilential sheds despite the provision providing that "the wives and children of merchants are allowed to come to America" (46). After the Geary Act, immigration officials assumed all Chinese testimony to be fraudulent. They judged arriving Chinese to be "suspected criminals"— illegal aliens—until proven otherwise, in flagrant disregard of the due process protections of the Fifth and Fourteenth Amendments, specifically in the presumption of innocence.[147] Chinese seeking admission into the U.S. thus bore the burden of proof to establish their right to entry. It "is the practice for custom officers," observed a pro-Chinese pamphlet, "to look upon their [the Chinese's] attempt to enter the country as criminal offences, and treat them worse than thieves or robbers."[148] Chinese activists and immigration reformers insisted that it was "tantamount to a high crime or felony to be a Chinese alien," and the boycott novel often recast these conflicts in terms of a racial struggle between the "yellow race" and the "white race."[149] For example, *The Bitter Society* couches confrontations over U.S.-China foreign policy in terms of this racial conflict. "In today's world," proclaims one protagonist, "there is no freedom for the yellow race; there is only freedom for the white race."[150]

The Bitter Society meditates on this connection between Asiatic "foreignness" and criminality in the U.S. The novel's detailed accounts of shed detention, particularly of detained women and children, sought to cultivate the sympathetic identification of its Chinese readers. The dramatization of Zilan's domestic plight reveals the disjuncture between the letter of the law and its abusive administration. Because "one word in a street name had been incorrectly given," immigration officials, as in the case of Ju Toy, exert their authority to lawfully detain Zilan's wife and nephew for an indefinite period without bail, effectively treating the two as criminals (47). In arguing for the repeal of the Geary Act before the House Committee on Foreign Affairs, Wong Chin Foo critiqued this presumption of guilt criminalizing all Chinese. He avowed that it violated "the spirit and principles of the Constitution," for it "branded and classified" Chinese in the U.S. "as criminals simply because they were of Chinese birth."[151] In the novel, after bribing an immigration inspector, Zilan gains entry into the shed to discover his ailing wife "on the floor," "shackled hand and foot," sharing "a low, dank room" with "over ten people" (47). In failing to protect his wife, Zilan, like He Jintang before him, is given but one option by immigration officials: "if Zilan will declare his intention to take his wife back to China, she'll be released immediately" (49). *The Bitter Society* repeatedly dramatizes the tragedy of Chinese characters faced with the "choice" of immediate deportation (and loss of property) or familial separation. In every instance, characters select self-deportation to remain with their families. In taking leave of Zilan aboard his China-bound vessel, Li Xinchun and Gu Zifeng run into yet another merchant, Mianfu, who faces deportation. Immigration authorities had arbitrarily declared Mianfu's passport "incorrect" and denied him reentry, threatening to imprison him "based on the new rules" if he "protested further" (50).

The Bitter Society's San Francisco chapters emphasize the tenuousness of Chinese home life as they position the reader as helpless witness to repeated instances of state-sanctioned violence. These pathos-inducing scenes of familial separation—a commonplace of sentimental novels such as *Uncle Tom's Cabin*—stress the victimization of innocent Chinese characters, revealing the punitive nature of Chinese exclusion and its abusive administration. The chapter "Separation from a Young Son Poses a Dilemma" richly illustrates the political aesthetics of racial pain and injury, for it involves Wang, one of the three original Chinese merchants, who offers some structure and coherence to these episodic chapters. An elderly childless widower, the merchant Wang adopts the U.S.-born son of his first cousin as his heir. The cousin is a common laborer who "had a child" with "a local woman" from Mexico, since "no laborer was allowed to bring over his wife or children" (52). In this, the novel also limns the extent to which Chinese exclusion reshaped the racial regulations of neighboring Mexico and Canada. Between 1895 and 1926, Chinese immigration to Mexico grew exponentially, from roughly one thousand to over twenty four thousand.[152] The largest Chinese population was located in the Mexican state of Sonora along the Arizona-Mexico border. Many of these Chinese immigrants had fled the U.S. in the wake of increasingly stringent exclusion legislation and settled in Mexico, living in free or civil unions with Mexican women until the passage of anti-Chinese legislation in 1923, which included an antimiscegenation statute banning Chinese men (regardless of naturalization to Mexican citizenship) from marrying or living with Mexican women.[153] Wang's cousin is detained at the U.S.-Mexico border after a routine visit to his son's "family in Mexico," for "the immigration people said that he was a laborer and since he had left, he had no right to return and intended to deport him to China" (52). Born on U.S. soil, the eleven-year-old boy, however, "was considered an American, and if he wished, would be allowed to stay," in accordance with *U.S. v. Wong Kim Ark* (52).

Faced with an untenable dilemma, the fictional Wang Bofu of *The Bitter Society* must either relinquish his beloved heir or ask his aging cousin to face deportation alone. As a tearful Wang relates to his fellow merchants, Li Xinchun and Gu Zifeng: "If my cousin were to return alone—well, as he's so old and his son has been with him all along—the whole trip will be miserable." However, Wang cannot face the prospect of utter kinlessness in the U.S. "Though we didn't live together, we saw each other every day," he relates. "If he were to suddenly leave me, I would not have a single relative here. How can I bear to let him go?" (52–53). Such highly wrought emotional scenes linger on the racial pain and suffering inflicted by U.S. law and foreign policy, provoking Chinese readers into sympathetic identification and nationalist indignation against Western power. In the end, Wang urges the boy to return to China with his father, given the worsening conditions for Chinese in the U.S. "As the Americans are now bringing forth more unreasonable, harsh regulations," Gu Zifeng cautions Wang, "I'm afraid that sooner or later we'll be caught up in it. There's no stability for us here" (53). *The Bitter Society* ties the helplessness of these characters to a weak Chinese state incapable of protecting its subjects abroad. The novel's variously intersecting tragic subplots reveal the destruction of Chinese home life as a procedural norm of immigration administration, which created the conditions for de facto forms of self-deportation. According to the novel, Chinese migrants "had left against their will after insults and abuse" (64). Even so-called exempt merchants must face the decision of "choosing"—in the language of the novel—between kinship and U.S. residence.

As with Lin's translation of *Uncle Tom's Cabin*, *The Bitter Society* mobilizes the powerful images of the slave pen and coffle—popularized, in part, by Stowe's moving image of Uncle Tom with "chains on his wrists, chains on his feet," transported up the Red River to Legree's plantation (480)—in depicting the racialization of Chinese immigrants into illegal aliens. The Chinese protagonists in *The Bitter Society* witness in horror a routine police roundup of so-called illegal Chinese immigrants: "They saw a row of over ten horse-drawn carriages, full of Chinese chained by the necks. Policemen were still everywhere arresting men and women, young and old" (53). Moreover, these San Francisco chapters emphasize the mechanism of racial policing once associated with the "pass system" of the antebellum slave South. The Geary Act permitted the detention of any Chinese person pending confirmation of his or her legal status. Indeed, this policing power overrode even the supposed legal immunity that attached to Chinese diplomats. Another chapter draws on the well-known 1903 tragedy of the Chinese official Tom Kim Yung (Tan Jinyong), a military attaché of the Chinese legation who committed suicide after he was physically assaulted and arrested by San Francisco police officers.[154] A policeman accosts the official on his way to the Chinese consulate from Li's store and brutally clubs him for "daring to resist arrest" when the man attempts to explain his diplomatic office (57). Alerted by the uproar, Li and Wang run to assist the severely injured man, only to face the wide "blue eyes" of the policeman, who taunts, "This is a criminal who violated the curfew and resisted arrest. You say we can't hit him? You must be his accomplices!" (58). A semiotic marker for white hegemony in later African American writings, from Malcolm X's "How the 'Blue-Eyed Devil' Race was Created" to Toni Morrison's *Bluest Eye*, the policeman's "blue eyes" in *The Bitter Society* serve as an index of the violence of Chinese racialization. Only the timely intervention of a white bystander prevents the arrests of Li and Wang as well. The Chinese consul eventually secures Tan's release, but the policemen go unpunished, for they had acted only in accordance with the letter of the law.

The chapter illustrates how police abuse targeting Chinese in the U.S. functioned under cover of legal formalism. Angered by the Chinese consulate's efforts to seek justice for Tan's attack, the municipal police retaliate with a campaign of harassment, threatening the diplomatic couriers with arrest for their lack of identification papers. The courier's protest, "You have no authority over diplomats!" is met with the policemen's sneering rejoinder: "We are only doing our duty. Since you don't have any identification and say that you work for the consulate but have no proof, you must at least show us your card, so that we can discharge our duty" (59). Consular officials and other exempt Chinese were particularly vulnerable to arrest and deportation because the Immigration Bureau required them to leave their Section 6 certificates verifying their exempt status at ports of entry, thus stripping them of documentation in the event of the periodic raids conducted by immigration officials searching for illegal aliens.[155] In addition, as the Chinese American reformer Ng observes, since the Geary Act "did not require the exempt classes or their wives and children to obtain a certificate of legal residence, . . . any Chinese merchant, student or physician who was in this country at the time of registration and did not get a certificate is now liable to arrest and imprisonment."[156] This would also prove true for U.S. citizens of Chinese descent, as in the case of Ju Toy.

The boycott novel gave literary form to the transpacific sentimental politics first delineated in Lin's translation of *Uncle Tom's Cabin*. As in the example of *The Bitter Society*, the boycott novel dramatized the racial suffering and abuse that the U.S. inflicted on Chinese migrants. Emotionally wrought scenes of anti-Chinese violence also critiqued China's failure to ensure the welfare of its overseas subjects, provoking nationalistic outrage in urban Shanghai, where the 1905 boycott originated. Gu Zifeng of *The Bitter Society* exclaims with dismay that Chinese officials "view the American exclusion laws as merely empty words on paper" and do nothing for their mitigation (61). Li Xinchun adds that "there's nothing that can be done if China refuses to stand up for herself" (62). In condemning the shortfalls of Chinese foreign diplomacy and sovereignty, such novels channeled sentiment toward a powerful, if emergent, Chinese nationalism—one with the dangerous potential to redirect populist antiforeign animus from the U.S. to the Chinese government once in the hands of exiled revolutionaries such as Sun Yat-sen, the first president of the Republic of China.

In *The Bitter Society*, the escalation of anti-Chinese violence forces the three merchants to close their businesses in San Francisco and return to Shanghai. On the eve of their departure, the men offer a few parting words to their fellow Chinese Americans: "You are not like the people back home; with your eyes and ears you've seen and listened to everything. You're well informed—how can you not see through this! Nobody says it aloud, but everyone knows it deep inside. After a while, we forget and act as if Europeans and Americans are really heaven's favorites, and that we Chinese deserve their bullying" (65). Americanization entails a process of racialization that differentiates the Chinese in the U.S. from the "people back home." In this, *The Bitter Society* limns the tense push-pull of connection and disaffiliation in the Chinese diaspora even as its sentimental narrative of racialized suffering in the U.S. seeks to draw all Chinese together into a collective—indeed, national—identification. Indeed, the repeated trope of threatened familial separation imagines a Chinese racial nationalism in which filial piety fuses with Chinese patriotism. Sympathetic characters repeatedly choose kin over material gain in the U.S.[157] In the novel's episodic account of San Francisco Chinatown, *The Bitter Society* centers sentimentalism in the racialization and radicalization of transpacific Chinese identification. The next section builds on this discussion of the transpacific politics of sentimentalism in the struggle against Chinese exclusion and illuminates understudied aspects of Eaton's aesthetic politics in her contemporaneous short fictions on the North American Chinese.

Edith Maude Eaton and the Politics of Home Life

In the U.S., the promise of a household unscathed by market forces came to distinguish the postbellum era of contract freedom after the abolition of slavery.[158] In casting the morality of free market relations against the evils of chattel slavery, antebellum writers had made "home life, together with labor, central to the conflict over slavery and freedom."[159] For example, Stowe figured the corruption of the nation in the slave market's erosion of home life, domesticity, and familial relations.[160] After abolition, home life became the proving ground for postemancipation freedoms, as unprecedented forms of state authority were brought to bear on a personal sphere "once held to be self regulating."[161] This transformation held powerful implications for the administration of U.S. immigration law. As the Immigration Bureau routinized its administrative processes at the end of the century, it began concentrating "on the everyday lives of Chinese immigrants it interrogated," asking for details of a personal and household nature to ascertain the veracity of admission claims to the U.S.[162] *U.S. v. Ju Toy* further placed the interpretation of immigration laws in the hands of the administrators tasked to enforce them, facilitating the policing of home life as a key feature of Progressive-era immigration regulation. Immigration inspectors interrogated applicants on the quotidian details of their home life in making admission decisions that often resulted in the separation of families. Immigration law vested inspectors with the power to separate Chinese families—wives from husbands, children from parents. It recalled the ravages of antebellum slavery and slave law as depicted in *Uncle Tom's Cabin* and bore testimony to the failures of postemancipation freedom.

Home life also became a key concern for Progressive-era reformers such as Jacob Riis, a Danish immigrant. By the time Riis published his pioneering work of investigative photojournalism *How the Other Half Lives: Studies among the Tenements of New York* (1890), Chinese exclusion had become an established feature of his adopted country, although he remained ambivalent about "the law that shuts out the ... Chinaman."[163] Riis entertained no hope for Chinese assimilation, unlike for European immigrants; they remain "a constant and terrible menace to society," particularly given fears of racial miscegenation.[164] Riis attributed this failure to a lack of proper home life. "Rather than banish the Chinamen," he suggests, "I would have the door opened wider— for his wife; and make it a condition of his coming or staying that he bring his wife with him."[165] The author and journalist Edith Maude Eaton, better known by her penname, Sui Sin Far, exposed the racial ideologies underpinning both Progressive-era immigration regulation and mainstream reformism. Like the boycott novel, her Chinatown stories dramatize the detrimental effects of Chinese exclusion on Chinese American home life and the normalizing racial violence that attended

U.S. nation and empire building under the aegis of Christian benevolence, tutelage, and uplift.[166]

Earlier critics such as Sean McCann dismissed Eaton for her apolitical "anti-progressivism"; however, this section, in contrast, reads her detailed domestic milieus as calibrated responses to the state management of Chinese households as a feature of Progressive-era immigration control.[167] The eldest daughter of an English father and a Chinese mother, Eaton published in over forty different Canadian, U.S., and Jamaican periodicals between 1888 and 1914.[168] Unlike her younger sister, who assumed a less stigmatized Japanese identity and penname, Onoto Watanna, Eaton embraced her Chinese identity and openly addressed the "Chinese Question." In her Chinatown stories, Eaton often adapted sentimentalism and its middle-class ideologies into a powerful critique of U.S. immigration law and the state regulation of Chinese home life. Her almost-exclusive focus on the domestic lives of "Americanized" Chinese merchants strategically utilized the class consciousness that structured sentimentalism's appeal to sympathetic identification as well as the letter of Chinese exclusion law.[169] In the early Progressive era, realism, regionalism, and local-color fictions had begun to supplant literary sentimentalism's once enormous popularity, yet sentimentalism's ideological force remained undiminished, particularly in its representational powers of making political problems legible by their effects on the household.[170] In Eaton's Chinatown stories, merchant households serve as exotic yet familiar points of identification for middle-class American readers, particularly given the feminization of the short-story format and the mass press reader at century's end.[171]

As with *The Bitter Society*'s San Francisco chapters, Eaton's emphasis on the domestic vicissitudes of Chinese merchants was a political response to popular Yellow Peril perceptions of inassimilable Chinese aliens. The Chinese merchants and compradores depicted in Eaton's stories were neither the abject coolies nor the hostile foreign aggressors promulgated in Chinese invasion fiction. These characters embodied, as Arnold Pan argues, a kind of "transnational modernity" that militated against Yellow Peril depictions of Chinese as undifferentiated "coolie" masses facilitating the end of American industrialism and Christian civilization.[172] In Eaton's writings, merchant figures serve as agents of modernity's promise; they stand as representative figures for a Chinese modernity modeled on yet antagonistic to the West, as China underwent the transition from empire to nation.[173] Her writings humanize a Chinese populace long racialized as labor-saving machines incapable of feeling, domestic ties, and home life. Naturalist typologies often heightened this dehumanizing massification of Chinese otherness in what Colleen Lye terms Asiatic racial form.[174] Writers such as Jack London and Frank Norris popularized the overdetermined Asiatic racial types associated with emerging forms of Pacific Coast naturalism and helped drive Eaton's experiments with sentimental and realist conventions. Her complex portrayals of merchant families and home life offer powerful counterpoints to the Yellow Peril discourse of an inassimilable Chinese menace as well as to the politics and form of Chinese invasion fiction studied in chapter 3.

During the period covering *Ju Toy* and the Chinese boycott of U.S. goods, Eaton published a range of journalistic writings and short fictions about the North American Chinese at the height of protests against the "bureaucratic tyranny" of the Immigration Bureau.[175] These Chinatown stories made their way into her only book, *Mrs. Spring Fragrance* (1909–1912), a collection of new and previously published works featuring the wife of a Chinese merchant who sets out to write "a book about Americans" for a Chinese audience.[176] It saw publication just as news of the newly established Republic of China broke headlines, and it remains Eaton's only work in book form, given her death two years later at the age of forty-nine. Literary scholars, including Mary Chapman, Martha Cutter, Dominika Ferens, and June Howard, have recovered over two hundred previously unknown publications, revealing Eaton's diverse range, in addition to the Chinatown stories and journalism reprinted in *Mrs. Spring Fragrance and Other Writings* (edited by Amy Ling and Annette White-Park; 1995).

In Eaton's more familiar Chinatown writings, racialized forms of legal subjection lie at the edges of her tales of middle-class romantic love and home life, framing their interpretation and meaning. In the first stories introducing the book's eponymous character, Eaton embeds a critique of U.S. immigration law in a wry epistle that Jade Spring Fragrance addresses to her "Americanized" husband, "a young curio merchant." Details tangential to the tale's marriage plot between U.S.-born Kai Tzu and Mai Gwi Far (or Laura) inform readers that immigration officials have placed Mrs. Spring Fragrance's brother-in-law in a "Detention Pen" (23). After attending a "magniloquent lecture" on "America, the Protector of China!" in the company of "an American lady," Mrs. Spring Fragrance, in reference to the speaker's jingoistic "expression of benevolence," playfully chides her husband: "And murmur no more because your honored elder brother, on a visit to this country, is detained under the roof-tree of this great Government instead of under your own humble roof. Console him with the reflection that he is protected under the wing of the Eagle, the Emblem of Liberty. What is the loss of ten hundred years or ten thousand times ten dollars compared with the happiness of knowing oneself so securely sheltered?" (21). These seemingly unrelated details remain at the edges of the unfolding marriage plot. They reveal the subtle workings of a racially repressive state in the formation of Chinese home life in the U.S.

A milder version of Wong Chin Foo's trademark satire, Mrs. Spring Fragrance's wry remarks undercut the rhetoric of protection and benevolence that informed U.S. immigration policies and underwrote U.S. imperial rule in the Pacific. U.S. diplomacy often masked its neocolonial interests in the language of benevolent friendship, citing the Open Door policy as affirmation that "the United States is China's greatest friend," in the words of one American consul in Guangzhou (or Canton).[177] U.S. newspapers sympathetic to the 1905 Chinese boycott of U.S. goods had drawn attention to this profound contradiction in the U.S. policy of Chinese exclusion. "Our Department of State talked fluently of maintaining 'the open door' in China," noted one editorial, "but it also simultaneously slammed the Philippines door in China's face."[178] In Eaton's collected stories, marginal references to shed detention and "the indemnity money returned to the Dragon by Uncle Sam" (23) — federal redress to China for the pogroms against Pacific Coast Chinese — emerge as unresolved textual disturbances, interrupting the mechanics of sentimental closure and consumption. Like Lin Shu's transpacific politics of sentimentalism, Eaton does not "describe sorrow for the purpose of eliciting useless tears from readers." Aligned with realist conventions, these details reveal the attenuation and disruption of the Chinese American household not as a fundamental defining characteristic of Asiatic racial difference but as the consequence of the racializing imperatives of U.S. immigration law.

Eaton's Chinatown writings emphasize themes of familial separation, "self-deportation," and failed immigration in short narratives that center Chinese figures as agents in and interpreters of their experiences in the U.S. Her sentimentalized plots dramatize the conflict between Chinese home life and the racializing imperatives of immigration law, illuminating the state as a catalyst for familial dissolution and violence. As a political critique, the trope of ruined home life exposes the failure of U.S. benevolence and protectorate relations with China. Thus, the transpacific contours of the boycott movement provide another underexamined framework for reading the much-debated politics of Eaton's short fictions. In fact, Eaton explicitly situates her writings on North American Chinese life within the same transpacific networks of communication and exchange that enabled the 1905 boycott. These "Chinese, Chinese-Americans I call them," she writes, "are not unworthy of a little notice, particularly as they sustain throughout the period of their residence here, a faithful and constant correspondence with relations and friends in the old country, and what they think and what they write about Americans, will surely influence, to a great extent, the conduct of their countrymen towards the people of the United States" (233). By 1909, Chapman notes that Eaton had also begun "studying Chinese, interviewing people in Chinatown in Chinese, and publishing 'translations' of Chinese folktales," like her predecessor Wong Chin Foo.[179] Her Chinatown stories feature Chinese merchants struggling and failing to protect their households from state incursions, for U.S. immigration law suspends their so-called right to family.[180] They capture in largely understudied ways what Pan describes as the complex "geopolitical structures of power between China and the West."[181] Federal immigration and naturalization laws produced Chinese migrants as alien menaces to American society even as U.S. foreign policy insisted on friendly protectorate relations with China.

First published in William Hayes Ward's *New York Independent* (September 2, 1909), Eaton's oft-anthologized "In the Land of the Free" powerfully marshals the sentimental trope of familial separation to critique the abusive administration of U.S. immigration law. The *Independent* appended a notice to the story alerting its readers to "the autobiography of Sui Sin Far in [its] issue of January 21, entitled 'Leaves from the

Mental Portfolio of an Eurasian.'" The *Independent* described Eaton's life story, which frames the short fiction, as truth "cast in the form of fiction," for "fiction . . . is often less strange and cruel than the truth."[182] In embracing literary production as a means toward political mobilization, antebellum abolitionists such as Stowe had popularized the adage of "truth stranger than fiction." Indeed, this maxim became the title of the reprinted edition of Josiah Henson's slave narrative, *Truth Stranger than Fiction: Father Henson's Story of His Own Life* (1858), which capitalized on the popularity of Stowe's fictional rendering of Henson as Uncle Tom.[183] In recasting fact in the form of fiction, Eaton's "In the Land of the Free" adapts the familiar tropes of sentimental fiction to social realism and the political context of Chinese exclusion.

The story begins with the return of Lae Choo, a Chinese woman—the wife of a local merchant—after she gives birth to their son while on a visit to China. The Chinese merchant Hom Hing is the expectant husband and father "who had been waiting on the wharf for an hour," impatient to "board the steamer and welcome his wife and child" (93). However, immigration officials detain the child on board, claiming, "We cannot allow the boy to go ashore. There is nothing in the paper that you have shown us—your wife's papers and your own—having any bearing upon the child" (94). They proceed to administer the strict letter of the law against the Chinese merchant, for "the boy has no certificate entitling him to admission to this country," taking him into custody until they "hear from Washington" (94). A stray remark muttered by one of the officers, "I don't like this part of the business," speaks to the regularity of familial separation as a procedural norm of Chinese immigration administration (94). Hom Hing's repeated protestation, "he is my son," only elicits the officials' rote response, "We have no proof" (94). Lae Choo's maternal claim, "he my son too," gives the inspectors some pause; but she too must relinquish the child, for "'tis the law" (94–95). Immigration law supersedes the mother-child bond—the most powerful representation of ownership and emotional connection in the tradition of literary sentimentalism. "The Little One protested lustily against the transfer, but his mother covered her face with her sleeve and his father silently led her away," reports the narrator. "Thus was the law of the land complied with" (95). As in the case of Ju Toy, immigration inspectors demanded reproductive heterosexual home life as proof of Chinese assimilation to American social norms even as Chinese exclusion laws militated against this domestic ideal.

"In the Land of the Free" depicts U.S. immigration law as inimical to Chinese home life, for the child's arrival initiates a devastating separation from his parents. His "bereaved mother" wastes away as a day turns into months. Hom Hing's incredulous assertion, "There cannot be any law that would keep a child from its mother," is proven wrong (96). The story depicts a complex landscape of Chinese home life shaped by immigration law. "Beneath the flat occupied by" Lae Choo and Hom Hing lie the "quarters for a number of bachelor Chinamen"—an earlier generation of labor migrants whose bachelordom remains largely a condition imposed by long-standing immigration bans against "immoral Chinese women," since the Page Act (96). This extraneous detail, like others in Eaton's short fictions, works toward dispelling the specter of so-called bachelor societies as Chinese perversions of normative domesticity. Long subjected to class-based racialized legislation, these Chinese bachelors lurk at the edges of Eaton's domestic tale about middle-class home life. Indeed, their unspoken stories constitute the historical substratum of Eaton's critique—existing literally underneath Hom Hing and Lae Choo's apartment. Such details fuse classic sentimental tropes with realism's "detail-laden physical descriptions," revealing glimpses of the proletarian histories of Chinese labor migration underlying Eaton's depictions of middle-class Chinese domesticity.[184]

Whereas Eaton depicts intermeddling Christian missionaries and misplaced Christian benevolence as the agents of familial disunion in the Jamaican setting of "The Sugar Cane Baby" (1910), it is U.S. law and the bureaucratic state that separates parents and child in "In the Land of the Free." After five months, the Immigration Bureau transfers the child to a Christian mission, where "white women" care for him, as "Washington still delayed sending the answer which would return him to his parents" (97). In desperation, the father commits all their savings to a "keen-faced" young American lawyer, James Clancy, who lodges fifteen fruitless appeals to the government "Re Chinese child, alleged to be the son of Hom Hing, Chinese merchant" (98). In this figure, Eaton inveighs against the popular depictions of the avaricious "thirst for gold" driving early Chinese migration to the fabled "Gold Mountain" of the

Pacific Coast. She reverses this extraction metaphor, for Lae Choo barters her jewelry of "pure China gold" for Clancy's legal services. Eaton subtly manipulates English syntax in her depiction of Lae Choo, who leavens this exchange with an ethical critique. "You not one hundred man good," she angrily accuses Clancy; "you just common white man" (99). Ten months later, and the "paper had come at last—the precious paper which gave Hom Hing and his wife the right to the possession of their own child" (101). State authority supersedes *and* authorizes their parental claim to their own child. Eaton's critique draws on the inversion of domestic order long established in sentimental fiction, in which the parental claims of mother love—typified by characters such as Eliza Harris—should reign supreme. The parents finally arrive at the mission to reclaim their "Little One" but discover that he has been renamed "Kim," in a pointed reference to Rudyard Kipling's vagabond orphan.

The painful reunion between mother and child further illuminates the tragic force of U.S. immigration law. Lae Choo "fell on her knees and stretched out her hungry arms towards her son" (101). However, the long separation has remade mother into a stranger, for "the Little One shrunk from her and tried to hide himself in the folds of the white woman's skirt" (101). The story ends with the child rejecting his Chinese mother in English: "'Go'way, go'way!' he bade his mother" (101). In this pathos-inducing conclusion, Eaton uses sentimental tropology, yet she resists sentimental resolution or closure. Mother and child are reunited, but separation has wrought irreparable damage. In fusing sentimentalism's moral suasion with aspects of realist form, Eaton critiques the Christian ecumenical mission to Westernize Chinese children at home and in Asia.

In another tragic tale, "The Wisdom of the New," Eaton marshals the pathos-laden trope of infanticide to explore the consequences of familial separation from the perspective of Pau Lin, a sympathetic Chinese mother. Mother-love-driven infanticide harks back to the widely disseminated antebellum accounts of Margaret Garner, or the "Modern Medea," which Stowe anticipated in the fictional character of Cassy from *Uncle Tom's Cabin*. Set partially in China, "The Wisdom of the New" also serves as a corollary tale to "In the Land of the Free." The Chinese mother, Lae Choo, appears as one of Pau Lin's "women friends" in the "American Chinatown," linking the two stories (48, 49). In this powerful character study, Eaton rewrites literary sentimentalism and its trope of ruined home life to explore the limits of female sympathy. The story dramatizes Pau Lin's painful sense of alienation upon arrival to the U.S., for she had "left all her own relations" in China to join her merchant husband, Wou Sankwei, a "junior partner and bookkeeper of the firm of Leung Tang Wou and Co. of San Francisco" (43). The young son Yen brings husband and wife together, yet the parents disagree vehemently over the child's assimilation to U.S. social norms, namely, his enrollment in "American school." "They have drifted seven years of life apart," observes Mrs. Dean, Sankwei's American benefactress: "There is no bond of interest or sympathy between them, save the boy" (53).

In the U.S., Pau Lin becomes increasingly embittered by her husband's friendship with and admiration for an American "New Woman," Adah Charlton, Mrs. Dean's niece. Charlton expresses a powerful sympathetic identification with Pau Lin. "I do not believe there is any real difference between the feelings of a Chinese wife and an American wife," exclaims Charlton to her aunt; yet her female affinity remains largely one-sided, for the language barrier prevents Charlton from communicating it to Pau Lin (53). Rather, Charlton uses this sympathetic identification to authorize a private interview with Sankwei on Pau Lin's behalf, breaking from the social restraint that had long structured their interpersonal relations. To Sankwei's protests against Charlton's meddling in his domestic affairs, Charlton replies, "You promised to listen and heed. I do understand, even though I cannot speak to your wife nor find out what she feels and thinks" (57). In this fashion, Eaton exposes how sympathetic affinity reinforces existing asymmetries of racial power in the sentimental idiom.[185] Furthermore, Charlton's sympathetic revelations appear belated in a narrative that minimizes aesthetic distance by allowing readers to surmount the English-Chinese language divide and enter Pau Lin's consciousness. Eaton thus meditates on the forms of "sentimental benevolence" embraced by various middle-class women's reform movements (and crystallized in the pervasive trope of female enslavement to patriarchal power). She reveals how the sympathetic identification central to the sentimental idiom often reinforced the hierarchies of racial difference that it sought to overcome.[186]

These emotional undercurrents facilitate the chilling dénouement of the tale, in which Pau Lin, fearing the loss of her beloved son Yen to the contaminating influences of Westernization or the "Wisdom of the New," poisons him in a desperate act of mother love. As in "In the Land of the Free," the Chinese woman's tireless efforts to embody the domestic ideal of motherhood end in a failure that reinscribes Asiatic racial difference. In this fashion, Eaton explores the volatile and shifting dynamics of sentimental identification, testing the limits of affective attunement between reader and tragic Chinese heroine. In Eaton's characterization of Pau Lin, as earlier in Stowe's Cassy, external circumstances—here, the long separation between husband and wife enforced by Chinese exclusion—conspire to transform "the redemptive, generous motherhood of ideal domesticity" into "murderous maternity," as Gillian Brown argues in her reading of *Uncle Tom's Cabin*.[187] The child's death facilitates Pau Lin and Sankwei's return to China in an act of self-deportation, just as Lae Choo finds her motherhood usurped by the state and Christian missionaries. As stories of failed immigration, both stories dramatize the destruction of Chinese American households. Eaton introduces contradiction and failure into the normative discourses of Chinese motherhood and heterosexual home life to expose the contradiction and failure of U.S. protectorate relations with China.[188] Hence, the realist irresolution of these narratives accentuates the sentimental trope of ruined home life, revealing the aesthetic experimentation at the heart of Eaton's political critique.[189]

By emphasizing the plight of merchant figures, Eaton's North American Chinese stories sought to reveal the growing discrepancy between the formal letter of immigration law and its bureaucratic enforcement. Her Chinatown stories illuminate the destructive effects of "bureaucratic tyranny" in the Immigration Bureau's administration of Chinese exclusion.[190] The Supreme Court ruling in *U.S. v. Ju Toy* effectively unmoored the new Immigration Bureau from federal courts, placing the interpretation of immigration laws into the hands of administrators tasked to enforce them. Immigrants seeking admission into the U.S. became subject to the power of immigration officials such as Inspector Dunn in the case of Ju Toy. As illustrated in *The Bitter Society*, these bureaucratic officials exercised considerable discretion with little, if any, restraint.[191] Bureaucracy, according to the social theorist Max Weber, is the inevitable consequence and necessary condition of modernity; thus, the radical expansion of immigration administration also facilitated the coconstitutive rise of the U.S. as a bureaucratic state and overseas empire.[192]

Chinese writers and activists continued to press for broad reforms in immigration policy and procedure, demanding the judicial review of admission and deportation decisions. Protests against Chinese exclusion such as *Ju Toy* and the stalled negotiations over the Gresham-Yang Treaty became the focus of increasing anti-American sentiment in China, culminating in the popular mass movement of the 1905 boycott. From opposite sides of the Pacific, the boycott novelists and Eaton seized on the figure of the Chinese merchant as the contradictory exception to the racial rule of Chinese exclusion in fashioning their literary critiques of U.S. sovereignty and state power. Their varied writings across the English-Chinese language divide delineate the contours of a transpacific politics of literary sentimentalism attuned to the contradictions of Chinese exclusion and U.S. foreign policy on China. By dramatizing the destruction of Chinese home life (and, by extension, the Chinese nation), these various writers centered Chinese racial suffering and victimization by Western powers as constitutive of asymmetrical East-West relations at the dawn of the new century.

This transpacific revivification of literary sentimentalism emerged just as influential U.S. literary realists such as William Dean Howells began deriding the form as obsolete and incapable of expressing the truth of the modern experience. In the context of Progressive-era immigration control, literary sentiment—particularly in its arousal of suffering, shame, and frustration—limns a powerful transpacific counterdiscursive formation to Chinese exclusion and its attendant Yellow Peril discourses. For example, Eaton explores the regenerative qualities of racial shame in another Chinatown story, "The Son of Chung Wo" (1910), which features a young Chinese protagonist who passes as Japanese, because, according to his father, "he had a horror of himself as a Chinaman."[193] The story concludes with the return of the prodigal son, who confesses to his shameful ethnic masquerade, seeking redemption and reconciliation with his Chinese father. Sentiment also held particular appeal to Chinese translators and writers such as Lin Shu, given the emergence of the genre of New Fiction in China as late-Qing reformers began advocating the role of fiction in social and political change.[194] In militating against "useless tears," Lin's translation of *Uncle Tom's Cabin* radically transformed U.S. sentimentalism to advance emerging forms of Chinese national consciousness; he excised its Christian ideologies and adapted it to a "Confucian structure of feeling," as Lee argues.[195] In the context of Chinese exclusion, the protonationalism of Chinese sentimentalism differed from the sentimental politics of *Uncle Tom's Cabin*, in which white consumption of black suffering helped reestablish hierarchies of racial difference.

The analogous—if divergent—literary forms examined in this chapter limn the possibilities and limitations of sentimentalism as a vehicle for transpacific political protest and reform, as China began forging its cultural destiny in the modern world. In China's transition from empire to nation, Chinese leaders, following the May Fourth Movement, began disavowing Lin's classical Chinese translations and Confucian sentimentalism, which they deemed as archaic to the new modern China, just as American realists such as Howells overlooked the literary experimentations—indeed, the progressive modernism—of a writer such as Eaton. Like her Chinese contemporaries, Eaton's self-conscious use of sentimentalism centered racial pain and victimization while drawing its realist details from the legal text of Chinese exclusion.[196] In adapting sentimentalism to the politics of Chinese exclusion, these various writers sought to center China and Chinese suffering in a history of Western thinking on sympathy and humanity that deemed the Chinese outside what Eric Hayot calls the "sympathetic transformation of human life that founded modernity's dream of the universal subject."[197] Taken together, these writings responded to and challenged insidious and lasting Western discourses of Yellow Peril that imagined the limits of the "human" in China and in the failures of Chinese sentiment.[198]

Conclusion

Against Historicism: James D. Corrothers and Speculations on Our Racial Futures

Nineteenth-century America is commonly viewed as the era of free immigration before twentieth-century legal regulations put into place racialized restrictions and national-origins quotas; however, growing anxieties over the influx of foreigners and changing U.S. foreign policies, especially in regard to China, transformed America into what the historian Erika Lee calls a "gatekeeping nation" by the century's end.[1] The "Chinese Question" produced a vast archive of legislation, literature, and images that was made anomalous to the development of modern U.S. immigration history. It also directed the course of U.S. foreign relations in the Asia Pacific. The various Chinese test cases challenging the Exclusion Acts first identified the porous line between excludable (hence illegal) alien and citizen that continues to trouble U.S. immigration policy today.[2] The Chinese immigration case law from *Chae Chan Ping v. U.S.* (1889) to *U.S. v. Ju Toy* (1905) reveals how Chinese exclusion established the racialized category of the "alien ineligible to citizenship" that came to define all immigrants from the Asia Pacific as nonnaturalizable noncitizens. It facilitated the juridical and ideological production of "all people of Asian ancestry as presumptively foreign and thus un-American," as the legal scholar Devon Carbado argues.[3] The "Chinese Question" also helped establish national sovereignty and the regulation of territorial borders as the central premise of federal plenary power over immigration in ways that articulated nationalism with racism. The changing racial landscape of Reconstruction-era immigration, naturalization, and citizenship policies not only shaped Asian American cultural politics but also profoundly impacted African American life in the *longue durée*.

At the end of the century, *Plessy v. Ferguson* (1896) began the reentrenchment of legal whiteness, and Progressive-era immigration laws—modeled on Chinese exclusion—further secured this exclusionary category of racial whiteness. The 1917 Immigration Act expanded the racial exclusion of Chinese immigrants to South Asians and other inhabitants of the Middle East, East Asia, and the Pacific Islands into what became known as the "Asiatic Barred Zone."[4] In quick succession, two additional U.S. Supreme Court cases, *Takao Ozawa v. U.S.* (1922) and *U.S. v. Bhagat Singh Thind* (1923), applied the racially excluded category of the Asiatic to Japanese and South Asians, making them ineligible for naturalization according to precedents set in the earlier Chinese cases. In theorizing these so-called prerequisite cases, the legal scholar Ian Haney López charts the shifting ways in which whiteness functioned as a normative identity for citizenship, revealing the racialized terms of naturalization jurisprudence through which people became white by law.[5] Delivered right before the Johnson-Reed Immigration Act of 1924, the rulings in *Ozawa* and *Thind* completed the legal construction of the banned Asiatic, which was later extended to immigrants from Korea (in 1924) and the Philippines (in 1934).[6]

The Johnson-Reed Act further realigned race, nationality, and religion in complex new ways by establishing numerical limits on immigration and a globalized racial-national hierarchy favoring the admission of white European immigrants.[7] The Immigration Bureau tasked to administer the law also had grown into a powerful centralized agency with broad discretionary powers and control over all phases of immigration, according to Lucy Salyer.[8] The Johnson-Reed Act hardened into twentieth-century law the racial categories first forged during Chinese exclusion, as it sought to resolve the legal ambiguities and conflicts over the racial status of nonwhite, nonblack immigrants from the Asia Pacific.[9] It gave shape to the "peculiarly American racial category" of the banned Asiatic, which in turn helped to further solidify the boundaries of whiteness, particularly the whiteness of desirable European immigrants, notes Mae M. Ngai.[10] Such forms of Asiatic racialization continued well into the Cold War era with the 1952 Immigration and Nationality Act, or McCarran-Walter Act, which repealed existing measures against Asian immigration and naturalization yet continued to restrict Asian immigration according to an annual quota of one hundred new immigrants on the basis of race rather than nationality.[11]

Against the rising tide of Progressive-era white nativism, black writers and activists such as W. E. B. Du Bois, Sutton E. Griggs, and James D. Corrothers drew on the intersecting histories of black and Asian racializations to craft powerful critiques of the U.S. "racial state," active in the perpetuation of social inequities through the manipulation of race and racial categories, as Michael Omi and Howard Winant have shown.[12] Writing at the nadir of U.S. race relations, Griggs and Corrothers envisioned the U.S. racial state as the site of violent future struggle. Griggs, in a supplement to his self-published black conspiracy novel *The Hindered Hand* (1905), condemned the "cultivation of race hatreds on the part of Mr. [Thomas] Dixon and others who labor with him" and linked U.S. empire in the Asia Pacific with racial segregation and the institutional divestment of constitutional rights and protections from black citizens. To illustrate this point, Griggs considers the interconnected global economies structuring U.S. market relations with the non-Western world: "The wonderful activity of American industries call[s] loudly for the world as a market for their goods. . . . The dark races of world, now backward in the manner of manufacturing, must largely furnish those markets," he observed. "The cloven foot of America's race prejudice will make itself manifest, and its owner will find it increasingly difficult to secure a ready purchaser for his goods."[13]

Resurgent fears over U.S. domestic overproduction stimulated the search for international markets capable of absorbing American surplus. This economic rationale drove U.S. incursions into the Asia Pacific as demands for Chinese "cheap" labor waned after the completion of the transcontinental railroad. Immigration, as Lisa Lowe argues, "has been a crucial locus through which U.S. interests have recruited and regulated both labor and capital from Asia."[14] For Griggs, the nationalization of the anti-Chinese movement in the U.S. was of one piece with the antiblack national imaginary espoused in Thomas Dixon's *The Leopard's Spots* (1901), the first novel in his Ku Klux Klan trilogy. For the likes of Dixon, overseas empire helped shore up the idea of the U.S. as fundamentally white and descended from European immigrant stock. A fantasy of U.S. race and empire, Dixon's *Leopard's Spots* brought into alignment white supremacy and imperial rule in its depiction of the

Spanish-American War as the realization of the "beautiful dream called *E Pluribus Unum*" for a long-sectionalized "Anglo-Saxon" America.[15]

Writers such as Du Bois, Griggs, and Corrothers began articulating black protest against Jim Crow America with Asian anticolonial resistance abroad. In *The Souls of Black Folk* (1903), Du Bois cast his global color-line thesis within this twofold context of race and empire: the "problem of the twentieth century is the problem of the color-line, the relation of the darker to lighter races of men in Asia and Africa, in America and the islands of the sea."[16] He later gave fictional form to his color-line thesis in his much-maligned utopian romance *Dark Princess* (1928), which envisions a "Great Council of the Darker Peoples" that includes the African American protagonist Matthew Townes and representatives from the "Asiatic Barred Zone," who are committed to the overthrow of white imperialism throughout the world.[17] For Griggs, the 1905 Chinese boycott against U.S. goods (studied in the previous chapter) serves as a precursor to U.S. economic ruination—the dire consequences of the white supremacist ideologies fostered by the likes of Dixon. "We have a hint of what will happen in the awakened darker world," writes Griggs, "in the boycott of American goods by the Chinese, because of the rude treatment by American custom officials, of unoffending Chinese, a treatment born of the spirit of race hatred."[18] Building on the example of the Chinese boycott, Griggs envisions the revolutionary possibilities of an alternate future, in which U.S. industrial modernity finds itself at the mercy of the "dark races of the world."

On the eve of World War I, Corrothers gave powerful fictional form to Griggs's speculations about the political-economic futures of the "awakened darker world" arrayed against the U.S. racial state. For Corrothers, race war is no longer a contingent future possibility but is a foregone conclusion of modern American life. A former Chicago newspaperman turned Methodist minister and writer "of Scotch-Irish, [Cherokee] Indian, and Negro stock," according to one contemporaneous account, Corrothers serialized his two-part short story "A Man They Didn't Know" in the December 1913 and January 1914 issues of the NAACP's *Crisis*.[19] Du Bois, during his long tenure as editor, dictated the uncompromising direction of the *Crisis*, which he set forth in his opening editorial: "The object of this publication is to set forth those facts and arguments which show the danger of race prejudice, particularly as manifested today towards colored people."[20] In this spirit, Corrothers's "A Man They Didn't Know" charts the complex converging processes of racial formations that structured African American and Asian American life in the U.S. Mentioned briefly in chapter 3, "A Man They Didn't Know" is one of Corrothers's lesser-studied stories in a varied corpus that often "exploit[ed] and subvert[ed] minstrelsy" to illustrate "the complexities and contradictions within assimilation and racial uplift ideology," according to the historian Kevin Gaines.[21] Corrothers's story recasts the popular subgenre of Chinese invasion fiction to imagine the possibility of an alternate racial future uncoupled from the historicism of past precedent.

The denial of African American progress has long been linked to the threat of an Asiatic future in the U.S. cultural imaginary. The idea of black backwardness emerged alongside and through equally denigrating Yellow Peril discourses of aggressive Asiatic difference. The future that Corrothers imagines in "A Man They Didn't Know" is informed by this past but seeks neither to reiterate nor to resemble it. In resisting historicism, Corrothers crafts an alternate world in which the racialized structures of economic, political, and social oppression have unified Griggs's "awakened darker world" into a heterogeneous alliance against U.S. imperialism and white supremacy. His future fantasy begins in medias res with the startling yet disorienting admission, "The opposition was right."[22] In plying the negation and avowal of knowledge, "A Man They Didn't Know" expresses a keen desire for historical reinvention, as it forces readers to confront their lack of knowledge in a plot that moves backward to illuminate the circumstances unfolding in the narrative present. Set in an unspecified future, "A Man They Didn't Know" challenges the multiform nature of white supremacy and the class-based ideology of racial uplift in its exploration of black identifications inimical to the U.S. racial state. It entertains the idea of black treason in counterrepresentation to what Stephen Knadler describes as a long-standing romantic discourse of black national loyalty and "organic citizenship" as an inborn racial instinct.[23] Racial uplift ideology often utilized depictions of black patriotism in advocating the "spread of civilization and the interests of the American nation" as a means of overcoming racial barriers at home, according to Gaines.[24] Corrothers, like Griggs before him, resisted the idea of black Americans as willing agents of white imperial enterprise and the U.S. racial state.

"A Man They Didn't Know" links together critiques of U.S. incursions into Mexico and the Asia Pacific with structural racism and white supremacy at home. A bungling President Martin Carlos Nefferman has brought the U.S. to the brink of national catastrophe. The narrator derides Nefferman's failure of statesmanship as he unveils the global contours of an incipient race war poised to erupt from both within and without the U.S.:

> Already the Orientals, through their secret treaties with Mexico, were at the beginnings of things. The American consulate in Mexico City had been damaged; several Americans in Mexico had been imprisoned, tortured and killed; shots, always "random shots," had been fired across the border into the United States, wounding our citizens and destroying property; American soldiers had been hit, and skirmishes were frequent until forbidden by the American government. Then began the desertions of our Negro soldiers to Mexican ranks. There these trained men, of a race never before disloyal to their land or flag, manned the machine guns for the "Mexicans," and sent vindictive volleys crashing back into American homes and towns. (85)

As in Griggs's militant black conspiratorial fantasy *Imperium in Imperio* (1899), Corrothers reworks a range of historical materials into his plot of future Asiatic invasion and race war. In the Treaty of Guadalupe Hidalgo (1848), Mexico ceded the vast territories that later became Arizona and parts of New Mexico and Nevada, but this did not end U.S. territorial aggrandizement along the southwestern borderlands. Corrothers alludes to the 1910 revolution against the Mexican autocrat Porfirio Díaz, whose regime had been long supported by the U.S. government. He envisions "Negro soldiers," deployed to suppress the border uprising, breaking away from the U.S. Army and finding common cause with Mexican anticolonial revolutionaries—a fiction informed, in part, by the racial histories of the "Jim Crow Southwest," which ranged from Indian boarding schools aimed to "civilize" Native Americans to mass deportations of Mexican nationals from border states.[25]

Corrothers then proceeds to bring together Mexican independence struggles with the political mobilizations of black and Asian populations in the U.S. The narrator continues, "Next came the California 'land law' movement, against which Japan formally protested to this government—*her only open move*" (85). The California Alien Land Law (1913) worked in concert with the racial ban against Asiatic naturalization to prohibit "aliens ineligible for citizenship"—namely, nonwhite, nonblack Japanese immigrants—from owning land or property in the state.[26] In crafting a fictional Japan-Mexico alliance, Corrothers, like Jack London in his dystopian fiction *Iron Heel* (1908), may have drawn on rumors originated by Kaiser Wilhelm II of Germany—infamous, as Gary Okihiro observes, for disseminating the racialized threat of Yellow Peril—who claimed to have evidence of Japanese soldiers dispersed throughout Mexico with orders to seize the Panama Canal.[27] In Corrothers's alternate history, racial restrictions further politicize these various minoritized constituencies in the U.S., who join in "the remarkable '*votes for Negroes;' justice NOW!*' movement of the blacks throughout the country" (86). In thus limning the political contours of the national "crisis . . . at hand," Corrothers envisions a future in which racialized U.S. citizens long subject to white hegemony join forces with the foreign subjects of U.S. colonial and economic expansion.[28]

In imagining politicized black Americans joining with anticolonial Mexican revolutionaries and dissident Nisei and Chinese Americans, Corrothers offers a counternarrative to the revolutionary cross-racial alliance first envisioned in William Ward Crane's earlier Chinese invasion fiction "The Year 1899" (1893), in which a disaffected black citizenry leagues with Chinese and Native Americans in an unsuccessful attempt to overthrow the U.S. and global white supremacy.[29] Published in the *Overland Monthly*, Crane's tale purports to be a historical record of the past like the Chinese invasion fictions studied in chapter 3. A precursor to Fu Manchu's international Si-fan organization, Crane's cross-racial confederacy originates in Caribbean emancipation from colonial rule. In the neighboring U.S., the unification of the Chinese and African American populations becomes a growing source of white anxiety, especially after a white refugee confirms the radical portent of the Afro-Asian rituals that he witnesses, echoing similar fears voiced by Cuban planters such as Eliza McHatton Ripley (studied in chapter 1) over the possible revolutionary alliances between black Creole slaves and Chinese contract laborers. The "reservation Indians," according to Crane's tale, "had generally entered into the plot, and . . . the Southern negroes had also gone into the league in vast numbers," while "the whole of Asia and Malaysia and all northern Africa . . . join[ed] in a holy war against the white race everywhere" (580, 582). Arrayed in black uniform and carrying "black felt banners," this heterogeneous coalition unifies under the universalized sign of blackness: "'The blacks are coming!' was the horrified cry in their front" (583). However, it also advances the reentrenchment of legal whiteness as factionalized European countries unite along the global color line to defeat the "black and tan combination," thus ending the "human inundation from the East" and returning the white race to power (586, 589).

Whereas Crane's vision of an (ultimately thwarted) allied Asiatic invasion sought to affirm the ideologies of white supremacy and Western colonialism, Corrothers's "A Man They Didn't Know" seizes on the radical imaginary of a black alliance with foreign powers to challenge the U.S. racial state and its white supremacist order. Corrothers's imagination of future race war does not reconsolidate categorical "whiteness" as racial eligibility for citizenship, for the struggle at hand also includes "certain renegade whites" along with black and Asian birthright citizens. In Corrothers's tale, President Nefferman's sneering indifference toward the racialized protest and revolutionary struggle erupting across the U.S. abruptly ends with the "'peaceful' revolution of Hawaii," in which "20,000 Hawaiian-born Japanese youths, real 'American citizens,' who had the right to vote, . . . together with certain renegade whites and a wholesale importation of Negroes, formed a new political balance of power in the islands" (85). Corrothers roots in Hawaii the cross-racial combination that precipitates the U.S. into defensive action against an Asiatic invasion. He charts the fictional course of Hawaiian independence that serves as a counterpart to the ongoing Mexican Revolution. "The yellow peril is upon us," reports an official communiqué. "Behind all that has happened may *now* be discerned the hand of the plotting East" (86). In protest against the U.S. nation-state, black Americans offer a near-unanimous response to this impending race war: "The Negroes declared . . . they would not bear arms in the impending conflict unless the national government took steps for their relief" (86).

Facing this formidable alliance, President Nefferman is shocked to encounter the "unprecedented attitude which [the] colored citizens" have assumed toward "the national government," for the defense of the U.S. requires full African American participation in the war effort (87). In this, Corrothers explores the racialization of different nonwhite minorities in relation to the state. The president must appeal to a council of representative black leaders for their help and sympathy: "I *know* your race has been abused; I know we have lost its confidence. *Can it be restored*?" (87). The only remedy for black disaffection from the nation, as the protagonist Grant Noble, a Baptist minister, emphatically insists, is "simply, *inspiring JUSTICE*" (136). A possible alter ego for Corrothers, Noble first appeared in another short story, titled "At the End of the Controversy" (1914) and published in the *American Magazine*. In this earlier tale, Noble is an honest man betrayed by both the white religious establishment and the members of his own black congregation in a series of tragic events that lead to the untimely deaths of his wife and son.[30] As the plot unfolds in "A Man They Didn't Know," the now-disaffected Noble has nearly yielded to enemy recruitment, and only Nefferman's timely appeal prevents his treasonous betrayal. "The subjugation of the whole country is planned," informs Noble: "The yellow race has shaken hands upon the prospect" (137). Nefferman tasks Noble with the recruitment of the "discredited negro boxer" Jed Blackburn, based on the African American heavyweight champion John Arthur "Jack" Johnson (1878–1946), to lead the black citizenry to war. Blackburn initially refuses to "fight fer *this* country," claiming, "Fightin' fer white folks is what ruined *me!*" and "I'm just whut white men *developed* me into" (137). However, Noble convinces Blackburn to accept the commission as a means to personal redemption and not (as it might appear) to prove his fitness for citizenship and inclusion within the imagined community. Dialect marks Blackburn's regionalized class origins, and his backstory reveals the centrality of white power in such "sporting" violence among blacks. Corrothers thus weaves into the plot of Asiatic invasion a structural critique of the corrosive impact of the U.S. racial state and its white supremacist order on black life.

Unlike earlier Chinese invasion fiction, Corrothers's "A Man They Didn't Know" explicitly emphasizes the racialized structures of U.S. foreign and domestic policies as provocation for allied Asiatic attack.

Corrothers locates the origins of the ensuing war in the country's histories of racialized violence toward its domestic and colonial subjects, and the plot of Asiatic invasion allows Corrothers to contemplate the radical possibilities of black political progress in an alternate future. The impending war brings together African Americans with European immigrants into a multiethnic army: "The country responded gallantly to the President's call for volunteers—Germans, Jews, Irish, Italians, Negroes, men of nearly every race, a million Americans sprang bravely to arms, proudly augmenting the regular troops" (137). However, this show of patriotism does not elide the dissident blacks, "renegade whites," and Nisei who helped precipitate the crisis at hand by seeking common cause with Mexican and Hawaiian anticolonial revolutionaries. Corrothers's invocation of figures inimical to the nation—aliens barred from naturalization, anticolonial revolutionaries, and traitors—pushes beyond citizenship as the horizon of national inclusion. For Corrothers, black national identity is forged in relation to these divergent yet interlinked racial formations and in the global contexts of U.S. continental and overseas empire.

In the penultimate pages, Blackburn leads an advance troop of ten thousand black volunteers into a victorious counterattack against the Japanese invasion of Southern California. He ends the Japanese invasion but dies in the bloody battle, which arrayed "400,000 yellow men against 10,000 blacks." Proclaimed the "man of the hour," the now-chastened President Nefferman "generously avowed that much credit was due to a colored man of the name of Grant Noble," who in turn seeks out the slain Blackburn, declaring, "There, gentlemen ... is a man they didn't know" (138). Corrothers makes white recognition of black masculine national participation contingent on Blackburn's death. He serves as a representative figure for the black "masses" and remains the unnamed subject of the story's enigmatic title. The belated recognition that the state extends to Blackburn (and mediated through Noble) further illuminates the simulacrum of black racial inclusiveness against the backdrop of Asiatic exclusion.[31] It too comes at a terrible human cost, given the horrific losses suffered by the "army of Nippon," warning us that gains against racism are often accompanied by the broadening of other forms of racial thinking.[32] Corrothers offers a deeply ambivalent vision of black national assimilation forged in violent bloodshed and precipitated by nativist antiblack and anti-immigrant violence and imperialist intervention. It limns the push-pull of black political weddedness to and alienation from the U.S. In rewriting the Chinese invasion subgenre, Corrothers meditates on the occulted black presence—in the rhetorical figure of "a man they didn't know"—essential to the establishment and preservation of U.S. modernity in the global world order. As with Vachel Lindsay (studied in chapter 3), Corrothers manipulates the radical, counterfactual possibilities embedded in the form of Chinese invasion fiction while challenging the white supremacist ideologies that underpinned the subgenre's Orientalist imaginary of the racialized Asiatic "Other."

Specifically, "A Man They Didn't Know" reimagines how U.S. immigration law, foreign policy, and empire writ large might offer a glimpse of America's possible racial futures. Rather than a testament to black patriotism, Corrothers's story critically recasts the interlocking racial formation forged in the previous century: the dialectical configuration of black inclusion/Chinese (or Asiatic) exclusion. His bitter fantasy of belated black inclusion questions the necessary exclusion—indeed, destruction—of an Asiatic presence encroaching on Nefferman's white America. In thus alluding to an earlier moment of historical convergence, Corrothers draws out a tale of African American identity formation from the Yellow Peril subgenre of Asiatic invasion to challenge the racialization of U.S. citizenship and national inclusion. Writing in Jim Crow America, Corrothers dramatizes the conflicts over citizenship and immigration studied in this book and anticipates the era of the Johnson-Reed Act and beyond. Beginning in the nineteenth century, the racialization of Chinese difference as the basis of nonwhite, nonblack racial exclusion continued into the twentieth century. Chinese exclusion remained in force until 1943, when Congress repealed the law as a wartime measure to stem Japanese war propaganda; however, this did not end America's policy of racial restriction against the Chinese. In lieu of Chinese exclusion, Congress set the annual Chinese quota at 105 and further constructed it according to an idea of Chinese racial difference that applied to all Chinese in the world (not just to those originating from China), unlike the immigration quotas for all other nations, as Ngai points out.[33] This anomalous quota system based on race rather than nation remained active until the Immigration and

Nationality Act of 1965 repealed the national-origins quota system, including the one against the Chinese (although it maintained the policy of numerical limitations).[34]

The measured utopianism of "A Man They Didn't Know" opens up a generative space for rethinking citizenship and the processes of racial formation through struggle and contestation. It too limns alternate forms of cross-racial and transpacific connections in an unspecified American future. In imagining the potential demise of the U.S. racial state, Corrothers reexamines the role of history and precedent in determining the future course of race and racialization in the U.S. Moreover, the lack of narrative closure dramatizes racialization as an ongoing epistemological problem. Blackburn remains unknown and unknowable to the disembodied "they" of Corrothers's fictional U.S. racial state, suggesting the limits of U.S. citizenship and its additive logic of greater racialized inclusion. Furthermore, Corrothers represents Nisei, Hawaiian, Mexican, and African American characters as more than the subjects of racial segregation, restriction, and exclusion; they appear as powerful—indeed, treasonous—agents of revolutionary political transformation. In a post-1960s milieu, Corrothers's tale might be understood to limn a kind of coalitional politics in its "recognition of differential and relational racialization"; yet this reading is too limiting, for the story also suggests the unknowability—indeed, the opacity—of race while charting "the sociohistorical process by which racial categories are created, inhabited, transformed, and destroyed" in what Omi and Winant call racial formation.[35] In the end, Blackburn eludes capture by the racial state, for he remains "a man they didn't know." Thus, Corrothers provides a fitting conclusion to *Racial Reconstruction* in his vision of an alternate future in which racialized political subjectivities need not be narrated through the limiting national discourse of citizenship in the U.S. racial state.[36]

Corrothers's recasting of the invasion subgenre also offers a powerful counterrepresentational antecedent to resurgent forms of American Yellow Peril, in which China—among the so-called Asian Tigers—serves as a collective figure for the contradictions, perils, and disjunctive temporalities of U.S. globalization and economic neoliberalism today.[37] Political pundits and advocacy groups such as the nonpartisan Citizens Against Government Waste have revived the specter of Asiatic invasion, in the service of political persuasion in our current globalized order, asking Americans to imagine our failed national future—indeed, our economic enslavement to China, currently the largest single holder of U.S. government debt.[38] In the face of such revivified Yellow Peril discourse, the critical interrogation of the U.S. racial state that Corrothers crafts in "A Man They Didn't Know" remains as prescient today as in the late Progressive era, particularly as the racialized immigration struggles that first gave rise to American Yellow Peril have again seized the public consciousness in the current conjuncture.

The structural transformation of a globalized U.S. economy continues to produce demands for "cheap" immigrant labor in the face of the resurgent specter of economic race war with China. In providing for the punitive enforcement of alien registration, the notorious Arizona statute euphemistically entitled Support Our Law Enforcement and Safe Neighborhoods Act (S.B. 1070) harks back to the notorious 1892 Geary Act, which criminalized all Chinese as illegal aliens until documentation proved otherwise. It also popularized the doctrine of "self-deportation" that resurfaced in the 2012 Republican presidential platform. Enacted in 2010, S.B. 1070 was one of the most restrictive anti-illegal-immigration measures passed in recent U.S. history. It established an official state policy of "attrition through enforcement," which required aliens to carry registration papers at all times on penalty of a state misdemeanor, charged undocumented aliens seeking work or holding a job with a state misdemeanor, and allowed law enforcement to arrest suspected undocumented immigrants without warrants. Similar laws were passed in Alabama, Georgia, Indiana, South Carolina, and Utah. In the test case that followed, the U.S. Supreme Court struck down three key provisions but upheld the most controversial aspect of the law, which required police officers to verify the status of suspected illegal immigrants, clearing a path for racial profiling and rights abuses against Latinos, Asian Americans, and all others presumed to be criminally "foreign."

Immigration law is governed by the central premise that the government owes nothing to aliens except the privileges that it explicitly grants to them, unlike the constitutional rights accorded to citizens.[39] As in the case of *Ju Toy* in 1905, S.B. 1070 exposes the racialized mechanisms of establishing and policing the still-porous line between alien and citizen as well as the differential treatment—the suspension of legal norms—accorded to suspected illegal aliens. As in earlier Chinese immigration case law, state exclusion facilitates even greater incorporation into an expanding system of bureaucratic management.[40] The U.S. racial state persists despite the increasingly popular concept of a postracial America. In the face of resurgent Yellow Peril and S.B. 1070, this postracial designation might serve more aptly as a mark of the predicament of identifying "the nature and forms of racialization in the present" than as a sign of its transcendence, as Susan Koshy argues.[41] The epistemological problem of racial knowledge that ends Corrothers's "A Man They Didn't Know" might offer an alternative way to conceptualize the relationship between the past and our possible racial futures. It speaks to the contingencies of racial formation and suggests that our racial paradigms must move beyond the internal opposition of white and nonwhite to include racial minorities outside the nation-state, as new immigrants and class divisions within minoritized groups facilitate new and unexpected global realignments of race and racialization.[42] In a comparative fashion, Corrothers's "A Man They Didn't Know" illuminates the mutually constitutive nature of racial formations in national and transnational contexts. It challenges citizenship as the limit of national inclusion while opening up a sense that the history of race and racialization in the U.S. might not be inevitable or determined. Past precedent informs but does not dictate the course of our racial futures. As Congress inches toward a comprehensive reformation of the U.S. immigration system for the twenty-first century, such an epistemic shift in orientation toward our racial past becomes ever more significant in our political present.

NOTES

INTRODUCTION

1. In 1908, the Asiatic Exclusion League reprinted the pamphlet with a new introduction that expanded the Yellow Peril menace to include "all the Asiatic races, Chinese, Japanese, Koreans, and Hindoos." Samuel Gompers and Herman Gutstadt, *Meat vs. Rice. American Manhood against Asiatic Coolieism. Which Shall Survive?* (San Francisco: Asiatic Exclusion League, 1908), 3.

2. Devon W. Carbado, "Racial Naturalization," *American Quarterly* 57.3 (2005): 637.

3. Ibid., 646.

4. *Truth versus Fiction; Justice versus Prejudice: Meat for All, Not for a Few* (Washington, DC, c. 1902), 36.

5. Carbado 645.

6. Lisa Lowe, *Immigrant Acts: On Asian American Cultural Politics* (Durham: Duke University Press, 1996), 2.

7. Howard Winant, *The New Politics of Race: Globalism, Difference, Justice* (Minneapolis: University of Minnesota Press, 2004), 25.

8. Brook Thomas, *American Literary Realism and the Failed Promise of Contract* (Berkeley: University of California Press, 1997), 201, 207.

9. John Marshall Harlan, dissent in *Plessy v. Ferguson*, in *Plessy v. Ferguson: A Brief History with Documents*, ed. Brook Thomas (Boston: Bedford / St. Martin's, 1997), 58.

10. George Washington Cable, "The Freedman's Case in Equity," *Century Magazine* (January 1885): 412.

11. Arif Dirlik, "Race Talk, Race, and Contemporary Racism," *PMLA* 123.5 (2007): 1370.

12. Amy Dru Stanley, *From Bondage to Contract: Wage Labor, Marriage, and the Market in the Age of Slave Emancipation* (Cambridge: Cambridge University Press, 1998), ix.

13. Erika Lee, *At America's Gate: Chinese Immigration during the Exclusion Era, 1882–1943* (Chapel Hill: University of North Carolina Press, 2003), 24.

14. For comparative methodologies emerging out of queer of color critique, see Grace Hong and Roderick Ferguson, eds., *Strange Affinities: The Gender and Sexual Politics of Comparative Racialization* (Durham: Duke University Press, 2011).

15. Nayan Shah, *Stranger Intimacy: Contesting Race, Sexuality, and the Law in the North American West* (Berkeley: University of California Press, 2011), 6.

16. Lisa Lowe, "The International within the National: American Studies and Asian American Critique," *Cultural Critique* 40 (Autumn 1998): 29.

17. Ibid., 30, 42.

18. Carbado 653.

19. Leslie Bow, *Partly Colored: Asian Americans and Racial Anomaly in the Segregated South* (New York: NYU Press, 2010); Natalia Molina, *How Race Is Made in America: Immigration, Citizenship, and the Historical Power of Racial Scripts* (Berkeley: University of California Press, 2014).

20. Vijay Prashad, *Everybody Was Kung Fu Fighting: Afro-Asian Connections and the Myth of Cultural Purity* (Boston: Beacon, 2001); Bill Mullen, *Afro-Orientalism* (Minneapolis: University of Minnesota Press, 2004); Andrew Jones and Nikhil Singh, eds., *The Afro-Asian Century*, special issue, *positions: east asia cultures critique* 11.1 (Spring 2003).

21. Crystal Anderson, *Beyond the Chinese Connection: Contemporary Afro-Asian Cultural Production* (Jackson: University of Mississippi Press, 2013); Helen Jun, *Race for Citizenship: Black Orientalism and Asian Uplift from Pre-Emancipation to Neoliberal America* (New York: NYU Press, 2011); Julia Lee, *Interracial Encounters: Reciprocal Representations in African and Asian American Literatures, 1896–1937* (New York: NYU Press, 2011).

22. Jun 8.

23. Najia Aarim-Heriot, *Chinese Immigrants, African Americans, and Racial Anxiety in the United States, 1848–82* (Urbana: University of Illinois Press, 2004).

24. Mae M. Ngai, *Impossible Subjects: Illegal Aliens and the Making of Modern America* (Princeton: Princeton University Press, 2003).

25. Lucy E. Salyer, *Law Harsh as Tigers: Chinese Immigrants and the Shaping of Modern Immigration Law* (Chapel Hill: University of North Carolina Press, 1995), 208.

26. Carbado 641.

27. Salyer 207–208.

28. Juan R. Torruella, "The *Insular Cases*: The Establishment of a Regime of Political Apartheid," *University of Pennsylvania Journal of International Law* 29.2 (2007): 286. Also see Amy Kaplan's suggestive reading of "foreign in a domestic sense" in *The Anarchy of Empire in the Making of U.S. Culture* (Cambridge: Harvard University Press, 2002).

29. Grace Hong and Roderick Ferguson, introduction to *Strange Affinities: The Gender and Sexual Politics of Comparative Racialization*, ed. Hong and Ferguson (Durham: Duke University Press, 2011), 12.

30. Mae M. Ngai, "Transnationalism and the Transformation of the 'Other': Response to the Presidential Address," *American Quarterly* 57.1 (2005): 60.

CHAPTER 1. "COSA DE CUBA!"

1. George W. Williams, *Sketches of Travel in the Old and New World* (Charleston, SC: Walker, Evans and Cogswell, 1871), 20–21.

2. Moon-Ho Jung, *Coolies and Cane: Race, Labor, and Sugar in the Age of Emancipation* (Baltimore: Johns Hopkins University Press, 2006), 12.

3. Harold F. Smith, "A Bibliography of American Travellers' Books about Cuba Published before 1900," *Americas* 22.4 (1966): 405–406.

4. Lisa Lowe, *Critical Terrains: French and British Orientalism* (Ithaca: Cornell University Press, 1991), 30–31.

5. See Sara Mills, *Discourses of Difference: An Analysis of Women's Travel Writing and Colonialism* (London: Routledge, 1993); Susan Morgan, *Place Matters: Gendered Geography in Victorian Women's Travel Books about Southeast Asia* (New Brunswick: Rutgers University Press, 1996); and Inderpal Grewal, *Home and Harem: Nation, Gender, Empire and the Cultures of Travel* (Durham: Duke University Press, 1996).

6. Jung 224–225.

7. Samuel Hazard, *Cuba with Pen and Pencil* (Hartford, CT: Hartford, 1871), 508.

8. Evelyn Hu-DeHart, "'La Trata Amarilla': The 'Yellow Trade' and the Middle Passage, 1847–1884," in *Many Middle Passage: Forced Migration and the Making of the Modern World*, ed. Emma Christopher, Cassandra Pybus, and Marcus Rediker, 166–183 (Berkeley: University of California Press, 2007), 167.

9. Richard Henry Dana, *To Cuba and Back* (1859; repr., Warwick, NY: 1500 Books, 2007), 128; hereafter cited parenthetically in the text.

10. Rebecca J. Scott, *Degrees of Freedom: Louisiana and Cuba after Slavery* (Cambridge: Harvard University Press, 2008), 23.

11. Ibid., 29, 95.

12. Sidney Mintz, *Sweetness and Power: The Place of Sugar in Modern History* (New York: Penguin Books, 1985), 50; Denise Helly, introduction to *The Cuba Commission Report: A Hidden History of the Chinese in Cuba*, trans. Sidney W. Mintz, 3–30 (Baltimore: Johns Hopkins University Press, 1993), 4.

13. John S. Thrasher, *Cuba and Louisiana: Letter to Samuel J. Peters, Esq.* (New Orleans: Picayune Print, 1854), 8; and Jung 76.

14. Evelyn Hu-DeHart, "Chinese Coolie Labour in Cuba in the Nineteenth Century: Free Labour or Neo-Slavery?," *Slavery and Abolition* 14.1 (1993): 70.

15. Demoticus Philalethes, *Yankee Travels through the Island of Cuba; or, The Men and Government, the Laws and Customs of Cuba, as Seen by American Eyes* (New York: D. Appleton, 1856), 75.

16. Lisa Lowe, "Autobiography Out of Empire," *Small Axe* 28 (March 2009): 99.

17. Gaiutra Bahadur, *Coolie Woman: The Odyssey of Indenture* (Chicago: University of Chicago Press, 2014), 22.

18. Helly 11.

19. Lisa Lowe, "The Intimacies of Four Continents," in *Haunted by Empire: Geographies of Intimacy in North American History*, ed. Ann Stoler, 191–212 (Durham: Duke University Press, 2006), 197.

20. Lowe, "Intimacies" 194–195.

21. Jung 9; and Kathleen Lopez, *Chinese Cubans: A Transnational History* (Chapel Hill: University of North Carolina Press, 2013), 85–87.

22. Evelyn Hu-DeHart and Kathleen López, "Asian Diasporas in Latin America and the Caribbean: An Historical Overview," *Afro-Hispanic Review* 27.1 (2008): 14.

23. Hu-DeHart, "La Trata" 167.

24. Lisa Yun, *The Coolie Speaks: Chinese Indentured Laborers and African Slaves of Cuba* (Philadelphia: Temple University Press, 2008), 8.

25. Joseph Conrad, "Typhoon," *Pall Mall Magazine* 26 (January–April 1902): 96.

26. Ibid., 106.

27. "The Coolie Trade," *Merchants' Magazine and Commercial Review* (May 1, 1856): 649; and "The Coolie Slave Trade," *Liberator* (April 18, 1856): 1.

28. Quoted in Yun 25–26.

29. Ibid., 26–27.

30. "The Coolie Slave Trade" 1.

31. "The Coolie Trade," *Flag of Our Union* (April 3, 1858): 109.

32. Jung 23–24.

33. Renee C. Redman, "From Importation of Slave to Migration of Laborers: The Struggle to Outlaw American Participation in the Chinese Coolie Trade and the Seeds of United States Immigration Law," *Albany Government Law Review* 3 (2010): 26.

34. Ibid., 4.

35. Jung 88, 40, 79.

36. Ibid., 37.

37. Redman 54.

38. Louis A. Perez, Jr., introduction to *Slaves, Sugar, and Colonial Society: Travel Accounts of Cuba, 1801–1899*, xi–xxvi (Wilmington, DE: Scholarly Resources, 1992), xxv.

39. Rodrigo Lazo, *Writing to Cuba: Filibustering and Cuban Exiles in the United States* (Chapel Hill: University of North Carolina Press, 2005), 3, 10; Kirsten Silva Gruesz, *Ambassadors of Culture: The Transamerican Origins of Latino Writing* (Princeton: Princeton University Press, 2002), 143–144.

40. Gruesz 143; Thrasher 2.

41. Helly 7.

42. "Negotiation Concerning the Annexation of Cuba—Extraordinary Disclosures," *National Era* (April 5, 1849).

43. Matthew Pratt Guterl, *American Mediterranean: Southern Slaveholders in the Age of Emancipation* (Cambridge: Harvard University Press, 2008), 98–99.

44. Walter Johnson, *River of Dark Dreams: Slavery and Empire in the Cotton Kingdom* (Cambridge: Harvard University Press, 2013), 306–308.

45. Matthew Pratt Guterl, "An American Mediterranean: Haiti, Cuba, and the American South," in *Hemispheric American Studies*, ed. Caroline F. Levander and Robert S. Levine, 96–115 (New Brunswick: Rutgers University Press, 2008), 100.

46. Caroline Levander, "Confederate Cuba," *American Literature* 78.4 (2006): 821–822.

47. Maturin M. Ballou, *History of Cuba; or, Notes of a Traveller in the Tropics* (Boston: Phillips, Sampson, 1854), 199; hereafter cited parenthetically in the text. Ballou

also wrote an 1858 drama based on Cuban folklore, entitled *Miralda; or, The Justice of Tacon*.

48. Philalethes ii.
49. Levander 837.
50. Amar Wahab, "Mapping West Indian Orientalism: Race, Gender and Representations of Indentured Coolies in the Nineteenth-Century British West Indies," *Journal of Asian American Studies* 10.3 (2007): 288.
51. Ibid., 288–289.
52. W. M. L. Jay [Julia Woodruff], *My Winter in Cuba* (New York: Dutton, 1871), 221.
53. Led by Julián Zulueta, a large-scale Cuban landowner involved in the contraband African slave trade, the Real Junta de Fomento y de Colonización sent an agent to China in 1844 to study the possibilities of importing Chinese laborers. In 1846, Zulueta and the planter interest that he represented struck an agreement with the British in Amoy, and the first transport ship of Chinese contract laborers arrived in Havana the following year (Hu-DeHart, "Chinese" 69). Cuba suspended the importation of Chinese laborers after the first contract with Zulueta to experiment with other forms of immigrant labor (Yucatecos from Mexico, Gallegos, Catalans and Canary Islanders from Europe) but officially resumed it in 1853 (ibid., 69–70).
54. "Commerce in Coolies," *Friends' Intelligencer* (May 31, 1856): 174.
55. Jung 20.
56. Wahab 303.
57. Johnson 14.
58. "Commerce in Coolies" 174.
59. Ibid.
60. "The Coolie System," *Friends' Review* (January 31, 1857): 334.
61. Review of *To Cuba and Back*, *Littell's Living Age* (October 29, 1859): 315.
62. The unnumbered stand-alone chapter on the subject of "slavery" in Cuba was the most widely reprinted selection from Dana's travelogue, but extracts often excised his lengthy discussion of Chinese coolieism as a variant of Cuban racial slavery.
63. Review of *To Cuba and Back* 315.
64. Fernando Ortiz, *Cuban Counterpoint: Tobacco and Sugar* (Durham: Duke University Press, 1995), 98.
65. Lowe, "Intimacies" 197.
66. J. Milton Mackie, *From Cape Cod to Dixie and the Tropics* (New York: G. P. Putnam, 1864), 313.
67. Wahab 291.
68. Hazard 149–150, 165–166, 169, 273, 359, 446.
69. Guterl, *American* 102.
70. "Chinese Coolie Trade at Havana," *Merchants' Magazine and Commercial Review* (October 1, 1857): 518.
71. Guterl, *American* 99.

72. Amy Dru Stanley, *From Bondage to Contract: Wage Labor, Marriage, and the Market in the Age of Slave Emancipation* (Cambridge: Cambridge University Press, 1998), 19.

73. William Ashmore, "Article II.—The Chinese Coolie Trade," *Christian Review* (April 1, 1862): 212.

74. Ibid., 213.

75. Richard H. Chinn to Eliza McHatton Ripley, July 23, 1874, Series 13, Carton 10, File 149, Thomas Hubbard McHatton Family Papers, Hargrett Rare Books and Manuscript Library, University of Georgia Libraries.

76. Ibid.

77. Stephanie Smallwood, "Commodified Freedom: Interrogating the Limits of Anti-Slavery Ideology in the Early Republic," *Journal of the Early Republic* 24 (Summer 2004): 292.

78. Ibid., 295.

79. Stanley x.

80. Ibid., ix.

81. Ibid., x–xi.

82. Ibid., 15–16.

83. Ibid., 17.

84. Ibid., 3, 5.

85. John Locke, *Second Treatise of Civil Government* (1690), ed. C. B. Macpherson (Indianapolis: Hackett, 1980), 17.

86. "Chinese Coolie Trade," *New York Times*, reprinted in *Friend* (April 1, 1874): 28.

87. James J. O'Kelly, *The Mambi-Land; or, Adventures of a Herald Correspondent in Cuba* (Philadelphia: Lippincott, 1874), 42.

88. Ibid., 66.

89. Stanley 87, 93.

90. Ibid., 73.

91. Ibid., 85.

92. Richard Samuel West, *The San Francisco Wasp: An Illustrated History* (Easthampton, MA: Periodyssey, 2004), 63.

93. Ibid., 62.

94. Ashmore 222.

95. Ibid., 224.

96. Yun 65; *The Cuba Commission Report: A Hidden History of the Chinese in Cuba* (Baltimore: Johns Hopkins University Press, 1993); hereafter cited parenthetically in the text.

97. Yun 125–126.

98. Cuba's racial system included whites and *raza de color* (race of color) or *clase de color* (class of color) that encompassed blacks and mulattoes. (My thanks to Ryan Kernan for pointing this out to me.) The *cedula*'s color designation "*su clase*" does not specify José as chino, but we might surmise this on the basis of Ripley's professed

preference for Chinese cooks and an entry dated October 1, 1868, in the Desengaño Account Book noting the rehiring of a chino named José after he completed the term of his original contract: "19 of the Rozo Chinos have expired today—Rehired Ramon at $30 and José at $18 per month." Account Book of Desengaño Plantation 1868, Series 13, Carton 10, File 59, Thomas Hubbard McHatton Family Papers.

99. O'Kelly 44–45.
100. Yun 126.
101. Ibid., 123.
102. Ibid., xxi.
103. Stanley 59.
104. Jung 29, 30.
105. O'Kelly 71.
106. Jung 26.
107. Matthew Pratt Guterl, "'I Went to the West Indies': Race, Place, and the Antebellum South," *American Literary History* 18.3 (2006): 462; and Guterl, *American* 87.
108. "From Flag to Flag," *Critic: A Weekly Review of Literature and the Arts* (January 5, 1889): 5.
109. Eliza Ripley, *Social Life in Old New Orleans: Being Recollections of My Girlhood* (1912; repr., Gretna, LA: Pelican, 1998).
110. Coleman Hutchison, *Apples and Ashes: Literature, Nationalism, and the Confederate States of America* (Athens: University of Georgia Press, 2012), 175–176.
111. Guterl, *American* 109.
112. Eliza McHatton Ripley, *From Flag to Flag: A Woman's Adventures and Experiences in the South during the War, in Mexico, and in Cuba* (1889; repr., Slough, UK: Dodo, 2010), 1; hereafter cited parenthetically in the text.
113. Review of *From Flag to Flag*, *Eclectic Magazine of Foreign Literature* (January 1889): 137.
114. Review of *From Flag to Flag*, *Critic: A Weekly Review of Literature and the Arts* 262 (January 5, 1889): 5.
115. In an affidavit filed on February 15, 1872, McHatton relates that he and Douglas had entered into a partnership to establish a plantation in Washington County, Mississippi. Douglas's heirs solicited McHatton's aid in presenting a congressional petition for compensation for the loss of the plantation and cotton seized by Union troops after the fall of Vicksburg in 1863. Affidavit, James A. McHatton, Douglas Claim, 1872, Series 13, Carton 10, File 113, Thomas Hubbard McHatton Family Papers.
116. Jung 76, 58, 60.
117. Eliza McHatton to Anna, October 31, 1864, Series 13, Carton 10, File 30, Thomas Hubbard McHatton Family Papers; emphasis in original.
118. The lenient terms of President Andrew Johnson's postwar Reconstruction, which included amnesty for all but the highest-ranking leaders of the Confederacy, restoration of all private property excepting slaves, and the appointment of provisional governors with the power of assembling a convention to amend state constitutions facilitated the return of many ex-Confederates to the U.S. Guterl, *American* 136.

119. The term *desengaño* has no perfect equivalent in English, for it refers to a complex process of spiritual enlightenment or of being undeceived. I thank Ryan Kernan for assistance with the translation.

120. Hazard 463–464.

121. Sarah L. Franklin, *Women and Slavery in Nineteenth-Century Colonial Cuba* (Rochester, NY: University of Rochester Press, 2012), 9.

122. Jung 52, 189, 214.

123. Ibid., 104.

124. Siempre Fiel, "Chinese Servants," supplement to *New Orleans Times* (February 11, 1871); "Planting in Cuba," *Hearth and Home* (August 20, 1870): 548–549.

125. Siempre Fiel, "Chinese."

126. Ibid.

127. Ibid.

128. Lowe, "Intimacies" 194.

129. Siempre Fiel, "Chinese."

130. I thank Shuang Shen for assistance with the Chinese translation.

131. Hu-DeHart, "Chinese" 72.

132. Jung 213.

133. Account Book, Desengaño Plantation, Cuba 1868, entry dated August 21, 1866, Series 13, Carton 10, File 70, Thomas Hubbard McHatton Family Papers.

134. Account Book, Desengaño Plantation, Cuba 1868, entries dated May 13, 1867, and May 18, 1867, Series 13, Carton 10, File 70, Thomas Hubbard McHatton Family Papers.

135. Account Book, Desengaño Plantation, Cuba 1868, 1870, Series 13, Carton 10, File 70, Thomas Hubbard McHatton Family Papers; Barnet quoted in Guterl, *American* 106.

136. Cited in Jung 68–71.

137. Jay [Woodruff] 234.

138. Wahab 303.

139. "Havana," *Frederick Douglass' Paper* (October 5, 1855).

140. The holograph manuscript of *From Flag to Flag* struck out a sentence that revealed the fate of the cook Rita: "her untidy ways and Cuban messes was relegated to the fields." Series 13, Carton 9, File 26, Thomas Hubbard McHatton Family Papers.

141. Plantation Diary, Cuba, 1870, entries dated September 11, 1870, and September 15, 1870, Series 13, Carton 10, File 70, Thomas Hubbard McHatton Family Papers.

142. Plantation Diary, Cuba, 1870, entry dated July 21, 1868, Series 13, Carton 10, File 70, Thomas Hubbard McHatton Family Papers.

143. Julia Ward Howe, *A Trip to Cuba* (Boston: Ticknor and Fields, 1860); W. M. L. Jay [Julia Woodruff], *My Winter in Cuba* (New York: Dutton, 1871).

144. Jung 16.

145. Scott 96.

146. Eliza McHatton Ripley to Robert and Anna, August 26, 1866, Series 13, Carton 10, File 42, Thomas Hubbard McHatton Family Papers.

147. Helly 16.

148. On the basis of the handwritten holographs, Ripley had originally intended this sentence for the introduction to *From Flag to Flag* but later moved it to the end of her narrative.

149. Stanley 188–190.

150. Guterl, *American* 111.

151. In January 1874, Richard H. Chinn took over management of Desengaño from Ripley's nephew Charles M. Jackson, who had administered the plantation since Ripley's relocation to New York. Jackson's steady stream of letters kept Ripley updated on the status of her Cuban investment. Charles M. Jackson to Eliza McHatton Ripley, January 19, 1874, Series 13, Carton 10, File 149, Thomas Hubbard McHatton Family Papers.

152. Certification of Henry McHatton's Attendance of Norwich Free Academy, 1874, Series 13, Carton 10, File 139, Thomas Hubbard McHatton Family Papers; and Correspondences, Henry McHatton, 1875, Carton 10, File 151, Thomas Hubbard McHatton Family Papers.

153. Anastasio Millet, Havana, to Mrs. Eliza McHatton, Desengaño, January 8, 1871, Series 13, Carton 10, File 83, Thomas Hubbard McHatton Family Papers.

154. Anastasio Millet, Havana, to Mrs. Eliza McHatton, Desengaño, January 8, 1871, Series 13, Carton 10, File 83, Thomas Hubbard McHatton Family Papers. My thanks to Matt Cohen for his assistance with the translation.

155. Richard H. Chinn to Eliza McHatton Ripley, April 20, 1874, Series 13, Carton 10, File 149, Thomas Hubbard McHatton Family Papers.

156. Ibid.

157. Ibid.

158. Ibid.

159. Ibid.

160. Enclosure to letter from Richard H. Chinn to Eliza McHatton Ripley, April 11, 1874, Series 13, Carton 10, File 149, Thomas Hubbard McHatton Family Papers; emphasis in original.

161. Richard H. Chinn to Eliza McHatton Ripley, July 9, 1874, Series 13, Carton 10, File 149, Thomas Hubbard McHatton Family Papers.

162. Ann Laura Stoler, "Tense and Tender Ties: The Politics of Comparison in North American History and (Post) Colonial Studies," in *Haunted by Empire: Geographies of Intimacy in North American History*, ed. Stoler, 23–67 (Durham: Duke University Press, 2006), 24.

163. Ripley, *Social Life* 192.

164. Helly 10.

165. Richard H. Chinn to Eliza McHatton Ripley, July 23, 1874, Series 13, Carton 10, File 149, Thomas Hubbard McHatton Family Papers.

166. Account Book of Desengaño Plantation 1868, Series 13, Carton 10, File 59, Thomas Hubbard McHatton Family Papers.

167. Jung 90–91.

168. Yun 54.

169. Yen Ching-Hwang, *Coolies and Mandarins: China's Protection of Overseas Chinese during the Late Ch'ing Period (1851–1911)* (Singapore: Singapore University Press, 1985), 123–124; and Yun 39.

170. China sent a second Commission headed by Yung Wing, the first Chinese graduate of Yale University and associate commissioner of the short-lived Chinese Educational Mission to investigate Chinese working conditions in Peru.

171. Yun 36.

172. "Personal," *Harper's Bazaar* (March 14, 1874): 171.

173. "The Coolie Trade in Cuba," *Hartford Daily Courant* (February 12, 1874): 2.

174. "The Chinese in Connecticut," *Inter-Ocean* (March 7, 1874): 3; and Yun 40, 286nn11–12.

175. "Distinguished Visitors: The Chinese Commission to Cuba," *Daily Picayune* (March 7, 1874): 2.

176. Yun 45.

177. Ching-Hwang 125.

178. "Summary of News," *Philadelphia Friends' Review: A Religious, Literary and Miscellaneous Journal* (July 10, 1875): 752.

179. Ching-Hwang 127.

180. Ibid., 231.

181. Hu-DeHart, "Chinese" 72; Stanley 14.

182. Yun 5, 30, 86.

183. Saidiya Hartman, *Scenes of Subjection: Terror, Slavery, and Self-Making in Nineteenth-Century America* (New York: Oxford University Press, 1997), 119.

184. Yun 126–127.

185. Ibid., 29.

186. Jung 192–193.

187. Guterl, *American* 129.

188. Ibid., 133, 182.

189. Ibid., 130.

190. Yun 106–107.

191. Sean Metzger, "Ripples in the Seascape: The *Cuba Commission Report* and the Idea of Freedom," *Afro-Hispanic Review* 27.1 (2008): 112.

192. William Goodell, *The American Slave Code in Theory and Practice: Its Distinctive Features Shown by Its Statutes, Judicial Decisions, and Illustrative Facts*, 2nd ed. (New York: American and Foreign Anti-Slavery Society, 1853), 89.

193. Orlando Patterson, *Slavery and Social Death: A Comparative Study* (Cambridge: Harvard University Press, 1982), 22.

194. Stanley 74.

195. Royal Decree of 1860, Section II, 34, stipulates, "It is understood that immigrants, when signing and accepting their contracts, renounce all civil right which may not be compatible with the accomplishment of the obligations to which they engage

themselves, unless it be a right expressly conferred upon them by these Regulations." *Cuba Commission Report* 134.

196. Colin Dayan, *The Law Is a White Dog: How Legal Rituals Make and Unmake Persons* (Princeton: Princeton University Press, 2011), 57.

197. Ibid., 45.

198. Ibid., 99, 109.

199. Henry McHatton to Eliza McHatton Ripley, April 15, 1875, Series 13, Carton 10, File 151, Thomas Hubbard McHatton Family Papers.

200. Henry McHatton to Eliza McHatton Ripley, November 13, 1876, Correspondences, Henry McHatton, 1876, Series 13, Carton 11, File 10, Thomas Hubbard McHatton Family Papers; and Diary, Henry McHatton, 1875–1876, entry dated May 3, 1875, Series 13, Carton 10, File 155, Thomas Hubbard McHatton Family Papers.

201. Diary, Henry McHatton, 1875–1876, entry dated June 24, 1875, Series 13, Carton 10, File 155, Thomas Hubbard McHatton Family Papers.

202. "The Coolie Trade," *Maine Farmer* (August 5, 1875): 2.

203. Stanley 35.

204. Wong Chin Foo, "The Chinese in Cuba (His Story of Chung Young Hing's Sufferings as a Slave in Cuba)," *New York Times* (August 17, 1874): 2.

205. "Chinese Coolies," *Inter-Ocean* (August 25, 1874): 4.

206. The *New Hampshire Patriot* attributed its version of Wong's account of "Chun Yung Hing" to the *Boston Journal*, in which the "simple story is given to Mr. [James] Redpath by Wong Chin Foo, Chinese rebel chief, who makes it the occasion of complaint against the Tartar rulers of his country." "Coolie Slavery in Cuba," *New Hampshire Patriot* (August 26, 1874): 2. A slightly earlier version appeared as "Chinese Slavery in Cuba," *Chicago Daily Tribune* (August 18, 1874): 7. It was reprinted on the front page of the *Sacramento Daily Union* (August 25, 1874).

207. C. P. Bush, "The Chinese in New York," *New York Evangelist* (August 5, 1875): 1.

208. "Says We Are Wrong," *Daily Inter-Ocean* (December 14, 1896): 7.

209. Scott D. Seligman, *The First Chinese American: The Remarkable Life of Wong Chin Foo* (Hong Kong: University of Hong Kong Press, 2013), 52.

210. Wong 2.

211. Metzger 112.

212. "News of the Week," *Prairie Farmer* (August 22, 1874): 272.

213. "Coolie Slavery in Cuba" 2.

214. Wong 2.

215. Frederick Douglass, *Narrative of the Life of Frederick Douglass* (New York: Signet Classics, 2005), 106–107.

216. In the U.S., the idea of personal freedom associated with the ideology of contract entailed a right to an inviolate body. To make the case for the miscarriage of contract, the *Cuba Commission Report* marshaled a numbing catalogue of wounds evidenced on the bodies of interviewed Chinese: "fractured and maimed limbs, blindness, the heads full of sores, the teeth struck out, the ears mutilated, and the skin and flesh lacerated, proofs of cruelty patent to the eyes of all" (33).

217. Ching-Hwang 41–42.
218. Wong 2.
219. Ibid.
220. Ibid.
221. Ibid.
222. Lowe, "Intimacies" 204. The Cuban-born American novelist Cristina García reimagined this occulted "conjunction of 'new world modernity,'" in *Monkey Hunting* (New York: Ballantine Books, 2003), which explores the dispersal, in time and space, of five generations of Afro-Chinese Cubans—the hapless descendants of a Chinese contract laborer or "coolie" and an enslaved black Creole Cuban woman, herself the unhappy child of paternal rape and incest. See Ruthanne Lum McCunn's historical novel *God of Luck* (New York: Soho, 2007) for a fictional account of the Chinese coolie trade to Peru.
223. Lisa Lowe, "Insufficient Difference," *Ethnicities* 5.3 (2005): 412.

CHAPTER 2. FROM EMANCIPATION TO EXCLUSION

1. John Kuo Wei Tchen, *New York before Chinatown: Orientalism and the Shaping of American Culture, 1776–1882* (Baltimore: Johns Hopkins University Press, 1999), 182–183.
2. First elected to the House of Representatives in 1862, Blaine served as Speaker of the House from 1869 to 1875 before his election to the Senate, where he served from 1876 to 1881. He was later appointed secretary of state (1889–1892) after an unsuccessful presidential campaign as the Republican candidate against Democrat Grover Cleveland in 1884.
3. Joshua Paddison, *American Heathens: Religion, Race, and Reconstruction in California* (Berkeley: University of California Press, 2012), 142.
4. James G. Blaine, "Chinese Immigration: Letter from Senator Blaine," *New-York Tribune* (February 24, 1879), 5, http://chroniclingamerica.loc.gov/lccn/sn83030214/1879-02-24/ed-1/seq-5/.
5. Ibid.
6. Ibid.
7. Moon-Ho Jung, *Coolies and Cane: Race, Labor, and Sugar in the Age of Emancipation* (Baltimore: Johns Hopkins University Press, 2006), 6, 13.
8. Blaine 5.
9. Eric Foner, *Reconstruction: America's Unfinished Revolution, 1863–1877* (New York: Harper and Row, 1988), 586.
10. Paddison 26.
11. "The Chinese Panic," *New-York Tribune* (February 24, 1879): 4.
12. Ibid.
13. "Blaine on the Chinese Bill," *Georgia Weekly Telegraph* (March 4, 1879): 4.
14. Paddison 51.
15. Qingsong Zhang, "The Origins of the Chinese Americanization Movement: Wong Chin Foo and the Chinese Equal Rights League," in *Claiming America:*

Constructing Chinese American Identities during the Exclusion Era, ed. K. Scott Wong and Sucheng Chan, 41–63 (Philadelphia: Temple University Press, 1998), 42.

16. Jun defines this variant of nineteenth-century American Orientalism as "a discursive formation that was determined by and determining of U.S. economic and political engagements with East Asia and the Pacific and that provided the ideological structure for producing and managing Asian racial difference in the United States." Helen Heran Jun, *Race for Citizenship: Black Orientalism and Asian Uplift from Pre-Emancipation to Neoliberal America* (New York: NYU Press, 2011), 17–18.

17. For a detailed examination of "racial scripts," see Natalia Molina, *How Race Is Made in America* (Berkeley: University of California Press, 2014).

18. "Christ or Confucius," *New Haven Evening Register* (February 15, 1879): 1.

19. Gordon H. Chang, "China and the Pursuit of America's Destiny," *Journal of Asian American Studies* 15.2 (June 2012): 153.

20. Blaine 5.

21. William Lloyd Garrison, "William Lloyd Garrison Once More: A Reply to Senator Blaine's Letter to the Tribune," *New-York Tribune* (February 27, 1879): 2, http://chroniclingamerica.loc.gov/lccn/sn83030214/1879-02-27/ed-1/seq-2/.

22. Ibid., 2.

23. Tchen 207.

24. Gwendolyn Mink, *Old Labor and New Immigrants in American Political Development: Union, Party, and State, 1875–1920* (Ithaca: Cornell University Press, 1986), 89–90.

25. Paddison 3–4.

26. Limited by form and politics, the binary structure of the "Afro-Asian analogy" too often subsumes Asian American racial logics and racisms to a foundational anti-black white supremacy forged in relation to chattel slavery. Colleen Lye, "The Afro-Asian Analogy," *PMLA* 123 (October 2008): 1733.

27. Paddison 6.

28. The newspaper's emphases on regional news and a variety of nonfictional short-form genres, including letters, editorial, travelogues, biographies, and essays, helped facilitate the obscurity of black western writers, especially given print culture studies' focus on long-format books. Eric Gardner, "Early African American Print Culture and the American West," in *Early African American Print Culture*, ed. Lara Langer Cohen and Jordan Alexander Stein, 75–89 (Philadelphia: University of Pennsylvania Press, 2012), 75.

29. Leigh Dana Johnsen, "Equal Rights and the 'Heathen "Chinee"': Black Activism in San Francisco," *Western Historical Quarterly* 11 (January 1980): 59.

30. "Chinese Immigration," *San Francisco Elevator* (April 26, 1873); and "The Chinese: Shall He Be Welcome?," *San Francisco Elevator* (March 8, 1873).

31. Paddison 20.

32. Jun 29–30; and Jeff Diamond, "African-American Attitudes towards United States Immigration Policy," *International Migration Review* 32 (Summer 1998): 453–454.

33. "We Are in Error of the Remark," *Philadelphia Christian Recorder* (April 6, 1882).
34. "The New Outrage," *Philadelphia Christian Recorder* (March 23, 1882).
35. Ibid.
36. For example, Jennie Carter, a regular contributor to the *Elevator* (known as "Semper Fidelis" and "Ann Trask") voiced similar cross-racial "sympathy" when she parted from editor Bell on the "Chinese Question" and rejected "the anti-Chinese plank of the [Democratic] platform," admonishing her black readers "to remember those in bonds as being bound with them." Jennie Carter, letter to the editor, *San Francisco Elevator*, August 30, 1873, in *Jennie Carter: A Black Journalist of the Early West*, ed. Eric Gardner (Jackson: University of Mississippi Press, 2007), 109–110.
37. Molina 6–7.
38. Eve Tavor Bannet, "Analogy as Translation: Wittgenstein, Derrida, and the Law of Language," *New Literary History* 28 (Autumn 1997): 655.
39. "Report of the Committee on the Governor's Special Message in Regard to Asiatic Emigration," *State of California, Journal of the Senate*, 3rd sess. (1852), appendix, 734, 735. In 1872, San Francisco police arrested Williams for an arson fire that led to the death of Elizabeth Thompson. After two weeks in jail, Williams was discharged, but he faced slander and criticism in the black press, particularly in the *Pacific Appeal*. Eric Gardner, "Williams, James," in *African American National Biography*, ed. Henry Louis Gates and Evelyn Brooks Higginbotham, Oxford African American Studies Center, http://www.oxfordaasc.com/article/opr/t0001/e4082 (accessed March 6, 2015).
40. Vijay Prashad, "Bruce Lee and the Anti-Imperialism of Kung Fu: A Polycultural Adventure," *positions* 11 (Spring 2003): 53–54.
41. Houston A. Baker Jr., *Long Black Song: Essays in Black American Literature and Culture* (1972; repr., Charlottesville: University of Virginia Press, 1990), 2; also quoted in Gardner, introduction to *Jennie Carter* xxviii.
42. James Williams, *Fugitive Slave in the Gold Rush: Life and Adventures of James Williams* (Lincoln: University of Nebraska Press, 2002), 2; hereafter cited parenthetically in the text.
43. The year after Williams's arrival, California passed its own Fugitive Slave Law policing the racial character of migrants into the state, prompting Williams to flee to Mexico for a time. Williams reports that he "could take the Spanish language," but his accounts of Mexico, Panama, and South America are surprisingly free of ethnographic detail. They focus primarily on his picaresque adventures with "a chum, a white man," shipping aboard American vessels plying between San Francisco and Mazatlán and Talcahuano, Chile (*Fugitive Slave* 25). See Stephen Knadler, *Remapping Citizenship and the Nation in African-American Literature* (New York: Routledge, 2010) for a discussion of Williams in relation to a "pre-national" borderland Southwest (125–131).
44. Alan Trachtenberg, *The Incorporation of America: Culture and Society in the Gilded Age* (New York: Hill and Wang, 1982), 17.
45. Jean Fagan Yellin, *Harriet Jacobs: A Life* (New York: Basic Civitas Books, 2004), 108.

46. Rudolph Lapp, *Archy Lee: A California Fugitive Slave Case* (San Francisco: Book Club of California, 1969), 29.

47. Williams is notably cryptic about his role in the Archy Lee case, although he mentions rooming with Lee in Sacramento after their return from Vancouver.

48. Nat Love, *The Life and Adventures of Nat Love* (1907; repr., Lincoln: University of Nebraska Press, 1995), 45, 13.

49. With a population of four hundred miners in 1855, "Nigger Hill contained the largest collection of black miners, but Chinese, Portuguese, and Anglo-American miners could also be found there." Sucheng Chan, "A People of Exceptional Character: Ethnic Diversity, Nativism, and Racism in the California Gold Rush," *California History* 79 (Summer 2000): 69.

50. Alexander Saxton, *The Indispensable Enemy: Labor and the Anti-Chinese Movement in California* (Berkeley: University of California Press, 1971), 46–48; Charles Howard Shinn, *Mining Camps: A Study in American Frontier Government* (New York: Charles Scribner's Sons, 1885), 3.

51. Gardner, introduction to *Jenny Carter* xix.

52. Daniel Widener, "'Perhaps the Japanese Are to Be Thanked?': Asia, Asian Americans, and the Construction of Black California," *positions* 11 (Spring 2003): 136.

53. "Chinese Emigration," *Frederick Douglass' Paper* (June 17, 1852).

54. Najia Aarim-Heriot, *Chinese Immigrants, African Americans, and Racial Anxiety in the United States, 1848–82* (Urbana: University of Illinois Press, 2003), 56.

55. John Bigler, "Governor Bigler's Special Message in Regard to Chinese Coolie Emigration," *State of California, Journal of the Senate*, 3rd sess. (1852), 378.

56. Ibid., 377.

57. "Negro Citizenship," *North Star* (November 23, 1849); and Bigler 377, 374.

58. Bigler 373.

59. Ibid., 374.

60. In thus conflating racial identity with political status, Bigler also anticipated the shape of Chief Justice Roger Taney's infamous *Dred Scott v. Sandford* (1857) ruling, which denied U.S. citizenship (and, consequently, the right to bring suit in U.S. courts) to all people of African descent. In the majority opinion, Taney relied heavily on a similar interpretation of the 1790 Naturalization Act to illustrate the long-standing "repudiation of the African race" as an "alien" to "the political family of the United States." *Dred Scott v. Sandford*, 60 U.S. 393, 416, 407 (1856).

61. "Chinese Emigration."

62. Ibid.

63. "The United States of the United Races," *National Era* (September 15, 1853).

64. Ibid.

65. "Report of the Committee," 734, 735.

66. Aarim-Heriot 44.

67. Michael Omi and Howard Winant, *Racial Formation in the United States from the 1960s to the 1990s*, 2nd ed. (New York: Routledge, 1994), 82.

68. "From Our San Francisco Correspondent," *Frederick Douglass' Paper* (October 26, 1855).

69. *People v. Hall*, 4 Cal. 399, 403–404 (1854).

70. The ban against Chinese testimony lasted until the passage of section 16 of the Civil Rights Act of 1870, but it was unevenly enforced in California courts, which continued the testimony ban until 1872. Charles J. McClain, *In Search of Equality: The Chinese Struggle against Discrimination in Nineteenth-Century America* (Berkeley: University of California Press, 1994), 40–42.

71. Ariela J. Gross, *What Blood Won't Tell: A History of Race on Trial in America* (Cambridge: Harvard University Press, 2008), 216.

72. Editorial, *Provincial Freeman* (May 19, 1855).

73. Martin Delany, "Political Aspect of the Colored People of the United States," *Provincial Freeman* (October 13, 1855).

74. "Rapid Strides towards Slavery," *Liberator* (December 15, 1854).

75. Samuel A. S. Lowery, "Correspondence: For the Provincial Freeman," *Provincial Freeman* (March 17, 1855).

76. "Chinese Emigration."

77. "Have the Chinese Any Rights Which Americans Are Bound to Respect," *San Francisco Elevator* (May 24, 1873).

78. Priscilla Wald, *Constituting Americans: Cultural Anxiety and Narrative Form* (Durham: Duke University Press, 1995), 2.

79. Colleen Lye, *America's Asia: Racial Form and American Literature, 1893–1945* (Princeton: Princeton University Press, 2005), 5.

80. Devon W. Carbado "Racial Naturalization," *American Quarterly* 57.3 (2005): 637.

81. Mae M. Ngai, *Impossible Subjects: Illegal Aliens and the Making of Modern America* (Princeton: Princeton University Press, 2004), 5.

82. John C. McWilliams, "'Men of Colour': Race, Riots, and Black Firefighters' Struggle for Equality from the AFA to the Valiants," *Journal of Social History* 41 (Fall 2007): 110; Matt Cohen and Edlie Wong, introduction to *The Killers: A Narrative of Real Life in Philadelphia*, by George Lippard, 1–41 (Philadelphia: University of Pennsylvania Press, 2014), 15–34.

83. Mifflin Wistar Gibbs, *Shadow and Light: An Autobiography* (Lincoln: University of Nebraska Press, 1995), 19.

84. Ibid., 23.

85. Paddison 78.

86. Rudolph Lapp, *Blacks in Gold Rush California* (New Haven: Yale University Press, 1977), 242.

87. Hsuan L. Hsu, "Vagrancy and Comparative Racialization in *Huckleberry Finn* and 'Three Vagabonds of Trinidad,'" *American Literature* 81 (December 2009): 701.

88. For example, Knadler argues for an expanded understanding of the black cowboy as a complicated transnational figure "identified with . . . American nationalism" who "spoke from multiple sites of cultural and political attachment and participation" (118).

89. Love 130.
90. Ibid., 162.
91. Renato Rosaldo, "Imperialist Nostalgia," *Representations* 26 (Spring 1989): 107–122.
92. Paddison 60–61.
93. Claire Jean Kim, "The Racial Triangulation of Asian Americans," *Politics and Society* 27 (March 1999): 107.
94. Paddison 60–61.
95. "The Modoc War: Report from the Seat of Hostilities," *New York Herald* (January 9, 1873), http://docs.newsbank.com/s/HistArchive/ahnpdoc/EANX/1294998EF1A8 A580/10497FA79919C158.
96. Jacques Derrida, "The Force of Law: The 'Mystical Foundation of Authority,'" in *Deconstruction and the Possibility of Justice*, ed. Drucilla Cornell, Michel Rosenfeld, and David Gray Carlson, 3–67 (New York: Routledge, 1992), 6, 35.
97. Paddison 3.
98. Frederick Douglass, "Our Composite Nationality: An Address Delivered in Boston, Massachusetts, on 7 December 1869," in *The Frederick Douglass Papers, Series One: Speeches, Debates, and Interviews*, ed. John W. Blassingame and John R. McKivigan, vol. 4, 240–259 (New Haven: Yale University Press, 1991); hereafter cited parenthetically in the text.
99. "Lecture by Frederick Douglass," *Delaware County American* (January 12, 1870); "Happenings Here and There," *Pomeroys Democrat* (December 1, 1869): 2; "Connecticut News," *Hartford Daily Courant* (December 16, 1869): 4; "Notices," *Trenton (NJ) Daily State Gazette* (March 3, 1873): 3.
100. James Redpath established the Boston Lyceum Bureau in 1868. Lyceum lecturing became Douglass's primary source of income in the 1860s to 1870s, and the Redpath Bureau received a commission of 10 percent of Douglass's lecturing fees. Angela Ray, "Frederick Douglass on the Lyceum Circuit: Social Assimilation, Social Transformation?," *Rhetoric and Public Affairs* 5.4 (2002): 628.
101. Numerous versions of Douglass's speech exist. It was often excerpted and reprinted, but the most complete version is a typescript version titled "Composite Nation: Delivered in the Parker Fraternity Course, Boston, 1867 [sic]." John W. Blassingame and John R. McKivigan, headnote to Douglass, "Our Composite Nationality," 240.
102. Secretary of State William Seward favored free immigration and was the actual, albeit unacknowledged, author of the Burlingame Treaty, which offered China the most equitable and favorable terms of any treaty with a Western nation in the century. Gordon H. Chang, "China and the Pursuit of America's Destiny," *Journal of Asian American Studies* 15.2 (2012): 162.
103. *Text of the Treaty between China & the United States, Generally Known as the "Burlingame Treaty of 1868"* (San Francisco, 1879), 6.
104. John Hayakawa Torok, "Reconstruction and Racial Nativism: Chinese Immigrants and the Debates on the Thirteenth, Fourteenth, and Fifteenth Amendments and Civil Rights Law," *Asian Law Journal* 3.55 (1996): 56.

105. Ibid., 57.
106. McClain 280.
107. Foner 446–447.
108. Paddison 22.
109. Ibid., 91.
110. Foner 233.
111. Torok 82, 91–92.
112. Ibid., 79–80.
113. Paddison 23.
114. Ibid., 24. The deviant religious practices of Mormonism, which included polygamy, had also authorized the federal government to launch a military attack on Mormon pioneers in Utah territory, which lasted from 1857 to 1858.
115. Paddison 24.
116. "Suffrage for the Negro, Indian, and Chinaman," *New York Herald* (December 9, 1869): 7.
117. Ray 632.
118. Robert Levine, *Dislocating Race and Nation: Episodes in Nineteenth-Century American Literary Nationalism* (Chapel Hill: University of North Carolina Press, 2008), 213.
119. Frederick Douglass, "The Future of the Negro," *Christian Recorder* (June 26, 1884): 3.
120. Levine 212–213.
121. Eric Gardner, "Newby, William H.," in *African American National Biography*, ed. Henry Louis Gates Jr. and Evelyn Brooks Higginbotham, *Oxford African American Studies Center*, http://www.oxfordaasc.com/article/opr/t0001/e4637 (accessed March 6, 2015).
122. Ibid. See Gardner, "Early African American" 75–89, for a detailed discussion of the *Mirror of the Times*.
123. Newby was an enthusiastic supporter of Douglass's newspaper. In one correspondence, he excitedly announced that the "*Frederick Douglass' Paper* came to us by the last steamer in a new dress, and looked beautifully and worthy of the ability and talent with which it is conducted." Nubia [William Newby], "From Our San Francisco Correspondent: San Francisco, July 14, 1855," *Frederick Douglass' Paper* (August 24, 1855): 3.
124. Nubia [William Newby], "Progress of the Colored People of San Francisco: San Francisco, Aug. 10, 1854," *Frederick Douglass' Paper* (September 22, 1854): 4.
125. Eric Gardner, *Unexpected Places: Relocating Nineteenth-Century African American Literature* (Jackson: University Press of Mississippi, 2009), 4.
126. Nubia, "Progress" 4.
127. Nubia [William Newby], "From Our California Correspondent: San Francisco, Feb. 6th, 54," *Frederick Douglass' Paper* (March 16, 1855): 1.
128. Ngai 51.
129. Ibid.

130. Nubia [William Newby], "From Our San Francisco Correspondent: San Francisco, Aug. 14, 1855," *Frederick Douglass' Paper* (September 28, 1855): 3.

131. Nubia [William Newby], "San Francisco, Feb. 28, 1855," *Frederick Douglass' Paper* (April 6, 1855): 3.

132. Jun 6.

133. Nubia, "Progress" 4.

134. Nubia [William Newby], "From Our San Francisco Correspondent: San Francisco, May 14, 1855," *Frederick Douglass' Paper* (June 15, 1855): 3.

135. Tchen 182–183.

136. Wendell Phillips, "The Chinese: An Editorial in the 'National (Antislavery) Standard,' July 30, 1870," in *Speeches, Lectures, and Letters* (Boston: Lee and Shepard, 1891), 145–151.

137. Ibid., 148.

138. Frederick Douglass, "The Races," in *The Lyceum and Public Culture in the Nineteenth-Century United States,* by Angela G. Ray, 207–220 (East Lansing: Michigan State University Press, 2005), 214, 219.

139. Ibid., 219.

140. Quoted in Ray, "Frederick" 639.

141. Douglass, "Races" 219.

142. Ray, "Frederick" 639.

143. Ngai 233.

144. W. E. B. Du Bois, *The Souls of Black Folk* (1903; repr., New York: Pocket, 2005), 17–18.

145. Martin goes so far as to argue that "Douglass unequivocally advocated total Negro assimilation into the white, Anglo-Saxon Protestant-dominated political culture." Waldo E. Martin Jr., *The Mind of Frederick Douglass* (Chapel Hill: University of North Carolina Press, 1984), 219, 220.

146. Scott D. Seligman, *The First Chinese American: The Remarkable Life of Wong Chin Foo* (Hong Kong: University of Hong Kong Press, 2013), x.

147. Hsuan Hsu, "Wong Chin Foo's Periodical Writings and Chinese Exclusion," *Genre* 39 (Fall 2006): 83.

148. Seligman xi.

149. James Mussell, "Cohering Knowledge in the Nineteenth Century: Form, Genre and Periodical Studies," *Victorian Periodical Review* 42.1 (2009): 93, 95.

150. Saxton 18.

151. Ibid., 48.

152. Wong Chin Foo, "The Chinese in New York," *Cosmopolitan* (June 1888): 297.

153. Hsuan Hsu, "A Connecticut Yankee in the Court of Wu Chih Tien: Mark Twain and Wong Chin Foo," *Common-Place* 11.1 (2010), http://www.common-place.org/vol-11/no-01/hsu/.

154. Seligman 1.

155. Ibid., 17, 20.

156. Ibid., 27–28.

157. Ibid., 43.
158. Ibid., 44–45; "Editorial Notes," *New York Evangelist* (July 30, 1874): 4.
159. "Who Are the Heathen?," *Boston Investigator* (March 8, 1876): 2; "Turning the Tables," *Milwaukee Daily Sentinel* (February 3, 1876): 2; "Wong Chin Foo," *Milwaukee Daily Sentinel* (December 8, 1876): 3.
160. Paddison 9.
161. "A Roland for an Oliver," *North American and United States Gazette* (December 3, 1874); "Personal Notes," *Christian Union* (October 7, 1874): 274.
162. "Philadelphia Letter," *New York Evangelist* (December 3, 1874): 2.
163. "A Chinese Mandarin on a Missionary Tour through the United States," *St. Louis Globe-Democrat* (October 17, 1875): 10.
164. Marjorie Harrell Eubank, "The Redpath Lyceum Bureau from 1868 to 1901" (Ph.D. diss., University of Michigan, Ann Arbor, 1968), 303–306.
165. "A Chinese Mandarin" 10.
166. Eubank 305.
167. Seligman 63, 67, 249; Hsu, "Wong" 87.
168. Hsu, "Wong" 84.
169. "A Chinese Mandarin" 10. The *North American Review* published Wong's essay as one of an ongoing series of theological polemics, which included Edward Everett Hale's "Why Am I a Unitarian?" (1886), John Hall's "Why Am I a Presbyterian?" (1886), George R. Crook's "Why Am I a Methodist?" (1886), S. M. Brandi's "Why Am I a Catholic?" (1886), Thomas Armitage's "Why I Am a Baptist?" (1887), Gail Hamilton's "Why I Am a Congregationalist?" (1887), Pereira Mendes's "Why Am I a Jew?" (1887), A. E. Newton's "Why I Am a Spiritualist?" (1888), Iba Abbas's "Why Am I a Moslem?" (1888), J.A.R.'s "Why Am I a Quaker?" (1889), Frederic William Farrar's "Why Am I an Episcopalian?" (1889), and Robert G. Ingersoll's "Why I Am I an Agnostic?" (1889–1890).
170. Hsu, "Wong" 94.
171. Wong Chin Foo, "Why Am I a Heathen?," *North American Review* (August 1887): 169; hereafter cited parenthetically in the text.
172. Jackson Lears, "The Mormon Ethic and the Spirit of Capitalism," *New Republic* (Oct. 10, 2012), http://www.newrepublic.com/article/books-and-arts/magazine/108787/the-mormon-ethic-and-the-spirit-capitalism.
173. See Jean Pfaelzer, *Driven Out: The Forgotten War against Chinese Americans* (New York: Random House, 2007).
174. "College Notes," *Christian Union* (July 7, 1887): 7.
175. Amy Ling, "Yan Phou Lee on the Asian American Frontier," in *Re-Collecting Early Asian America: Essays on Cultural History*, ed. Josephine Lee, Imogene Lim, and Yuko Matsukawa, 273–287 (Philadelphia: Temple University Press, 2002), 279.
176. K. Scott Wong, "Cultural Defenders and Brokers: Chinese Responses to the Anti-Chinese Movement," in *Claiming America: Constructing Chinese American Identities during the Exclusion Era*, ed. K. Scott Wong and Sucheng Chan, 3–40

(Philadelphia: Temple University Press, 1998); and Edward J. M. Rhoads, *Stepping Forth into the World: The Chinese Educational Mission to the United States, 1872–81* (Hong Kong: Hong Kong University Press, 2011), 62.

177. Paddison 53.
178. Ibid., 55.
179. Yan Phou Lee, *When I Was a Boy in China* (Boston: D. Lothrop, 1887), 41.
180. Yan Phou Lee, "Why I am Not a Heathen," *North American Review* (September 1887): 1307.
181. Ibid., 1312.
182. Ibid., 1310; Paddison 128.
183. K. Wong 6.
184. Paddison 127.
185. Ibid., 106.
186. Ibid., 49.
187. Quoted in Zhang 46.
188. Pan, "Sayings and Doings," *Puck* (May 2, 1877): 4.
189. Michael Warner, *The Letters of the Republic: Publication and the Public Sphere in Eighteenth-Century America* (Cambridge: Harvard University Press, 1990), xii.
190. Kirsten Silva Gruesz *Ambassadors of Culture: The Transamerican Origins of Latino Writing* (Princeton: Princeton University Press, 2002), 9.
191. Tchen 167–168.
192. Gruesz 117.
193. "A Chinese Newspaper," *San Francisco Daily Evening Bulletin* (February 3, 1883).
194. Notice, *Christian Recorder* (March 29, 1883): 4.
195. "Morning Dispatches. Difficulties of Publishing a Chinese Newspaper," *San Francisco Daily Evening Bulletin* (April 14, 1883): 4.
196. "The First Chinese Newspaper in New York," *St. Louis Globe-Democrat* (February 9, 1883): 5; reprinted from the *New York World*.
197. Ibid.
198. Yumei Sun, "San Francisco's *Chung Sai Yat Po* and the Transformation of Chinese Consciousness, 1900–1920," in *Print Culture in a Diverse America*, ed. James P. Danky and Wayne A. Wiegand, 85–97 (Urbana: University of Illinois Press, 1998), 88.
199. "The First Chinese Newspaper in New York," *Fayetteville Observer* (February 15, 1883); "That Chinese Paper," *St. Louis Globe-Democrat* (May 5, 1883): 7.
200. Seligman 99.
201. Notice, *Friend's Review* (March 22, 1888): 541.
202. "Literature," *Christian Recorder* (January 15, 1885): 2.
203. Lee took over the editorship of a local newspaper in Wood Ridge, New Jersey, after his second marriage to an American woman. From 1918 to 1927, Lee served as managing editor for the *American Banker*, a financial journal, before he returned to China, where he became editor of the *Canton Gazette* (*Guangdong Bao*) in 1931, until

the government ended its subsidy. It is presumed that Lee was killed during a Japanese bombing raid sometime during the second Sino-Japanese War (1937–1945) (Ling 278–279).

204. "The Geary Act," *Boston Daily Advertiser* (October 18, 1892); "Our Chinese Brethren," *Boston Daily Advertiser* (November 18, 1892): 5.

205. "Chinamen Kick in 'Melican Fashion,'" *New York Herald* (September 23, 1892); Seligman 200.

206. "Want Recognition of the Chinese," *Chicago Tribune* (July 9, 1896).

207. Quoted in Zhang 55.

208. "A Chinese League," *San Francisco Call* (May 26, 1897): 6.

209. "Turning the Tables," *Milwaukee Daily Sentinel* (February 3, 1876): 2; "Who Are the Heathen?," *Boston Investigator* (March 8, 1876): 2; "Wong Chin Foo," *Milwaukee Daily Sentinel* (December 18, 1876): 3; "An Oriental Missionary," *Lowell Daily Citizen* (September 30, 1874).

210. Pan 4.

211. "Would Cut Off Heads," *Denver Evening Post* (December 14, 1896).

212. Hsu, "Wong" 85.

213. Seligman 247.

214. Jane Hwang Degenhardt, "Situating the Essential Alien: Sui Sin Far's Depiction of Chinese-White Marriage and the Exclusionary Logic of Citizenship," *MFS: Modern Fiction Studies* 54.4 (Winter 2008): 657.

215. Lee, *When* 106.

216. Lee was one of only three Chinese students who managed to return to the U.S. after the end of the Chinese Educational Mission (Ling 276).

217. Lee, *When* 107.

218. Ibid., 107–108.

219. Ibid., 108.

220. Paddison 58–59.

221. Ibid., 139.

222. Lee, *When* 108.

223. Jun 16. In the struggles for political inclusion, the black press, argues Jun, marshaled the "Orientalist logic of the anti-Chinese movement" to help consolidate "black identification as U.S. national subjects" (17).

224. See Shu-mei Shih, "Comparative Racialization: An Introduction," *PMLA* 123 (October 2008): 1347–1362.

CHAPTER 3. AMERICAN FUTURES PAST

1. *Text of the Treaty between China and the United States, Generally Known as the "Burlingame Treaty 1868"* (San Francisco: n.p., 1879), 6.

2. *The Labor Agitators; or, The Battle for Bread* (San Francisco: Geo. W. Green, 1879), 5.

3. Eric Hayot, *The Hypothetical Mandarin: Sympathy, Modernity, and Chinese Pain* (Oxford: Oxford University Press, 2009), 140.

4. Lisa Lowe, *Immigrant Acts: On Asian American Cultural Politics* (Durham: Duke University Press, 1996), 5.

5. Frederic Jameson, "Reification and Utopia in Mass Culture," *Social Text* 1 (Winter 1979): 140.

6. Max Horkheimer and Theodor W. Adorno, *The Dialectic of Enlightenment* (New York: Continuum, 1996), 234.

7. Darko Suvin, "On the Poetics of the Science Fiction Genre," *College English* 34.3 (1972): 378, 379.

8. I. F. Clarke, *Voices Prophesying War: Future Wars, 1763–3749*, 2nd ed. (Oxford: Oxford University Press, 1992), 42–43.

9. Catherine Gallagher, "Telling It Like It Wasn't," *Pacific Coast Philology* 45 (2010): 13, 15.

10. See John Kuo Wei and Dylan Yeats, *Yellow Peril! An Archive of Anti-Asian Fear* (London: Verso, 2014), for a critical compendium of Yellow Peril images, essays, and ephemera.

11. G. B. Densmore, *The Chinese in San Francisco: Description of Chinese Life in San Francisco* (San Francisco: Pettit and Russ, 1880), 121.

12. On the "credit-ticket system," see Him Mark Lai, Joe Huang, and Don Wong, *The Chinese of America, 1785–1980* (San Francisco: Chinese Culture Foundation, 1980).

13. Moon-Ho Jung, *Coolies and Cane: Race, Labor, and Sugar in the Age of Emancipation* (Baltimore: Johns Hopkins University Press, 2006), 5, 222.

14. In the *Slaughterhouse Cases* (1873), Justice Samuel Freeman Miller's interpretation of the Thirteenth Amendment constructed "Chinese coolieism" as a form of racialized labor that was distinct from both free white labor and black chattel slavery: "If Mexican peonage or the Chinese coolie labor system shall develop slavery of the Mexican or Chinese race within our territory, this amendment may safely be trusted to make it void" (83 U.S. [16 Wall.] 36, 69, 72 [1873]). On the legal impact of Miller's interpretation of the Thirteenth Amendment, see Hoang Gia Phan, "'A Race So Different': Chinese Exclusion, the *Slaughterhouse Cases*, and *Plessy v. Ferguson*," *Labor History* 45.2 (2004): 145.

15. Lorelle, "The Battle of The Wabash: A Letter from the Invisible Police," *Californian* 2.10 (1880): 365; hereafter cited parenthetically in the text.

16. Emma J. Teng, "Artifacts of a Lost City: Arnold Genthe's Pictures of Old Chinatown and Its Intertexts," in *Re/collecting Early Asian America: Essays in Cultural Criticism*, ed. Josephine Lee, Imogene L. Lim, and Yuko Matsukawa, 54–77 (Philadelphia: Temple University Press, 2002), 56.

17. Densmore 21.

18. M. P. Shiel, *The Yellow Danger* (London: Grant Richards, 1898), 12.

19. John P. Jones, *Chinese Immigration: Speech of Hon. John P. Jones, of Nevada, in the Senate of the United States, Thursday, March 9, 1882* (Washington, DC: n.p., 1882), 18.

20. Clarke 33.

21. Ibid., 64.

22. Ibid., 3.

23. Colleen Lye, *America's Asia: Racial Form and American Literature, 1893–1945* (Princeton: Princeton University Press, 2005), 22–24.

24. Marsden Manson, *The Yellow Peril in Action: A Possible Chapter in History* (San Francisco: Britton and Rey, 1907), 17; hereafter cited parenthetically in the text.

25. Chinese invasion fiction also found its way to Australia, where news of a gold strike in the 1850s catalyzed the large-scale immigration of Chinese laborers. Australia's earliest Chinese invasion narratives included the anonymous *The Battle of Mordialloc; or, How We Lost Australia* (1888) and the Irish socialist William Lane's first foray into fiction, *White or Yellow? A Story of the Race War of A.D. 1908* (1888), serialized in his journal *Boomerang* under the pseudonym "Sketcher." In the following decades, novels such as Kenneth MacKay's *The Yellow Wave: A Romance of the Asiatic Invasion of Australia* (1895) and Vincent Joyce's *The Celestial Hand: A Sensational Story* (1903) helped establish a parallel Australian tradition of Yellow Peril. Russell Blackford, Van Ikin, and Sean McMullen, *Strange Constellations: A History of Australian Science Fiction* (Westport, CT: Greenwood, 1999), 37–39.

26. Susan Gillman, *Blood Talk: American Race Melodrama and the Culture of the Occult* (Chicago: University of Chicago Press, 2003), 83; Fredric Jameson, "Progress versus Utopia; or, Can We Imagine the Future?," *Science Fiction Studies* 9.2 (1982): 151, 152.

27. P. W. Dooner, *Last Days of the Republic* (San Francisco: Alta California Publishing House, 1880), 128; hereafter cited parenthetically in the text.

28. Wong Chin Foo, "Why Am I a Heathen?," *North American Review* (August 1887): 169.

29. Hsuan L. Hsu, *Geography and the Production of Space in Nineteenth-Century American Literature* (Cambridge: Cambridge University Press, 2010), 104, 105.

30. For example, Atwell Whitney's anti-Chinese novel *Almond Eyed: A Story of the Day* (1878) lampooned this idea that immigration to the U.S. made Chinese heathens more receptive to Christianity and civilization.

31. Hayden White, *Tropics of Discourse: Essays in Cultural Criticism* (Baltimore: Johns Hopkins University Press, 1978), 49.

32. Gallagher 15.

33. Hayden White, *Metahistory: The Historical Imagination in Nineteenth-Century Europe* (Baltimore: Johns Hopkins University Press, 1973), 49.

34. Gallagher 12.

35. White, *Metahistory* x.

36. Robert Woltor, *A Short and Truthful History of the Taking of California and Oregon by the Chinese in the Year A.D. 1899 by Robert Woltor, a Survivor* (San Francisco: A. L. Bancroft, 1882), 10; hereafter cited parenthetically in the text.

37. "'The Californian,'" *Idaho Avalanche* (October 2, 1880): 4.

38. Jameson, "Progress" 151, 152.

39. Carl Freedman, *Critical Theory and Science Fiction* (Middletown, CT: Wesleyan University Press, 2000), xvi.

40. Ignatius Donnelly, *Caesar's Column: A Story of the Twentieth Century* (1891; repr., Middletown, CT: Wesleyan University, 2003), 14.

41. "Counterfactual," *Oxford English Dictionary*, 2nd ed. (1989), online version, November 2010, http://www.oed.com:80/Entry/42781 (accessed January 30, 2011).

42. Stephen M. Best, *The Fugitive's Properties: Law and the Poetics of Possession* (Chicago: University of Chicago, 2004), 211, quoting H. L. A. Hart and A. M. Honoré, *Causation in the Law* (Oxford, UK: Clarendon, 1959), 15.

43. *Labor Agitators* 12.

44. John Rieder, *Colonialism and the Emergence of Science Fiction* (Middletown, CT: Wesleyan University Press, 2008), 3.

45. "A Compliment," *Weekly Arizona Miner* (July 8, 1871): 4; "The Pioneer Press," *Arizona Weekly Star* (December 4, 1879): 1. For an excavation of Dooner's rather checkered career in early Arizona journalism, see Kenneth Hufford, "P. W. Dooner: Pioneer Editor of Tucson," *Arizona and the West* 10.1 (1968): 25–42.

46. Notice, *Weekly Arizona Miner* (November 1, 1873): 2; Notice, *Weekly Arizona Miner* (November 8, 1873): 2; Notice, *Arizona Miner* (April 17, 1874): 1.

47. Richard Samuel West, *The San Francisco "Wasp": An Illustrated History* (Easthampton, MA: Periodyssey, 2004), 18.

48. Gallagher 23.

49. "News and Notes," *Queries* 6.10 (1890): 330; "Fiction," *Publisher's Weekly* (January 24, 1891): 148.

50. Hayot, *Hypothetical* 118.

51. "Literary Notes," *Daily Alta California* (October 26, 1890): 6.

52. Hayot, *Hypothetical* 131, 142.

53. Ibid., 149.

54. Lucy E. Salyer, *Law Harsh as Tigers: Chinese Immigrants and the Shaping of Modern Immigration Law* (Chapel Hill: University of North Carolina Press, 1995), 10.

55. Arthur Dudley Vinton, *Looking Further Backward: Being a Series of Lectures Delivered to the Freshman Class at Shawmut College, by Professor Won Lung Li* (New York: Albany Book Company, 1890), 8; hereafter cited parenthetically in the text.

56. White, *Metahistory* x.

57. Eric Hayot, "Chinese Bodies, Chinese Futures," *Representations* 99.1 (2007): 99, 100.

58. Anthony Grafton, *The Footnote: A Curious History* (Cambridge: Harvard University Press, 1997), 51.

59. Edward Bellamy, *Looking Backward, 2000–1887* (Boston: Ticknor, 1888), 205.

60. Jing Tsu, "Extinction and Adventure on the Chinese Diasporic Frontier," *Journal of Chinese Overseas* 2.2 (2006): 260.

61. *Facts upon the Other Side of the Chinese Question: With a Memorial to the President of the U.S. from Representative Chinamen in America* (San Francisco: n.p., 1876), 24.

62. Densmore 1.

63. Meredith K. Olafson, "The Concept of Limited Sovereignty and the Immigration Law Plenary Power Doctrine," *Georgetown Immigration Law Journal* 13 (1999): 433.

64. Teemu Ruskola, "Canton Is Not Boston: The Invention of American Imperial Sovereignty," *American Quarterly* 57.3 (2005): 877.

65. Gabriel J. Chin, "Segregation's Last Stronghold: Race Discrimination and the Constitutional Law of Immigration," *UCLA Law Review* 46 (1998): 15.

66. Mae M. Ngai, *Impossible Subjects: Illegal Aliens and the Making of Modern America* (Princeton: Princeton University Press, 2004), 213.

67. Gabriel J. Chin, "Chae Chan Ping and Fong Yue Ting: The Origins of Plenary Power," in *Immigration Stories*, ed. David A. Martin and Peter H. Schuck, 7–29 (New York: Foundation Press, 2005).

68. Ibid., 12.

69. Densmore 14.

70. *Chae Chan Ping v. United States*, 130 U.S. 581, 603–604 (1889).

71. Ibid., 606.

72. Elliott C. Cowdin, "Chinese Immigration: Maintain the National Faith; Speech of Mr. Elliot C. Cowdin before the Chamber of Commerce of the State of New York" (New York: n.p., c. 1879), 2.

73. Ngai 11, 12.

74. Salyer 23.

75. *Facts upon the Other Side* 7. Field later dissented from *Fong Yue Ting v. United States*, which upheld the Geary Act, arguing against its "despotic power" to deport lawful resident aliens (Salyer 53).

76. *Fong Yue Ting v. United States*, 149 U.S. 698, 705, 13 S. Ct. 1016, 1019, 37 L. Ed. 905 (1893).

77. Chin, "Chae Chan Ping" 19.

78. The state of exception, writes Agamben, "appears as the legal form of what cannot have legal form," and "a theory of the state of exception is the preliminary condition for any definition of the relation that binds and, at the same time, abandons the living being to law." It is an ambiguous zone in which we might understand the stakes involved in the supposed difference between the political and juridical, law and living life. Giorgio Agamben, *State of Exception*, trans. Kevin Attell (Chicago: University of Chicago Press, 2005), 1–2.

79. *United States v. Kagama*, 118 U.S. 375, 380 (1886).

80. Priscilla Wald, *Contagious: Cultures, Carriers, and the Outbreak Narrative* (Durham: Duke University Press, 2008), 60.

81. Walter Benn Michaels, *Our America: Nativism, Modernism, and Pluralism* (Durham: Duke University Press, 1995), 34.

82. Jack London, *The Valley of the Moon* (New York: Review of Reviews, 1917), 155.

83. Mae M. Ngai, "From Colonial Subject to Undesirable Alien: Filipino Migration, Exclusion, and Repatriation," in *Re/collecting Early Asian America*, ed. Josephine Lee, Imogene L. Lim, and Yuko Matsukawa, 111–126 (Philadelphia: Temple University Press, 2002), 116.

84. Lye 51, 52.

85. Deborah L. Madsen, "The Exception That Proves the Rule? National Fear, Racial Loathing, Chinese Writing in 'UnAustralia,'" *Antipodes* 23.1 (2009): 17.

86. Washington Irving, "The Men of the Moon," in *Future Perfect: American Science Fiction of the Nineteenth Century*, ed. H. Bruce Franklin, 251–254 (New Brunswick: Rutgers University Press, 1995), 252. Using superior technology, the Lunatics violently seize the U.S. and initiate a benevolent mission of converting the "infidel savages from the darkness of Christianity . . . to enjoy the blessings of civilization and the charms of lunar philosophy" in Irving's satire of America's founding and the "right of the early colonists to the possession of this country" (254).

87. Eugene Casserly, *Speech of Eugene Casserly of California, Delivered in the Senate of the United States, July 8, 1870* (Washington, DC, 1870), 6.

88. London completed the story in 1907 but was unable to place it with a publisher until 1910. Lawrence I. Berkove, "A Parallax Correction in London's 'The Unparalleled Invasion,'" *American Literary Realism, 1870–1910* 24.2 (1992): 39n1.

89. Berkove notes that the colors of the diseases associated with the U.S.-based bacteriological warfare loosed on China, including scarlet fever, yellow fever, and the black death, heighten London's rather grim reflections on Yellow Peril and the course of white Western imperialism (35).

90. Jack London, "The Unparalleled Invasion: Excerpts from Walt. Nervin's 'Certain Essays in History,'" *McClure's Magazine* 35 (New York: McClure, 1910), 308, 314.

91. For discussions of the "outbreak narrative" and the racialization of Asian populations, see Wald; and Nayan Shah, *Contagious Divides: Epidemics and Race in San Francisco's Chinatown* (Berkeley: University of California Press, 2001).

92. Lye 22.

93. Helen Heran Jun, *Race for Citizenship: Black Orientalism and Asian Uplift from Pre-Emancipation to Neoliberal America* (New York: NYU Press, 2011), 6; Lye 9.

94. Lye 9.

95. Ibid., 5.

96. Jack London, "Yellow Peril," in *Revolution and Other Essays*, 267–289 (New York: Macmillan, 1910), 277.

97. Lye 3; Clarke 10.

98. M. B. Starr, *The Coming Struggle; or, What the People on the Pacific Coast Think of the Coolie Invasion* (San Francisco: Bacon, 1873), 106; hereafter cited parenthetically in the text.

99. In the 1870s, Starr, a Congregationalist minister, became the "Appointed Lecturer" of the anti-Chinese People's Protective Alliance of California, a coalition of local nativist organizations dedicated to oppose "the Emigration or Immigration of Heathen Idolators or any kind of servile labor into the United States." "Rev. M. B. Starr," *Sacramento Daily Union* (May 24, 1873): 1; Joshua Paddison, *American Heathens: Religion, Race, and Reconstruction in California* (Berkeley: University of California Press, 2012), 45.

100. Hayot, *Hypothetical* 167.

101. William Wu, *The Yellow Peril: Chinese Americans in American Fiction, 1850–1940* (Hamden, CT: Archon, 1982), 33.

102. Phan 133.

103. Bellamy 85–86.

104. Ibid., 456.

105. Thomas Dixon Jr., "A Friendly Warning to the Negro," in *Dixon's Sermons Delivered in the Grand Opera House, 1898–99* (New York: F. L. Bussey, 1899), 114; quoted in Gretchen Murphy, *Shadowing the White Man's Burden: U.S. Imperialism and the Problem of the Color Line* (New York: NYU Press, 2010), 66.

106. Best 261.

107. Donnelly 32.

108. Phan 150; Casserly 5.

109. Jones 12.

110. Claire Jean Kim, "The Racial Triangulation of Asian Americans," *Politics and Society* 27 (March 1999): 112.

111. *United States v. Wong Kim Ark*, 169 U.S. 649, 650 (1898).

112. Lowe 5–6.

113. Gillman 99.

114. Samuel Otter, *Philadelphia Stories: America's Literature of Race and Freedom* (New York: Oxford University Press, 2010), 339n86.

115. Sutton E. Griggs, *Imperium in Imperio* (1899; repr., New York: Modern Library, 2003), 167–168; Griggs, *The Hindered Hand* (1905; repr., New York: Echo Library, 2009), 125. The plot of *Hindered Hand* reveals a pan-Slavic conspiracy with a plan for germ warfare that involved unleashing a yellow-fever epidemic among white southerners, which resembles similar plot devices used in Chinese invasion tales such as Shiel's *Yellow Danger* and London's "Unparalleled Invasion."

116. London, "Yellow" 282–283.

117. Ibid., 285.

118. Ibid., 283.

119. Sibylle Fischer, *Modernity Disavowed: Haiti and the Cultures of Slavery in the Age of Revolution* (Durham: Duke University Press, 2004), 37–38.

120. London, "Yellow" 283.

121. James D. Corrothers, "A Man They Didn't Know: A Story; Part I," *Crisis* 7.2 (1913): 84–87; Corrothers, "A Man They Didn't Know: A Story; Part II," *Crisis* 7.3 (1914): 136–138; Ray Stannard Baker, introduction to *In Spite of the Handicap: An Autobiography by James D. Corrothers*, 7–9 (New York: George H. Doran, 1916), 8.

122. Kevin Gaines, "Assimilationist Minstrelsy as Racial Uplift Ideology: James D. Corrothers' Literary Quest for Black Leadership," *American Quarterly* 45.3 (1993): 345.

123. Yu-Fang Cho, "Domesticating the Aliens Within: Sentimental Benevolence in Late-Nineteenth-Century California Magazines," *American Quarterly* 61.1 (2009): 119.

124. James Robert Payne, "Griggs and Corrothers: Historical Reality and Black Fiction," *Explorations in Ethnic Studies* 6.1 (1983): 5.

125. [Nicholas] Vachel Lindsay, "The Golden-Faced People: A Story of the Chinese Conquest of America," *Crisis* 9.1 (1914): 36–42; hereafter cited parenthetically in the text.

126. Corrothers was born in the "Chain Lake Settlement," a free black colony in Cass County, Michigan, bordering northern Indiana, and the autobiography's first sentence establishes his connection to the young "Abraham Lincoln . . . in Springfield, Illinois." James D. Corrothers, *In Spite of the Handicap: An Autobiography* (New York: George H. Doran, 1916), 17.

127. Nancy Bentley, "The Fourth Dimension: Kinlessness and African American Narrative," *Critical Inquiry* 35 (2008): 286.

128. The fifteen men and teenage boys indicted in the case of Walker's gruesome death were eventually acquitted of all charges, and the outrage that this provoked became a catalyst for the NAACP's national antilynching campaign.

129. Vachel Lindsay to W. E. B. Du Bois, reprinted in "A Poem on the Negro: Vachel Lindsay's Congo," *Crisis* 10.1 (1915): 19.

130. Ibid., 18.

131. John C. Ward, "The Background of Lindsay's 'The Chinese Nightingale,'" *Western Illinois Regional Studies* 8.1 (1985): 70.

132. Vachel Lindsay and Joel Spingarn, "Editorial: A Letter and an Answer," *Crisis* 13.3 (1917): 113–114.

133. Ward 72.

134. Marjorie A. Taylor, "Vachel Lindsay and the Ghost of Abraham Lincoln," *CR: The Centennial Review* 22 (1978): 113.

135. W. E. B. Du Bois, *The Souls of Black Folk* (1903; repr., New York: Pocket, 2005), 7.

136. Henry Billings Brown, majority opinion in *Plessy v. Ferguson*, in *Plessy v. Ferguson: A Brief History with Documents*, ed. Brook Thomas, 41–51 (Boston: Bedford / St. Martin's, 1997), 50.

137. Best 214.

138. Vachel Lindsay, "Abraham Lincoln Walks at Midnight," in *Modern American Poetry*, by Louis Untermeyer, rev. and enl. ed., 232–234 (New York: Harcourt, Brace, 1921), 234.

139. Quoted in Taylor 116.

140. Yan Phou Lee, "The Chinese Must Stay," *North American Review* (April 1889): 476.

141. Murphy 5, 10.

142. Jing Tsu, *Failure, Nationalism, and Literature: The Making of Modern Chinese Identity, 1895–1937* (Stanford: Stanford University Press, 2005), 97.

143. L. P. Hartley, *The Go-Between* (New York: New York Review of Books, 2002), 17.

CHAPTER 4. BOYCOTTING EXCLUSION

1. Gordon H. Chang, "China and the Pursuit of America's Destiny," *Journal of Asian American Studies* 15.2 (2012): 147.

2. Gretchen Murphy, *Shadowing the White Man's Burden: U.S. Imperialism and the Problem of the Color Line* (New York: NYU Press, 2010), 152.

3. Mae M. Ngai, "From Colonial Subject to Undesirable Alien: Filipino Migration, Exclusion, and Repatriation," in *Re/collecting Early Asian America*, ed. Josephine Lee, Imogene L. Lim, and Yuko Matsukawa, 111–126 (Philadelphia: Temple University Press, 2002), 111.

4. Jing Tsu, *Failure, Nationalism, and Literature: The Making of Modern Chinese Identity, 1895–1937* (Stanford: Stanford University Press, 2005), 5–7.

5. Joanne Dobson, "Reclaiming Sentimental Literature," *American Literature* 69.2 (1997): 266.

6. Lucy E. Salyer, *Law Harsh as Tigers: Chinese Immigrants and the Shaping of Modern Immigration Law* (Chapel Hill: University of North Carolina Press, 1995), 20; Amy Dru Stanley, *From Bondage to Contract: Wage Labor, Marriage, and the Market in the Age of Slave Emancipation* (Cambridge: Cambridge University Press, 1998), 151.

7. Kitty Calavita, "Chinese Exclusion and the Open Door with China: Structural Contradictions and the 'Chaos' of Law, 1882–1920," *Social and Legal Studies* 10.2 (2001): 206, 219.

8. Quoted in Ng Poon Chew, "The Treatment of the Exempt Classes of Chinese in the United States" (San Francisco: n.p., 1908), 4.

9. Ibid., 8.

10. "Chinese Restriction," *San Francisco Evening Bulletin* (January 24, 1888): 1.

11. The 1891 Immigration Act established federal control over immigration policy by forming the Office of the Superintendent of Immigrants within the Treasury Department. In 1903, the Immigration Bureau was reorganized under the Department of Commerce and Labor, under the Department of Labor after 1913, and again under the Department of Justice after 1940.

12. *In re Jung Ah Lung* involved a Chinese immigrant who had established U.S. residency before traveling to China. The U.S. Attorney and collector of customs sought to prohibit Jung Ah Lung from reentering the U.S. because he had lost his return certificate during a robbery. When the case came to trial before the U.S. district court in 1885, the case against Jung Ah Lung argued that only documents officially issued and recognized by federal immigration authorities, such as the return certificate, were acceptable as evidence of U.S. residency.

13. Salyer 139.

14. Case file 10025/36 (Ju Toy), Records of the Immigration and Naturalization Service (Record Group 85), San Francisco, National Archives at San Francisco.

15. Ibid.

16. Ibid.

17. Ibid.

18. Born in China, John Endicott Gardner Jr. was the son of an American missionary and a Eurasian mother. He became the first immigration interpreter and inspector of Chinese descent hired by the Immigration Bureau. Mae M. Ngai, "'A Slight

Knowledge of the Barbarian Language': Chinese Interpreters in Late-Nineteenth- and Early-Twentieth-Century America," *Journal of American Ethnic History* 30.2 (2011): 14.

19. Case file 10025/36 (Ju Toy).

20. Susan M. Ryan, "Charity Begins at Home: Stowe's Antislavery Novels and the Forms of Benevolent Citizenship," *American Literature* 72.4 (2000): 772.

21. Case file 10025/36 (Ju Toy).

22. Ibid.

23. Acting Immigration Commissioner, San Francisco, California, to Chinese Inspector in Charge, San Francisco, California, November 5, 1905, ARC 296454, 21A, in ibid.

24. Commissioner E. H. Heacock presided over this court from 1892 to 1910 and often ruled in favor of Chinese petitioners (Salyer 77).

25. Ibid., 111–112.

26. Ibid., 163.

27. Ibid., 111.

28. The Chinese Six Companies engaged the San Francisco attorney Henry Dibble to represent Ju Toy before the U.S. Supreme Court (ibid., 112).

29. Neil Gotanda, "'Other Non-Whites' in American Legal History: A Review of *Justice at War*," *Columbia Law Review* 85.5 (1985): 1191.

30. Ibid., 1190.

31. *United States v. Ju Toy*, 198 U.S. 253, 263 (1905).

32. Devon W. Carbado, "Racial Naturalization," *American Quarterly* 57.3 (2005): 633, 638.

33. Nikhil Pal Singh, *Black Is a Country: Race and the Unfinished Struggle for Democracy* (Cambridge: Harvard University Press, 2004), 67.

34. *Ju Toy*, 198 U.S. at 269, 273.

35. Salyer 118.

36. Quoted in ibid., 154.

37. Salyer 113–114, 117, 143. The Chinese case *Ng Fung Ho v. White* (1922) went before the Supreme Court during what became known as the "Red Raids," the name given to U.S. Department of Justice efforts to arrest and deport radical leftists after World War I. The ruling in the case reversed aspects of *U.S. v. Ju Toy* by permitting alleged citizens to have judicial hearings before being deported (ibid., 240–241).

38. "Putative Native Sons Are Banished to China," *San Francisco Call* (August 11, 1905); "Chinese Ordered to Be Sent Back Home," *San Francisco Call* (August 12, 1905).

39. Salyer 170; "Chinese Send Protest to President," *Los Angeles Herald* (February 10, 1909).

40. Salyer 140.

41. "Chinese Civilization Encounters American Barbarism," *Outlook* (June 24, 1905): 456.

42. Editorial, *Grand Forks Herald* (August 12, 1905): 4; "The Chinese Boycott," *Watchman* (June 1, 1905): 1.

43. "A Shameful Law," *New York Observer and Chronicle* (July 20, 1905): 71.
44. Michael L. Krenn, *The Color of Empire: Race and American Foreign Relations* (Washington, DC: Potomac Books, 2006), 56–57.
45. Linda Papageorge, "American Diplomats Response to Chinese Nationalism: China's Anti-American Boycott, 1905–1906, for Patriotism or Profit?," *Proceedings and Papers of the Georgia Association of Historians* (1983): 99.
46. Chang-fang Chen, "Barbarian Paradise: Chinese Views of the United States, 1784–1911" (Ph.D. diss., Indiana University, 1985).
47. Guanhua Wang, *In Search of Justice: The 1905–1906 Chinese Anti-American Boycott* (Cambridge: Harvard University Press, 2002), 89.
48. Ibid., 190.
49. Amitav Ghosh, *River of Smoke* (New York: Farrar, Straus and Giroux, 2011), 355.
50. "The Chinese Boycott," *Puck* (June 28, 1905): 4.
51. Hsuan L. Hsu, "Sitting in Darkness: Mark Twain and America's Asia," *American Literary History* 25.1 (2013): 80.
52. S. B. Partridge, "The Chinese Boycott," *Watchman* (October 19, 1905): 13. This is not to say that American diplomats did not initially support the development of Chinese nationalism. A "strong China" worked to American interests by removing other Western threats to the Open Door, but only as long as China remained friendly with the U.S (Papageorge 100).
53. "The Chinese Boycott," *Chicago Daily Tribune* (June 14, 1905): 8.
54. Richard Weightman, "China's Retaliation Hits America Hard Blow in Her Tenderest Spot," *Chicago Daily Tribune* (June 24, 1905); "Chinese Boycott Threatens South," *Fort Worth Star-Telegram* (May 28, 1905): 1; "The Chinese Boycott," *Advocate of Peace* (August–September 1905): 166.
55. Ng 13; Delber L. McKee, "The Chinese Boycott of 1905–1906 Reconsidered: The Role of Chinese Americans," *Pacific Historical Review* 55.2 (1986): 179.
56. "Chinese Boycott Threatens South," *Fort Worth Star-Telegram* (May 28, 1905): 1.
57. "The President's Visit to the South," *Christian Observer* (November 1, 1905): 24.
58. "The Chinese Boycott," *Independent* (September 14, 1905): 601.
59. Wong Sin Kiong, *China's Anti-American Boycott Movement in 1905: A Study in Urban Protest* (New York: Peter Lang, 2002), 73–74.
60. "News of the Week (Friday, June 23)," *Christian Advocate* (June 29, 1905): 1040.
61. "We May Lose Chinese Trade," *Los Angeles Times* (June 12, 1905): 12.
62. "Chinese Boycott Ended," *Los Angeles Times* (October 20, 1905): 114.
63. "The President Demands Reform of Chinese Law," *St. Louis Post-Dispatch* (June 24, 1905): 2.
64. "The Chinese Puzzle," *Duluth News Tribune* (August 4, 1905): 4.
65. At Roosevelt's insistence, Metcalf's agency gradually eliminated the photographing of exempt Chinese in transit through the U.S. as well as the Bertillon system of identification. Exempt Chinese were also released on $2,000 bond while their cases were under investigation (Salyer 164–165, 221).
66. Kiong 21.

67. Ibid., 160.
68. "Labor Aroused," *Boston Daily Globe* (August 9, 1905): 6.
69. "Philippine Conditions," *San Francisco Chronicle* (July 7, 1905): 6; "An Illuminating Dispatch," *San Francisco Chronicle* (June 29, 1905): 6.
70. "Illuminating Dispatch" 6.
71. *St Louis Post-Dispatch* (June 24, 1905).
72. "The Chinese Boycott," *Advocate of Peace* (August–September 1905): 166.
73. "That Chinese Boycott: Not Nearly as Funny as It Looks," *Philadelphia Inquirer* (February 6, 1906): 2.
74. Arnold Pan, "Transnationalism at the Impasse of Race: Sui Sin Far and U.S. Imperialism," *Arizona Quarterly* 66.1 (2010): 95–96.
75. Kiong 156.
76. "Would Protect Chinese Trade," *Atlanta Constitution* (June 14, 1905): 3.
77. "The Chinese Boycott," *Current Literature* 39.3 (1905): 254.
78. "Fearful Finale of the Great Chinese Boycott," *Puck* (August 30, 1905): 11.
79. Kiong 159–160.
80. Jing Tsu, "Extinction and Adventure on the Chinese Diasporic Frontier," *Journal of Chinese Overseas* 2.2 (2006): 248; Wang, *In Search* 171.
81. "The Chinese Boycott: Opinion in China," *Outlook* (August 26, 1905): 992.
82. "Talk of Chinese Boycott on United States Goods," *San Francisco Chronicle* (June 15, 1905): 21; "Canadian Chinese Boycott America," *Duluth News-Tribune* (June 25, 1905): 15; "Chinese Boycott," *Dallas Morning News* (June 25, 1905): 14.
83. "Chinese Will Retaliate by Boycott on Our Goods," *Los Angeles Herald* (June 1, 1905): 2; "Chinese Boycott in Hawaii," *Idaho Statesman* (June 30, 1905): 1.
84. McKee 169, 179, 181.
85. "Chinese Boycott Extending," *Wilkes-Barre Times* (June 26, 1905): 1.
86. "Sailors Join Boycott," *Los Angeles Herald* (December 10, 1905).
87. Wang, *In Search* 141, 183–184.
88. Bob Adamson, *China's English: A History of English in Chinese Education* (Hong Kong: Hong Kong University Press, 2004), 18; Guanhua Wang, "Between Fact and Fiction: Literary Portraits of Chinese Americans in the 1905 Anti-American Boycott," in *Re-Collecting Early Asian America: Essays in Cultural History*, ed. Josephine Lee, Imogene L. Lim, and Yuko Matsukawa, 143–158 (Philadelphia: Temple University Press, 2002), 143, 147; and Wang, *In Search* 135.
89. Murphy 173.
90. David S. Reynolds, *Mightier than the Sword: Uncle Tom's Cabin and the Battle for America* (New York: Norton, 2011), xi.
91. Lin Shu, "Translator's Notes to *Uncle Tom's Cabin*," in *Land without Ghosts: Chinese Impressions of American from the Mid-Nineteenth Century to the Present*, trans. and ed. David R. Arkush and Leo O. Lee, trans. and eds., 77–80 (Berkeley: University of California Press, 1989), 77. Wei Yi most likely encountered *Uncle Tom's Cabin* while studying English at St. John's University, a missionary institution in Shanghai. Wei was later appointed to serve on the Translation Bureau of the Board of Education, where

he continued to collaborate with Lin Shu. Critics consider Wei to be the best of Lin's collaborators, in both his choice of texts and his command of English. Michael Gibbs Hill, *Lin Shu, Inc.: Translation and the Making of Modern Chinese Culture* (New York: Oxford University Press, 2013), 56, 58, 242–243.

92. Reynolds 213, 217, 219.

93. Mandarin Duck and Butterfly fiction derived its pejorative name from the genre's frequent invocations of these traditional symbols of romantic fidelity, and the term came to encompass all genres of pulp fiction. Haiyan Lee, *Revolution of the Heart: A Genealogy of Love in China, 1900–1950* (Stanford: Stanford University Press, 2007), 4, 61.

94. Hill 26, 32, 35, 38.

95. Vicente L. Rafael, *The Promise of the Foreign: Nationalism and the Technics of Translation in the Spanish Philippines* (Durham: Duke University Press, 2005), xvii.

96. A Chinese translation of Edward Bellamy's *Looking Backward*—in the form of a condensation of the original—appeared in serial installments in the *Globe Magazine* from December 1891 to April 1892 (Tsu, *Failure* 45).

97. Reynolds 41–42.

98. Lee 63.

99. Hill; also see Martha P. Y. Cheung, "The Discourse of Occidentalism? Lin Shu and Wei Yi's Version of *Uncle Tom's Cabin*," in *Translation and Creation: Readings of Western Literature in Early Modern China, 1840–1918*, ed. David Pollard, 127–149 (Amsterdam: John Benjamins, 1998), for a detailed comparison between the original and the Chinese translation.

100. Tsu, *Failure* 197.

101. Meg Wesling, *Empire's Proxy: American Literature and U.S. Imperialism in the Philippines* (New York: NYU Press, 2011), 72.

102. Ibid., 76–77.

103. Ibid., 32.

104. Ibid., 8.

105. Ibid., 93, 97.

106. Hill 51.

107. Chen 27.

108. Stanley 254.

109. Lin 77.

110. Ibid., 77–78.

111. Ibid., 78.

112. Tsu, *Failure* 21–22, 196–198; Lin 79.

113. Lin 79.

114. Harriet Beecher Stowe, *Uncle Tom's Cabin; or, Life among the Lowly* (New York: Penguin Books, 1981), 185; hereafter cited parenthetically in the text.

115. Chen 392–393.

116. Hill 2; and Lee 64.

117. Lin 78.

118. Ibid.
119. Chen 397.
120. Reynolds 124.
121. Hill 77.
122. Lee 10.
123. Susan M. Ryan, "Charity Begins at Home: Stowe's Antislavery Novels and the Forms of Benevolent Citizenship," *American Literature* 72.4 (2000): 751, 761–762.
124. Tsu, *Failure* 55–56, 63–64.
125. Hill 70.
126. Arthur Riss, "Racial Essentialism and Family Values in 'Uncle Tom's Cabin,'" *American Quarterly* 46.4 (1994): 515.
127. Lauren Berlant, "Poor Eliza," *American Literature* 70.3 (1998): 636.
128. Lin 79–80.
129. "Uncle Tom in Other Tongues!," *Topeka Plaindealer* (May 19, 1905): 1.
130. "Sherlock Holmes in China: The Mongolians Are Delighted with the Exploits of the Great Detective," *Kansas City Star* (November 3, 1911): 9.
131. Betty E. M. Ch'maj, "Foreword: The Strange Inscrutable Career of *Uncle Tom's Cabin* in China," *Prospects* 18 (1993): 507.
132. Reynolds 209.
133. Shiao-ling Yu, "Cry to Heaven: A Play to Celebrate One Hundred Years of Chinese Spoken Drama by Nick Rongjun Yu," *Asian Theatre Journal* 26.1 (2009): 1–10.
134. Reynolds 210–211, 214; Berlant 640–641.
135. Lee 3.
136. Ibid., 12.
137. Wang, *In Search* 146.
138. Ibid., 161.
139. June Mei and Jean Pang Yip, trans., "*The Bitter Society: Ku Shehui*: A Translation, Chapters 37–46," *Amerasia Journal* 8.1 (1981): 66; hereafter cited parenthetically in the text.
140. Wang, *In Search* 147; Hill 51.
141. Salyer 57.
142. Ibid., 63.
143. Wang, *In Search* 141–142.
144. *Ju Toy*, 198 U.S. at 263.
145. Chen 287.
146. Quoted in Chinese Equal Rights League, *Appeal of the Chinese Equal Rights League to the People of the United States for Equality of Manhood* (New York: Chinese Equal Rights League, 1893), 4.
147. Salyer 58, 149.
148. *Truth versus Fiction; Justice versus Prejudice: Meat for All, Not for a Few* (Washington, DC, c. 1902), 12.
149. Ibid., 44.
150. Quoted in Wang, *In Search* 149.

151. "Against the Geary Bill: Wong Chin Foo's Appeal for His Countrymen before the House Foreign Affairs Committee," *Philadelphia Inquirer* (January 27, 1893): 5.

152. Kif Augustine-Adams, "Making Mexico: Legal Nationality, Chinese Race, and the 1930 Population Census," *Law and History Review* 27.1 (2009): 119.

153. Ibid., 120–121.

154. Wang, *In Search* 37.

155. Salyer 152.

156. Ng 10–11.

157. Lee 81, 92.

158. Stanley 138.

159. Ibid., 267.

160. Gillian Brown, "Getting in the Kitchen with Dinah: Domestic Politics in *Uncle Tom's Cabin*," 36.4 (1984): 511.

161. Stanley 268.

162. Andrew Hebard, "Law, Literature, and the 'Situation' of Immigration," *Law, Culture and the Humanities* (December 14, 2011): 7.

163. Jacob A. Riis, *How the Other Half Lives: Studies among the Tenements of New York* (1890; repr., New York: Charles Scribner's Sons, 1914), 81.

164. Ibid., 80.

165. Ibid., 102.

166. Wesling 97, 99.

167. Sean McCann, "Connecting Links: The Anti-Progressivism of Sui Sin Far," *Yale Journal of Criticism* 12.1 (1999): 82.

168. Mary Chapman, "Finding Edith Eaton," *Legacy: A Journal of American Women Writers* 29.2 (2012): 264.

169. Pan 89.

170. Wesling 80.

171. Jean Marie Lutes, "Beyond the Bounds of the Book: Periodical Studies and Women Writers of the Late Nineteenth and Early Twentieth Centuries," *Legacy* 27.2 (2010): 338; Bonnie James Shaker, *Coloring Locals: Racial Formation in Kate Chopin's "Youth's Companion" Stories* (Iowa City: University of Iowa Press, 2003), 6.

172. Pan 91.

173. Rafael 11.

174. Colleen Lye, *America's Asia: Racial Form and American Literature, 1893–1945* (Princeton: Princeton University Press, 2005), 6.

175. Salyer 144, 185.

176. Dominika Ferens, *Edith and Winnifred Eaton: Chinatown Missions and Japanese Romances* (Urbana: University of Illinois Press, 2002), 54, 80; Sui Sin Far [Edith Maude Eaton], *Mrs. Spring Fragrance and Other Writings*, ed. Amy Ling and Annette White-Parks (Urbana: University of Illinois Press, 1995), 28; hereafter cited parenthetically in the text.

177. Quoted in Kiong 153.

178. Quoted in ibid., 158.

179. Chapman 265.
180. Stanley 142.
181. Pan 88.
182. Sui Sin Far [Edith Maude Eaton], "In the Land of the Free," *Independent* (September 2, 1909): 504.
183. Josiah Henson, *Truth Stranger than Fiction: Father Henson's Story of His Own Life* (Boston: John P. Jewett, 1858).
184. June Hee Chung, "Asian Object Lessons: Orientalist Decoration in Realist Aesthetics from William Dean Howells to Sui Sin Far," *Studies in American Fiction* 36.1 (2008): 47.
185. Gillian Silverman, "Sympathy and Its Vicissitudes," *American Studies* 43.3 (2002): 6.
186. Yu-Fang Cho, "Domesticating the Aliens Within: Sentimental Benevolence in Late-Nineteenth-Century California Magazines," *American Quarterly* 61.1 (2009): 116, 121.
187. Brown 522.
188. Cho 126.
189. Pan 101, 104.
190. Salyer 154.
191. Ibid., 152.
192. Max Weber, *Economy and Society*, ed. Guenther Roth and Claus Wittich, vol. 2 (Berkeley: University of California Press, 1978), 956.
193. Sui Sin Far [Edith Maude Eaton], "The Son of Chung Wo: *Leslie's Weekly* 16 June 1910: 592, 601, 602, 604," *Legacy* 28.1 (2011): 130.
194. Lee 77.
195. Ibid., 81.
196. Hill 6–8.
197. Eric Hayot, *The Hypothetical Mandarin: Sympathy, Modernity, and Chinese Pain* (Oxford: Oxford University Press, 2009), 6.
198. David L. Eng, Teemu Ruskola, and Shuang Shen, "Introduction: China and the Human," *Social Text* 109 (Winter 2012): 5.

CONCLUSION

1. Erika Lee, *At America's Gate: Chinese Immigration during the Exclusion Era, 1882–1943* (Chapel Hill: University of North Carolina Press, 2003), 24.
2. Mae M. Ngai, *Impossible Subjects: Illegal Aliens and the Making of Modern America* (Princeton: Princeton University Press, 2004), 6.
3. Devon W. Carbado, "Racial Naturalization," *American Quarterly* 57.3 (2005): 641.
4. Ngai 18, 237.
5. For a discussion of these racial prerequisite cases, see Ian F. Haney López, *White by Law* (New York: NYU Press, 1997).
6. Ngai 46.
7. Ibid., 3.

8. Lucy E. Salyer, *Law Harsh as Tigers: Chinese Immigrants and the Shaping of Modern Immigration Law* (Chapel Hill: University of North Carolina Press, 1995), 245.

9. Ngai 7.

10. Ibid., 37.

11. Ibid., 238; Lisa Lowe, *Immigrant Acts: On Asian American Cultural Politics* (Durham: Duke University Press, 1996), 9.

12. Michael Omi and Howard Winant, *Racial Formation in the United States from the 1960s to the 1990s*, 2nd ed. (New York: Routledge, 1994), 81–82.

13. Sutton E. Griggs, "A Hindering Hand," supplement to *The Hindered Hand*, 164–178 (1905; repr., New York: Echo Library, 2009), 164.

14. Lowe 7.

15. Thomas Dixon Jr., *The Leopard's Spots* (New York: Doubleday, Page, 1903), 406.

16. W. E. B. Du Bois, *The Souls of Black Folk* (1903; repr., New York: Pocket, 2005), 17–18.

17. W. E. B. Du Bois, *Dark Princess: A Romance* (1928; repr., Oxford: University Press of Mississippi, 1995), 150–151.

18. Griggs 164.

19. Ray Stannard Baker, introduction to *In Spite of the Handicap: An Autobiography*, by James D. Corrothers, 7–9 (New York: George H. Doran, 1916), 8.

20. Quoted in Michael Fultz, "'The Morning Cometh': African-American Periodicals, Education, and the Black Middle Class, 1900–1930," in *Print Culture in a Diverse America*, ed. James P. Danky and Wayne A. Wiegand, 129–148 (Urbana: University of Illinois Press, 1998), 132.

21. Kevin Gaines, "Assimilationist Minstrelsy as Racial Uplift Ideology: James D. Corrothers' Literary Quest for Black Leadership," *American Quarterly* 45.3 (1993): 344.

22. James D. Corrothers, "A Man They Didn't Know: A Story, Part I," *Crisis* 7.2 (1913): 85; Corrothers, "A Man They Didn't Know: A Story, Part II," *Crisis* 7.3 (1914): 136–138; hereafter cited parenthetically in the text.

23. Stephen Knadler, "Sensationalizing Patriotism: Sutton Griggs and the Sentimental Nationalism of Citizen Tom," *American Literature* 79.4 (2007): 674, 679.

24. Gaines 345.

25. Kristina M. Campbell, "Rising Arizona: The Legacy of the Jim Crow Southwest on Modern Immigration Law and Policy" (paper presented at "'We Must First Take Account': A Conference on Race, Law, and History in the Americas," University of Michigan Law School, April 1–2, 2011).

26. Ngai 39–40. Given restrictions on Chinese labor migration, Japanese immigration to the U.S. began to steadily increase in the 1890s, reaching 127,000 by the end of the century (Salyer 125). The informal 1907 "Gentleman's Agreement" between the U.S. and Japan helped reduce Japanese immigration, although it did not ban women—the so-called picture brides—from joining their husbands already resident in the U.S. Many of these Japanese migrants settled in the agricultural regions of California and became the focus of intensifying racial nativism when they began to purchase land and establish families (ibid., 126).

27. James Robert Payne, "Griggs and Corrothers: Historical Reality and Black Fiction," *Explorations in Ethnic Studies* 6.1 (1983): 6; Gary Y. Okihiro, *Margins and Mainstreams: Asians in American History and Culture* (Seattle: University of Washington Press, 1994), 118–119.

28. Payne 5.

29. William Ward Crane, "The Year 1899," *Overland Monthly and Out West Magazine* 21.126 (1893): 579–589; hereafter cited parenthetically in the text.

30. Like Noble, Corrothers also suffered the deaths of his first wife, Fannie Clemens, and younger son. After sacrificing his savings to rescue his debt-ridden Hackensack, New Jersey, parsonage, Corrothers, now a single father, was stunned when the "Negro church" "accused [him] of plotting to ruin" his bishop, brought legal proceedings against him, and effectively excommunicated him. James D. Corrothers, *In Spite of the Handicap: An Autobiography* (New York: George H. Doran, 1916), 183, 194.

31. Lowe 5.

32. Arif Dirlik, "Race Talk, Race, and Contemporary Racism," *PMLA* 123.5 (2007): 1364.

33. Ngai 203.

34. Ibid., 212.

35. James Kyung-Jin Lee, "The Transitivity of Race and the Challenge of the Imagination," *PMLA* 123.5 (2008): 1555, 1551; Omi and Winant 55.

36. Lowe 33.

37. The four "Asian Tigers" are Hong Kong, Singapore, South Korea, and Taiwan.

38. See Edlie Wong, "In a Future Tense: Immigration Law, Counterfactual Histories, and Chinese Invasion Fiction," *American Literary History* 26.3 (2014): 1–25. During the final weeks of the November 2010 elections, Citizens Against Government Waste, the nation's largest taxpayer watchdog group, released a controversial sixty-second television advertisement titled "Chinese Professor." It aired on CNN, FoxNews, AMC, and CNBC and on local broadcast stations in states with key gubernatorial and Senate races, including Florida, Ohio, Pennsylvania, and Wisconsin. It was run again in January and March 2011 and in the month before the 2012 presidential election. Since its original broadcast, "Chinese Professor" has become the subject of heated debate, praise, and parody, receiving nearly 2.7 million hits on YouTube alone.

39. Salyer 250.

40. Andrew Hebard, "Law, Literature, and the 'Situation' of Immigration," *Law, Culture and the Humanities* (December 14, 2011): 7.

41. Susan Koshy, "Why the Humanities Matter for Race Studies Today," *PMLA* 123.5 (2008): 1542.

42. Ibid., 1546–1547.

INDEX

Page numbers in italics refer to illustrations.

Aarim-Heriot, Najia, 10, 85
Abbott, John, *South and North; or, Impression Received during a Trip to Cuba and the South*, 18
abolitionism: Chinese exclusion represented as, 6, 70, 72–73, 155–56, 159–60, 197; and contract ideology, 31–32
Adorno, Theodor, 125
Afro-Asian analogy: in Chinese exclusion debates, 27, 83–86; and *Cuba Commission Report* (1876), 19; emergence in public discourse, 75–76; influence on California law and jurisprudence, 84–87; in Nast cartoons, 73–75, *74*, 122–23, *123*; in slavery debates, 19–20; in *Uncle Tom's Cabin* (Lin), 196–200; and James Williams's comparative framework, 78–79, 83
Agamben, Giorgio, 146, 264n78
Alien Contract Labor Law (1885) (Foran Act), 6
American Federation of Labor: response to 1905 Chinese boycott, 190; *Some Reasons for Chinese Exclusion*, 1, 138, 239n1
Americanization: as assimilation, 103–4, 217–18; as entailing reciprocal diversification, 104–6, 118
Anderson, Crystal, 9
Angell Treaty (U.S.-China Treaty 1880), 11, 142, 177
Ashmore, William, 30

assimilation, Americanization as, 103–4, 217–18

Baker, Houston, 79
Ballou, Maturin Murray, 13; on Chinese contract labor, 22–23; and Cuban annexation, 24; *Due South; or, Cuba Past and Present*, 18, 25, 32; *History of Cuba; or, Notes of a Traveller in the Tropics*, 18, 26, 35
Bamford, Mary, *Ti: A Story of San Francisco's Chinatown*, 130
Banks, Nathaniel, 38
"Battle of the Wabash: A Letter from the Invisible Police" (in *Californian* magazine): aboriginal whiteness in, 149–50; black effacement in, 160; capitalism tied to Chinese infiltration, 127–28; dangers of Chinese enfranchisement in, 164; historical references in, 149, 150
Bell, Philip Alexander, 76–77
Bellamy, Edward, *Looking Backward 2000–1887*, 137–39, 157–58
Bentley, Nancy, 168
Berlant, Lauren, 201
Bertillon system, 205
Best, Stephen, 132, 160
Bierce, Ambrose, 33, 134
Bigler, John, 78, 83–84, 87, 253n60
Bitter Society, The (anonymous, translation by June Mei and Jean Pang Yip): and Chinese diaspora, 211; Chinese

Bitter Society, The (continued)
government criticized in, 210; and Chinese immigration to Mexico, 208; and criminalizing of Chinese immigrants, 206–7, 209–10; denial of judicial review in, 204; depiction of shed detention, 206–7; documentation requirements in, 210; dramatization of deportation and family separation, 207–9; emphasis on racial pain, 208, 211; home life as focus of immigration inspection in, 176, 204; social impact of anti-Chinese laws, 203–5. *See also* Chinese boycott novels

black chattel slavery: analogized to labor migrants, 6, 14, 19–20, 22, 27, 29, 32, 69–70; as interpretive framework in *Uncle Tom's Cabin* (Lin), 196–200; as reform metaphor, 197, 200

black effacement: in Chinese invasion fiction, 159–61, 164, 228; in "A Man They Didn't Know" (Corrothers), 228, 234; and Thomas Dixon Jr., 160

black inclusion / Chinese exclusion dialectic: Blaine's espousal of, 72, 73, 115; and citizenship, 3–5, 14; satirized by Thomas Nast, 73–75, 74; sustained by heathenism discourse, 14, 71, 76, 98, 107, 110, 118, 120; and "A Man They Didn't Know" (Corrothers), 233–34; in *Truth versus Fiction* pamphlet, 2–3

black press: comparative racialization approach, 77–78; criticism of racialized citizenship, 84–85, 87; opposition to race-based immigration exclusion, 77–78; response to *People v. Hall*, 87

Black Slave's Cry to Heaven, A. See Uncle Tom's Cabin; or, Life among the Lowly (translation by Lin Shu)

Blackstone, William, 31, 98

black suffrage, and Reconstruction Amendments, 1, 96

black westward migration, and Fugitive Slave Bill, 79

Blaine, James: defense of Chinese exclusion, 69–75, 98, 114–15, 197; heathenism discourse, 98, 110, 114–15, 122; satirized in Thomas Nast cartoon, 73–75, 74; James Williams on, 88

Bow, Leslie, 8

Bridgman, Eliza, *Daughters of China; or, Sketches of Domestic Life in the Celestial Empire*, 130

Brown, Gillian, 221

Brown, Henry Billings, 171

Burlingame Treaty (1868): attacked by Chinese exclusion advocates, 70, 97, 124, 155; China as "most favored" nation under, 96, 124, 255n102; in Chinese invasion fiction, 131, 135–36, 155; immigration encouraged by, 70, 96, 97, 124, 187, 193; and Nast cartoon, 73–75, 74; vs. state sovereignty, 141. *See also* U.S.-China relations

Cable, George Washington, 4

California: antebellum black exclusion bills, 90; antebellum debates over racialized immigration restrictions, 83–87; Workingmen's Party, 69–89, 115, 124

California House riot, 89

Canby, E. R. S. (Edward Richard Sprigg), 93

capitalism: linked to Chinese infiltration in invasion fiction, 127–28, 154–59; linked to Christian doctrine by Wong, 112–13

Captain Jack (Kientpoos, or Kintpuash, Modoc Indian), 93, 94

Carbado, Devon, 8, 224

Cedulas de Libres de Color, 29–31, 34–36, 35

Chae Chan Ping v. U.S. (1889) (Chinese Exclusion Case): background, 143;

counterfactual thinking in, 132, 145, 171; and plenary power doctrine, 10, 142, 145; Yellow Peril trope invoked in ruling, 144–45
Chapman, Mary, 214, 216
Chen Lan-Pin (Chen Lanpin): and the Chinese Educational Mission, 57, 113–14, 193; and the Cuba Commission, 57–58, 193
Chesney, George, "The Battle of Dorking" (in *Blackwood's Magazine*), 119
Cheung, Martha, 195
Chinatown stories (Edith Maude Eaton): Christian missionaries criticized in, 218–19; contradictions in U.S. policy exposed, 213, 216; as counter to Chinese invasion fiction, 213–14; critique of U.S. foreign policy, 221; family separation as theme, 212–13, 215–21; historical context, 214; merchant figure in, 213–14, 221, 222; "self-deportation" as theme in, 216; shed detention satirized, 214–15; social realism, 217–21; transpacific dimensions of, 216. *See also* Chinese boycott novels; Eaton, Edith Maude (Sui Sin Far)
Chinese boycott (1905): characterized as capitalist conspiracy, 189–91; and Chinese invasion tropes, 191; Chinese support for, 191–92; Griggs on, 227; historical context, 187; immigration policies blamed for, 188–89; labor movement response to, 189–90; Roosevelt's response to, 188–89, 270n65; U.S. media coverage of, 187–88. *See also* U.S.-China relations
Chinese boycott novels: Chinese exclusion laws as source material, 176, 223; critique of Chinese government, 210–11; merchant figure in, 222; as records of diaspora experiences, 203; transpacific dimensions, 222; use of shared racial pain, 176, 194, 202. See also *Bitter Society, The* (anonymous); Chinatown stories (Edith Maude Eaton); *Uncle Tom's Cabin; or, Life among the Lowly* (translation by Lin Shu)
Chinese contract labor: analogized to black chattel slavery, 19–20, 22, 27, 29, 32; categorical ambivalence of, 13, 17, 20, 21; contract features, 29–31, 34–36, 35, 43–47, 50; and contract ideology, 13, 26–27, 29–36; "coolie-slave" applied to, 32–34, 33, 63, 67–68; and Cuban travelogues, 13, 17; Dana on, 20, 28–30; linked with wage slavery, 32–34, 33; as model for New South, 59, 60, 62; outlawed in U.S., 6; records of noncompliance, 46–48; Ripley's defense of, 41–42. *See also* Cuba; *Cuba Commission Report* (1876); *From Flag to Flag* (Eliza McHatton Ripley)
Chinese Educational Mission (1872–1881), 57, 113–14, 121
Chinese Equal Rights League, 63, 117–18
Chinese exclusion debates: and Afro-Asian analogy, 27, 83–86; "coolie-slave" figure in, 6, 13, 19, 27, 69–70, 124, 127; and influence of Cuban travelogues on, 13, 18–20, 23–26
Chinese exclusion laws: and birthright citizens, 182–83; challenged by habeas corpus suits, 96–97, 143, 163, 175, 178, 185; Chinese Exclusion Act (1882), 75; and Chinese immigration to Mexico, 208; and "fifteen passenger bill," 69–71, 75; Geary Act, 117, 142, 179, 183, 187, 206–9, 236; impact on home life in Chinatown stories (Eaton), 212–13, 215–21; impact on U.S.-China relations, 15, 183, 188, 222; labor union support of, 189–90; Naturalization Acts, 4–5, 77, 84, 96, 97; Page Act, 6, 7, 71, 78, 218; replaced by race-based quota system, 234; restriction by class, 177; and Roosevelt, 189; Scott Act, 142,

Chinese exclusion laws (*continued*) 143, 144; social impact revealed in *The Bitter Society*, 206–9

Chinese exclusion law test cases: and *Chae Chan Ping v. U.S.*, 10, 142, 144–45; and Chinese Exclusion Act (1882), 75; and *Elk v. Wilkins*, 163; and *U.S. v. Ju Toy*, 184–86; and *U.S. v. Wong Kim Ark*, 162–63

Chinese exclusion policy: and American Federation of Labor, 1, 138, 190; in antebellum California, 83–87, 90; Blaine's defense of, 69–75, 98, 114–15, 197; challenged by *Uncle Tom's Cabin* (Lin), 197–98; collective identification enabled by, 192; extended to U.S. overseas territories, 11–12, 175; heathenism as justification for, 5, 14, 110, 114–15, 119–20; Irish immigrant support of, 89–90; as precedent-setting, 224–25, 234–35; promoted by Chinese invasion fiction, 125; represented as abolitionist, 6, 70, 72–73, 155–56, 159–60, 197; Republican divisions over, 70, 73, 97–98, 103–4; James Williams on, 88

Chinese immigrants: cast as "coolie-slaves," 6, 13, 19, 27, 69–70, 124, 127; classified as "aliens ineligible to citizenship," 75, 224; criminalized by 1892 Geary Act, 206–9; as military agents, 154, 156–57; reentry certificates canceled, 142; used as strike breakers, 103

Chinese immigration: and Burlingame Treaty, 70, 73–75, *74*, 96, 97, 193; to Mexico, 208; as prelude to colonization in invasion fiction, 128; and Reconstruction Amendments, 96–97; as threat to home life, 104; transformed into a national concern, 141–42, 145

"Chinese in New York, The" (Wong Chin Foo), 108–9

Chinese invasion fiction: aboriginal whiteness in, 148, 149–50, 152; authors of, 14–15, 126; black effacement in, 159–61, 164, 228; capitalism linked with Chinese infiltration in, 127–28, 154–59; Chinese exclusion aligned with abolition, 159–60; Chinese immigrants as "coolie-slaves" / military agents, 15, 127, 154, 156–57; Chinese translations of, 173; compared with missionary literature, 130; and contemporary politics, 277n38; and Corrothers, 228; counterfactual thinking in, 131–33; dangers of enfranchisement in, 161–62, 164–66; as histories of the future, 130–32; influence on immigration case law, 142–47; internal enemy trope in, 129, 133, 135–36, 161–62, 166; literary context, 125–26, 129; Manifest Destiny inverted in, 15, 128, 150–52; modification of nativist ideologies, 148; and 1905 Chinese boycott, 191; overview, 173–74; popularity of, 126, 128; "slumbering volcano" metaphor in, 165–66, *165*; white dispossession in, 15, 127–28, 147, 150–52, 154, 157–59, 170–71. *See also* "Golden-Faced People, The: A Story of the Chinese Conquest of America" (Vachel Lindsay); *Last Days of the Republic* (Pierton W. Dooner); *Looking Further Backward* (Arthur Dudley Vinton)

Chinese labor immigrants: analogized to black chattel slavery, 6, 14, 69–70; depicted in Chinese invasion fiction, 15, 154, 156–57

Chinese Six Companies, 127, 141, 143, 186

Chinn, Richard, 52, 53, 54, 56

Christianity: and Grant's Native American policy, 122; Wong Chin Foo's critique of, 111–13; Yan Phou Lee's defense of, 114

INDEX | 283

Christian morality discourse: Blaine's use of, 98, 114–15; Douglass on, 105–6; Garrison on, 72; and Page Act (1875), 71; and racialized citizenship, 5, 14, 71–72, 98, 111; Wong Chin Foo on, 111–13. *See also* heathenism

Chun Young Hing. *See* "Story of Chun Young Hing's Sufferings as a Slave in Cuba" (Wong Chin Foo)

citizenship: assimilation as precondition for, 103–4, 217; and black inclusion / Chinese exclusion dialectic, 3–5, 14; heathenism as disqualification for, 5, 14, 110, 114–15, 119–20; and immigration policies, 10–11; linked with whiteness, 1, 3–4, 72, 85–87, 225; and racial formation, 1–4, 11–12, 122, 235, 236–37; and Reconstruction radicalism, 97

citizenship, racialization of: and Chinese exclusionary discourse, 5, 14, 71–72, 84, 98, 111; in Chinese invasion fiction, 161–62, 164–66, 171–72; detention shed as symbol of, 205–6; and exclusion law test cases, 10, 11–12, 142, 144–46, 162–63, 184–86, 224; and Naturalization Acts, 4–5, 77, 94, 96, 97

Clarke, I. F., 125, 129

colonialism. *See* white dispossession

comparative racialization: black and Chinese writers' use of, 12, 14, 75–78, 119–23; and Douglass's "composite nationality," 99–100, 101, 103–6; as framework for inquiry, 7–12; and immigration law, 9–10; James Williams's use of, 78–79, 81–83, 89–90, 120–21, 122–23. *See also* racial formation

Confucianism. *See* heathenism

Conrad, Joseph, *Typhoon*, 22, 206

contract ideology: and Chinese contract labor practices, 13, 26–27, 29–36; and concept of consent, 31, 60; and *Cuba Commission Report* (1876), 59, 60, 62–63

coolieism. *See* Chinese contract labor

"coolie-slave" figure: applied to Chinese contract laborer, 32–34, *33*, 63, 67–68; in Chinese exclusion debates, 6, 13, 19, 27, 69–70, 124, 127; and Cuban travelogues, 13, 17–20; influence on U.S. imperialism, 17–18, 26

coolie trade: American participation in, 21–22; analogized to slave trade, 60–61; China's response to, 57; media criticism of, 22–23; and slavery debates, 13, 19, 22–23

Coolie Trade Prohibition Act (1862), 23

Corrothers, James D. *See* "Man They Didn't Know, A" (James D. Corrothers)

counterfactual thinking: in Chinese invasion fiction, 131–33; in legal texts, 132, 145, 171, 184–85

Cowan, Edgar, 97

Crane, William Ward, "The Year 1899," 230–31

Cuba: and black chattel slavery, 20, 51, 56; independence movement, 24, 50, 56; policy on Chinese contract labor, 51, 243n53; as refuge for slaveholders, 24–25, 39, 40; and U.S. sugar market, 24. *See also* Chinese contract labor

Cuba Commission Report (1876), 13, 19, 34, 56–63, 249n216. *See also* Chinese contract labor

Cuban travelogues: Chinese contract labor depictions, 28; and "coolie-slave" figure, 13, 17–20; examples of, 18; genre characteristics, 20–21, 25–26; influence of, 18–20, 23–26. *See also* Ballou, Maturin Murray; *From Flag to Flag* (Eliza McHatton Ripley); *To Cuba and Back* (Richard Henry Dana)

Dana, Richard Henry. See *To Cuba and Back* (Richard Henry Dana)

Dayan, Colin, 62
Delany, Martin: *Blake; or, The Huts of America*, 166; response to *People v. Hall*, 87
Densmore, G. B., *The Chinese in California*, 127, 143
Derrida, Jacques, 94
Desengaño: forced recontracting at, 62–63; management after Ripley's relocation, 52–54, 247n151; records of Chinese noncompliance, 47, 48; size of labor force at, 56. See also *From Flag to Flag* (Eliza McHatton Ripley)
Dirlik, Arif, 4
Dixon, Thomas, Jr., 160, 194, 226–27
Donnelly, Ignatius, *Caesar's Column: A Story of the Twentieth Century*, 132, 160
Dooner, Pierton W. See *Last Days of the Republic* (Pierton W. Dooner)
Douglass, Frederick: immigration as human right, 98–99, 103; influence of western racial exclusions on, 95; monogenesis, 99–100; *Narrative* (1845), 65; "The Races" lecture, 99–100, 104; transnational humanism, 100; and W. E. B. Du Bois, 105. See also *Frederick Douglass' Paper*; "Our Composite Nationality" lecture (Frederick Douglass)
Du Bois, W. E. B.: color-line thesis, 227; *Dark Princess*, 227; on "double-consciousness," 170; *The Souls of Black Folk*, 105, 227
Due South; or, Cuba Past and Present (Maturin Murray Ballou), 18, 25, 32
Dunn, John, 179, 181–83

Eaton, Edith Maude (Sui Sin Far), 15; biographical details, 213, 214, 216; "In the Land of the Free," 216–19; "Mrs. Spring Fragrance," 214–15; publications of, 214; "The Son of Chung Wo," 222; "The Sugar Cane Baby," 218; "The Wisdom of the New," 219–21. See also Chinatown stories (Edith Maude Eaton)
Elk v. Wilkins (1884), 163
emancipation: and contract ideology, 31–32; and labor market, 5–6
Emancipation Proclamation, 23

family separation: in abolitionist literature, 211–12; dramatized in *The Bitter Society*, 207–9; as effect of immigration regulation, 181–82, 204, 212, 218; and literary sentimentalism, 176–77, 213, 217; as Progressive-era reform focus, 212; as theme in Chinatown stories (Eaton), 212–13, 215–21
Field, Stephen, 144–45
"fifteen passenger bill," 69–71, 75
Fifteenth Amendment, 97, 120
Fifth Amendment, 206
Fish, Hamilton, 53
Foner, Eric, 97
Fong Yue Ting v. U.S. (1893): counterfactual thinking in, 132; and plenary power doctrine, 10, 142, 146
Foran Act (1885) (Alien Contract Labor Law), 6
Fourteenth Amendment, 12, 96–97, 206
Frederick Douglass' Paper: criticism of California racial regulations, 84–85, 87, 95–96; Newby as correspondent for, 100–101; Nubia's reports in, 101–3. See also Douglass, Frederick; "Our Composite Nationality" lecture (Frederick Douglass)
free labor: Chinese contract labor as transition to, 13, 17, 19, 20, 21; vs. "coolie-slave" in Chinese exclusion debates, 6, 69–70
From Flag to Flag (Eliza McHatton Ripley), 18; biographical background, 38–39; Chinese contract labor as "modernization," 41, 42; labor contract discussed, 43–47, 44, 45; on labor

relations, 38–39, 40, 48, 49, 51–56; as plantation romance, 37–38, 40, 46–50, 51, 53; publication context, 37–38, 48; racial differentiation in, 42, 43, 48–49; reception history, 37–38. *See also* Cuban travelogues; Desengaño; Ripley, Eliza McHatton
"fugitive coolie." *See* "Story of Chun Young Hing's Sufferings as a Slave in Cuba" (Wong Chin Foo)
Fugitive Slave Act (1850): and black westward migration, 79; and Dana, 27; and Stowe, 197, 199

Gaines, Kevin, 228
Gallagher, Catherine, 125, 131
Gardner, Eric, 82, 251n28
Garrison, William Lloyd: compared with Stowe, 195; on coolie trade, 22; exchange with Blaine, 70, 72–73; response to *People v. Hall*, 87
Geary Act (1892), 117, 142, 179, 183, 187, 206–9, 236
Gibbs, Mifflin Wistar, *Shadow and Light: An Autobiography*, 89
Gibbs, R. W., *Cuba for Invalids*, 18
"Golden-Faced People, The: A Story of the Chinese Conquest of America" (Vachel Lindsay): antiblack and anti-immigrant violence linked in, 172–73; black-white racial hierarchy inverted in, 171–73; "double-consciousness" in, 170, 171–72; historical and literary sources, 168–69; influence of *Plessy v. Ferguson* on, 171; Lincoln referenced in, 170–71, 172–73; Booker T. Washington referenced in, 171; white dispossession and enslavement in, 170–71. *See also* Lindsay, Vachel
Gompers, Samuel, 190
Goodell, William, *The American Slave Code in Theory and Practice*, 61
Gotanda, Neil, 184

Grant, Ulysses S., 92, 122, 141
Gray, Horace, 146
Gresham-Yang Treaty (1894), 183, 204, 222
Griggs, Sutton. *See Hindered Hand, The* (Sutton Griggs)
Gruesz, Kirsten Silva, 116
Guterl, Matthew Pratt, 24, 28, 245n118

habeas corpus: Chinese exclusion laws challenged by, 15, 96–97, 143, 163, 175, 178, 185; and *In re Jung Ah Lung*, 178, 183; and *U.S. v. Ju Toy*, 175–76, 178, 185
Hall, Henry, 5, 53
Haney López, Ian, 225
Harlan, John Marshall, 3–4
Harris, Joel Chandler, 40, 49
Hartley, L. P., 174
Hawaiian-U.S. Treaty of Annexation (1898), 11
Hay, John, 153, 186
Hayes, Rutherford B., 69, 75, 143
Hayot, Eric, 156, 223
Hazard, Samuel, *Cuba with Pen and Pencil*, 18, 19, 28
heathenism: attributed to Chinese and Native Americans, 5, 72, 92, 98; black inclusion / Chinese exclusion sustained by, 14, 71, 76, 98, 107, 110, 118, 120; and Garrison-Blaine exchange, 72–73; as justification for Chinese exclusion, 5, 14, 110, 114–15, 119–20; racial difference recoded as, 71–72, 107–9, 110, 113, 114–15; rejected as rationale for exclusion by Douglass, 106; as theme in Chinese invasion fiction, 130; Wong Chin Foo's focus on demystifying, 14, 76, 107–9, 110, 118–19. *See also* Christian morality discourse
Higby, William, 97
Hill, Michael Gibbs, 195–97, 200
Hindered Hand, The (Sutton Griggs): black and Asian racializations linked,

Hindered Hand, The (continued)
226–27; on the Chinese boycott, 227; internal enemy trope recast, 166; U.S. imperialism and black inequality linked, 226
Holden, Edgar, "A Chapter on the Coolie Trade," 47
Holmes, Oliver Wendell, 184–85
Horkheimer, Max, 125
Howe, Julia Ward, *A Trip to Cuba*, 18, 49
Hsu, Hsuan, 107, 109, 111, 119, 130
Hu-DeHart, Evelyn, 7, 17, 21

Immigration Act (1917), 225
Immigration and Nationality Act (1952) (McCarran-Walter Act), 225
Immigration and Nationality Act (1965), 234–35
Immigration Bureau: bureaucratic evolution, 221–22, 268n11; expansion of authority by *U.S. v. Ju Toy*, 183–85, 221, 225; features of investigations, 205; focus on Chinese home life, 181–82, 204, 212, 218; interrogation techniques portrayed in *The Bitter Society*, 204, 221; limitation of exemptions from exclusion, 177; public criticism of, 189. *See also* immigration regulation
immigration law: and Chinese home life, 204, 212–13, 215–21; and comparative racialization studies, 9–10; as context for African American racial formation, 8; and Coolie Trade Prohibition Act (1862), 23; expansion to "Asiatics," 224–25; influence of Chinese invasion fiction on, 142; and plenary power doctrine, 10, 142–43, 145, 224; quota systems, 225–26, 234
immigration regulation: and bodily measurements, 205; documentation requirements, 210; and growth of bureaucracy, 221–22; and plenary power doctrine, 10, 142–43, 145–46, 224; and shed detention, 205–6. *See also* Immigration Bureau
imperialism, Chinese, in invasion fiction, 15, 128, 150–53
imperialism, U.S.: aligned with white supremacy, 11–12, 226–27, 229; and Cuban annexation, 24–27; influence of "coolie-slave" figure on, 17–18, 26; rhetoric of friendship, 186–87, 200, 215–16; satirized in "The Unparalleled Invasion" (London), 153; *Uncle Tom's Cabin* (Lin) as response to, 197
Imperium in Imperio (Sutton Griggs), 166
indentured labor. *See* Chinese contract labor
In re Ah Yup (1878), 11
In re Jung Ah Lung (1885), 178, 183
Insular Cases (1901–1922), 11–12
internal enemy trope: in Chinese invasion fiction, 129, 133, 135–36, 161–62, 166; in *U.S. v. Wong Kim Ark*, 162–63
"In the Land of the Free" (Edith Maude Eaton), 216–19
Irish immigrants: differentiated by heathenism discourse, 115; as proslavery, 89; support of Chinese exclusion, 89–90
Irving, Washington, "The Men of the Moon," 152, 265n86

Jenks, Cornelia H., *The Land of the Sun; or, What Kate and William Saw There*, 18
Johnson-Reed Immigration Act (1924), 225
Jones, Andrew, 9
judicial review of immigration decisions: Chinese demands for, 222; termination of, 15, 142, 145, 175–76, 221
Jun, Helen, 9, 102
Jung, Moon-Ho, 7, 23, 41, 46, 70, 127

K'ang Yu-wei, 192
Kearney, Denis: in *Last Days of the Republic* (Dooner), 135; James Williams on, 88; and Workingmen's Party of California, 69, 89, 115, 133
Keller, George Frederick: "A Fresh Eruption of the Pacific Coast Vesuvius" (in the *Wasp*), 165; "San Francisco A.D. 1900" cartoon (in the *Wasp*), 134
Kientpoos (Kintpuash, or Captain Jack, Modoc Indian), 93, 94
Kim, Claire Jean, 92
Kohler, Max J., 2, 185
Koshy, Susan, 237

labor movement: and Chinese exclusion, 1, 6, 69–70; and "coolie-slave" figure, 18, 32–34, 33, 58; and emancipation, 5–6; response to 1905 Chinese boycott, 189–90
Lai, Walton Look, 7
Last Days of the Republic (Pierton W. Dooner): Chinese exclusion laws justified, 136–37; "coolie-slave" / military agent figure in, 156; as counterfactual history, 130, 133, 135–37; dangers of Chinese enfranchisement in, 165; internal enemy trope in, 129, 135–36, 166; neoabolitionism in, 157; partisanship as weakness in, 130; *People v. Hall* recontextualized by, 87, 136–37; publication of, 134; racialization of citizenship in, 161–62; use of documentary empiricism, 135–36
Lee, Archy, 90
Lee, Erika, 6, 224
Lee, Haiyan, 195, 200, 202
Lee, Julia, 9
Lee, Yan Phou: on anti-Chinese laws, 173; and Chinese Educational Mission, 113, 121; defense of Christian universalism ("Why I Am Not a Heathen"), 114; print career, 117, 259n203; Protestant conversion, 113–14; Transcontinental Railroad journey, 121–22
Leopard's Spots, The (Thomas Dixon Jr.), 194, 226–27
Levander, Caroline, 25
Levine, Robert, 100
Life and Adventures of James Williams (James Williams): on antebellum Philadelphia, 80, 89–90; and California racial exclusion policies, 88, 90–91; comparative racialization approach, 78–79, 81–83, 89–90, 91, 92, 93, 95, 121, 122; historical context, 78, 79, 83–87; Modoc War, 91–94; narrative style, 80–81, 82, 88, 94; publication history, 80, *81*; skepticism of the law, 82, 91–94. *See also* Williams, James
Lindsay, Vachel: "Abraham Lincoln Walks at Midnight," 170, 172; African American reception, 169; "Booker T. Washington Trilogy," 169; "The Chinese Nightingale," 169, 172; "Congo," 169; influence of Lincoln on, 170; "Study of the Negro Race," 169. *See also* "Golden-Faced People, The: A Story of the Chinese Conquest of America" (Vachel Lindsay)
Ling, Amy, 117
Lin Shu. See *Uncle Tom's Cabin; or, Life among the Lowly* (translation by Lin Shu)
literary sentimentalism: adapted to social realism, 217–19; and Chinese national consciousness, 195–96, 222–23; as counter to Chinese exclusion discourse, 222; emphasis on shared racial pain, 194, 198, 213; focus on home life, 176–77, 213, 217
Locke, John, *Second Treatise of Civil Government*, 31
London, Jack: on Chinese capitalism, 154; *Iron Heel*, 230; and racial typologies, 214; "The Unparalleled Invasion," 153;

London, Jack (*continued*)
"Valley of the Moon," 150; "Yellow Peril," 166–67
Looking Further Backward (Arthur Dudley Vinton): capitalist exploitation in, 157–58; danger of constitutional limits portrayed in, 146–47; dangers of Chinese enfranchisement in, 165; effacement of blacks in, 159–60; as history lesson, 139–41; loss of individualism faulted, 138–39; as sequel to *Looking Backward 2000–1887* (Bellamy), 137–38, 157–58, 272n96; white dispossession and enslavement in, 157–59
López, Narciso, 13, 23–24
Love, Nat, *Life and Adventures*, 82, 91
Lowe, Lisa, 7–8, 21, 67, 163, 226
Lye, Colleen, 75, 154–55, 214

Mackie, J. Milton, *From Cape Cod to Dixie and the Tropics*, 18
Manifest Destiny: inverted in Chinese invasion fiction, 15, 128, 150–52; satirized in "The Unparalleled Invasion" (London), 153; James Williams's skepticism of, 82
Manson, Marsden, *The Yellow Peril in Action*, 129, 164, 191
"Man They Didn't Know, A" (James D. Corrothers): ambivalent view of black inclusion, 233–34; black treason in, 228–29; and Chinese invasion trope, 15, 16, 228; imperialism and white supremacy linked, 229; overview, 167–68; racialized violence as origin of war, 232–33; reference to "At the End of the Controversy," 232, 277n30; relevance to current immigration debates, 236–37; and rethinking citizenship and racial formation, 235, 236–37; white supremacy challenged by cross-racial alliance in, 167–68, 228, 229–31, 233

Martin, Waldo E., Jr., 106
McCann, Sean, 213
McCarran-Walter Act (1952 Immigration and Nationality Act), 225
McClain, Charles, Jr., 185
McHatton, Henry, 52, 62
McHatton, James A., 38, 52, 245n115
Metzger, Sean, 61
Michaels, Walter Benn, 148
Mintz, Sidney, 20
Modoc War (1872–1873), 91–94, 122
Molina, Natalia, 8, 77
Moret Law, 51, 52
Moyamensing Killers, 89
"Mrs. Spring Fragrance" (Edith Maude Eaton), 214–15
Mrs. Spring Fragrance and Other Writings (Edith Maude Eaton, edited by Amy Ling and Annette White-Park). See Chinatown stories (Edith Maude Eaton)
Mullen, Bill, 9
Murray, Hugh, 86–87, 136

Nast, Thomas: "The Civilization of Blaine" cartoon, 73–75, *74*, 122; "The Nigger Must Go" / "The Chinese Must Go" cartoon, 122–23, *123*
national consciousness: racial difference as catalyst for, 98–99, 103–6; shared racial pain as foundation for, 194, 195–96, 198–99, 201, 202, 222–23
Native Americans: coerced dislocation of, 91–93, 103; and Grant's Peace Policy, 122; and Modoc War, 91–94; and *People v. Hall*, 86; plenary power doctrine applied to, 147–48; racial exclusion of, 5; and Removal Act (1830), 92
Naturalization Act (1790), 4, 77, 84
Naturalization Act (1870), 4–5, 96, 97
Newby, William H. ("Nubia"): as California journalist, 100–101; linkage of Chinese exclusion with slavery, 14, 76.

See also Nubia's reports (in *Frederick Douglass' Paper*)
Ngai, Mae M., 10, 143, 175, 225, 234
Ng Poon Chew, 177, 210
Nubia's reports (in *Frederick Douglass' Paper*): influence on Douglass, 101, 103; Native American dislocation, 103; racial affiliation through sympathy, 102–3; status of Spanish Mexicans, 101–2; white hegemony, 101, 102. *See also* Newby, William H. ("Nubia")

O'Kelly, James, *The Mambi-Land; or, Adventures of a Herald Correspondent in Cuba*, 18, 32, 34, 35
Okihiro, Gary, 126, 230
Omi, Michael, 7, 226, 235
Open Door policy, 153, 186–87, 215
Opium Wars: and attacks on missionaries, 203; and Christian capitalism, 112–13; and Cuba Commission Report, 57
"Our Composite Nationality" lecture (Frederick Douglass): concept of nationality, 99–100, 101, 103–6; endorsement of Chinese and Native American citizenship, 96, 97, 98; historical context, 96–98; immigration justified as human right, 98–99. *See also* Douglass, Frederick; *Frederick Douglass' Paper*

Paddison, Joshua, 75, 89–90, 95, 98, 110, 113–14, 115
Page Act (1875), 6, 7, 71, 78, 218
Pan, Arnold, 213
People v. Hall (1854): Afro-Asian analogy influence on, 85–87; black press response to, 87; and Native Americans, 86; prohibition of Chinese legal testimony, 84, 85–86, 254n70; recontextualized in *Last Days of the Republic* (Dooner), 87, 136–37
Pfaelzer, Jean, 113

Phillips, Wendell, "The Chinese," 103–4
plenary power doctrine: applied to Native Americans, 147–48; in immigration regulation, 10, 142–43, 145, 224; and state of exception, 146–47
Plessy v. Ferguson (1896): applied to overseas territories, 11–12; counterfactual thinking in, 171; and "The Golden-Faced People" (Lindsay), 171; whiteness linked with citizenship, 3–5, 16, 225
Prashad, Vijay, 9

"Races, The," lecture (Douglass), 99–100, 104
racial difference: as catalyst for national consciousness, 98–99, 103–6; heathenism recoded as, 71–72, 107–9, 110, 113, 114–15
racial formation: and black inclusion / Chinese exclusion dialectic, 3–5; and citizenship, 1–4, 11–12, 122, 235, 236–37; influence of Chinese invasion fiction on, 125–26; need for comparative approach to, 7–8, 11–12; as relational process, 8–9, 119–23; as transnational, 11–12. *See also* comparative racialization
Rafael, Vicente, 195
Ranke, Leopold von, 139
Ray, Angela, 105
Reconstruction Amendments, 1, 96–97
Redpath, James, 95, 255n100
Redpath Lyceum Bureau, 110, 255n100
religious difference. *See* heathenism
Removal Act (1830), 92
Riis, Jacob, *How the Other Half Lives: Studies among the Tenements of New York*, 212
Riordan, Thomas, 143
Ripley, Dwight, 51
Ripley, Eliza McHatton, 13; background information, 38–39, 50–51; Confederate attitudes of, 20, 24; defense of

Ripley, Eliza McHatton (*continued*)
Chinese contract labor, 41–42; *Social Life in New Orleans*, 37; as woman traveler, 18, 37. See also *From Flag to Flag* (Eliza McHatton Ripley)
Roosevelt, Alice, 189
Roosevelt, Theodore, 186, 188, 189, 255n100
Rosaldo, Renato, 92

Salyer, Lucy, 185, 225
Saxton, Alexander, 108
Schmitt, Carl, 146
Scott Act (1888), 142, 143, 144
"self-deportation": and Arizona statute Support Our Law Enforcement and Safe Neighborhoods Act (S.B. 1070), 236; in *The Bitter Society*, 207–9; as theme in Chinatown stories (Eaton), 216
Seligman, Scott D., 107, 109, 118
Shah, Nayan, 7
shed detention: and immigration regulation, 205–6; and Ju Toy, 183; satirized in Chinatown stories (Eaton), 214–15; as symbol of Chinese racialization, 205–6
Shiel, M. P. *Yellow Danger*, 153
Shinn, Charles Howard, *Mining Camps: A Study in American Frontier Government*, 82
Short and Truthful History of the Taking of California and Oregon by the Chinese in the Year A.D. by Robert Woltor, a Survivor, A (Robert Woltor): aboriginal whiteness in, 152; "coolie-slave" / military agent figure in, 156–57; as historical record, 131–32; Manifest Destiny inverted in, 150–52
Singh, Nikhil, 9
slave trade: analogized with coolie trade, 22–23, 32; and Cuba, 20–21; Slave Trade Act (1808), 22

Smallwood, Stephanie, 30
Some Reasons for Chinese Exclusion (American Federation of Labor), 1, 138, 239n1
sovereignty, national: and immigration regulation, 141–43, 145–46; and plenary power doctrine, 142–43, 145–46, 224; and regulation of Indian affairs, 147–48
Stanley, Amy Dru, 5, 31, 51, 197
Starr, Milton B., *The Coming Struggle: or, What the People on the Pacific Coast Think of the Coolie Invasion*, 155–56
state of exception, 146–47, 264n78
Steele, J. W., *Cuban Sketches*, 18
Still, William, *Underground Rail Road*, 82
Stoler, Ann Laura, 55
"Story of Chun Young Hing's Sufferings as a Slave in Cuba" (Wong Chin Foo): Chinese coolie humanized in, 63–67; exploitation of Chinese and slave labor compared, 66; media interest in, 63–64; slave narrative as model, 64–65, 67; summary, 65–67
Stowe, Harriet Beecher: "feel right" injunction, 67, 200–201. See also *Uncle Tom's Cabin; or, Life among the Lowly* (Harriet Beecher Stowe)
Straus, Oscar, 177
Sui Sin Far. *See* Eaton, Edith Maude (Sui Sin Far)
Sumner, Charles, 97
Sun, Yumei, 116
Sun Yat-sen, 192, 211
Support Our Law Enforcement and Safe Neighborhoods Act (S.B. 1070), 236–37
sympathetic identification: boycott novel's use of, 194; and Chinatown stories (Eaton), 213, 220–21; and *The Bitter Society*, 206–9

Taft, William Howard, 189
Takao Ozawa v. U.S. (1922), 225
Tchen, John Kuo Wei, 69, 116, 126
Thrasher, John, 20
To Cuba and Back (Richard Henry Dana), 18; on Chinese contract labor, 20, 28–30; image of plantation life, 25; influence of, 27, 243n62
Torok, John, 96
Tourgée, Albion, 3
Transcontinental Railroad, 120, 121–22
Treaty of Guadalupe Hidalgo, 101, 229
Treaty of Tianjin (1858), 135
Truth versus Fiction; Justice versus Prejudice: Meat for All, Not for a Few, 1–3, 2
Tsu, Jing, 173, 176, 195, 196, 198
Turner, Frederick Jackson, 153

Uncle Tom's Cabin; or, Life among the Lowly (Harriet Beecher Stowe): parallels with *The Bitter Society*, 209; sentimentalism in, 200–201, 219, 221; use in Philippines colonial administration, 196–97
Uncle Tom's Cabin; or, Life among the Lowly (translation by Lin Shu): background, 194–97; black chattel slavery as interpretive framework, 196–200; emphasis on statelessness, 198–200; influence in China, 201–2; and national consciousness in, 195–96, 198–99, 201, 202, 222–23; as response to U.S. imperialism, 197; U.S. readers' response to, 201. See also Chinese boycott novels
U.S.-China relations: Chinese exclusion laws impact on, 15, 183, 188, 222; and Chinese market, 175; Open Door policy, 186–87, 200, 215; Scott Act (1888), 142, 143, 144; U.S.-China Treaty (1880), 11, 142, 177. See also Burlingame Treaty (1868); Chinese boycott (1905)

U.S.-China Treaty (1880) (Angell Treaty), 11, 142, 177
U.S. v. Bhagat Singh Thind (1923), 225
U.S. v. Ju Toy (1905), 178–86; and birthright citizenship, 181–83; counterfactual thinking in, 184–85; dissenting opinion, 185; effect on Chinese habeas corpus suits, 185; expansion of Immigration Bureau authority, 185, 221; home life as focus of immigration inspection, 181–82, 204, 212, 218; influence on jurisprudence, 184–86; *jus soli* vs. *jus sanguinis* in, 184; presumption of "foreignness," 184; public criticism of, 186; San Francisco case file, *180*; termination of judicial review of immigration decisions, 15, 175–76, 178, 185; and "There's Millions in It" (Solly H. Walter in the *Wasp*), 179
U.S. v. Kagama (1886), 147–48
U.S. v. Wong Kim Ark (1898): analogized to *Elk v. Wilkins*, 163; counterfactual thinking in, 132; internal enemy trope in, 162–63; *jus soli* vs. *jus sanguinis* in, 163–64; and nonnaturalizable immigrants in, 11

Vinton, Arthur Dudley. See *Looking Further Backward* (Arthur Dudley Vinton)

Wahab, Amar, 25
Wald, Priscilla, 148
Wang, Guanhua, 191, 193, 201
Washington, Booker T., 171
Wasp, the: and Ambrose Bierce, 134; "Celestial Cubans," 33; "A Fresh Eruption of the Pacific Coast Vesuvius" (Keller), *165*; "There's Millions in It" (Solly H. Walter), *179*
Weber, Max, 112, 221
Wesling, Meg, 196
White, Hayden, 131

white dispossession: in Chinese invasion fiction, 15, 127–28, 147, 150–52, 154, 157–59, 170–71. *See also* white supremacy

whiteness, aboriginal: in invasion fiction, 149–50, 151–52; linked with rhetoric of racial extinction, 152

whiteness, linked with citizenship, 1, 3–4, 72, 85–87, 225

white supremacy: affirmed by "The Year 1899" (Crane), 230–31; challenged in "A Man They Didn't Know" (Corrothers), 167–68, 228, 229–31, 233; challenged in "The Golden-Faced People" (Lindsay), 170–73; U.S. imperialism aligned with, 11–12, 226–27, 229. *See also* white dispossession

"Why Am I a Heathen?" (Wong Chin Foo), 108; critique of Christianity, 111–13; and Garrison, 72–73; publication of, 111

"Why I Am a Pagan" (revised as "The Great Spirit") (Zitkala-Sa), 111

"Why I Am Not a Heathen" (Yan Phou Lee), 114

Williams, George, *Sketches of Travel in the Old and New World*, 17, 26

Williams, James: biographical information, 78, 79–80; linkage of Chinese exclusion with slavery, 14, 76. See also *Life and Adventures of James Williams* (James Williams)

Winant, Howard, 3, 7, 226, 235

Woltor, Robert. See *Short and Truthful History of the Taking of California and Oregon by the Chinese in the Year A.D. by Robert Woltor, a Survivor, A*

Wong Chin Foo: advocacy of U.S. intervention in coolie trade, 67; biographical details, 109–10, 121; and Chinese Equal Rights League, 63, 117–18; "The Chinese in New York," 108–9; and Confucianism, 108, 110, 118–19; and "coolie-slave" figure, 19, 67–68; criticism of Chinese government, 64; critique of Christianity, 111–13, 114, 119; deconstruction of East-West dichotomies, 108–9; disarticulation of immigration from citizenship, 117–18; focus on demystifying heathenism, 14, 76, 107–9, 110–11; as lecturer, 109–10, 115; as newspaper editor, 116–17; use of comparative approach, 118; use of periodical form, 76, 107, 108, 109; "Why Am I a Heathen?," 72–73, 108, 111–13. *See also* "Story of Chun Young Hing's Sufferings as a Slave in Cuba" (Wong Chin Foo)

Wong Sin Kong, 191

Woodruff, Julia (W. M. L. Jay), *My Winter in Cuba*, 18, 25, 47, 49

Workingmen's Party of California, 69, 89, 115, 124, 133

Wu, William, 126

Wu Ting Fang, 190

Yun, Lisa, 7, 34, 56, 60

Zeng Xiaogu, 201–2

Zitkala-Sa, "Why I Am a Pagan" (revised as "The Great Spirit"), 111

ABOUT THE AUTHOR

Edlie Wong is Associate Professor at the University of Maryland and author of *Neither Fugitive nor Free: Atlantic Slavery, Freedom Suits, and the Legal Culture of Travel* and coeditor of George Lippard's *The Killers*. Her work has also appeared in *American Literary History*, *American Literature*, and *African American Review*.

www.ingramcontent.com/pod-product-compliance
Lightning Source LLC
Chambersburg PA
CBHW020356080526
44584CB00014B/1046